Study Guide

SEASONS OF LIFE
STUDY GUIDE
FOURTH EDITION

by

Richard O. Straub
University of Michigan-Dearborn

Worth Publishers

Seasons of Life Study Guide, Fourth Edition
by Richard O. Straub

This *Study Guide* is part of a full college course, which also includes five one-hour television programs; 26 half-hour audio programs; and **The Developing Person Through the Life Span**, Fifth Edition, by Kathleen Stassen Berger (Worth Publishers). For information about licensing the course, purchasing video and audiocassettes, or course print components, call 1-800-LEARNER, or write Annenberg/CPB Multimedia Collection, P.O. Box 2345, South Burlington, VT 05407.

Funding for **Seasons of Life** is provided by the Annenberg/CPB Project.

ISBN: 0-7167-5156-9

Printing: 1 2 3 4 5
Year: 04 03 02 01

Worth Publishers
41 Madison Avenue
New York, New York 10010

Contents

Preface

Seasons of Life is an introductory telecourse in life-span development—an exploration of the fascinating biological, social, and psychological changes that occur from the beginning of life to its end. In *Seasons of Life* you'll meet dozens of people in all stages of life and hear the views of nearly 50 leading social scientists.

Each of the twenty-six lessons of the telecourse consists of a thirty-minute audio program hosted by psychologist John Kotre; a chapter from *The Developing Person Through the Life Span, Fifth Edition,* by Kathleen Stassen Berger; and an assignment in this *Study Guide.*

Seasons of Life also features five one-hour television programs hosted by David Hartman, formerly of ABC's "Good Morning, America." Each program looks at a particular stage, or "season" of life. Program One introduces the "clocks" that influence biological, social, and psychological development throughout life and explores development during the first six years. Program Two covers development during childhood and adolescence (ages 6–20), and Program Three looks at early adulthood (ages 20–24). Program Four focuses on middle adulthood (ages 40–60) and Program Five concludes with late adulthood (ages 60+).

This *Study Guide* is designed to help you evaluate and enhance your understanding of the telecourse material. Your instructor will inform you of the lessons and assignments to be completed. At the end of the course you will be asked to complete a Television Term Project. The purpose of the project is to help you to integrate the material presented in the audio, video, and textbook components of the telecourse and to interpret your own experiences in view of what you have learned.

This *Study Guide* also includes a section, "How to Manage Your Time Efficiently and Study More Effectively" (page xi), which provides information on how to use the *Study Guide* for maximum benefit. It also offers additional study suggestions for time management, effective note-taking, evaluation of exam performance, and ways to improve your reading comprehension.

We are grateful to everyone who has contributed to this project. Special thanks go to our core group of advisors: Urie Bronfenbrenner of Cornell University, David Gutmann of Northwestern University, Bernice Neugarten of the University of Chicago, Anne Petersen of Penn State University, Alice Rossi of the University of Massachusetts–Amherst, and Sheldon White of Harvard University. Jack Mitchell of WHA at the University of Wisconsin provided much wise counsel regarding audio programming. Janet Whitaker of Rio Salado Community College was especially helpful in the design of our supplementary materials. Margie Moeller of WQED wrote excellent descriptions of the people in the television programs. Wilbert McKeachie and Elizabeth Douvan of the University of Michigan offered help close to home, and the staff of Worth Publishers supplied patience and professionalism. Major funding for *Seasons of Life* was provided by the Annenberg/CPB Project.

In preparing the materials that make up the *Seasons of Life* project, we were guided by a simple idea: that by examining the stories people tell about their lives, we can come to an understanding not only of these lives but of the life cycle itself, and of its "seasons." We hope your journey through the telecourse experience will be an enjoyable one and will provide you with information that enhances your insight into your own life story and those of others.

Richard O. Straub, Ph.D.
Professor of Psychology
University of Michigan–Dearborn

The Seasons of Life Study Guide

This study guide has many features that will help you study more effectively. Part I of this introduction describes these features. Part II provides suggestions that can help you to use your study time more effectively.

Part I FEATURES OF THIS STUDY GUIDE

THE LESSONS

Each Study Guide lesson consists of nine sections designed to help direct your study activities. After a while, you will discover which sections are the most helpful for you, and you can concentrate on them.

Orientation This section provides an overview of the lesson, highlighting important themes, placing facts in context, and integrating the audio program with the textbook. It also introduces the experts and stories that appear in each audio program and helps you relate its content to important ideas covered in other lessons.

Lesson Goals These goals—typically four or five for each lesson—identify the major themes of each lesson. They are drawn from both the textbook and the audio program.

Audio Assignment This section contains several specific questions drawn from the important facts and concepts covered in the lesson's audio program. Once you have finished listening to the program, try to answer the questions in your own words. Completing this section will help you to identify concepts you may need to review by replaying portions of the program.

Textbook Assignment This section contains a series of fill-in-the-blank questions drawn from important facts and concepts presented in the textbook chapter. Once you have finished reading the chapter, try to answer all the questions. Completing the questions will help you to identify those points you may need to review.

Testing Yourself This section consists of between 15 and 20 multiple-choice questions drawn from both the audio program and the textbook chapter. They should be answered only after you have listened to the program, read the chapter, and completed the audio and textbook assignments. Correct answers, along with explanations and textbook page references (as appropriate), are provid-

ed at the end of the chapter. If you miss a question, read the explanation and, if you need to, review the appropriate text pages or portion of the audio program.

Exercise This section contains a short assignment that you are to complete and hand in to your instructor. The exercise will help you make meaningful connections between the lesson content and your own life story. In some cases the exercise involves gathering information from a relative or friend. In others, it is based on applying important lesson concepts to your own experiences.

Lesson Guidelines Organized into separate sections for the audio program and the textbook, this section will help you to evaluate your answers to question in the "Audio Assignment" and "Textbook Assignment" sections of the Study Guide. Taken together, the items provide a summary of the main points covered in the lesson.

Answers to Testing Yourself This section can be used to evaluate your performance on the questions in the "Testing Yourself" section of the Study Guide. For each question, the correct answer is given, along with the question's source—whether material in the audio program or the text. For questions based on the text, page references are given where the answer can be found.

References In this section, you are referred to journals, magazine articles, and books that contain additional information on topics discussed in the lesson.

THE TELEVISION TERM PROJECT

The Television Term Project consists of 25 essay questions designed to integrate the audio, video, and print components of the telecourse. The questions are divided into two categories. For each television program, there are four questions which should be answered soon after the program is viewed. For the entire series, there are five additional questions that cover major themes and help you to make meaningful connections between the telecourse and your own life experiences.

KEEPING TRACK

The following grid will help you keep track of your progress through the *Seasons of Life* telecourse. Your actual assignments, of course, will depend on your instructor.

Lesson	Exercise Score	Quiz Score
1	|——————|	|——————|
2	|——————|	|——————|
3	|——————|	|——————|
4	|——————|	|——————|
5	|——————|	|——————|
6	|——————|	|——————|
7	|——————|	|——————|
8	|——————|	|——————|
9	|——————|	|——————|
10	|——————|	|——————|
11	|——————|	|——————|
12	|——————|	|——————|
13	|——————|	|——————|
14	|——————|	|——————|
15	|——————|	|——————|
16	|——————|	|——————|
17	|——————|	|——————|
18	|——————|	|——————|
19	|——————|	|——————|
20	|——————|	|——————|
21	|——————|	|——————|
22	|——————|	|——————|
23	|——————|	|——————|
24	|——————|	|——————|
25	|——————|	|——————|
26	|——————|	|——————|
Total	|——————|	|——————|

Average

Exercise average _____

Quiz average _____

Mid-term exam _____

Final exam _____

Television term project _____

Overall Average _____

Final Grade _____

Part II HOW TO MANAGE YOUR TIME EFFICIENTLY AND STUDY MORE EFFECTIVELY

Students who are new to college life or who are returning after a long absence may be unsure of their study skills. Suggestions for making the best use of your time and improving your skills may be found in the following section of the Study Guide. These suggestions will help you not only with *Seasons of Life*, but also with many of your other college courses.

How effectively do you study? Good study habits make the job of being a college student much easier. Many students, who could succeed in college, fail or drop out because they have never learned to manage their time efficiently. Even the best students can usually benefit from an in-depth evaluation of their current study habits.

There are many ways to achieve academic success, of course, but your approach may not be the most effective or efficient. Are you sacrificing your social life or your physical or mental health in order to get A's on your exams? Good study habits result in better grades *and* more time for other activities.

EVALUATE YOUR CURRENT STUDY HABITS

To improve your study habits, you must first have an accurate picture of how you currently spend your time. Begin by putting together a profile of your present living and studying habits. Answer the following questions by writing "yes" or "no" on each line.

_____ 1. Do you usually set up a schedule to budget your time for studying, recreation, and other activities?

_____ 2. Do you often put off studying until time pressures force you to cram?

_____ 3. Do other students seem to study less than you do, but get better grades?

_____ 4. Do you usually spend hours at a time studying one subject, rather than dividing that time between several subjects?

_____ 5. Do you often have trouble remembering what you have just read in a textbook?

_____ 6. Before reading a chapter in a textbook, do you skim through it and read the section headings?

_____ 7. Do you try to predict exam questions from your lecture notes and reading?

_____ 8. Do you usually attempt to paraphrase or summarize what you have just finished reading?

_____ 9. Do you find it difficult to concentrate very long when you study?

_____ 10. Do you often feel that you studied the wrong material for an exam?

Thousands of college students have participated in similar surveys. Students who are fully realizing their academic potential usually respond as follows: (1) yes, (2) no, (3) no, (4) no, (5) no, (6) yes, (7) yes, (8) yes, (9) no, (10) no.

Compare your responses with those of successful students. The greater the discrepancy, the more you could benefit from a program to improve your study habits. The questions are designed to identify areas of weakness. Once you have identified your weaknesses, you will be able to set specific goals for improvement and implement a program for reaching them.

MANAGE YOUR TIME

Do you often feel frustrated because there isn't enough time to do all the things you must and want to do? Take heart. Even the most productive and successful people feel this way at times. But they establish priorities for their activities and they learn to budget time for each of them. There's much in the saying, "If you want something done, ask a busy person to do it." A busy person knows how to get things done.

If you don't now have a system for budgeting your time, develop one. Not only will your academic accomplishments increase, but you will actually find more time in your schedule for other activities. And you won't have to feel guilty about "taking time off," because all your obligations will be covered.

Establish a Baseline

As a first step in preparing to budget your time, keep a diary for a few days to establish a summary, or baseline, of the time you spend in studying, socializing, working, and so on. If you are like many students, much of your "study" time is nonproductive; you may sit at your desk and leaf through a book, but the time is actually wasted. Or you may procrastinate. You are always getting ready to study, but you rarely do.

Table 1   Sample Time-Management Diary

Activity	Time Completed	Duration Hours: Minutes
	Monday	
Sleep	7:00	7:30
Dressing	7:25	:25
Breakfast	7:45	:20
Commute	8:20	:35
Coffee	9:00	:40
French	10:00	1:00
Socialize	10:15	:15
Videogame	10:35	:20
Coffee	11:00	:25
Psychology	12:00	1:00
Lunch	12:25	:25
Study Lab	1:00	:35
Psych. Lab	4:00	3:00
Work	5:30	1:30
Commute	6:10	:40
Dinner	6:45	:35
TV	7:30	:45
Study Psych.	10:00	2:30
Socialize	11:30	1:30
Sleep		

Prepare a similar chart for each day of the week. When you finish an activity, note it on the chart and write down the time it was completed. Then determine its duration by subtracting the time the previous activity was finished from the newly entered time.

Besides revealing where you waste time, your diary will give you a realistic picture of how much time you need to allot for meals, commuting, and other fixed activities. In addition, careful rec-ords should indicate the times of the day when you are consistently most productive. A sample time-management diary is shown in Table 1.

Plan the Term

Having established and evaluated your baseline, you are ready to devise a more efficient schedule. Buy a calendar that covers the entire school term and has ample space for each day. Using the course outlines provided by your instructors, enter the dates of all exams, term paper deadlines, and other important academic obligations. If you have any long-range personal plans (concerts, weekend trips, etc.), enter the dates on the calendar as well. Keep your calendar up to date and refer to it often. I recommend carrying it with you at all times.

Develop a Weekly Calendar

Now that you have a general picture of the school term, develop a weekly schedule that includes all of your activities. Aim for a schedule that you can live with for the entire school term. A sample weekly schedule, incorporating the following guidelines, is shown in Table 2.

1. Enter your class times, work hours, and any other fixed obligations first. *Be thorough.* Using information from your time-management diary, allow plenty of time for such things as commuting, meals, laundry, and the like.

2. Set up a study schedule for each of your courses. The study habits survey and your time-management diary will direct you. The following guidelines should also be useful.

   a. Establish regular study times for each course. The 4 hours needed to study one subject, for example, are most profitable when divided into shorter periods spaced over several days. If you cram your studying into one 4-hour block, what you attempt to learn in the third or fourth hour will interfere with what you studied in the first 2 hours. Newly acquired knowledge is like wet cement. It needs some time to "harden" to become fixed in your memory.

   b. Alternate subjects. The type of interference just mentioned is greatest between similar topics. Set up a schedule in which you spend time on several *different* courses during each study session. Besides reducing the potential for interference, alternating subjects will help to prevent mental fatigue with one topic.

   c. Set weekly goals to determine the amount of study time you need to do well in each course. This will depend on, among other things, the difficulty of your courses and the effectiveness of your methods. Many professors recommend studying at least 1 to 2 hours for each hour in class. If your time-management diary indicates that you presently study less time than that, do not plan to jump immediately to a much higher level. Increase study time from your baseline by setting weekly goals [see (4)] that will gradually bring you up to the desired level. As an initial schedule, for example, you might set aside an amount of study time for each course that matches class time.

Table 2   Sample Weekly Schedule

Time	Mon.	Tues.	Wed.	Thurs.	Fri.	Sat.
7–8	Dress Eat	Dress Eat	Dress Eat	Dress Eat	Dress Eat	
8–9	Psych.	Study Psych.	Psych.	Study Psych.	Psych.	Dress Eat
9–10	Eng.	Study Eng.	Eng.	Study Eng.	Eng.	Study Eng.
10–11	Study French	Free	Study French	Open Study	Study French	Study Stats.
11–12	French	Study Psych. Lab	French	Open Study	French	Study Stats.
12–1	Lunch	Lunch	Lunch	Lunch	Lunch	Lunch
1–2	Stats.	Psych. Lab	Stats.	Study or Free	Stats.	Free
2–3	Bio.	Psych. Lab	Bio.	Free	Bio.	Free
3–4	Free	Psych.	Free	Free	Free	Free
4–5	Job	Job	Job	Job	Job	Free
5–6	Job	Job	Job	Job	Job	Free
6–7	Dinner	Dinner	Dinner	Dinner	Dinner	Dinner
7–8	Study Bio.	Study Bio.	Study Bio.	Study Bio.	Free	Free
8–9	Study Eng.	Study Stats.	Study Psych.	Open Study	Open Study	Free
9–10	Open Study	Open Study	Open Study	Open Study	Free	Free

This is a sample schedule for a student with a 16-credit load and a 10-hour-per-week part-time job. Using this chart as an illustration, make up a weekly schedule, following the guidelines outlined here.

d. Schedule for maximum effectiveness. Tailor your schedule to meet the demands of each course. For the course that emphasizes lecture notes, schedule time for a daily review soon after the class. This will give you a chance to revise your notes and clean up any hard-to-decipher shorthand while the material is still fresh in your mind. If you are evaluated for class participation (for example, in a language course), allow time for a review just *before* the class meets. Schedule study time for your most difficult (or least motivating) courses during hours when you are the most alert and distractions are fewest.

e. Schedule open study time. Emergencies, additional obligations, and the like could throw off your schedule. And you may simply need some extra time periodically for a project or for review in one of your courses. Schedule several hours each week for such purposes.

3. After you have budgeted time for studying, fill in slots for recreation, hobbies, relaxation, household errands, and the like.

4. Set specific goals. Before each study session, make a list of specific goals. The simple note "7–8 PM.: study psychology" is too broad to ensure the most effective use of the time. Formulate your daily goals according to what you know you must accomplish during the term. If you have course outlines with advance assignments, set systematic daily goals that will allow you, for example, to cover fifteen chapters before the exam. And be realistic: Can you actually expect to cover a 78-page chapter in one session? Divide large tasks into smaller units; stop at the most logical resting points. When you complete a specific goal, take a 5- or 10-minute break before tackling the next goal.

5. Evaluate how successful or unsuccessful your studying has been on a daily or weekly basis. Did you reach most of your goals? If so, reward yourself immediately. You might even make a list of five to ten rewards to choose from. If you have trouble studying regularly, you may be able to motivate yourself by making such rewards contingent on completing specific goals.

6. Finally, until you have lived with your schedule for several weeks, don't hesitate to revise it. You may need to allow more time for chemistry, for example, and less for some other course. If you are trying to study regularly for the first time and are feeling burned-out, you probably have set your initial goals too high. Don't let failure cause you to despair and abandon the program. Accept your limitations and revise your schedule so that you are studying only 15 to 20 minutes more each evening than you are used to. The point is to *identify a regular schedule with which you can achieve some success.* Time management, like any skill, must be practiced to become effective.

TECHNIQUES FOR EFFECTIVE STUDY

Knowing how to put study time to best use is, of course, as important as finding a place for it in your schedule. Here are some suggestions that should enable you to increase your reading comprehension and improve your note-taking. A few study tips are included as well.

Using SQ3R to Increase Reading Comprehension

How do you study from a textbook? If you are like many students, you simply read and reread in a passive manner. Studies have shown, however, that most students who simply read a textbook cannot remember more than half the material ten minutes after they have finished. Often, what is retained is the unessential material rather than the important points upon which exam questions will be based.

This Study Guide employs a program known as SQ3R (Survey, Question, Read, Recite, and Review) to facilitate, and allow you to assess, your comprehension of the important facts and concepts in the *Seasons of Life* telecourse. It will help you to integrate material from the audio and television programs with that in Kathleen Berger's text, *The Developing Person Through the Life Span, 5/e.*

Research has shown that students using SQ3R achieve significantly greater comprehension of textbooks than students reading in the more traditional passive manner. Once you have learned this pro-

gram, you can improve your comprehension of any textbook.

Survey   Before reading a chapter, determine whether the text or the Study Guide has an outline or list of objectives. Read this material and the summary at the end of the chapter. Next, read the textbook chapter fairly quickly, paying special attention to the major headings and subheadings. This survey will give you an idea of the chapter's content and organization. You will then be able to divide the chapter into logical sections in order to formulate specific goals for a more careful reading of the chapter.

In this Study Guide, the "Orienta-tion" summarizes the major topics of the audio program and the textbook chapter. This section also provides a few suggestions for approaching topics you may find difficult.

Question   You will retain material longer when you have a use for it. If you look up a word's definition in order to solve a crossword puzzle, for example, you will remember it longer than if you merely fill in the letters as a result of putting other words in. Surveying the chapter will allow you to generate important questions that the chapter will proceed to answer. These questions correspond to "mental files" into which knowledge will be sorted for easy access.

As you survey, jot down several questions for each chapter section. One simple technique is to generate questions by rephrasing a section heading. For example, the "Preoperational Thought" head could be turned into "What is preoperational thought?" Good questions will allow you to focus on the important points in the text. Examples of good questions are those that begin as follows: "List two examples of" "What is the function of?" "What is the significance of?" Such questions give a purpose to your reading. The audio assignment questions in this Study Guide can be used for this purpose. Similarly, you can formulate questions based on the chapter outline.

Read   When you have established "files" for each section of the chapter, review your first question, begin reading, and continue until you have discovered its answer. If you come to material that seems to answer an important question you don't have a file for, stop and write down the question.

Be sure to read everything. Don't skip photo or art captions, graphs, or marginal notes. In some cases, what may seem vague in reading will be made clear by a simple graph. Keep in mind that test questions are sometimes drawn from illustrations and charts.

Recite When you have found the answer to a question, close your eyes and mentally recite the question and its answer. Then *write* the answer next to the question. It is important that you recite an answer in your own words rather than the author's. Don't rely on your short-term memory to repeat the author's words verbatim.

In responding to the questions, pay close attention to what is called for. If you are asked to identify or list, do just that. If asked to compare, contrast, or do both, you should focus on the similarities (compare) and differences (contrast) between the concepts or theories. Answering the questions carefully will not only help you to focus your attention on the important concepts of the audio program, but it will also provide excellent practice for essay exams. For the textbook assignment, after completing all the questions on a topic you should try to summarize the material in your own words.

Recitation is an extremely effective study technique, recommended by many learning experts. In addition to increasing reading comprehension, it is useful for review. Trying to explain something in your own words clarifies your knowledge, often by revealing aspects of your answer that are vague or incomplete. If you repeatedly rely upon "I know" in recitation, you really *may not know.*

Recitation has the additional advantage of simulating an exam, especially an essay exam; the same skills are required in both cases. Too often students study without ever putting the book and notes aside, which makes it easy for them to develop false confidence in their knowledge. When the material is in front of you, you may be able to *recognize* an answer, but will you be able to *recall* it later, when you take an exam that does not provide these retrieval cues?

After you have recited and written your answer, continue with your next question. Read, recite, and so on.

Review When you have answered the last question on the material you have designated as a study goal, go back and review. Read over each question and your written answer to it. Your review might also include a brief written summary that integrates all of your questions and answers. This review need not take longer than a few minutes, but it is important. It will help you retain the material longer and will greatly facilitate a final review of each chapter before the exam.

An excellent way to review your understanding of the chapters of *The Developing Person Through the Life Span, 5/e,* is to complete the "Key Questions" at the end of each textbook chapter. Then go through

the "Lesson Guidelines" section of this Study Guide. You may be surprised to discover that you didn't know the chapter as well as you thought you did!

Also provided to facilitate your review are multiple-choice questions in the "Testing Yourself" section of the Study Guide. These questions cover both audio program and textbook content and should *not* be answered until you have listened to the program, read the chapter, and completed the audio and textbook assignments in the Study Guide. Correct answers, along with explanations of why each alternative is correct or incorrect, are provided at the end of the chapter. The relevant text page numbers for each question are also given. If you miss a question, read these explanations and, if you need to, review the text pages to further understand why. The questions do not test every aspect of a concept, so you should treat an incorrect answer as an indication that you need to review the concept.

One final suggestion: Incorporate SQ3R into your time-management calendar. Set specific goals for completing SQ3R with each assigned chapter. Keep a record of chapters completed, and reward yourself for being conscientious. Initially, it takes more time and effort to "read" using SQ3R, but with practice, the steps will become automatic. More important, you will comprehend significantly more material and retain what you have learned longer than passive readers do.

Listening to the Audio Programs

Using audio tapes and television programs for learning requires much more active attention to their content than when these media are used simply for entertainment.

In following the steps outlined in each Study Guide lesson, you will gain the most from each program by applying the SQ3R method to your audio tape listening. You will find it helpful to read the lesson orientation, lesson goals, and audio review questions before listening to the program. You may choose to listen to the entire program first and then answer the questions, replaying portions of the program as necessary. Or you may find it works better for you to answer the questions as you go along, stopping the tape as necessary. Soon after listening to the program, you should compare your answers with material in the "Lesson Guidelines" section of the Study Guide. Make sure that you have a good grasp of the answer to each audio question before you continue with the lesson.

Watching the Television Programs

The five television programs illustrate many of the facts and concepts of the course. They may be viewed any time during the semester and perhaps more than once. Before watching each program, you will find it helpful to read the program synopsis and story descriptions which appear in the Television Term Project chapter at the end of the Study Guide. To help focus your viewing on important series and program themes, you also should review the four essay questions that follow the story descriptions for each program.

Evaluating Your Exam Performance

How often have you received a grade on an exam that did not do justice to the effort you spent preparing for the exam? This is a common experience that can leave one feeling bewildered and abused. "What do I have to do to get an A?" "The test was unfair!" "I studied the wrong material!"

The chances of this happening are greatly reduced if you have an effective time-management schedule and use the study techniques described here. But it can happen, even to the best-prepared student. It is most likely to occur on your first exam in a new course.

Remember that there are two main reasons for studying. One is to learn for your own general academic development. Many people believe that such knowledge is all that really matters. Of course it is possible, though unlikely, to be an expert on a topic without achieving commensurate grades, just as one can, occasionally, earn an excellent grade without truly mastering the course material. During a job interview or in the workplace, however, your A in Java won't mean much if you can't actually program a computer.

In order to keep career options open after you graduate, you must both know the material *and* maintain competitive grades. In the short run, this means performing well on exams, which is the second main objective in studying.

Probably the single best piece of advice to keep in mind when studying for exams is to *try to predict exam questions*. This means ignoring the trivia and focusing on the important questions and their answers (with your instructor's emphasis in mind).

A second point is obvious. How well you do on exams is determined by your mastery of *both* lecture (or, in this case, audio tape) and textbook material. Many students (partly because of poor time management) concentrate too much on one at the expense of the other.

To evaluate how well you are learning the audio tape and textbook material, analyze the questions you missed on the first exam. Divide the questions into two categories, those drawn primarily from the audio tapes and those drawn primarily from the textbook. Determine the percentage of questions you missed in each category. If your errors are evenly distributed and you are satisfied with your grade, you have no problem. If you are weaker in one area, you will need to set goals for increasing and/or improving your study of that area.

Similarly, note the percentage of test questions drawn from each category. While your instructor may not be entirely consistent in making up future exams, you may be able to tailor your studying by placing *additional* emphasis on the appropriate area.

Exam evaluation will also point out the types of questions your instructor prefers. Does the exam consist primarily of multiple-choice or essay questions? You may also discover that an instructor is fond of wording questions in certain ways. For example, an instructor may rely heavily on questions that require you to draw an analogy between a theory or concept and a real-world example. Evaluate both your instructor's style and how well you do with each format. Use this information to guide your future exam preparation.

Important aids, not only in studying for exams but also in determining how well prepared you are, are the "Testing Yourself" sections of the Study Guide. If these tests don't include all of the types of questions your instructor typically writes, make up your own practice exam questions. Spend extra time testing yourself with question formats that are most difficult for you. There is no better way to evaluate your preparatin for an upcoming exam than by testing yourself under the conditions most likely to be in effect during the actual test.

A FEW PRACTICAL TIPS

Even the best intentions for studying sometimes fail. Some of these failures occur because students attempt to work under conditions that are simply not conducive to concentrated study. To help ensure the success of your time-management program, here are a few suggestions that should assist you in reducing the possibility of procrastination or distraction.

1. If you have set up a schedule for studying, make your roommate, family, and friends aware of this commitment, and ask them to honor your quiet study time. Close your door and post a "Do Not Disturb" sign.

2. Set up a place to study that minimizes potential distractions. Use a desk or table, not your bed or

an extremely comfortable chair. Keep your desk and the walls around it free from clutter. If you need a place other than your room, find one that meets as many of the above requirements as possible—for example, in the library stacks.

3. Do nothing but study in this place. It should become associated with studying so that it "triggers" this activity, just as a mouth-watering aroma elicits an appetite.

4. Never study with the television on or with other distracting noises present. If you must have music in the background in order to mask outside noise, for example, play soft instrumental music. Don't pick vocal selections; your mind will be drawn to the lyrics.

5. Study by yourself. Other students can be distracting or can break the pace at which *your* learning is most efficient. In addition, there is always the possibility that group studying will become a social gathering. Reserve that for its own place in your schedule.

If you continue to have difficulty concentrating for very long, try the following suggestions.

6. Study your most difficult or most challenging subjects first, when you are most alert.

7. Start with relatively short periods of concentrated study, with breaks in between. If your attention starts to wander, get up immediately and take a break. It is better to study effectively for 15 minutes and then take a break than to fritter away 45 minutes out of an hour. Gradually increase the length of study periods, using your attention span as an indicator of successful pacing.

SOME CLOSING THOUGHTS

I hope that these suggestions help make you more successful academically, and that they enhance the quality of your college life in general. Having the necessary skills makes any job a lot easier and more pleasant. Let me repeat my warning not to attempt to make too drastic a change in your lifestyle immediately. Good habits require time and self-discipline to develop. Once established they can last a lifetime.

Introduction

AUDIO PROGRAM: Of Seasons, Stories, and Lives

ORIENTATION

Developmental psychology is concerned with how people change as they grow older and how they remain the same. According to the **life-span perspective**, development is a lifelong process. Far from believing that our fates are sealed by the end of childhood, as some earlier theorists proposed, experts today believe that development continues throughout the life span and is unpredictable. The message is simple: you cannot tell how a life story will end just by knowing how it began.

Lesson 1 of the *Seasons of Life* series introduces the three **developmental clocks** that govern our progress through the seasons of life. The **biological clock** is a metaphor for the body's way of timing its physical development. The **social clock** reflects society's age norms for when certain life events should occur. The **psychological clock** represents each person's inner timetable for development. In Chapter 1 of *The Developing Person Through the Life Span, 5/e,* Kathleen Berger discusses the three domains of development that form the basis for the text organization, the many contexts of development, and the strategies developmentalists use in their research. The final section discusses the ethics of research with humans.

Audio program 1, "Of Seasons, Stories, and Lives," describes a basic method of developmental research: the interpretation of **life stories**. We hear several people recall their earliest memories and their memories of **nuclear episodes**: the most significant moments in their life stories. Through the expert commentary of psychologist Dan McAdams, we learn what such **autobiographical memories** tell researchers about a person's life story. With the help of commentary by psychologist Richard Lerner, we come to a fuller appreciation of the life-span perspective.

As the program opens, we hear a woman recounting her earliest memory—the opening scene of her life story.

LESSON GOALS

By the end of this lesson you should be prepared to:

1. Define developmental psychology, and explain the life-span and ecological perspectives.

2. Identify several controversies that echo throughout the study of development, and describe the scientific method.

3. Discuss the significance of the three developmental clocks through the life span.

4. Describe the components of an experiment and three basic research designs used by developmental psychologists.

5. Explain how the interpretation of life stories and autobiographical memories helps psychologists to understand development through the life span.

Audio Assignment

Listen to the audio tape that accompanies Lesson 1: "Of Seasons, Stories, and Lives." Write answers to the following questions. You may replay portions of the program if you need to refresh your memory. Answer guidelines may be found in the Lesson Guidelines section at the end of this chapter.

1. Explain the "life-span perspective" in developmental psychology and the concept that there are "seasons" of life.

2. Compare and contrast the three developmental clocks.

3. Explain the significance of first memories and nuclear episodes in the interpretation of life stories.

Textbook Assignment

Read Chapter 1: "Introduction," pages 3–35 in *The Developing Person Through the Life Span, 5/e*, then work through the material that follows to review it. Complete the sentences and answer the questions. As you proceed, evaluate your performance for each secdtion by consulting the answers on page 11. Do not continue with the next section until you understand each answer. If you need to, review or reread the appropriate section in the textbook before continuing.

The Study of Human Development (pp. 3–6)

1. The scientific study of human development can be defined as the science that seeks to understand

_____

_____ .

Central to this science is the _____-

_____ _____ , which recognizes the sources of continuity and discontinuity from the beginning of life to the end.

The five developmental characteristics embodied within the life-span perspective are that development is

a. _____

b. _____

c. _____

d. _____

e. _____

2. One of the most encouraging aspects of the life-span perspective is that development is characterized by _____ , or the capability of change.

3. The study of human development can be separated into three domains: _____ , _____ , and _____ .

4. The study of brain and body changes and the social influences that guide them falls within the _____ domain.

5. Thinking, perception, and language learning fall mainly in the _____ domain of development.

6. The study of emotions, personality, and interpersonal relationships falls within the _____ domain.

7. All three domains _____ (are/are not) important at every age. Each of the domains _____ (is/is not) affected by the other two. While development is organized into domains, each person is an integrated whole; that is, development is

_____ .

Contexts and Systems (pp. 6–15, 16–17)

8. Forces outside the individual that influence development make up the _____ of development.

9. The approach that emphasizes the influence of the systems, or contexts, that support the developing person is called the _____ model of development. This approach was first emphasized by _____ .

10. According to this model, the family, the peer group, and other aspects of the immediate social setting constitute the _____ .

11. Systems that link one microsystem to another constitute the _____ .

12. Community structures and local educational, medical, employment, and communications systems make up the _____ .

13. Cultural values, political philosophies, economic patterns, and social conditions make up the

_____ .

14. A recent addition to this model is the _____ , which emphasizes the importance of historical time on development.

15. The ecological model emphasizes the _____ (unidirectional/multidirectional) and _____ nature of social influences.

16. This idea is most clearly expressed in two theories from the natural sciences: _____ theory and _____ theory, which stress the unpredictability and dynamism of all natural systems.

17. The phenomenon of the _____ _____ refers to the fact that the ecosystems _____ (act/do not act) in isolation; even a tiny change in one system can have a profound effect on the other systems of development.

18. A group of people born within a few years of each other is called a _____ . These people tend to be affected by history in _____ (the same way/different ways).

19. One such group is the huge "_____ _____" generation of children born just after World War II. The historical circumstances of their youth may have promoted greater _____ and _____ than did those of older and younger adults.

20. In addition to being influenced by the particular social contexts in which they develop, cohorts can be affected by differences in their relative _____ .

21. A widely shared idea about the way things are, or should be, is a _____ . An important point about such ideas is that they _____ (often change/are very stable) over time.

22. The life stage of _____ is also an example of a social construction.

23. A contextual influence that is determined by a person's income, education, place of residence, and occupation is called _____ _____ , which is often abbreviated _____ .

24. The values, assumptions, and customs as well as the physical objects that a group of people have adopted as a design for living constitute a _____ .

25. One example of the impact of cultural values on development is the greater tendency for children to be viewed as an economic asset in _____ _____ communities. In such communities, infant care is designed to maximize _____ and emphasize family _____ . By contrast, middle-class parents in _____ nations are less worried about infant mortality and thus focus care on fostering _____ growth and emotional _____ . For these reasons, most women in developed nations want _____ (how many?) children and most women in developing countries want _____ children.

26. (A Life-Span View) The minimum income needed to pay for a family's basic necessities is called the _____ _____ . Among the hazards and pressures of poverty are higher rates of _____ _____ , _____ _____ , inadequate _____ , and adolescent _____ .

27. (A Life-Span View) Fifty years ago, the poorest age group in most nations of the world were the _____ . Today, poverty rates are highest in the _____ _____ age group.

28. (A Life-Span View) Although poverty is a useful signal for severe problems throughout life, other variables, such as the presence of _____ _____ within a family, play a crucial role in determining individual development. For example, some children

seem resilient to the hazards of poverty, especially those whose parents are _____ and involved. As another example, there are likely to be fewer social problems among poor people who work to keep up their _____ .

29. A collection of people who share certain attributes, such as ancestry, national origin, religion, and language and, as a result, tend to have similar beliefs, values, and cultural experiences is called a(n) _____ _____ . In distinguishing racial identity, _____ traits are less important than are the _____ and _____ that arise from ethnic or racial consciousness. Thus, race is actually a _____ _____ .

30. (In Person) Because his mother contracted the disease _____ during her pregnancy, David was born with a heart defect and cataracts over both eyes. Thus, his immediate problems centered on the _____ domain. However, because he was born at a particular time, he was already influenced by the larger _____ context. His physical handicaps later produced _____ and _____ handicaps.

Developmental Study as a Science (pp. 15, 18)

31. In order, the basic steps of the scientific method are:

    a. _____

    b. _____

    c. _____

    d. _____

    e. _____

32. A specific, testable prediction that forms the basis of a research project is called a _____ .

33. To repeat an experimental test procedure and obtain the same results is to _____ the test of the hypothesis.

34. The people who are studied in a research project are called the _____ .

35. Age, sex, education, and other quantities that may differ during an investigation are called _____ . Developmental researchers deal with both _____ variation, which occurs from day to day in each person, and _____ variation, which occurs between people or groups.

36. The nature/nurture controversy concerns how much, and which aspects, of development are affected by _____ and how much by _____ . The _____/_____ controversy concerns whether development is largely gradual in nature or characterized by sudden transformations. The _____/_____ controversy focuses on when individual differences in development are celebrated or considered problems that need correcting.

Research Methods (pp. 18–30)

37. In designing research studies, scientists are concerned with four issues: _____ , or whether a study measures what it purports to measure; _____ , or whether its measurements are correct; _____ , or whether the study applies to other populations and situations; and _____ , or whether it solves real-life problems.

38. When researchers observe and record, in a systematic and unbiased manner, what research subjects do, they are using _____ _____ . People may be observed in a _____ setting or in a _____ .

39. A chief limitation of observation is that it does not indicate the _____ of the behavior being observed.

40. (Research Report) To be sure that trained observers are viewing the traits of interest, each trait has be described in a precise behavioral manner, that is, it has to be _____ .

41. (Research Report) To determine whether a difference between two groups occurred purely by

coincidence, or chance, researchers apply a math-ematical test of _____ _____ . Generally, coincidence is ruled out if there is less than 1 possibility in _____ that the difference could have occurred by chance.

42. A statistic that indicates whether two variables are related to each other is a _____ . To say that two variables are related in this way _____ (does/does not) necessarily imply that one caused the other.

43. A correlation is _____ if the occur-rence of one variable makes it more likely that the other will occur, and _____ if the occurrence of one makes it less likely that the other will occur.

44. The method that allows a scientist to test a hypothesis in a controlled environment, in which the variables can be manipulated, is the _____ . In this method, researchers manipulate a(n) _____ variable to determine its effect on a(n) _____ variable.

45. Although this research method enables researchers to uncover the links between _____ and _____ , it is sometimes criticized for studying behavior in a situation that is _____ .

46. Another limitation is that participants in this research technique (except very young children) who know they are research subjects may attempt to _____ _____ . A final limitation is that most research studies of this type are of very limited _____ .

47. In a(n) _____ _____ , scientists collect information from a large group of people by personal interview, written ques-tionnaire, or by some other means.

48. A potential problem with this research method is that respondents may give answers they think the researcher _____ .

49. An intensive study of one individual is called a(n) _____ . An advantage of this

method is that it provides a rich _____ description of development, rather than relying only on _____ data. Another important use is that it provides a good _____ _____ for other research.

50. Research that involves the comparison of people of different ages is called a _____-_____ research design.

51. With cross-sectional research it is very difficult to ensure that the various groups differ only in their _____ . In addition, every cross-sec-tional study will, to some degree, reflect _____ .

52. Research that follows the same people over a rel-atively long period of time is called a _____ research design.

State three drawbacks of this type of research design.

53. The research method that combines the longitudi-nal and cross-sectional methods is the _____-_____ research method.

Ethics and Science (pp. 30–33)

54. Researchers who study humans must ensure that their subjects are not _____ and that their participation is _____ and _____ .

55. The most complex matter in research with humans is ensuring that the _____ of a proposed study outweigh its _____ . Complicating this issue is the fact that research with the greatest potential benefit often involves groups that are the most _____ .

56. A research study that is a compilation of data from many other sources is called a _____-_____ .

Testing Yourself

After you have completed the audio and text review questions, see how well you do on the following quiz. Correct answers, with text and audio references, may be found at the end of this chapter.

1. Which of the following statements most accurately expresses the life-span perspective on development?
   a. Human development reflects the interaction of three developmental clocks.
   b. Human development is a continuous process rather than a series of stages.
   c. Human development occurs in discontinuous stages.
   d. Human development is a lifelong process of change.

2. The research method in which the same group of people is studied over a long period of time is called the:
   a. cross-sectional method.
   b. longitudinal method.
   c. survey method.
   d. naturalistic method.

3. Culturally determined age norms for when to enter school, when to start a family, and when to retire, are set according to:
   a. the biological clock.
   b. the social clock.
   c. the psychological clock.
   d. all three developmental clocks.

4. Memories of especially significant events in a life story are called:
   a. flashbulb memories.
   b. iconic memories.
   c. nuclear episodes.
   d. eidetic images.

5. Dan McAdams studies autobiographical memories by:
   a. coding them for the presence of certain motives.
   b. interviewing relatives of the subject of a case study.
   c. using the cross-sectional method.
   d. interpreting art produced by subjects at different stages in their life span.

6. The scientific study of human development is defined as the study of:
   a. how and why people change or remain the same over time.
   b. psychosocial influences on aging.
   c. individual differences in learning over the life span.
   d. all of the above.

7. The cognitive domain of development includes:
   a. perception.
   b. thinking.
   c. language.
   d. all of the above.

8. Changes in height, weight, and bone thickness are part of the _____ domain.
   a. cognitive   c. psychosocial
   b. biosocial   d. physical

9. Psychosocial development focuses primarily on personality, emotions, and:
   a. intellectual development.
   b. sexual maturation.
   c. relationships with others.
   d. perception.

10. The ecological model of developmental psychology focuses on the:
    a. biochemistry of the body systems.
    b. cognitive domain only.
    c. internal thinking processes.
    d. overall environment of development.

11. Researchers who take a life-span perspective on development focus on:
    a. the sources of continuity from the beginning of life to the end.
    b. the sources of discontinuity throughout life.
    c. the "nonlinear" character of human development.
    d. all of the above.

12. During the 1960s, American society tilted toward a youth culture. This is a vivid example of the effect of _____ on society.
    a. the "baby boom" cohort
    b. the biosocial domain
    c. the cognitive domain
    d. the microsystem

13. A hypothesis is a:
    a. conclusion.
    b. prediction to be tested.
    c. statistical test.
    d. correlation.

14. A developmentalist who is interested in studying the influences of a person's immediate environment on his or her behavior is focusing on which system?
    a. mesosystem
    b. macrosystem
    c. microsystem
    d. exosystem

15. Socioeconomic status is determined by a combination of variables, including:
    a. age, education, and income.
    b. income, ethnicity, and occupation.
    c. income, education, and occupation.
    d. age, ethnicity, and occupation.

16. A disadvantage of experiments is that:
    a. people may behave differently in the artificial environment of the laboratory.
    b. control groups are too large to be accommodated in most laboratories.
    c. they are the method most vulnerable to bias on the part of the researcher.
    d. proponents of the ecological approach overuse them.

17. In an experiment testing the effects of group size on individual effort in a tug-of-war task, the number of people in each group is the:
    a. hypothesis.
    b. independent variable
    c. dependent variable.
    d. level of significance.

18. Which research method would be most appropriate for investigating the relationship between parents' religious beliefs and their attitudes toward middle school sex education?
    a. experimentation
    b. longitudinal research
    c. naturalistic observation
    d. the survey

19. In which type of community are children generally valued most highly as economic assets?
    a. developing agricultural communities
    b. developed postindustrial nations
    c. low-income families in developed countries
    d. middle-income families in developing nations

20. Developmentalists who carefully observe the behavior of schoolchildren during recess are using a research method known as:
    a. the case study.
    b. cross-sectional research.
    c. naturalistic observation.
    d. cross-sequential research.

NAME _____   INSTRUCTOR _____

LESSON 1: FIRST MEMORIES

Exercise

The audio program notes that one way of understanding an individual's life is by listening to his or her life story. In order to make sense of **life stories**, psychologists are beginning to probe **autobiographical memory**. This kind of memory begins with each individual's very first memory of life. Although first memories are often a mixture of fact and fiction, they are especially revealing glimpses into each person's current identity.

To further your understanding of the material presented in this lesson, the Exercise asks you to reflect on the first memories of characters heard in the audio program. Answer the following questions and hand the completed exercise in to your instructor.

1. How did Mary's first memory relate to the rest of her life story? How did it express her identity?

2. How did Arnelle Douglas's first memory relate to the rest of his life story? How did it express his identity?

3. Of course, not all first memories relate to the rest of a person's story. Ask someone you know about his or her earliest memory (or try to remember your own). Do you see any connection between the memory and the rest of the person's life story? between the memory and your subject's sense of who he or she is?

LESSON GUIDELINES

Audio Question Guidelines

1. The life-span perspective states that development is not fixed early in the life span, as earlier theorists had proposed, but continues throughout the seasons of life.

   Developmental psychologists recognize separate life-span seasons of infancy, childhood, adolescence, early adulthood, middle adulthood, and late adulthood.

   The life-span perspective emphasizes that people become more diverse as they age, that they are capable of controlling their development, that is, of being the authors of their own life stories.

   The life-span perspective has also made experts aware of the three developmental clocks—the biological, social, and psychological clocks—that interact to pace human development.

2. The developmental clocks are metaphors for the three ways in which people change during the seasons of life. To begin with, people change because their bodies change. The **biological clock** represents the body's mechanisms for timing physical development. It times birth, growth, the reproductive cycle, and aging.

   People also change because the world around them changes. The **social clock** represents each society's age norms for when certain life events should occur—for example, when people should enter school, start a family, and retire.

   Finally, people change because their own inner needs change. The **psychological clock** represents a person's inner timetable for development, that is, his or her own way of determining the right time for certain life events.

3. One way of understanding life-span development is to listen to a specific person's **life story**. The story, although continually evolving and being rewritten, may be what gives each life continuity and purpose. It may represent each individual's sense of who he or she is.

   The interpretation of **autobiographical memory**, including nuclear episodes and first memories, is especially interesting. Cognitive psychologists suggest that what we remember from the past is reconstructed over time so that such memories are generally combinations of fact and fantasy.

   Early memories, whether true or not, say something about a person's current identity and highlight significant themes in his or her entire life story.

Nuclear episodes are personal memories that are very significant to the individual. How people describe nuclear episodes often reveals important personality traits—for example, a desire for intimacy.

Textbook Question Answers

1. how and why people change as they grow older, as well as how and why they remain the same; life-span perspective
   a. multidirectional
   b. multicontextual
   c. multicultural
   d. multidisciplinary
   e. plastic
2. plasticity
3. biosocial; cognitive; psychosocial
4. biosocial
5. cognitive
6. psychosocial
7. are; is; holistic
8. contexts (or systems or environments)
9. ecological; Urie Bronfenbrenner
10. microsystem
11. mesosystem
12. exosystem
13. macrosystem
14. chronosystem
15. multidirectional; interactive
16. complexity; chaos
17. butterfly effect; do not act
18. cohort; the same way
19. baby boom; assertiveness; independence
20. sizes
21. social construction; often change
22. childhood
23. socioeconomic status; SES
24. culture
25. developing agricultural; survival; cooperation; postindustrial; cognitive; intellectual; independence, one or two; three to five
26. poverty level; child neglect; infant mortality; schools; violence
27. old; youngest
28. supportive relationships; nurturant; neighborhoods

29. ethnic group; biological; attitudes; experiences; social construction

30. rubella; biosocial; social; cognitive; psychosocial

31. **a.** formulate a research question;
    b. develop a hypothesis;
    c. test the hypothesis;
    d. draw conclusions;
    e. make the findings available.

32. hypothesis

33. replicate

34. subjects

35. variables; intrapersonal; interpersonal

36. genes; environment; continuity/discontinuity; difference/deficit

37. validity; accuracy; generalizability; usefulness

38. scientific observation; naturalistic; laboratory

39. cause

40. operationally defined

41. statistical significance; 20

42. correlation; does not

43. positive; negative

44. experiment; independent; dependent

45. cause; effect; artificial

46. produce the results they believe the experimenter is looking for; duration

47. scientific survey

48. expects

49. case study; qualitative; quantitative; starting point

50. cross-sectional

51. ages; cohort differences

52. longitudinal

Over time, some subjects may leave the study. Some people may change simply because they are part of the study. Longitudinal studies are time-consuming and expensive.

53. cross-sequential

54. harmed; confidential; voluntary

55. benefits; costs; vulnerable

56. meta-analysis

Answers to Testing Yourself

1. **d.** In contrast to earlier views that development was largely fixed early in life, the life-span perspective views development as continuing throughout the seasons of life. (audio program)

2. **b.** The *long*itudinal method studies development over a *long* period of time. (audio program)

3. **b.** The social clock represents society's way of telling us to "act our age." (audio program)

4. **c.** The nucleus is "at the center." Nuclear episodes are central to our sense of who we are. (audio program)

5. **a.** In McAdams's view, autobiographical memories reflect each person's sense of identity. (audio program)

6. **a.** is the answer. (textbook, p. 4)

   b. & c. The study of development is concerned with a broader range of phenomena, including biosocial aspects of development, than these answers specify.

7. **d.** is the answer. (textbook, p. 5)

8. **b.** is the answer. (textbook, p. 5)

   a. This domain is concerned with thought processes.

   c. This domain is concerned with emotions, personality, and interpersonal relationships.

   d. This is not a domain of development.

9. **c.** is the answer. (textbook, p. 5)

   a. This falls within the cognitive and biosocial domains.

   b. This falls within the biosocial domain.

   d. This falls within the cognitive domain.

10. **d.** is the answer. This approach sees development as occurring within four interacting levels, or environments. (textbook, p. 7)

11. **d.** is the answer. (textbook, p. 23)

12. **a.** is the answer. (textbook, pp. 8–9)

    b. The biosocial domain is concerned with brain and body changes.

    c. The cognitive domain is concerned with thought processes in individuals and the factors that influence them.

    d. The microsystem is the immediate social setting that surrounds an individual.

13. **b.** is the answer. (textbook, p. 15)

14. **c.** is the answer. (textbook, p. 7)

    a. This refers to systems that link one microsystem to another.

    b. This refers to cultural values, political philosophies, economic patterns, and social conditions.

    d. This includes the community structures that affect the functioning of smaller systems.

15. **c.** is the answer. (textbook, p. 10)

16. **a.** is the answer. (textbook, p. 23)

17. **b.** is the answer. (textbook, p. 23)

    a. A possible hypothesis for this experiment would be that the larger the group, the less hard a given individual will pull.

    c. The dependent variable is the measure of individual effort.

    d. Significance level refers to the numerical value specifying the possibility that the results of an experiment could have occurred by chance.

18. **d.** is the answer. (textbook, pp. 24–25)

    a. Experimentation is appropriate when one is seeking to uncover cause-and-effect relationships; in this example the researcher is only interested in determining whether the parents' beliefs *predict* their attitudes.

    b. Longitudinal research would be appropriate if the researcher sought to examine the development of these attitudes over a long period of time.

    c. Mere observation would not allow the researcher to determine the attitudes of the subjects.

19. **a.** is the answer. (textbook, p. 11)

20. **c.** is the answer. (textbook, p. 19)

    a. In this method, *one* subject is studied over a period of time.

    b. & d. In these research methods, two or more *groups* of subjects are studied and compared.

Reference

Kotre, John (1995). *White gloves: How we create ourselves through memory*. New York: Free Press.

Professor Kotre, creator of the *Seasons of Life* series, discusses autobiographical memory and the insights it yields into each person's sense of him- or herself.

Theories

AUDIO PROGRAM: The Story of Erik Erikson

ORIENTATION

Lesson 1 introduced the subject matter of developmental psychology, described the three clocks that govern development, and introduced the many contexts of development. Lesson 2 deals with theories of human development, including that of Erik Erikson, who is the subject of the audio program, and explains the various research methods used in life-span psychology.

Theories provide a useful way of organizing ideas about behavior into testable hypotheses. In Chapter 2 of *The Developing Person Through the Life Span, 5/e*, five theories that have significantly influenced life-span psychology are described, evaluated, and compared. The theories complement one another: each emphasizes different aspects of development and is too restricted to be used on its own to explain the diverse ways in which development occurs. **Psychoanalytic theory** focuses on early experiences and distinguishable stages of growth, and **learning theory** emphasizes environmental influences. **Cognitive theory** emphasizes the influence of thinking on behavior, and **sociocultural theory** explains human development in terms of the support provided by one's culture. **Epigenetic systems theory** emphasizes the genetic origins of behavior but also stresses that genes, over time, are directly and systematically affected by environmental forces.

Most developmental psychologists today take an *eclectic perspective*, applying insights from various theories rather than limiting themselves to only one school of thought. The final test of a theory is its usefulness in clarifying observations and suggesting new hypotheses.

One theory that has withstood this test is that of Erik Erikson. A student of Freud, Erikson was one of the first psychologists to devote attention to the entire life cycle—to adulthood as well as to childhood.

Erikson spent his childhood in Germany and came to America when Adolf Hitler became Chancellor and Freud's writings were publicly burned in Berlin. In America, Erikson practiced as one of the first psychoanalysts for children, studying people as diverse as the Native American Sioux and soldiers who suffered emotional trauma during World War II. Erikson's experiences led him to the conclusion that Freud's **psychosexual stages** were too limited. In Erikson's view there were eight important challenges, or *crises*, in life and, hence, eight (rather than five) stages of development. Unlike Freud's stages, Erikson's reflect social and cultural influences; as a result, they are called **psychosocial stages**. In the program, these stages are outlined and contrasted with those embodied in Freud's theory.

The program begins with Erikson himself describing how he came to create one of psychology's most influential theories of the life cycle.

LESSON GOALS

By the end of this lesson you should be prepared to:

1. Explain the role theories play in developmental psychology, and differentiate grand theories, minitheories, and emergent theories.

2. Outline the basic terms and themes of the five major theories of human development: psychoanalytic theory, learning theory, cognitive theory, sociocultural theory, and epigenetic systems theory.

3. Discuss Harlow's research with infant monkeys and the ethology of infant social instincts and adult caregiving impulses.

4. Summarize the contributions and criticisms of the major developmental theories, and explain the eclectic perspective in developmental psychology.

5. Describe Erikson's eight stages of psychosocial development, and discuss the significance of Erikson's theory in life-span psychology.

Audio Assignment

Listen to the audio tape that accompanies Lesson 2: "The Story of Erik Erikson."

Write answers to the following questions. You may replay portions of the program if you need to refresh your memory. Answer guidelines may be found in the Lesson Guidelines section at the end of this chapter.

1. Outline Freud's five stages of psychosexual development.

2. Outline Erikson's eight stages of psychosocial development.

3. Describe how Erikson's psychosocial theory has contributed to the study of development, noting how it diverges from that of Freud; then, cite criticisms of it.

Textbook Assignment

Read Chapter 2: "Theories of Development," pages 37–67 in *The Developing Person Through the Life Span*, 5/e, then work through the material that follows to review it. Complete the sentences and answer the questions. As you proceed, evaluate your performance for each secdtion by consulting the answers on page 25. Do not continue with the next section until you understand each answer. If you need to, review or reread the appropriate section in the textbook before continuing.

What Theories Do (pp. 37–38)

1. A systematic set of principles and generalizations that explains behavior and development is called a(n) _____ _____ .

2. Developmental theories provide a broad and _____ view of the influences on development; they form the basis for educated guesses, or _____ , about behavior; and they provide a framework for future research.

3. Developmental theories fall into three categories: _____ theories, which offer a comprehensive view of development but have proven to be outdated; _____ theories, which explain a specific area of development; and _____ theories, which may be the comprehensive theories of the future.

Grand Theories (pp. 38–51, 52–53)

4. Psychoanalytic theories interpret human development in terms of intrinsic _____ and _____ , many of which are _____ (conscious/ unconscious) and _____ .

5. According to Freud's _____ theory, children experience sexual pleasures and desires during the first six years as they pass through three _____ _____ . From infancy to early childhood to the preschool years, these stages are the _____ stage, the _____ stage, and the _____ stage. Finally, after a period of sexual _____ , which lasts for about _____ years, the individual enters the _____ stage, which begins at about age _____ and lasts throughout adulthood.

Specify the focus of sexual pleasure and the major developmental need associated with each of Freud's stages.

oral _____

_____

anal _____

_____

phallic _____

_____

genital _____

_____

6. Erik Erikson's theory of development, which focuses on social and cultural influences, is called a(n) _____ theory. In this theory, there are _____ (number) developmental stages, each characterized by a particular developmental _____ related to the person's relationship to the social environment. Unlike Freud, Erikson proposed stages of development that _____ (span/do not span) a person's lifetime.

Complete the following chart regarding Erikson's stages of psychosocial development.

Age Period	Stage
Birth to 1 yr.	trust vs. _____
1–3 yrs.	autonomy vs. _____
3–6 yrs.	initiative vs. _____
7–11 yrs.	_____ vs. inferiority
Adolescence	identity vs. _____
Young adulthood	_____ vs. isolation
Middle adulthood	_____ vs. stagnation
Older adulthood	_____ vs. despair

7. A major theory in American psychology, which directly opposed psychoanalytic theory, was _____ . This theory, which emerged early in the twentieth century under the influence of _____ , forms the basis for contemporary _____ theory because of its emphasis on how we learn specific behaviors.

8. Learning theorists have formulated laws of behavior that are believed to apply

_____ (only at certain ages/at all ages). The basic principles of learning theory explore the relationship between an experience or event (called the _____) and the behavioral reaction associated with it (called the _____). The learning process, which is called _____ , takes two forms _____ _____ and

_____ _____ .

9. In classical conditioning, which was discovered by the Russian scientist _____ and is also called _____ conditioning, a person or an animal learns to associate a(n) _____ stimulus with a meaningful one.

10. According to _____ , the learning of more complex responses is the result of _____ conditioning, in which a person learns that a particular behavior produces a particular _____ , such as a reward. This type of learning is also called _____ conditioning.

11. The process of repeating a consequence to make it more likely that the behavior in question will recur is called _____ . The consequence that increases the likelihood that a behavior will be repeated is called the

_____ .

12. The extension of learning theory that emphasizes the ways that people learn new behaviors by observing others is called _____ _____ . The process whereby a child patterns his or her behavior after a parent or teacher, for example, is called

_____ .

13. This process is most likely to occur when an observer is _____ and when the model is _____ . This type of learning is also affected by the individual's

_____ .

14. (Research Report) The behavior of infant monkeys separated from their mothers led researcher _____ to investigate the origins of _____ in infant monkeys. These studies, which demonstrated that infant monkeys clung more often to "surrogate" mothers that provided _____ (food/contact comfort), disproved _____ theory's idea that infants seek to satisfy oral needs and _____ theory's view that reinforcement directs behavior.

15. The structure and development of the individual's thought processes and the way those thought processes affect the person's understanding of the world are the focus of _____ theory. A major pioneer of this theory is _____ .

16. In Piaget's first stage of development, the _____ stage, children experience the world through their senses and motor abilities. This stage occurs between birth and age _____ .

17. According to Piaget, during the preschool years (up to age _____), children are in the _____ stage. A hallmark of this stage is that children begin to think _____ . Another hallmark is that sometimes the child's thinking is _____ , or focused on seeing the world solely from his or her own perspective.

18. Piaget believed that children begin to think logically in a consistent way at about _____ years of age. At this time, they enter the _____ stage.

19. In Piaget's final stage, the _____ stage, reasoning expands from the purely concrete to encompass _____ thinking. Piaget believed most children enter this stage by age _____ .

20. According to Piaget, cognitive development is guided by the need to maintain a state of mental balance, called _____ _____ .

21. When new experiences challenge existing understanding, creating a kind of imbalance, the individual experiences _____ _____ , which eventually leads to mental growth.

22. According to Piaget, people adapt to new experiences either by reinterpreting them to fit into, or _____ with, old ideas. Some new experiences force people to revamp old ideas so that they can _____ new experiences.

Identify two psychoanalytic ideas that *are* widely accepted.

Identify one way in which the study of human development has benefited from learning theory.

Identify one way in which the study of human development has benefited from cognitive theory.

23. Today, hypotheses and concepts from

    _____ theory are more often the

    topic of research than those from the other two

    grand theories.

24. The idea that every person passes through fixed

    stages, as proposed by _____ ,

    _____ , and _____

    cannot account for the diversity of human devel-

    opment worldwide. Similarly, the idea that every

    person can be conditioned in the same way, as

    proposed by _____ ,

    _____ , and _____ has

    also been refuted.

25. Research has demonstrated that the grand theo-

    ries focus too much on the _____

    context of development and underestimate the

    role of _____ and _____

    influences.

26. (Changing Policy) The debate over the relative

    influence of heredity and environment in shaping

    personal traits and characteristics is called the

    _____-_____ contro-

    versy. Traits inherited at the moment of concep-

    tion give evidence of the influence of

    _____ ; those that emerge in

    response to learning and environmental influ-

    ences give evidence of the effect of

    _____ .

27. (Changing Policy) Developmentalists agree that,

    at every point, the _____

    between nature and nurture is the crucial influ-

    ence on any particular aspect of development.

28. (Changing Policy) All the grand theories tended

    to explain homosexuality in terms of

    _____ (nature/nurture). However,

    new research suggests that it is at least partly due

    to _____ (nature/nurture).

(Changing Policy) Briefly summarize two research
findings concerning homosexuality and the nature-
nurture controversy.

Emergent Theories (pp. 51, 54–64)

29. In contrast to the grand theories, the two emerg-

    ing theories draw from the findings of

    _____ (one/many) discipline(s).

30. Sociocultural theory sees human development as

    the result of _____

    _____ between developing persons

    and their surrounding _____ .

31. A major pioneer of this perspective was

    _____ , who was primarily interest-

    ed in the development of

    _____ competencies.

32. Vygotsky believed that these competencies result

    from the interaction between _____

    and more mature members of the society, acting

    as _____ , in a process that has been

    called an _____ _____

    _____ .

33. In Vygotsky's view, the best way to accomplish

    the goals of apprenticeship is through

    _____ _____ , in

    which the tutor engages the learner in joint activi-

    ties.

34. (A Life-Span View) According to Vygotsky, a

    mentor draws a child into the _____

    _____ _____

    _____ , which is defined as the

    range of skills that the child can exercise with

    _____ but cannot perform indepen-

    dently.

Cite several contributions and several criticisms of
sociocultural theory.

35. The newest of the theories, epigenetic systems theory emphasizes the interaction between _____ and the _____ .

36. In using the word *genetic*, this theory emphasizes that we have powerful _____ and abilities that arise from our _____ heritage.

37. The prefix "epi" refers to the various _____ factors that affect the expression of _____ _____ . These include _____ factors such as injury, temperature, and crowding. Others are _____ factors such as nourishing food and freedom to play.

38. Some epigenetic factors are the result of the evolutionary process called _____ _____ , in which, over generations, genes for useful traits that promote survival become more prevalent.

39. "Everything that seems to be genetic is actually epigenetic." This statement highlights the fact that _____ (some/most/all) genetic instructions are affected by the environment.

40. The "systems" aspect of this theory points out that changes in one part of the individual's system _____ _____ .

41. (In Person) The study of animal behavior as it is related to the evolution and survival of a species is called _____ . Newborn animals and human infants are genetically programmed for _____ _____ as a means of survival. Similarly, adult animals and humans are genetically programmed for _____ _____ .

The Theories Compared (pp. 64–65)

42. Which major theory of development emphasizes:
    a. the importance of culture in fostering development? _____
    b. the ways in which thought processes affect actions? _____

    c. environmental influences? _____
    d. the impact of "hidden dramas" on development? _____

    e. the interaction of genes and environment ____ _____

43. Which major theory of development has been criticized for:
    a. being too mechanistic? _____
    b. undervaluing genetic differences? _____
    c. being too subjective? _____
    d. neglecting society? _____
    e. neglecting individuals? _____

44. Because no one theory can encompass all of human behavior, most developmentalists have a(n) _____ perspective, which capitalizes on the strengths of all the theories.

Testing Yourself

After you have completed the audio and text review questions, see how well you do on the following quiz. Correct answers, with text and audio references, may be found at the end of this chapter.

1. Erik Erikson's theory of development:
    a. is based on eight crises all people are thought to face.
    b. emphasizes cultural and social influences on development.
    c. was one of the first to emphasize that development is lifelong.
    d. includes all of the factors listed above.

2. Freud's stages of development are called _____ stages; Erikson's are called _____ stages.
    a. psychosexual; psychosocial
    b. psychosocial; psychosexual
    c. psychosexual; social learning
    d. psychoanalytic; neo-Freudian

3. According to Freud's theory, the correct sequence of stages of development is:
   a. oral, anal, genital, latent, phallic.
   b. anal, oral, phallic, latent, genital.
   c. genital, oral, anal, latent, phallic.
   d. oral, anal, phallic, latent, genital.

4. The zone of proximal development refers to:
   a. the control processes by which information is transferred from the sensory register to working memory.
   b. the range of skills that a child can exercise with assistance but cannot perform independently.
   c. the influence of a pleasurable stimulus on behavior.
   d. the mutual interaction of a person's internal characteristics, the environment, and behavior.

5. Freud believed that sexual forces become dormant between ages 7 and 11; Erikson, on the other hand, saw this age period as a critical time of conflict between:
   a. autonomy and shame.
   b. trust and mistrust.
   c. industry and inferiority.
   d. identity and role confusion.

6. The purpose of a developmental theory is to:
   a. provide a broad and coherent view of the complex influences on human development.
   b. offer guidance for practical issues encountered by parents, teachers, and therapists.
   c. generate testable hypotheses about development.
   d. do all of the above.

7. Which developmental theory emphasizes the influence of unconscious drives and motives on behavior?
   a. psychoanalytic   c. cognitive
   b. learning   d. sociocultural

8. Which of the following is the correct order of the psychosexual stages proposed by Freud?
   a. oral stage; anal stage; phallic stage; latency; genital stage
   b. anal stage; oral stage; phallic stage; latency; genital stage
   c. oral stage; anal stage; genital stage; latency; phallic stage
   d. anal stage; oral stage; genital stage; latency; phallic stage

9. Erikson's psychosocial theory of human development describes:
   a. eight crises all people are thought to face.
   b. four psychosocial stages and a latency period.
   c. the same number of stages as Freud's, but with different names.
   d. a stage theory that is not psychoanalytic.

10. Which of the following theories does *not* belong with the others?
    a. psychoanalytic   c. sociocultural
    b. learning   d. cognitive

11. An American psychologist who explained complex human behaviors in terms of operant conditioning was:
    a. Lev Vygotsky.   c. B. F. Skinner.
    b. Ivan Pavlov.   d. Jean Piaget.

12. Pavlov's dogs learned to salivate at the sound of a bell because they associated the bell with food. Pavlov's experiment with dogs was an early demonstration of:
    a. classical conditioning.
    b. operant conditioning.
    c. positive reinforcement.
    d. social learning.

13. (Changing Policy) The nature-nurture controversy considers the degree to which traits, characteristics, and behaviors are the result of:
    a. early or lifelong learning.
    b. genes or heredity.
    c. heredity or experience.
    d. different historical concepts of childhood.

14. Modeling, an integral part of social learning theory, is so called because it:
    a. follows the scientific model of learning.
    b. molds character.
    c. follows the immediate reinforcement model developed by Bandura.
    d. involves people's patterning their behavior after that of others.

15. Which developmental theory suggests that each person is born with genetic possibilities that must be nurtured in order to grow?
    a. sociocultural   c. learning
    b. cognitive   d. epigenetic systems

16. Vygotsky's theory has been criticized for neglecting:
    a. the role of genes in guiding development.
    b. developmental processes that are not primarily biological.
    c. the importance of language in development.
    d. social factors in development.

17. Which is the correct sequence of stages in Piaget's theory of cognitive development?
    a. sensorimotor, preoperational, concrete operational, formal operational
    b. sensorimotor, preoperational, formal operational, concrete operational
    c. preoperational, sensorimotor, concrete operational, formal operational
    d. preoperational, sensorimotor, formal operational, concrete operational

18. When an individual's existing understanding no longer fits his or her present experiences, the result is called:
    a. a psychosocial crisis.
    b. equilibrium.
    c. disequilibrium.
    d. negative reinforcement.

19. (Changing Policy) In explaining the origins of homosexuality, the grand theories have traditionally emphasized:
    a. nature over nurture.
    b. nurture over nature.
    c. a warped mother-son or father-daughter relationship.
    d. the individual's voluntary choice.

20. (A Life-Span View) The zone of proximal development refers to:
    a. the control process by which information is transferred from the sensory register to working memory.
    b. the influence of a pleasurable stimulus on behavior.
    c. the range of skills a child can exercise with assistance but cannot perform independently.
    d. the mutual interaction of a person's internal characteristics, the environment, and the person's behavior.

NAME _____ INSTRUCTOR _____

LESSON 2: THEORIES OF HUMAN DEVELOPMENT

Exercise

Four major theories of human development are described, compared, and evaluated in Chapter 2. These are the **psychoanalytic theories** of Freud and neo-Freudians such as Erikson; the **learning** and **social learning theories** of Pavlov, Skinner, and Bandura; the **cognitive theories of** Piaget and the information-processing theorists; and the **sociocultural theory** of Vygotsky. Although each theory is too restricted to account solely for the tremendous diversity in human development, each has made an important contribution to life-span psychology.

To help clarify your understanding of the major **developmental theories**, this exercise asks you to focus on the similar, contradictory, and complementary aspects of the four theories. Answer the following questions and hand the completed exercise in to your instructor.

1. Which of the major developmental theories are stage theories? Which are not?

2. Which theories emphasize individual conscious organization of experience? unconscious urges? observable behavior? individuality? social and cultural influences?

3. Which theories emphasize the impact of early experience on development?

4. How does each theory view the child?

5. Do the theories use the same methodology? What is the relationship of the research strategies to the various theories?

6. How does each theory view adult development?

LESSON GUIDELINES

Audio Question Guidelines

1. According to Freud's **psychoanalytic theory** of **childhood sexuality**, children have sexual pleasures and fantasies long before adolescence.

   During the first five or six years, development progresses through three **psychosexual stages**, characterized by the focusing of sexual interest and pleasure, successively, on the mouth (**oral stage**), the anus (**anal stage**), and the sexual organs (**phallic stage**).

   Freud believed that personality was well established by the end of stage three, about the age of 6.

   Following a five- or six-year period of sexual **latency**, the individual enters the **genital stage**, which lasts throughout adulthood.

2. Erikson's **psychosocial theory** emphasizes each person's relationship to the social environment. Erikson proposed eight developmental stages, each characterized by a particular crisis that must be resolved in order for the individual to progress developmentally.

   During the first stage (*trust versus mistrust*), babies learn either to trust or to mistrust that others will meet their basic needs.

   During the second and third years of life (*autonomy versus shame and doubt*) children learn either to be self-sufficient in many activities or to doubt their own abilities.

   During the third stage (*initiative versus guilt*) children begin to envisage goals and to undertake many adultlike activities, sometimes experiencing guilt as they overstep the limits set by their parents.

   During the years from 6 to 12 (*industry versus inferiority*) children busily learn to feel useful and productive; failing that, they feel inferior and unable to do anything well.

   At adolescence (*identity versus role confusion*) individuals establish sexual, ethnic, and career identities or become confused about who they are.

   Young adults (*intimacy versus isolation*) seek companionship and love from another person or become isolated from others.

   Middle-aged adults (*generativity versus stagnation*) feel productive in their work and family or become stagnant and self-absorbed.

   Older adults (*integrity versus despair*) try to make sense of their lives; they either see life as meaningful or they feel despair in their failure to attain goals.

3. Erikson was one of the first psychologists to view development as a life-long process, not one largely fixed by the end of childhood, as Freud had proposed.

   Erikson also emphasized the importance of cultural and social influences on development.

   Some critics say that Erikson's theory is biased toward male development.

   The principal objection to Erikson's theory is its basic outline of life as a sequence of fixed stages. Critics argue that development is much more variable and flexible than this discontinuous, stage approach implies.

Textbook Question Answers

1. developmental theory
2. coherent; hypotheses
3. grand; mini; emergent
4. motives; drives; unconscious; irrational
5. psychoanalytic; psychosexual stages; oral; anal; phallic; latency; 5 or 6; genital; 12

Oral stage: The mouth is the focus of pleasurable sensations as the baby becomes emotionally attached to the person who provides the oral gratifications derived from sucking.

Anal stage: Pleasures related to control and self-control, initially in connection with defecation and toilet training, are paramount.

Phallic stage: Pleasure is derived from genital stimulation; interest in physical differences between the sexes leads to the development of gender identity, sexual orientation, and the child's development of moral standards.

Genital stage: Mature sexual interests that last throughout adulthood emerge.

6. psychosocial; 8; crisis (challenge); span

Age Period	Stage
Birth to 1 yr.	trust vs. **mistrust**
1–3 yrs.	autonomy vs. **shame and doubt**
3–6 yrs.	initiative vs. **guilt**
7–11 yrs.	**industry** vs. inferiority
Adolescence	identity vs. **role confusion**
Young adulthood	**intimacy** vs. isolation
Middle adulthood	**generativity** vs. stagnation
Older adulthood	**integrity** vs. despair

7. behaviorism; John B. Watson; learning

8. at all ages; stimulus; response; conditioning; classical conditioning; operant conditioning

9. Ivan Pavlov; respondent; neutral

10. B. F. Skinner; operant; consequence; instrumental

11. reinforcement; reinforcer

12. social learning; modeling

13. uncertain or inexperienced; admired, powerful, or similar to the observer; self-understanding

14. Harry Harlow; attachment; contact comfort; psychoanalytic; learning

15. cognitive; Jean Piaget

16. sensorimotor; 2

17. 6; preoperational; symbolically; egocentric

18. 7; concrete operational

19. formal operational; abstract (hypothetical); 12

20. cognitive equilibrium

21. cognitive disequilibrium

22. assimilate; accommodate

Two widely accepted psychoanalytic ideas are that (1) unconscious motives affect our behavior, and (2) the early years are a formative period of personality development.

Learning theory's emphasis on the causes and consequences of behavior has led researchers to see that many seemingly inborn problem behaviors may actually be the result of learning.

By focusing attention on active mental processes, cognitive theory has led to a greater understanding of the different types of thinking that are possible at various ages.

23. cognitive

24. Freud; Erikson; Piaget; Watson; Skinner; Pavlov

25. social; biological; genetic

26. nature-nurture; nature; nurture

27. interaction

28. nurture; nature

A man is more likely to be gay if his mother's brother or his own brother is gay. Most children who were raised by lesbian mothers are heterosexual.

29. many

30. dynamic interaction; culture

31. Lev Vygotsky; cognitive

32. novices; mentors (or tutors); apprenticeship in thinking

33. guided participation

34. zone of proximal developmental; assistance

Sociocultural theory has deepened our understanding of the diversity in the pathways of development. It has also emphasized the need to study development in the specific cultural context in which it occurs. The theory has been criticized for neglecting the importance of developmental processes that are not primarily social, such as the role of biological maturation in development.

35. genes; environment

36. instincts; biological

37. environmental; genetic instructions; stress; facilitating

38. selective adaptation

39. all

40. cause corresponding changes and adjustments in every other part

41. ethology; social contact; infant caregiving

42. a. sociocultural

    b. cognitive

    c. learning

    d. psychoanalytic

    e. epigenetic systems

43. a. learning

    b. cognitive

    c. psychoanalytic

    d. epigenetic systems

    e. sociocultural

44. eclectic

Answers to Testing Yourself

1. **d.** is the answer. All of these are true of Erikson's theory. (audio program; textbook, pp. 40–41)

2. **a.** is the answer. Freud's psychosexual stages focus on gratification of sexual pleasure; Erikson's psychosocial stages focus on each person's relationship with the social environment. (audio program; textbook, p. 40)

3. **d.** is the answer. (audio program; textbook, p. 40)

4. **b.** is the answer. In Vygotsky's theory, the mentor draws the learner into this zone. (textbook, p. 56)

5. **c.** During this stage, according to Erikson, children learn to be competent and productive or feel inferior and unable to do anything well. (audio program)

6. **d.** is the answer (textbook, p. 37)

7. **a.** is the answer. (textbook, p. 39)

   b. Learning theory emphasizes the influence of the immediate environment on behavior.

   c. Cognitive theory emphasizes the impact of *conscious* thought processes on behavior.

   d. Sociocultural theory emphasizes the influence on development of social interaction in a specific cultural context.

8. **a.** is the answer. (textbook, p. 39)

9. **a.** is the answer. (textbook, pp. 40–41)

   b. & c. Whereas Freud identified four stages of psychosexual development, Erikson proposed eight psychosocial stages.

   d. Although his theory places greater emphasis on social and cultural forces than Freud's did, Erikson's theory is nevertheless classified as a psychoanalytic theory.

10. **c.** is the answer. Sociocultural theory is an emergent theory. (textbook, p. 38)

    a., b., & d. Each of these is an example of a grand theory.

11. **c.** is the answer. (textbook, p. 43)

12. **a.** is the answer. In classical conditioning, a neutral stimulus—in this case, the bell—is associated with a meaningful stimulus—in this case, food. (textbook, p. 43)

    b. In operant conditioning, the consequences of a voluntary response determine the likelihood of its being repeated. Salivation is an involuntary response.

    c. & d. Positive reinforcement and social learning pertain to voluntary, or operant, responses.

13. **c.** is the answer. (textbook, p. 52)

    a. These are both examples of nurture.

    b. Both of these refer to nature.

    d. The impact of changing historical concepts of childhood on development is an example of how environmental forces (nurture) shape development.

14. **d.** is the answer. (textbook, p. 46)

    a. & c. These can be true in all types of learning.

b. This was not discussed as an aspect of developmental theory.

15. **d.** is the answer. (textbook, p. 55)

    a. & c. Sociocultural and learning theories focus almost entirely on environmental factors (nurture) in development.

    b. Cognitive theory emphasizes the developing person's own mental activity but ignores genetic differences in individuals.

16. **a.** is the answer. (textbook, p. 55)

    b. Vygotsky's theory does not emphasize biological processes.

    c. & d. Vygotsky's theory places considerable emphasis on language and social factors.

17. **a.** is the answer. (textbook, p. 48)

18. **c.** is the answer. (textbook, p. 49)

    a. This refers to the core of Erikson's psychosocial stages, which deals with people's interactions with the environment.

    b. Equilibrium occurs when existing schemes *do* fit a person's current experiences.

    d. Negative reinforcement is the removal of a stimulus as a consequence of a desired behavior.

19. **b.** is the answer. (textbook, p. 53)

    c. This is only true of psychoanalytic theory.

    d. Although the grand theories have emphasized nurture over nature in this matter, no theory suggests that sexual orientation is voluntarily chosen.

20. **c.** is the answer. (textbook, p. 56)

    a. This describes attention.

    b. This describes positive reinforcement.

    d. This describes reciprocal determinism.

Reference

Erikson, Erik H. (1963). *Childhood and society* (2nd ed.). New York: Norton.

   This is Erikson's landmark publication, which outlines the eight stages of psychosocial development.

Heredity and Environment

AUDIO PROGRAM: And Then We Knew: The Impact of Genetic Information

---

ORIENTATION

Lessons 1 and 2 of *Seasons of Life* examined the meaning of life stories and the methods and theories of life-span development. Now we turn to the journey through life itself. Lesson 3 focuses on the mechanisms of biological inheritance and the interaction of those mechanisms with environmental influences. The audio program and text explain how physical characteristics are inherited from our parents through **genes**, **chromosomes**, and **DNA**. They also describe **genetic** and **chromosomal abnormalities**, which occur when a fertilized egg has destructive genes or too few or too many chromosomes, and the physical and mental disorders that may result.

As described in Chapter 3 of the text, and by the experts in the audio program, genetic testing can help to predict whether a couple will produce a child with a genetic problem. In addition, the emerging field of **genetic counseling** plays a vital role in helping people to understand and cope with genetic information. The audio program further notes that through the new experimental techniques of **gene mapping** and **gene replacement therapy**, researchers are gaining a deeper understanding of the causes of many genetic disorders and of how to prevent them.

As the audio program illustrates, the price of advances in genetic technology is increased knowledge, the implications of which many individuals would rather not confront. Knowing that the husband, Don, is a **carrier** of a deleterious gene, a young couple faces the difficult decision of whether or not to have children. In addition to its potentially devastating impact on Don's self-esteem, the genetic "news" deeply affects both his wife, Karen, and his mother. As the story unfolds, we learn from geneticist Dr. Donald Rucknagel and genetic counselor Diane Baker of the incredible technological advances that have made genetic counseling possible, and of the impact this technology has on a real couple and their extended families.

LESSON GOALS

By the end of this lesson, you should be prepared to:

1. Describe the process of conception and the first hours of development of the zygote.

2. Explain the basic mechanisms of heredity, including the significance of chromosomes and genes.

3. Describe common causes of genetic and chromosomal abnormalities and several techniques of genetic testing for the presence of such disorders.

4. Discuss the process and importance of genetic counseling.

5. Explain how scientists distinguish the effects of genes and environment on development, and explain the role of molecular genetics in this process.

Audio Assignment

Listen to the audio tape that accompanies Lesson 3: "And Then We Knew."

Write answers to the following questions. You may replay portions of the program if you need to refresh your memory. Answer guidelines may be found in the Lesson Guidelines section at the end of this chapter.

1. What is the difference between a person's genotype and phenotype?

2. In the audio program, how was amniocentesis used to determine that Karen and Don's first child would have been mentally retarded and physically deformed?

3. What is the baseline genetic risk factor that is present in any pregnancy?

4. How can genetic counseling help in each of the following areas?

   a. prenatal diagnosis

   b. pediatric genetics

   c. adult-onset conditions

5. Describe each of the following techniques for treating genetic abnormalities, and explain its significance.

   a. chorionic villi sampling

   b. gene mapping

   c. gene replacement therapy

Textbook Assignment

Read Chapter 3: "Heredity and Environment," pages 69–95 in *The Developing Person Through the Life Span, 5/e*, then work through the material that follows to review it. Complete the sentences and answer the questions. As you proceed, evaluate your performance for each secdtion by consulting the answers on page 39. Do not continue with the next section until you understand each answer. If you need to, review or reread the appropriate section in the textbook before continuing.

Development Begins (pp. 69–76)

1. The human reproductive cells, which are called _____ , include the male's _____ and the female's _____ .

2. When the gametes' genetic material combines, a living cell called a _____ is formed.

3. Before the zygote begins the process of cellular division that starts human development, the combined genetic material from both gametes is _____ to form two complete sets of genetic instructions. Soon after, following a genetic timetable, the cells start to _____ , with various cells beginning to specialize and reproduce at different rates.

4. A complete copy of the genetic instructions inherited by the zygote at the moment of conception is found in _____ (every/most/ only a few) cell(s) of the body.

5. The basic units of heredity are the _____ , which are discrete segments of a _____ , which is a molecule of _____ .

6. Genetic instructions are "written" in a chemical code, made up of four pairs of bases: _____ , _____ , _____ , and _____ . The precise nature of a gene's instructions is determined by this _____ _____ , that is, by the overall _____ in which base pairs appear along each segment of the DNA molecule.

7. The _____ _____ _____ is the ongoing international effort to map and interpret the complete genetic code. This task is complicated by the fact that some genes appear in several versions, called _____ , and that most genes have _____ (only one/several different) function(s).

8. Genes direct the synthesis of hundreds of different kinds of _____ , including _____ , which are the body's building blocks and regulators. Genes direct not only the form and location of cells, but also life itself, instructing cells to _____ _____ .

9. Each normal person inherits _____ chromosomes, _____ from each parent.

10. During cell division, the gametes each receive _____ (one/both) member(s) of each chromosome pair. Thus, in number each gamete has _____ chromosomes.

11. The developing person's sex is determined by the _____ pair of chromosomes. In the female, this pair is composed of two _____-shaped chromosomes and is designated _____ . In the male, this pair includes one _____ and one _____ chromosome and is therefore designated _____ .

12. The critical factor in the determination of a zygote's sex is which _____ (sperm/ovum) reaches the other gamete first.

13. Genes ensure both genetic _____ across the species and genetic _____ within it.

14. When the twenty-three chromosome pairs divide up during the formation of gametes, which of the two pair members will end up in a particular gamete is determined by _____ .

15. Genetic variability is also affected by the _____-_____ of genes, and by the interaction of genetic instructions in ways unique to the individual. This means that any given mother and father can form approximately _____ genetically different offspring.

16. Identical twins, which occur about once in every _____ pregnancies, are called _____ twins because they come from one zygote. Such twins _____ (are/are not) genetically identical.

17. Twins who begin life as two separate zygotes created by the fertilization of two ova, are called _____ twins. Such twins have approximately _____ percent of their genes in common.

18. Dizygotic births occur naturally about once in every _____ births. Women in their _____ (what age?) are three times as likely to have dizygotic twins than women in their _____ .

19. The number of multiple births has _____ (increased/decreased/remained unchanged) in many nations because of the increased use of _____ . Generally, the more embryos that develop together, the _____ , less _____ , and more _____ each one is.

20. (Changing Policy) Worldwide, slightly more _____ (females/males) than _____ (females/males) are born each year. However, because _____ (females/males) have a slightly higher rate of childhood death, a balance occurs when men and women reach _____ age.

21. (Changing Policy) After about age _____ , the sex ratio now favors women. This is due to the fact that in the past many women died in _____ , whereas today more men than women die from _____ _____ .

22. (Changing Policy) Today, choosing the sex of children _____ (is/is not) feasible and _____ (is/is not) widespread.

Genotype to Phenotype (pp. 77–86)

23. Most human characteristics are affected by many genes, and so are _____ ; and by many factors, and so are _____ .

24. The sum total of all the genes a person inherits is called the _____ . The sum total of

all the genes that are actually expressed is called the _____ .

25. A person who has a gene in his or her genotype that is not expressed in the phenotype is said to be a _____ of that gene.

26. For any given trait, the phenotype arises from the interaction of the proteins synthesized from the specific _____ that make up the genotype, and from the interaction between the genotype and the _____ .

27. A phenotype that reflects the sum of the contributions of all the genes involved in its determination illustrates the _____ pattern of genetic interaction. Examples include genes that affect _____ and _____ _____ .

28. Less often, genes interact in a _____ fashion. In one example of this pattern, some genes are more influential than others; this is called the _____-pattern. In this pattern, the more influential gene is called _____ , and the weaker gene is called _____ . In one variation of this pattern, the phenotype is influenced primarily, but not exclusively, by the dominant gene; this is the _____ _____ pattern. Hundreds of _____ characteristics follow this basic pattern.

29. Some recessive genes are located only on the X chromosome and so are called _____-_____ .

Examples of such genes are the ones that determine _____ _____ .

Because they have only one X chromosome, _____ (females/males) are more likely to have these characteristics in their phenotype.

30. Complicating inheritance further is the fact that dominant genes sometimes do not completely _____ the phenotype. This may be caused by _____ ,

_____ , or other factors. Furthermore, chromosome pairs sometimes do not split precisely, resulting in a mixture of cells called a _____ .

31. Whether a gene is inherited from the mother or the father _____ (does/does not) influence its behavior. This tendency of genes is called _____ _____ , or tagging.

32. The complexity of genetic interaction is particularly apparent in _____ , which is the study of the genetic origins of _____ characteristics. These include _____ traits such as _____ ; psychological disorders such as _____ _____ ; and _____ traits such as _____ .

33. Most behavioral traits are affected by the _____ of large numbers of _____ with _____ factors. Traits that are plastic early in life _____ (always/do not always) remain plastic thereafter.

34. To identify genetic influences on development, researchers must distinguish genetic effects from _____ effects. To this end, researchers study _____ and _____ children.

35. If _____ (monozygotic/dizygotic) twins are found to be much more similar on a particular trait than _____ (monozygotic/dizygotic) twins are, it is likely that genes play a significant role in the appearance of that trait.

36. Traits that show a strong correlation between adopted children and their _____ (adoptive/biological) parents suggest a genetic basis for those characteristics.

37. The best way to try to separate the effects of genes and environments is to study _____ twins who have been raised in _____ (the same/different) environments.

38. Environment, as broadly defined in the text, affects _____ (most/every/ few) human characteristic(s).

39. The study of the chemical codes that make up a particular molecule of DNA is called

_____ _____ .

40. Researchers can now directly compare a pattern of genes shared by two individuals with a promising new statistical technique called

_____ _____

_____ .

Explain how social scientists define environment.

Briefly explain how shyness (or inhibition), which is influenced by genes, is also affected by the social environment.

41. Other psychological traits that have strong genetic influences but may be affected by environment include _____ ,

_____ , _____

_____ , _____ , and

_____ .

42. If one monozygotic twin develops schizophrenia, about _____ of the time the other twin does, too. Researchers have pinpointed a gene on chromosome _____ , which predisposes schizophrenia.

43. Environmental influences _____ (do/do not) play an important role in the appearance of schizophrenia. One predisposing factor is

birth during _____

_____ , probably because a certain

_____ is more prevalent at this time of year.

44. Another disease that develops from the complex interaction of genes and environmental conditions is _____ _____

45. (A Life-Span View) Alcoholism _____ (is/is not) partly genetic; furthermore, its expression _____ (is/is not) affected by the environment. Certain temperamental traits correlate with abusive drinking, including _____ . A person is most likely to become an active alcoholic between ages _____ and _____ .

(A Life-Span View) Briefly explain how genes for alcoholism might have evolved in certain groups.

Inherited Abnormalities (pp. 86–93)

Researchers study genetic and chromosomal abnormalities for three major reasons. They are:

46. (Research Report) When conception occurs in a laboratory dish, called _____ , cells can be analyzed for genetic defects before they are inserted into the uterus. This procedure is called _____ - _____

_____ . One test for neural-tube defects and Down syndrome analyzes the level of _____ in the mother's blood. An ultrasound, or _____ , uses high-frequency sound waves to produce an image of the fetus. Physicians use a device called a _____ to directly observe the fetus and the inside of the placenta.

47. (Research Report) The "mainstay" of prenatal diagnosis is _____ , in which a small amount of fluid surrounding the fetus, inside the placenta, is analyzed for chromosomal or genetic abnormalities. A test that provides the same information but can be performed much earlier during the pregnancy is called

_____ _____

_____ .

48. Chromosomal abnormalities occur during the formation of the _____ , producing a sperm or ovum that does not have the normal complement of chromosomes.

49. An estimated _____ of all zygotes have too few or too many chromosomes. Most of these _____ (do/do not) begin to develop, usually because a _____ occurs. Nevertheless, about 1 in every _____ newborns has one chromosome too few or one too many, leading to a cluster of characteristics called a

_____ .

50. The most common extra-chromosome syndrome is _____ , which is also called _____ .

List several of the physical and psychological characteristics associated with Down syndrome.

51. About 1 in every 500 infants has either a missing _____ chromosome or two or more such chromosomes. One such syndrome is _____ _____ , in

which a boy inherits the _____ chromosome pattern.

52. In some individuals, part of the X chromosome is attached by such a thin string of molecules that it seems about to break off; this abnormality is called _____-_____ syndrome.

53. The variable that most often correlates with chromosomal abnormalities is _____

_____ .

54. Chromosomal abnormalities such as Down syndrome _____ (rarely/almost always) follow an age-related pattern.

55. (In Person) Through _____

_____ _____ , couples today can learn more about their genes and about their chances of conceiving a child with chromosomal or other genetic abnormalities.

56. (In Person) List four situations in which genetic counseling is strongly recommended.

a. _____

b. _____

c. _____

d. _____

57. It is much _____ (more/less) likely that a person is a carrier of one or more harmful genes than that he or she has abnormal chromosomes.

58. Most of the known genetic disorders are _____ (dominant/recessive). Genetic disorders usually _____ (are/are not) seriously disabling.

59. Two exceptions are the central nervous system disease called _____ _____ and the disorder that causes its victims to exhibit uncontrollable tics and explosive outbursts, called _____

_____ .

60. Genetic disorders that are _____

and _____ claim more victims than

dominant ones. Three common recessive disor-

ders are _____

_____ , _____ , and

_____-_____

_____ .

Testing Yourself

After you have completed the audio and text review questions, see how well you do on the following quiz. Correct answers, with text and audio references, may be found at the end of this chapter.

1. A person who is a "carrier" of a genetic disorder but does not suffer from it manifests the abnormality:
   a. only in his or her genotype.
   b. only in his or her phenotype.
   c. in either the genotype or the phenotype.
   d. in both the genotype and the phenotype.

2. The experimental technique in which normal genes are cultivated and exchanged for abnormal genes is called:
   a. chorionic villi sampling.
   b. gene mapping.
   c. amniocentesis.
   d. gene replacement therapy.

3. In the audio program, Don and Karen decided to have a second child, even though Don was a carrier of a genetic condition in which there was a(n):
   a. dominant gene for Down syndrome.
   b. genetic incompatibility with Karen.
   c. excess of amniotic fluid.
   d. chromosome translocation.

4. Concerning gene mapping and gene replacement therapy, which of the following is true?
   a. At the present time, more advances have been made in gene mapping than in gene replacement therapy.
   b. More advances have been made in gene replacement therapy than in gene sampling.
   c. The technology is not yet sophisticated enough for gene replacement to be used.
   d. All of the above are true.

5. When a sperm and an ovum merge, a one-celled _____ is formed.
   a. zygote
   b. reproductive cell
   c. gamete
   d. monozygote

6. Genes are discrete segments that provide the biochemical instructions that each cell needs to become:
   a. a zygote.
   b. a chromosome.
   c. a specific part of a functioning human body.
   d. deoxyribonucleic acid.

7. In the male, the twenty-third pair of chromosomes is designated _____ ; in the female, this pair is designated _____.
   a. *XX; XY*   c. *XO; XXY*
   b. *XY; XX*   d. *XXY; XO*

8. Since the twenty-third pair of chromosomes in females is *XX*, each ovum carries an:
   a. *XX* zygote.   c. *XY* zygote.
   b. *X* zygote.   d. *X* chromosome.

9. When a zygote splits, the two identical, independent clusters that develop become:
   a. dizygotic twins.   c. fraternal twins.
   b. monozygotic twins.   d. trizygotic twins.

10. In scientific research, the *best* way to separate the effects of genes and the environment is to study:
    a. dizygotic twins.
    b. adopted children and their biological parents.
    c. adopted children and their adoptive parents.
    d. monozygotic twins raised in different environments.

11. Most of the known genetic disorders are:
    a. dominant.
    b. recessive.
    c. seriously disabling.
    d. sex-linked.

12. When we say that a characteristic is multifactorial, we mean that:
    a. many genes are involved.
    b. many environmental factors are involved.
    c. many genetic and environmental factors are involved.
    d. the characteristic is polygenic.

13. Genes are segments of molecules of:
    a. genotype.
    b. deoxyribonucleic acid (DNA).
    c. karyotype.
    d. phenotype.

14. The potential for genetic diversity in humans is so great because:
    a. there are approximately 8 million possible combinations of chromosomes.
    b. when the sperm and ovum unite, genetic combinations not present in either parent can be formed.
    c. just before a chromosome pair divides during the formation of gametes, genes cross over, producing recombinations.
    d. of all the above reasons.

15. A chromosomal abnormality that affects males only involves a(n):
    a. *XO* chromosomal pattern.
    b. *XXX* chromosomal pattern.
    c. *YY* chromosomal pattern.
    d. *XXY* chromosomal pattern.

16. Polygenic complexity is most apparent in _____ characteristics.
    a. physical
    b. psychological
    c. recessive gene
    d. dominant gene

17. Babies born with trisomy-21 (Down syndrome) are often:
    a. born to older parents.
    b. unusually aggressive.
    c. abnormally tall by adolescence.
    d. blind.

18. To say that a trait is polygenic means that:
    a. many genes make it more likely that the individual will inherit the trait.
    b. several genes must be present in order for the individual to inherit the trait.
    c. the trait is multifactorial.
    d. most people carry genes for the trait.

19. Some genetic diseases are recessive, so the child cannot inherit the condition unless both parents:
    a. have Kleinfelter syndrome.
    b. carry the same recessive gene.
    c. have *XO* chromosomes.
    d. have the disease.

LESSON GUIDELINES

Audio Question Guidelines

1. **Genotype** refers to an individual's entire genetic makeup, including those genes that are not expressed outwardly.

   When a trait is apparent, it means that the genes have expressed themselves in the person's **phenotype**.

2. **Amniocentesis** is a prenatal diagnostic test that can reveal genetic problems in a fetus months before birth. A needle is inserted into the uterus, where the fetus floats in a sac filled with amniotic fluid. Amniotic fluid contains cells shed by the fetus. A sample of fluid is withdrawn and the chromosomes of the cells are magnified, photographed, and examined for chromosomal abnormalities.

   In the case of Karen and Don's unborn fetus, an examination of its chromosomes showed that the child would not only be a carrier of the genetic abnormality called a **chromosome translocation** but would also develop the characteristic physical and mental abnormalities in its phenotype. On the basis of this information they decided to terminate the pregnancy.

3. When any healthy young couple undertakes a pregnancy, there is a two-to- three-percent baseline risk that the outcome could be abnormal—for example, a significant birth defect resulting in mental retardation or a shortened life span.

4. As in Karen and Don's case, prenatal diagnosis and counseling are available to prospective parents concerned that a genetic condition may run in their family.

   Pediatric genetic counseling is available to families whose children were born with significant birth defects, and children who, though apparently healthy at birth, later show a decline in development that suggests a genetic condition.

   Counseling for **adult-onset conditions** is available for genetic conditions such as Huntington's disease, presenile dementia, certain neuromuscular disorders, and other problems that do not begin to be expressed until the adult years.

5. **Chorionic villi sampling**: A catheter is inserted into the placenta parallel to the wall of the uterus. A sample of the villi—fingerlike projections that dip into the lining of the uterus—is removed through the catheter.

   The villi are composed of fetal tissue, the cells of which are dividing so rapidly that their chromosomes can be examined directly.

Two advantages of this technique over amniocentesis are that it can be done earlier in the pregnancy, and that the results are available to parents sooner.

Gene mapping: Gene mapping refers to techniques that identify the abnormal genes specifically causing a genetic disorder.

Through gene mapping, abnormal genes have been identified for Huntington's disease, cystic fibrosis, sickle-cell anemia, and other genetic conditions.

Gene replacement therapy: Gene replacement therapy refers to the experimental process in which "good" genes are cultivated and substituted for abnormal genes in a diseased person's tissue.

Still in the experimental stages, and not without possible negative effects, gene replacement therapy may eventually be available to treat some disorders.

Textbook Question Answers

1. gametes; sperm; ovum
2. zygote
3. duplicated; differentiate
4. every
5. genes; chromosome; DNA
6. adenine; guanine; cytosine; thymine; genetic code; sequence
7. Human Genome Project; alleles; several different
8. proteins; enzymes; grow, to repair damage, to take in nourishment, to multiply, to atrophy, and so forth
9. 46; 23
10. one; 23
11. twenty-third; *X*; *XX*; *X*; *Y*; *XY*
12. sperm
13. continuity; diversity
14. chance
15. crossing-over; 64 trillion
16. 270; monozygotic; are
17. dizygotic (fraternal); 50
18. 60; late 30s; early 20s
19. increased; fertility drugs; smaller; mature; vulnerable
20. males; females; males; reproductive
21. 45; childbirth; heart attacks
22. is; is not

23. polygenic; multifactorial

24. genotype; phenotype

25. carrier

26. genes; environment

27. additive; height; skin color

28. nonadditive; dominant-recessive; dominant; recessive; incomplete dominance; physical

29. X-linked; color-blindness, many allergies, several diseases, and some learning disabilities; males

30. penetrate; temperature; stress; mosaic

31. does; genetic imprinting

32. behavioral genetics; psychological; personality; sociability, assertiveness, moodiness, and fearfulness; schizophrenia, depression, and attention-deficit hyperactive disorder; cognitive; memory for numbers, spatial perception, and fluency of expression

33. interaction; genes; environmental; do not always

34. environmental; twins; adopted

35. monozygotic; dizygotic

36. biological

37. identical (or monozygotic); different

38. every

39. molecular genetics

40. quantitative trait loci

Social scientists define *environment* broadly to refer to the multitude of variables that can interact with the person's genetic inheritance at every point of life.

A genetically shy child whose parents are outgoing, for example, would have many more contacts with other people and would observe his or her parents socializing more freely than if this same child's parents were also shy. In growing up, the child might learn to relax in social settings and would become less observably shy than he or she would have been with more introverted parents, despite the genetic predisposition toward shyness. Culture plays a role in the expression of shyness.

41. intelligence; emotionality; activity level; aggression; religiosity

42. two-thirds; 6

43. do; late winter; virus

44. Alzheimer's disease

45. is; is; a quick temper, a willingness to take risks, and a high level of anxiety; 15; 25

Since the distillation process involved in producing alcohol killed the destructive bacteria that thrived in drinking water, being able to drink alcohol in quantity was adaptive for our ancestors in most of Europe.

Because east Asians boiled their water and drank it as tea, however, about half lack the gene for an enzyme necessary to fully metabolize alcohol.

By studying genetic disruptions of normal development, researchers (a) gain a fuller appreciation of the complexities of genetic interaction, (b) reduce misinformation and prejudice directed toward those afflicted by such disorders, and (c) help individuals understand the likelihood of occurrence and to become better prepared to limit their harmful effects.

46. in vitro; pre-implantation testing; alphafetoprotein; sonogram; fetoscope

47. amniocentesis; chorionic villi sampling

48. gametes

49. half; do not; spontaneous abortion; 200; syndrome

50. Down syndrome; trisomy-21

Most people with Down syndrome have certain facial characteristics—a thick tongue, round face, slanted eyes—as well as distinctive hands, feet, and fingerprints. Many also have hearing problems, heart abnormalities, muscle weakness, and short stature. Almost all experience some mental slowness.

51. sex; Klinefelter syndrome; XXY

52. fragile-X

53. maternal age

54. almost always

55. prenatal genetic counseling

56. Genetic counseling is recommended for (a) those who have a parent, sibling, or child with a serious genetic condition; (b) those who have a history of spontaneous abortions, stillbirths, or infertility; (c) couples who are from the same ethnic group or subgroup; and (d) women over age 34.

57. more

58. dominant; are not

59. Huntington's chorea; Tourette syndrome

60. recessive; multifactorial; cystic fibrosis, thalassemia, sickle-cell anemia

Answers to Testing Yourself

1. **a.** is the answer. A carrier manifests the abnormality only in his or her genotype. (audio program; textbook, p. 77)

2. **d.** is the answer. Although still in the experimental stage, gene replacement therapy may someday be a viable form of treatment for many genetic disorders. (audio program)

3. **d.** is the answer. A fragment from Don's chromosome 3 had broken off and become attached to his chromosome 15. (audio program)

4. **a.** is the answer. More advances have been made in genetic mapping. (audio program)

5. **a.** is the answer. (textbook, p. 69)

   b. & c. The reproductive cells (sperm and ova), which are also called gametes, are individual entities.

   d. *Monozygote* refers to one member of a pair of identical twins.

6. **c.** is the answer. (textbook, p. 70)

   a. The zygote is the first cell of the developing person.

   b. Chromosomes are molecules of DNA that *carry* genes.

   d. DNA molecules contain genetic information.

7. **b.** is the answer. (textbook, p. 72)

8. **d.** is the answer. When the gametes are formed, one member of each chromosome pair splits off; because in females both are *X* chromosomes, each ovum must carry an *X* chromosome. (textbook, p. 72)

   a., b., & c. The zygote refers to the merged sperm and ovum that is the first new cell of the developing individual.

9. **b.** is the answer. *Mono* means "one." Thus, monozygotic twins develop from one zygote. (textbook, p. 75)

   a. & c. Dizygotic, or fraternal, twins develop from two (*di*) zygotes.

   d. A trizygotic birth would result in triplets (*tri*), rather than twins.

10. **d.** is the answer. In this situation, one factor (genetic similarity) is held constant while the other factor (environment) is varied. Therefore, any similarity in traits is strong evidence of genetic inheritance. (textbook, p. 81)

11. **a.** is the answer. (textbook, p. 90)

c. & d. Most dominant disorders are neither seriously disabling, nor sex-linked.

12. **c.** is the answer. (textbook, p. 77)

   a., b., & d. *Polygenic* means "many genes"; *multifactorial* means "many factors," which are not limited to either genetic or environmental factors.

13. **b.** is the answer. (textbook, p. 70)

   a. Genotype is a person's genetic potential.

   c. A karyotype is a picture of a person's chromosomes.

   d. Phenotype is the actual expression of a genotype.

14. **d.** is the answer. (textbook, p. 73)

15. **d.** is the answer. (textbook, p. 89)

   a. & b. These chromosomal abnormalities affect females.

   c. There is no such abnormality.

16. **b.** is the answer. (textbook, p. 79)

   c. & d. The text does not equate polygenic complexity with either recessive or dominant genes.

17. **a.** is the answer. (textbook, p. 89)

18. **b.** is the answer. (textbook, p. 77)

19. **b.** is the answer. (textbook, p. 92)

   a. & c. These abnormalities involve the sex chromosomes, not genes.

   d. In order for an offspring to inherit a recessive condition, the parents need only be carriers of the recessive gene in their genotypes; they need not actually have the disease.

Reference

Plomin, R., DeFries, J. C., & McClearn, G. E. (1995). *Behavioral genetics: A primer* (2nd ed.). San Francisco: Freeman.

A helpful, readable introduction to genetic research.

Prenatal Development and Birth

AUDIO PROGRAM: When to Have a baby

ORIENTATION

Is 21 years of age too young to become a parent? Is 36 years of age too old? There are no simple answers to these questions. As Lesson 4 explains, the answers depend on the settings of three developmental clocks that tick through the seasons of life. The first is the biological clock, which is the body's timetable for growth and decline. The second is the social clock, a culturally set timetable that establishes when various events in life are most appropriate. The third is the psychological clock, our personal timetable of readiness for life's milestones. The clocks, which come into play in every major transition of life, are not always in synchrony. In addition, their settings have been changed over the course of history.

One of the themes of *Seasons of Life* is that the diversity of life-span development is due in part to the fact that the social and psychological clocks are not set the same for everyone. Just as each culture, subculture, and historical period establishes its own social clock, so each individual establishes his or her own psychological clock on the basis of individual life experiences.

In audio program 4, "When to Have a Baby," two couples about to have their first child discuss their impending parenthood. Because one of the expectant mothers is 21 and the other 36, the life-span consequences of their "early" and "late" births will be very different. Their stories, illuminated by the expert commentary of sociologist Alice Rossi and anthropologist Jane Lancaster, illustrate how the three developmental clocks influence the timing of births.

The birth of a child is one of life's most enriching experiences. Nine months of prenatal development culminate in the expectant couple assuming a new and demanding role as parents, and being transformed from a couple to a family. But, as discussed in Chapter 4 of the textbook, parental responsibilities begin long before birth, during the prenatal period. This development is outlined, together with a description of some of the problems that can occur, including prenatal exposure to disease, drugs, and environmental hazards, and **preterm** birth and **low birth weight**.

As the program opens we hear the voices of the two couples pondering their imminent transition to parenthood.

LESSON GOALS

By the end of this lesson you should be prepared to:

1. Discuss how the timing of births and the setting of the three developmental clocks have changed over the course of human history, and explain the significance of the three clocks.

2. Outline the rapid and orderly development that occurs between conception and birth.

3. Explain the general risk factors and specific hazards that may affect prenatal development.

4. Describe the normal process of birth and the test used to assess the neonate's condition.

5. Explain the concept of parent–newborn bonding and the current view of most developmentalists regarding bonding in humans.

Audio Assignment

Listen to the audio tape that accompanies Lesson 4: "When to Have a Baby."

Write answers to the following questions. You may replay portions of the program if you need to refresh your memory. Answer guidelines may be found in the Lesson Guidelines section at the end of this chapter.

1. Explain how the biological, social, and psychological clocks each affect the timing of births.

2. Discuss whether the settings of the three developmental clocks are different for different generations.

3. Explain how the pattern and timing of childbearing changed as humans shifted from a hunting-and-gathering society to a modern society.

4. Discuss some of the life-span consequences of births that occur early and late in parents' lives.

Textbook Assignment

Read Chapter 4: "Prenatal Development and Birth," pages 97–127 in *The Developing Person Through the Life Span*, *5/e*, then work through the material that follows to review it. Complete the sentences and answer the questions. As you proceed, evaluate your performance for each secdtion by consulting the answers on page 54. Do not continue with the next section until you understand each answer. If you need to, review or reread the appropriate section in the textbook before continuing.

From Zygote to Newborn (pp. 97–104)

1. Prenatal development is divided into _____ main periods. The first two weeks of development are called the _____ period; from the _____ week through the _____ week is known as the period of the _____ ; and from this point until birth is the period of the _____ . Some developmentalists prefer to divide pregnancy into 3-month periods called _____ .

2. At least through the _____ (how many?) doubling of cells following conception, each of the zygote's cells is identical. Soon after, clusters of cells begin to take on distinct traits. The first clear sign of this process, called _____ , occurs about _____ week(s) after conception, when the multiplying cells separate into outer cells that will become the _____ and inner cells that will become the

_____ .

3. The next significant event is the burrowing of the outer cells of the organism into the lining of the uterus, a process called _____ . This process _____ (is/is not) automatic.

4. At the beginning of the period of the embryo, a fold in the outer cells of the developing individual forms a structure that will become the _____ _____ , which will develop into the _____ _____ .

Briefly describe the major features of development during the second month.

5. Eight weeks after conception, the embryo weighs about _____ and is about _____ in length. The organism now becomes known as the _____ .

6. The first stage of development of the sex organs is the appearance in the _____ week of the _____ _____ , a cluster of cells that can develop into male or female sex organs.

7. If the fetus has a(n) _____ (X/Y) chromosome, a gene on this chromosome sends a biochemical signal that triggers the development of the _____ (male/female) sex organs. Without that gene, no signal is sent, and the fetus begins to develop _____ (male/female) sex organs. Not until the _____ week are the external male or female genital organs fully formed.

8. By the end of the _____ month, the fetus is fully formed, weighs approximately _____ , and is about _____ long. These figures _____ (vary/do not vary) from fetus to fetus.

9. The placenta connects the mother's _____ _____ with that of her growing embryo.

10. During the fourth, fifth, and six months the brain increases in size by a factor of _____ . This neurological maturation is essential to the regulation of such basic body functions as _____ and _____ .

11. The age at which a fetus has at least some chance of surviving outside the uterus is called the _____ _____ , which occurs _____ weeks after conception.

12. At about _____ weeks after conception, brain-wave patterns begin to resemble the _____ – _____ cycles of a newborn.

13. A 28-week-old fetus typically weighs about _____ and has more than a _____ percent chance of survival.

14. The normal due date is calculated at _____ days after conception.

15. Two crucial aspects of development in the last months of prenatal life are maturation of the _____ and _____ systems.

16. The average newborn weighs _____ .

17. An important part of the fetus's weight gain is the formation of body _____ , which will provide a layer of insulation to keep the newborn warm.

18. This weight gain also provides the fetus with _____ for use until the mother's breast milk is fully established.

Risk Reduction (pp. 104–112)

19. The scientific study of factors that contribute to birth defects is called _____ . Harmful agents that can cause birth defects, called _____ , include

_____

_____ .

20. Substances that impair the child's action and intellect by harming the brain are called _____ _____ .

21. Teratology is a science of _____ _____ , which attempts to evaluate the factors that can make prenatal harm more or less likely to occur.

22. Three crucial factors that determine whether a specific teratogen will cause harm, and of what nature, are the _____ of exposure, the _____ of exposure, and the developing organism's _____ _____ to damage from the substance.

23. The time when a particular part of the body is most susceptible to teratogenic damage is called its _____ _____ . For physical structure and form, this is the entire period of the _____ . However, for _____ teratogens, which damage the _____ and _____ _____ , the entire prenatal period is critical.

24. Two especially critical periods are at the beginning of pregnancy, when _____ can impede _____ , and during the final weeks, when the fetus is particularly vulnerable to damage that can cause _____ _____ .

25. Some teratogens have a _____ effect—that is, the substances are harmless until exposure reaches a certain frequency or amount. However, the _____ of some teratogens when taken together may make them more harmful at lower dosage levels than when taken separately.

26. Genetic susceptibilities to the prenatal effects of alcohol and to certain birth disorders, such as cleft palate, may involve defective _____ .

27. When the mother-to-be's diet is deficient in _____ _____ , neural-tube defects such as _____ _____ or _____ may result.

28. Genetic vulnerability is also related to the sex of the developing organism. Generally, _____ (male/female) embryos and fetuses are more vulnerable to teratogens. This sex not only has a higher rate of teratogenic birth defects and later behavioral problems, but also a higher rate of _____ _____ and later _____ _____ .

29. When contracted during the critical period, German measles, also called _____ , is known to cause structural damage to the heart, eyes, ears, and brain.

30. The most devastating viral teratogen is _____ _____ _____ , which gradually overwhelms the body's natural immune responses and leads to a host of diseases that together constitute _____ _____ _____ . About one in every four infants born to women with this virus acquire it from the mother during _____ or _____ . This disease's long incubation period—up to _____ years or more—complicates its prevention.

31. The best way to prevent pediatric AIDS is to prevent _____ _____ . The second best way is to _____ _____ . A third preventive measure is to administer the drug _____ to HIV-infected women during pregnancy and at birth.

32. Some widely used medicinal drugs, including _____ , are teratogenic in some cases.

33. Psychoactive drugs such as _____ _____ _____ slow fetal _____ and can trigger premature _____ . The potential long-term teratogenic effects of such drugs include _____ _____ .

34. (text and Table 4.3) Prenatal exposure to alcohol may lead to _____ _____ _____ , which includes such symptoms as abnormal facial characteristics, slowed physical growth, behavior problems, and mental

retardation. Likely victims of this syndrome are those whose mothers ingest more than

_____ drinks daily during pregnancy. Even more moderate alcohol consumption can be teratogenic, causing _____ .

_____ _____ .

(Table 4.3) List some of the effects of fetal exposure to tobacco.

35. (Table 4.3) Infants born to heavy users of marijuana often show impairment to their

_____ _____

system.

(Table 4.3) List some of the effects of fetal exposure to cocaine.

36. The specific effects of illicit drugs _____ (are/are not) difficult to document because users often use multiple drugs and have other problems, including

_____ _____ .

(Changing Policy) List five protective steps pregnant women should take to prevent drug damage to their offspring.

37. (Changing Policy) Babies born to women who recently emigrated to the United States often weigh _____ (more/less) than babies of native-born women of the same ethnicity. One likely reason is that these women are more often _____-_____ .

38. (Changing Policy) Teratogenic effects of psychoactive drugs _____ (do/do not) accumulate throughout pregnancy.

Low Birthweight (pp. 112–117)

39. Newborns who weigh less than

_____ are classified as

_____ _____ babies. Below 3 pounds, they are called _____

_____ _____ babies; at less than 2 pounds they are _____

_____ _____ babies. Worldwide, rates of this condition _____ (vary/do not vary) from nation to nation.

40. Many factors can cause low birthweight, including _____ and

_____ .

41. Babies who are born 3 or more weeks early are called _____ .

State several factors that increase the likelihood of early birth.

42. Infants who weigh substantially less than they should, given how much time has passed since conception, are called _____

_____ _____

_____ .

43. About 25 percent of all low-birthweight (LBW) births in the United States are linked to maternal use of _____ , which is responsible for about _____ percent of LBW in many European nations.

44. Virtually all the risk factors for low birthweight are related to _____ . Mothers of low-birthweight babies are more likely to be _____ , _____ , _____ , and _____ .

45. (A Life-Span View) Overall, rates of very-low-birthweight and extremely-low-birthweight babies in the United States are _____ (rising/falling/holding steady). Perhaps because LBW babies are more demanding and less responsive, the rates of child _____ and _____ are elevated for these children, especially if they are also _____ .

46. Low-birthweight infants are often raised in low-income homes, which increases family _____ and reduces the chance of the initial handicap being overcome. The best preventive medicine for LBW includes ongoing _____ , _____ , and _____ _____ .

The Normal Birth (pp. 117–121)

47. At about the 266th day, the fetal brain signals the release of certain _____ into the mother's bloodstream, which trigger her _____ _____ to contract and relax. The normal birth process begins when these contractions become regular. The average length of labor is _____ for first births and _____ for subsequent births.

48. The newborn is usually rated on the _____ _____ , which assigns a score of 0, 1, or 2 to each of the following five characteristics: _____

_____ . A score below _____ indicates that the newborn is in critical condition and requires immediate attention; if the score is _____ or better, all is well. This rating is made twice, at _____ minute(s) after birth and again at _____ minutes.

49. The mother's birth experience is influenced by several factors, including _____ _____ .

50. When a normal vaginal delivery is likely to be hazardous, a doctor may recommend a surgical procedure called a _____ _____ . Another common procedure, which involves a minor incision of the tissue at the opening of the vagina, is the _____ .

51. In many nations, increasing numbers of trained _____ preside over uncomplicated births. Even in hospital births, an increasing number of deliveries occur in the _____ _____ . An even more family-oriented environment is the _____ _____ .

Birth Complications (pp. 122–123)

52. The disorder _____ _____ , which affects motor centers in the brain, often results from _____ vulnerability, worsened by exposure to _____ and episodes of _____ , a temporary lack of _____ during birth.

53. Because they are often confined to an isolette or hooked up to medical machinery, low-birthweight infants may be deprived of normal kinds of _____ , such as _____ .

54. Providing extra soothing stimulation to vulnerable infants in the hospital _____ (does/does not) aid weight gain and

_____ (does/does not) increase overall alertness.

55. Among the minor developmental problems that accompany preterm birth are being late to

_____ .

High-risk infants are often more

_____ , less _____ ,

and slower to _____ .

56. The deficits related to low birthweight usually _____ (can/cannot) be

overcome.

The Beginning of Bonding (pp. 123–126)

57. The term used to describe the close relationship that begins within the first hours after birth is

the _____–_____

_____ .

58. (Research Report) The best evidence for such a

relationship comes from studies of various

species of _____ .

59. (Research Report) Three factors that contribute to

animal bonding are:

a. _____

b. _____

c. _____

60. Research suggests that such a period

_____ (does/does not) exist in

humans, leading some social scientists to con-

clude that bonding is a _____

_____ .

61. Some new mothers experience a profound feeling

of sadness called _____

_____ .

Testing Yourself

After you have completed the audio and text review questions, see how well you do on the following quiz. Correct answers, with text and audio references, may be found at the end of this chapter.

1. Among other things, the social clock tells us:
   a. the age at which having a child becomes bio-logically feasible.
   b. the average age for having a first child.
   c. the appropriate or "best" age for having a child in our society.
   d. the age at which having a child best correlates with the parents' well-being later on.

2. In contrast to hunter-gatherer women, sedentary women tend to have:
   a. more children.
   b. fewer children.
   c. fewer menstrual cycles.
   d. a shorter fertile period.

3. The audio program states that for the typical American woman today the biological and social clocks are out of sync. Which of the following statements explains why this is so?
   a. The average teenager today is sexually mature before she is psychologically interested in sex-ual activity.
   b. Although menarche occurs at a younger age than ever before, it takes longer than ever to achieve the social status of an adult.
   c. Most women today assume the social role of adults before their reproductive systems are optimally suited for childbearing.
   d. Because of the widespread use of oral contra-ceptives, the biological clock that governs menstruation has effectively been halted.

4. Two patterns of childbearing are common today. The one associated with "early" births favors the _____ clock, while the one associated with "late" births favors the _____ clock.
   a. social; biological
   b. social; psychological
   c. biological; social
   d. psychological; social

5. *Sedentism* refers to:
   a. the tendency for menarche to occur at an earli-er age in recent years.
   b. the process by which the biological clock gov-erns the optimal years for childbearing.
   c. the tendency of less active women to have a later menarche.
   d. the shift in human social organization from a nomadic life to a village-dwelling society.

6. The third through the eighth week after conception is called the:
   a. period of the embryo.
   b. period of the ovum.
   c. period of the fetus.
   d. germinal period.

7. The neural tube develops into the:
   a. respiratory system.
   b. umbilical cord.
   c. brain and spinal column.
   d. circulatory system.

8. To say that a teratogen has a "threshold effect" means that it is:
   a. virtually harmless until exposure reaches a certain level.
   b. harmful only to low-birthweight infants.
   c. harmful to certain developing organs during periods when these organs are developing most rapidly.
   d. harmful only if the pregnant woman's weight does not increase by a certain minimum amount during her pregnancy.

9. By the eighth week after conception, the embryo has almost all the basic organs except the:
   a. skeleton.   c. sex organs.
   b. elbows and knees. d. fingers and toes.

10. The most critical factor in attaining the age of viability is development of the:
    a. placenta.   c. brain.
    b. eyes.   d. skeleton.

11. An important nutrient that many women do not get in adequate amounts from the typical diet is:
    a. vitamin A.   c. guanine.
    b. zinc.   d. folic acid.

12. An embryo begins to develop male sex organs if _____ , and female sex organs if _____ .
    a. genes on the Y chromosome send a biochemical signal; no signal is sent from an X chromosome
    b. genes on the Y chromosome send a biochemical signal; genes on the X chromosome send a signal
    c. genes on the X chromosome send a biochemical signal; no signal is sent from an X chromosome
    d. genes on the X chromosome send a biochemical signal; genes on the Y chromosome send a signal

13. A teratogen:
    a. cannot cross the placenta during the period of the embryo.
    b. is usually inherited from the mother.
    c. can be counteracted by good nutrition most of the time.
    d. may be a virus, a drug, a chemical, radiation, or environmental pollutants.

14. Among the characteristics of babies born with fetal alcohol syndrome are:
    a. slowed physical growth and behavior problems.
    b. addiction to alcohol and methadone.
    c. deformed arms and legs.
    d. blindness.

15. The birth process begins:
    a. when the fetus moves into the right position.
    b. when the uterus begins to contract at regular intervals to push the fetus out.
    c. about 8 hours (in the case of firstborns) after the uterus begins to contract at regular intervals.
    d. when the baby's head appears at the opening of the vagina.

16. The Apgar scale is administered:
    a. only if the newborn is in obvious distress.
    b. once, just after birth.
    c. twice, 1 minute and 5 minutes after birth.
    d. repeatedly during the newborn's first hours.

17. Most newborns weigh about:
    a. 5 pounds.   c. 7 1/2 pounds.
    b. 6 pounds.   d. 8 1/2 pounds.

18. Low-birthweight babies born near the due date but weighing substantially less than they should:
    a. are classified as preterm.
    b. are called small for gestational age.
    c. usually have no sex organs.
    d. show many signs of immaturity.

19. Approximately 1 out of every 4 low-birthweight births in the United States is caused by maternal use of:
    a. alcohol.
    b. tobacco.
    c. crack cocaine.
    d. household chemicals.

20. (Research Report) The idea of a parent–newborn bond in humans arose from:

    a. observations in the delivery room.

    b. data on adopted infants.

    c. animal studies.

    d. studies of disturbed mother-newborn pairs.

LESSON 4: SAYING WHEN

Exercise

The three developmental clocks come into play in every major transition of life. No transition is greater than the change from being pregnant to being a parent. The setting of the developmental clocks can affect the timing of births and the adjustment of first-time parents to their new roles, and can have long-term life-span consequences on both parents and their children.

The stories of the two couples introduced in audio program 4 illustrate some of these effects and contrast two new patterns of childbearing in our species. Shelley and her husband Charles gave birth when Shelley was 21. Shelley's pregnancy was "on time" biologically, but "off time" socially and psychologically. The pregnancy was unexpected and came at a time when the young couple was still establishing their own relationship, completing their educations, and struggling to make a living.

Brett and Henry's child was born when Brett was 36. This biologically "late" birth is an example of an increasingly common pattern of childbearing that favors the social clock by allowing parents to establish careers and improve their financial security before having children. Brett and Henry's birth may have been "off time" biologically, but it was "on time" psychologically and "on time," or perhaps even a little late, in terms of the social clock.

The experts in the audio program point out that unlike the biological clock, which changes little from generation to generation, the social clock and psychological clocks can be reset. The settings of these clocks reflect each individual's culture, historical context, and life experiences.

To help you integrate the material in Lesson 4 into an actual life story, write answers to the questions that follow, then hand the completed exercise in to your instructor. Before completing the exercise, you may find it helpful to review Audio Guidelines 1–4 to make sure you understand the differences and interrelationships of the three developmental clocks.

1. If you (or your subject) are a parent, please discuss the timing of your child(ren)'s birth(s) by answering the following questions. If you (or your subject) are not a parent, skip to question 2.
   a. According to the settings of your social, biological, and psychological clocks, was the timing of your child(ren)'s, birth(s) "on-time" or "off-time"?
   b. If your child(ren)'s birth(s) was (were) not recent, would its (their) timing be considered different according to the present settings of the developmental clocks and the two new patterns of childbearing mentioned in the audio program?
   c. What factors (career, education, health concerns, and so on) influenced the timing of your child(ren)'s birth(s)?

2. If you (or your subject) are not a parent, but contemplate having children, at what developmental "time" do you foresee these births occurring according to your biological clock? your social clock? your psychological clock? How does this compare with the settings of your parents' developmental clocks when you were born?

3. In your opinion, what is the ideal timing for the birth of a child from the standpoint of the three developmental clocks? You may conclude that the ideal time is never. Whatever the case, please explain your reasoning.

4. What is your current age (or the age of your subject)?

LESSON GUIDELINES

Audio Question Guidelines

1. The biological clock governs physical development through the various mechanisms of heredity and physiology that program growth, fertility, and aging. For women, the biologically optimal period for having a child is between 22 and 32 years; for men the range is between 22 and 40 years.

   The social clock is a culturally set timetable that establishes when various events and behaviors in life are appropriate and called for. Today, the social clock prescribes "later" births, giving couples an opportunity to establish their careers and financial solvency.

   The psychological clock represents each person's inner timetable of development. It is the individual's way of determining when he or she is ready to marry, to become a parent, and to make the other transitions inherent in development.

2. Unlike the two other developmental clocks, which can be reset on the basis of the individual's life experiences, culture, and generation, the biological clock is relatively immutable. For most life events, however, the biological clock specifies a normal *range* of time rather than a precise moment. For example, although the biological clock was unchanged in our transition from a hunter-gatherer society to a sedentary society, because of better nutrition and living conditions in modern times, the average age of menarche has dropped to 12.5 years, which is the lower end of the range set by the biological clock.

   Even as young people are becoming sexually mature at younger ages, the social clock has moved in the opposite direction: it takes longer and longer to achieve the status of an adult in our society. The result is that today's society has created a lengthy period in which an individual may have the reproductive capacity of an adult but the social role of a child.

   The psychological clock, set as it is according to each individual's life experiences, shows the greatest diversity of the three developmental clocks. Because she lives at a time when the biological and social clocks are out of sync, the typical American woman today finds it very difficult to decide when to have a child. The burden generally falls on her individual psychological clock.

3. As recently as 10,000 years ago, our ancestors lived as hunter-gatherers. Unlike modern women, hunter-gatherer women nursed their children for three or four years. This continuous nursing tended to suppress ovulation and limit the number of children born. With the development of agriculture and the shift from a nomadic to a **sedentary** lifestyle, the numbers of children born increased. In addition, the average age of menarche—the beginning of the menstrual cycle—dropped from about age 16 in hunter-gatherer women to age 12.5 in today's sedentary women.

   For hunter-gatherer women, the biological and social clocks were in sync: by the time they had their first child they had already assumed their social role as adults. Because the social and biological clocks are not in sync today, two new patterns of childbearing have emerged. One, favoring the biological clock, is the bearing of children very early in the life cycle (at or before the age of 21). The second, favoring the social clock, is exemplified by women who postpone having children until age 35 or later in order to become established in a career.

4. During most of human history the peak reproductive years were between 20 and 30. The two new patterns of childbearing that have emerged today—"early" births and "late" births—are atypical of our species' history.

   As in the case of Shelley and Charles whom we met in the audio program, an "early" birth is one that may be on-time biologically but off-time socially and psychologically. When the three developmental clocks are out of sync, a difficult period of adjustment may follow.

   Once one moves outside the optimal biological range for having a baby—between 22 and 32 for women and between 22 and 40 for men—there is a greater risk of physiological impairment to the infant. Many early births (to mothers under age 16 or 17) result in low-birth-weight babies. Late births (to mothers over the age of 35) are associated with increased risk of conditions such as Down syndrome.

   Childbearing is delayed most often among better-educated segments of the population, who wish to complete their training or become established in a career before becoming parents. The late-timed baby may benefit from the parents' greater economic security and maturity.

   Because of the advancing ages of today's older parents, late-timed births are often only-births: the one-child family is becoming more and more common.

Textbook Question Answers

1. three; germinal; third; eighth; embryo; fetus; trimesters

2. third; differentiation; one; placenta; embryo

3. implantation; is not

4. neural tube; central nervous system

First, the upper arms, then the forearms, palms, and webbed fingers appear. Legs, feet, and webbed toes follow. At eight weeks, the embryo's head is more rounded, and the facial features are fully formed. The fingers and toes are distinct and separate. The "tail" is no longer visible.

5. 1/30 of an ounce (1 gram); 1 inch (2.5 centimeters); fetus

6. sixth; indifferent gonad

7. Y; male; female; twelfth

8. third; 3 ounces (87 grams); 3 inches (7.5 centimeters); vary

9. circulatory system

10. six; breathing; sucking

11. age of viability; 22

12. 28; sleep–wake

13. 3 pounds (1,300 grams); 90

14. 266

15. respiratory; cardiovascular

16. 7 1/2 pounds (3,400 grams)

17. fat

18. calories

19. teratology; teratogens; viruses, drugs, chemicals, pollutants, stressors, and malnutrition

20. behavioral teratogens

21. risk analysis

22. timing; amount; genetic vulnerability

23. critical period; embryo; behavioral; brain; nervous system

24. stress; implantation; learning disabilities

25. threshold; interaction

26. enzymes

27. folic acid; spina bifida; anencephaly

28. male; spontaneous abortions; learning disabilities

29. rubella

30. human immunodeficiency virus (HIV); acquired immune deficiency syndrome (AIDS); pregnancy; birth; 10

31. adult AIDS; prevent pregnancy in HIV-positive women; AZT

32. tetracycline, anticoagulants, phenobarbital, bromides, retinoic acid, most hormones, aspirin, antacids, diet pills

33. beer, wine, liquor, cigarettes, smokeless tobacco, heroin, methadone, LSD, marijuana, cocaine, inhalants, and antidepressant pills; growth; labor; learning difficulties, impaired self-control, poor concentration, overall irritability

34. fetal alcohol syndrome; three; fetal alcohol effects

Smoking increases the risk of abnormalities and reduces birthweight and size. Babies born to regular smokers tend to have respiratory problems and, in adulthood, increased risk of becoming smokers themselves.

35. central nervous

Cocaine use causes overall growth retardation, increases the risk of problems with the placenta, and often leads to learning problems in the first months of life.

36. are; malnutrition, stress, sickness, poor family support and health care

The five protective steps are:

    a. Abstain from drugs altogether, even before pregnancy.

    b. Abstain from drugs after the first month.

    c. Use drugs in moderation throughout pregnancy (if abstinence is impossible).

    d. Seek social support.

    e. Keep up with postnatal care.

37. more; drug-free

38. do

39. 2,500 grams (5 1/2 pounds); low birthweight; very low birthweight; extremely low birthweight; vary

40. malnutrition; poverty

41. preterm

The possible causes of early birth include infections, drugs, extreme stress, exhaustion, a placenta that becomes detached from the uterine wall, and a uterus that cannot accommodate further growth.

42. small for gestational age

43. tobacco; 50

44. poverty; ill, malnourished, teenaged, stressed

45. rising: abuse; neglect; disabled

46. stress; education, nutrition, family support

47. hormones; uterine muscles; 6 hours; 3 hours

48. Apgar scale; heart rate, breathing, muscle tone, color, and reflexes; 4; 7; 1; 5

49. the mother's preparation for birth, the physical and emotional support provided by birth attendants, the position and size of the fetus, the cultural context, the nature and degree of medical intervention

50. cesarean section; episiotomy

51. midwives; labor room; birthing center

52. cerebral palsy; genetic; teratogens; anoxia; oxygen

53. stimulation; rocking (or regular handling)

54. does; does

55. smile, hold a bottle, and to communicate; distractible; obedient; talk

56. can

57. parent–newborn bond

58. mammals

59. a. birth hormones that trigger maternal feelings

    b. the mother's identification of her infant by its smell

    c. the timing of the first contact between mother and newborn

60. does not; social construction

61. postpartum depression

Answers to Testing Yourself

1. **c.** is the answer. The social clock is a culturally set timetable that establishes when various events and behaviors in life are appropriate and called for. (audio program)

2. **a.** is the answer. The hunter-gatherer society is associated with greater restraint in the production of children. This is due, in part, to the tendency of women in hunter-gatherer societies to nurse continuously, which tends to suppress ovulation and prevent pregnancy. (audio program)

3. **b.** is the answer. Today's society has created a 10-year, or longer, period in which an individual may have the reproductive capacity of an adult but the social role of a child. (audio program)

4. **c.** is the answer. Early births favor the biological clock by occurring during the optimal period of biological fertility. Late births favor the social clock because they allow the couple to establish careers and attain greater financial security before having children. (audio program)

5. **d.** is the answer. The shift from a hunter-gatherer to village-dwelling society is referred to as sedentism. (audio program)

6. **a.** is the answer. (textbook, p. 97)

   b. This term, which refers to the germinal period, is not used in the text.

   c. The period of the fetus is from the ninth week until birth.

   d. The germinal period covers the first two weeks.

7. **c.** is the answer. (textbook, p. 98)

8. **a.** is the answer. (textbook, p. 106)

   b., c., & d. Although low birthweight (b), critical periods of organ development (c), and maternal malnutrition (d) are all hazardous to the developing person during prenatal development, none is an example of a threshold effect.

9. **c.** is the answer. The sex organs do not begin to take shape until the period of the fetus. (textbook, p. 100)

10. **c.** is the answer. (textbook, p. 101)

11. **d.** is the answer. (textbook, p. 107)

12. **a.** is the answer. (textbook, p. 100)

13. **d.** is the answer. (textbook, p. 105)

    a. In general, teratogens can cross the placenta at any time.

    b. Teratogens are agents in the environment, not heritable genes (although *susceptibility* to individual teratogens has a genetic component).

    c. Although nutrition is an important factor in healthy prenatal development, the text does not suggest that nutrition alone can usually counteract the harmful effects of teratogens.

14. **a.** is the answer. (textbook, p. 112)

15. **b.** is the answer. (textbook, p. 117)

16. **c.** is the answer. (textbook, p. 118)

17. **c.** is the answer. (textbook, p. 104)

18. **b.** is the answer. (textbook, p. 114)

19. b. is the answer. (textbook, p. 114)

20. c. is the answer. (textbook, p. 125)

Reference

Kitzinger, Sheila. (1995). *Birth over thirty five.* New York: Penguin.

Kitzinger examines various aspects of later pregnancies, including physical risks such as Down syndrome and Cesarean births, as well as psychological aspects such as how to adjust to the role of motherhood during middle age.

The First Two Years: Biosocial Development

AUDIO PROGRAM: The Biography of the Brain

ORIENTATION

This lesson is the first of a three-lesson unit that describes the developing person from birth to age 2 in terms of biosocial, cognitive, and psychosocial development. Lesson 5 examines biosocial development.

Biosocial development during the first two years is so rapid that infants often seem to change before their parents' very eyes. In Chapter 5 of *The Developing Person Through the Life Span, 5/e,* Kathleen Berger describes the typical patterns of growth in the body and nervous system and the timetables for **motor-skill**, **sensory**, and **perceptual development.** Although the developmental sequence is usually the same for all healthy infants, variation in the ages at which certain skills are mastered does occur, in part because development depends on the interaction of biological and environmental forces.

Audio program 5, "The Biography of the Brain," continues the stories of the two couples introduced in program 4. Both couples have now had their babies and in this lesson we follow the early months of the babies' biosocial development. Compared to other mammals, humans are physically quite immature at birth. Evolutionary biologist Stephen Jay Gould and anthropologist Barry Bogin suggest that during the course of human evolution, an increase in the size of the brain and skull required a corresponding reduction in the length of pregnancy. In this way, the infant can be born before its head has grown too large to pass through the birth canal. Brain development influences growth in a variety of ways. Attainment of adult body size and sexual maturity are delayed until the brain, too, is almost fully mature. Brain development continues throughout life, increasingly influenced by environmental factors and learning.

Another issue explored in this lesson is the importance of nutrition to the developing brain. In the program, anthropologist Jane Lancaster notes that mothers and babies store body fat in order to meet the nutritional needs of the developing brain. The mother's fat ensures a rich supply of milk, an ideal food with a special profile of nutrients that exactly matches the developmental needs of the infant.

Neuropsychologist Jill Becker describes brain development at the microscopic level as a process in which individual **neurons** grow and form synapses with other neurons. Laboratory research with animals indicates that being raised in a stimulating environment promotes the development of more of these neural connections.

As the program opens we hear one of the couples describe the birth of their first child and the tight fit of their baby's head through the birth canal.

LESSON GOALS

By the end of this lesson you should be prepared to:

1. Describe the size and proportion of an infant's body, including how they change furing the first two years and how they compare with those of an adult.

2. Describe normal patterns of brain, sensory, and motor-skill development during infancy.

3. Discuss how biological and environmental forces interact in the infant's brain maturation, acquisition of motor skills, and sensory and perceptual development.

4. Identify the competing evolutionary pressures that have led some anthropologists to argue that human babies are born "too soon."

5. Outline the nutritional needs of infants during the first year of life. Describe the significance of breast milk and body fat in ensuring adequate nutrition.

Audio Assignment

Listen to the audio tape that accompanies Lesson 5: "The Biography of the Brain."

Write answers to the following questions. You may replay portions of the program if you need to refresh your memory. Answer guidelines may be found in the Lesson Guidelines section at the end of this chapter.

1. Explain why some anthropologists believe that, compared with other mammals, human babies are very immature at birth.

2. Discuss the significance of body fat and breast milk in meeting the nutritional needs of the newborn.

3. Describe the ways in which the nervous system matures during childhood.

4. Compare development of the brain, body, and reproductive system during the first two years.

Textbook Assignment

Read Chapter 5: "The First Two Years: Biosocial Development," pages 131–157 in *The Developing*

Person Through the Life Span, 5/e, then work through the material that follows to review it. Complete the sentences and answer the questions. As you proceed, evaluate your performance for each secdtion by consulting the answers on page 67. Do not continue with the next section until you understand each answer. If you need to, review or reread the appropriate section in the textbook before continuing.

Physical Growth and Health (pp. 131–133, 134–135)

1. With the exception of _____ development, infancy is the period of the fastest and most notable increases in _____ and changes in _____ .

2. The average North American newborn measures _____ and weighs a little more than _____ .

3. In the first days of life, most newborns _____ (gain/lose) between 5 and 10 percent of their body weight.

4. By age 1, the typical baby weighs about _____ and measures almost _____ . The typical 2-year-old is almost _____ (what proportion?) of his or her adult weight and _____ (what proportion?) of his or her adult height.

5. Newborns often seem top-heavy because their heads are equivalent to about _____ (what proportion?) of their total length, compared to about _____ at 1 year and _____ in adulthood.

6. Newborns' legs represent about _____ (what proportion?) of their total length, whereas an adult's legs represent about _____ of it.

7. One common cause of infant death that is not related to any obvious problem is _____ _____ _____ _____ , also called _____ _____ in Great Britain or _____ _____ in the United States.

8. The cause of SIDS is an unsteady _____ _____ , usually between _____ and _____ months.

9. There is less of a risk for SIDS when healthy infants sleep on their _____ .

Identify several other preventive measures for reducing an infant's risk of SIDS.

10. (A Life-Span View) The chance of infants dying from infectious disease within the first year in North America and most developed nations is less than 1 in _____ . The single most important cause of the improvement in child survival is _____ .

11. Among the childhood diseases that have either been completely eradicated, or nearly so, are _____ , _____ , and _____ .

Brain Growth and Development (pp. 133, 136–138)

12. At birth, the brain has attained about _____ percent of its adult weight; by age 2 the brain is about _____ percent of its adult weight. In comparison, body weight at age 2 is about _____ percent of what it will be in adulthood.

13. The brain's communication system consists primarily of nerve cells called _____ connected by intricate networks of nerve fibers, called _____ and _____ . Each neuron has many _____ , but only a single _____ .

14. Neurons communicate with one another at intersections called _____ . After travelling down the length of the _____ , electrical impulses trigger chemicals called _____ that diffuse across the _____ _____ to the _____ of a "receiving" neuron. Most of the nerve cells _____

(are/are not) present at birth, whereas the fiber networks _____ (are/are not) rudimentary.

15. During the first months of life, brain development is most noticeable in its outer layer, which is called the _____ . This area of the brain controls _____ and _____ .

16. From birth until age 2, the density of dendrites in the cortex _____ (increases/ decreases) by a factor of _____ . The phenomenal increase in neural connections over the first two years has been called _____ .

17. The fibers that transmit impulses also become coated with the insulating substance called _____ that speeds neural transmission and enables _____ brain activity. This coating process proceeds most rapidly from birth to age _____ and continues through _____ .

18. The _____ area of the cortex, which assists in _____ and _____ , becomes more mature during infancy, giving infants greater regulation of their _____-_____ patterns and increasing control over their early _____ . With continued development in this area, _____ skills requiring deliberation begin to emerge, along with a basic capacity for _____ self-control.

19. Brain development _____ (is/is not) influenced by the infant's experiences.

20. Kittens that are _____ for the first several weeks of life never acquire normal vision. This visual deficit occurs because the _____ _____ of the brain fail to develop normally. Kittens who are temporarily blinded in one eye never acquire _____ _____ , which is the ability to focus two eyes together on an object.

21. Research studies involving sensory restriction or enriched stimulation demonstrate that the brain

retains some _____ as long as stimulating _____ continue.

Motor Skills (pp. 138–145)

22. The maturation of movement skills is called

_____ _____ .

23. An involuntary physical response to a stimulus is called a _____ .

24. The involuntary response of breathing, which causes the newborn to take the first breath even before the umbilical cord is cut, is called the

_____ _____ . Because breathing is irregular during the first few days, other reflexive behaviors, such as

_____ , _____ ,

and _____ , are common.

25. Shivering, crying, and tucking the legs close to the body are examples of reflexes that help to maintain _____

_____ .

26. A third set of reflexes fosters _____ . One of these is the tendency of the newborn to suck anything that touches the lips; this is the

_____ reflex. Another is the tendency of newborns to turn their heads and start to suck when something brushes against their cheek; this is the _____ reflex.

27. Large movements such as running and climbing are called _____

_____ skills.

28. Most infants are able to crawl on all fours (sometimes called creeping) between _____ and _____ months of age.

List the major landmarks in children's mastery of walking.

29. Babies who have just begun to walk are given the name _____ for the characteristic way they move their bodies from side to side.

30. Abilities that require more precise, small movements, such as picking up a coin, are called

_____ _____ skills. By _____ of age, most babies can reach for, grab, and hold onto almost any object of the right size.

31. Although the _____ in which motor skills are mastered is the same in all healthy infants, the _____ of acquisition of skills varies greatly.

32. The average ages at which most infants master major motor skills are known as

_____ . These averages are based on a large sample of infants drawn from

_____ (a single/many) ethnic group(s).

33. Motor skill norms vary from one

_____ group to another.

List several factors that account for the variation in the acquisition of motor skills.

34. Motor skill acquisition in identical twins _____ (is/is not) more similar than in fraternal twins, suggesting that genes _____ (do/do not) play an important role.

35. Most developmentalists would say that the age at which a particular baby first displays a particular skill depends on the interaction between _____ and _____ factors.

Sensory and Perceptual Capacities (pp. 145–151)

36. The process by which the visual, auditory, and other sensory systems detect stimuli is called

_____ ; _____

occurs when the brain tries to make sense out of a stimulus so that the individual becomes aware of it. At birth, both of these processes

_____ (are/are not) apparent.

Briefly describe the sensory abilities of the newborn.

37. Newborns' visual focusing is best for objects between _____ and _____ inches away, giving them distance vision of about 20/_____ . Distance vision improves rapidly, reaching 20/20 by _____ of age.

38. Increasing maturation of the visual cortex accounts for improvements in other visual abilities, such as the infant's ability to _____ an object and _____ to its critical areas. The ability to use both eyes together to focus on one object, which is called _____ _____ , develops at about _____ of age. As a result of these changes, _____ and _____ perception improve dramatically, as evidenced by infants' ability to _____ moving objects.

39. Color vision _____ (is/is not) present at birth.

40. Generally speaking, newborns' hearing is _____ (more/less) sensitive than their vision. By _____ of age, infants can perceive differences between very similar speech sounds.

41. An infant presented with an unfamiliar stimulus will respond with intensified sucking on a pacifier or concentrated gazing. When the stimulus becomes so familiar that these responses no longer occur, _____ is said to have occurred. If the infant reacts to a new stimulus,

researchers conclude that the infant _____ (can/cannot) perceive a difference between the stimuli.

42. Young infants _____ (can/cannot) distinguish between speech sounds that are not used in their native language.

43. About 1 in every _____ infants is profoundly deaf.

44. A common cause of temporary hearing loss during infancy is a middle ear infection, or _____ _____ . When this condition becomes chronic, the _____ ear fills with fluid. This condition may last for weeks or months, causing impairment in one or both ears.

45. (Research Report) Chronic otitis media may cause developmental lags in the ability to _____ , make _____ , and solve _____ problems, and deflect _____ . Treatments include the use of _____ drugs and placement of a _____ to drain fluid from the inner ear.

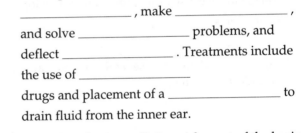

46. At birth, infants can distinguish most of the basic tastes except _____ tastes. Compared to their sense of taste, infants' sense of smell is _____ (more/less) acute. By _____ of age, taste and smell become quite sensitive.

47. The sense of touch _____ (is/is not) very acute during the first year. By 6 months, infants can distinguish objects on the basis of their _____ , _____ , _____ , and _____ .

Nutrition (pp. 151–155)

48. More important than an infant's feeding schedule in fostering development is the overall _____ and _____ of the infant's nutritional intake.

State several advantages of breast milk over cow's milk for the developing infant.

49. The most serious nutritional problem of infancy is _____-_____

_____ .

50. Severe protein-calorie deficiency in early infancy causes a disease called _____ . In toddlers, protein-calorie deficiency is more likely to cause a disease called

_____ , which involves swelling or bloating of the face, legs, and abdomen.

51. The primary cause of malnutrition in developing countries is _____

_____ .

(Changing Policy) Identify several possible causes of infant undernutrition.

52. Children who were undernourished as infants show impaired learning, especially in their ability to _____ and in their _____ skills.

Testing Yourself

After you have completed the audio and text review questions, see how well you do on the following quiz. Correct answers, with text and audio references, may be found at the end of this chapter.

1. According to experts in the audio program, why are human babies born so physically immature?
   a. As a result of better nutrition, the biological clock that times gestation has been reset.
   b. If prenatal development continued longer, infants' large heads would not fit through the birth canal.
   c. Humans are much less active than other mammals.
   d. All of the above are reasons for babies being born so physically immature.

2. In what order do parts of the human body mature?
   a. brain, body, reproductive system
   b. body, brain, reproductive system
   c. body, reproductive system, brain
   d. brain, reproductive system, body

3. Approximately 90 percent of the brain's growth is completed by the age of:
   a. 1 month.
   b. 6 months.
   c. 1 year.
   d. 5 years.

4. Laboratory research with animals has shown that one effect of being raised in a stimulating environment is:
   a. an increase in the number of neurons in the brain.
   b. a shortening of the time required for the brain to reach its full capacity.
   c. a reduction in the number of "extra" nerve cells that die.
   d. a reduction in nerve-cell insulation, which tends to slow neural communication.

5. Compared with that of other species, human milk has a high content of _____, which especially promotes development of _____ .
   a. protein; the brain
   b. protein; muscle
   c. sugar; muscle
   d. sugar; the brain

6. The average North American newborn:
   a. weighs approximately 6 pounds.
   b. weighs approximately 7 pounds.
   c. is "overweight" because of the diet of the mother.
   d. weighs 10 percent less than what is desirable.

7. Compared to the first year, growth during the second year:
   a. proceeds at a slower rate.
   b. continues at about the same rate.
   c. includes more insulating fat.
   d. includes more bone and muscle.

8. The major motor skill most likely to be mastered by an infant before the age of 6 months is:
   a. rolling over.
   b. sitting without support.
   c. turning the head in search of a nipple.
   d. grabbing an object with thumb and forefinger.

9. Norms suggest that the earliest walkers in the world are infants from:
   a. Western Europe.   c. Uganda.
   b. the United States.   d. Denver.

10. The interaction between inherited and environmental factors is responsible for:
    a. variation in the age at which infants master specific motor skills.
    b. physical growth, but not the development of motor skills.
    c. the fact that babies in the United States walk earlier than do Ugandan babies.
    d. the fact that infants master motor skills more slowly today than they did fifty years ago.

11. The development of binocular vision at about 14 months results in:
    a. a dramatic improvement in depth and motion perception.
    b. the rapid development of distance vision.
    c. the refinement of the ability to discriminate colors.
    d. both a. and b.

12. Proportionally, the head of the infant is about _____ of total body length; the head of an adult is about _____ of total body length.
    a. one-fourth; one-third
    b. one-eighth; one-fourth
    c. one-fourth; one-eighth
    d. one-third; one-fourth

13. Research has shown that young animals prevented from using their senses in a normal way experience:
    a. no significant impairment.
    b. harmful overstimulation.
    c. deficits in behavior only.
    d. permanent impairment.

14. Compared with formula-fed infants, breast-fed infants tend to have:
    a. greater weight gain.
    b. fewer allergies and digestive upsets.
    c. less frequent feedings during the first few months.
    d. more social approval.

15. Marasmus and kwashiorkor are caused by:
    a. bloating.
    b. protein-calorie deficiency.
    c. living in a developing country.
    d. poor family food habits.

16. The infant's first motor skills are:
    a. fine motor skills.   c. reflexes.
    b. gross motor skills.   d. unpredictable.

17. Babies are referred to as toddlers when:
    a. their newborn reflexes have disappeared.
    b. they can walk well unassisted.
    c. they begin to creep or crawl.
    d. they speak their first word.

18. Which of the following is true of motor-skill development in healthy infants?
    a. It follows the same basic sequence the world over.
    b. It occurs at different rates from individual to individual.
    c. It follows norms that vary from one ethnic group to another.
    d. All of the above are true.

19. Most of the nerve cells a human brain will ever possess are present:
    a. at conception.
    b. about 1 month following conception.
    c. at birth.
    d. at age 5 or 6.

20. (Research Report) Toddlers with a history of frequent ear infections are much more likely to:
    a. lag behind in language development.
    b. play by themselves.
    c. be uninterested in watching other children play.
    d. do all of the above.

LESSON 5: GROWTH RATES AND MOTOR-SKILL DEVELOPMENT IN THE FIRST TWO YEARS

Exercise

The text notes that weight gain and growth in early infancy are astoundingly rapid. The proportions of the human body change dramatically with maturation, especially in the first year of life. The growth that changes the baby's body shape follows the head-downward (cephalo-caudal) and center-outward (proximo-distal) direction of development. For instance, the percentage of total body length below the belly button is 25 percent at two months after conception, about 45 percent at birth, 50 percent by age 2, and 60 percent by adulthood. Questions 1–5 of this exercise will help you to gain some understanding of how rapid this growth is by projecting the growth patterns of the infant onto an adult, such as yourself or a friend.

Similarly, questions 6–10 of this exercise are designed to help you "feel" the progressively finer coordination achieved by the infant by having you work through the stages of development. A good place to start is with the mastery of motor skills involved in picking up objects. After you have answered the questions, hand the completed exercise in to your instructor.

1. Most newborns seem top-heavy because their heads are equivalent to about one-fourth of their total length, compared with one-fifth at a year and one-eighth in adulthood. Their legs, in turn, represent only about one-fourth of their total body length, whereas an adult's legs account for about one-half. Based on your present height in inches, what would be the lengths of your head and legs if they remained proportionally the same as when you were born?

2. If you were gaining weight at the rate of an infant, your weight would be tripled one year from today. Calculate how much you would weigh.

3. If you, like an infant, grew an inch a month, this would not mark such a significant growth rate—since you are much taller than an infant to begin with. Thus, every inch is a smaller percentage increase for you. Nevertheless, imagine that you are growing at the rate of an infant in the first year, adding an inch a month. What would your height be a year from today?

4. The same kind of calculations can help you make a less dramatic comparison between growth rates in the first and second years of life. In the first year, weight triples; thus an infant born at a little more than 7 pounds will weigh about 21 pounds at one year. If growth were to continue at this rate, how much would the child weigh at two years? (In fact, the average infant at two years weighs only 30 pounds.)

5. The average infant grows an inch a month in the first year. If a 30-inch one-year-old continued growing at this rate, how tall would he or she be at two years? (In fact, the faster growing child grows only 6 inches, to reach 36 inches at age two.)
Now try picking up objects as an infant would.

6. Pick up a piece of paper or some other small object with your whole hand, that is, with all fingers curled around it.

7. Now hold the paper between your middle fingers and the palm of your hand.

8. Pick up the paper with your index finger pressed against the side of your palm.

9. Finally, use your thumb and index finger to pick up the paper. When is this type of grasp achieved?

10. Which of these ways of grasping a small object felt most comfortable or natural to you?

LESSON GUIDELINES

Audio Question Guidelines

1. By mammalian standards, the nine-month gestation period in humans is relatively short. As a result, the human infant is exceedingly helpless and relatively less developed compared with most other animals. The relatively short gestation period may be a response to the evolution of a large brain, which, while providing humans with a high level of intelligence and cognitive flexibility, results in a large skull that makes birth difficult.

   Because of **bipedalism** (the upright posture of humans), the duration of prenatal development is somewhat of a compromise. Babies are born at a point when the brain is as big as it can be without requiring a wider birth canal, which would impair a female's ability to walk.

2. Compared with other primates, human infants are remarkably fat when they are born. Fat ensures that the developing brain—which has attained only one-quarter of its mature size at birth—is adequately nourished.

   Even before infants are born, their mothers begin storing fat for them. The mother's fat ensures a rich supply of breast milk for nursing. Each species' milk has a special profile of nutrients that exactly matches the species' specific developmental needs. Human milk is high in sugar, which provides energy for the baby's rapidly developing brain.

3. The brain consists of billions of nerve cells called **neurons**. All the neurons a human will ever possess are already present three months after conception. Some of the neurons will grow while others will die. Neuropsychologists estimate that humans start out with 20 to 40 percent more neurons than they end up with.

   During the first two years of life, neurons in the human brain become coated with insulation (which speeds their chemical communication) and hook up with other neurons by forming connections called synapses. The excess of neurons and synaptic connections creates redundancy that gives humans greater flexibility and insurance: if some neurons die, others can take over their functions.

   While 90 percent of the brain's growth is completed by age 5, synapses will be made and broken throughout life. Laboratory animals respond to stimulating environments by developing more synapses than those raised in normal or deprived environments. Even in old age, nerve cells respond to stimulation by growing extra connections.

4. The biological clock governs every aspect of physical growth. One of the peculiarities of human growth is that we grow slowly. Another is that we do not grow evenly. Development of the body and reproductive system is paced by development of the brain.

   Brain development is rapid, with 90 percent of growth completed by age 5.

   Body growth from birth to two years is very rapid and then levels off to a rate of 3 to 4 inches a year until puberty, when growth in height and weight again accelerates.

   The curve of growth for the reproductive system is very flat until the age of 12 or 14.

Textbook Question Answers

1. prenatal; size; proportion
2. 20 inches (51 centimeters); 7 pounds (3.2 kilograms)
3. lose
4. 22 pounds (10 kilograms); 30 inches (75 centimeters); one-fifth; half
5. one-fourth; one-fifth; one-eighth
6. one-fourth; one-half
7. sudden infant death syndrome; cot death; crib death
8. breathing reflex; 2; 4
9. backs

Other preventive measures include removing soft bedding, eliminating second-hand smoke, and prolonging breast-feeding.

10. 500; immunization
11. smallpox; polio; measles
12. 25; 75; 20
13. neurons; dendrites; axons; dendrites; axon
14. synapses; axon; neurotransmitters; synaptic gap; dendrites; are; are
15. cortex; perception; thinking
16. increases; five; transient exuberance
17. myelin; complex; 4; adolescence
18. frontal; self-control; self-regulation; sleep–wake; reflexes; cognitive; emotional
19. is
20. blindfolded; neural pathways; binocular vision
21. plasticity; experiences

22. developmental biodynamics

23. reflex

24. breathing reflex; hiccups, sneezes, thrashing

25. body temperature

26. feeding; sucking; rooting

27. gross motor

28. 8; 10

On average, a child can walk while holding a hand at 9 months, can stand alone momentarily at 10 months, and can walk well unassisted at 12 months.

29. toddler

30. fine motor; 6 months

31. sequence; age

32. norms; many

33. ethnic

Of primary importance in variations in the acquisition of motor skills are inherited factors, such as activity level, rate of physical maturation, and how fat the infant is. Particular patterns of infant care may also be influential.

34. is; do

35. inherited; environmental

36. sensation; perception; are

Although their sensory abilities are selective, newborns see, hear, smell, taste, and respond to pressure, motion, temperature, and pain.

37. 4; 30; 400; 1 year

38. scan; attend; binocular vision; 14 weeks; depth; motion; track

39. is not

40. more; 1 month

41. habituation; can

42. can

43. 1,000

44. otitis media; inner

45. learn; friends; social; aggression; antibiotic; tube

46. salty; more; 1 year

47. is; temperature; size; hardness; texture

48. quality; quantity

Breast milk is always sterile and at body temperature; it contains more iron, vitamin C, and vitamin A; it contains antibodies that provide the infant some protection against disease; it is more digestible than any formula; and it decreases the frequency of almost every common infant ailment.

49. protein-calorie malnutrition

50. marasmus; kwashiorkor

51. early cessation of breast-feeding

Undernutrition is caused by the interaction of many factors, with insufficient food as the immediate cause, and problems in the family and/or society as underlying causes. For example, depressed mothers tend to feed their infants erratically, and some may be ignorant of the infant's nutritional needs.

52. concentrate; language

Answers to Testing Yourself

1. **b.** is the answer. Human babies are born at a time when their brains are as big as they can be without requiring a wider birth canal, which would limit females' ability to walk. (audio program)

2. **a.** is the answer. Our slow, uneven growth—first the brain, then the body, then the reproductive system—is directed by the preeminent role of the brain. (audio program)

3. **d.** is the answer. Three-quarters of brain development occurs after birth; this may be the reason why humans store fat—that is, to ensure that the brain has adequate nutrition. (audio program)

4. **c.** is the answer. Environmental stimulation throughout the life span helps individuals, and their brains, grow. (audio program; textbook, pp. 137–138)

5. **d.** is the answer. Human milk has a high sugar content, which provides energy for the baby's rapidly developing brain. (audio program)

6. **b.** is the answer. (textbook, p. 131)

7. **a.** is the answer. (textbook, p. 132)

8. **a.** is the answer. (textbook, p. 143)

   b. The age norm for this skill is 7.8 months.

   c. This is a reflex, rather than an acquired motor skill.

   d. This skill is acquired between 9 and 14 months.

9. **c.** is the answer. (textbook, p. 143)

10. **a.** is the answer. (textbook, p. 145)

    b. Inherited and environmental factors are important for both physical growth *and* the development of motor skills.

    c. On average, Ugandan babies walk earlier than do babies in the United States.

    d. In fact, just the opposite is true.

11. **a.** is the answer. (textbook, p. 147)

12. **c.** is the answer. (textbook, p. 132)

13. **d.** is the answer. (textbook, p. 138)

    a. & c. Research has shown that deprivation of normal sensory experiences prevents the development of normal neural pathways that transmit sensory information.

b. On the contrary, these studies demonstrate harmful sensory *restriction.*

14. **b.** is the answer. This is because breast milk is more digestible than cow's milk or formula. (textbook, p. 152)

    a., c., & d. Breast- and bottle-fed babies do not differ in these attributes.

15. **b.** is the answer. (textbook, p. 153)

16. **c.** is the answer. (textbook, p. 139)

    a. & b. These motor skills do not emerge until somewhat later; reflexes are present at birth.

    d. On the contrary, reflexes are quite predictable.

17. **b.** is the answer. (textbook, p. 141)

18. **d.** is the answer. (textbook, p. 143)

19. **c.** is the answer. (textbook, p. 133)

20. **b.** is the answer. (textbook, p. 149)

Reference

Bogin, B. (1988). *Patterns of growth.* Cambridge, England: Cambridge University Press.

    Professor Bogin, who is heard on the audio program, presents a cross-cultural perspective on physical growth and discusses longitudinal studies of the effects of chronic malnourishment in early childhood on physical and intellectual development.

The First Two Years: Cognitive Development

AUDIO PROGRAM: First Words

ORIENTATION

During the first two years of life, cognitive development proceeds at a phenomenal pace as the infant is transformed from a baby who can know its world only through a limited set of basic reflexes into a toddler capable of imitating others, anticipating and remembering events, and pretending. Most significant among these advances is the development of language. By age 2, the average toddler has a relatively large vocabulary and is able to converse effectively with others.

Lesson 6 of *Seasons of Life* explores **cognitive development**—the ways in which individuals learn about, think about, and adapt to their surroundings—during the first two years. Chapter 6 of the textbook begins with a description of the infant's developing perceptual and memory abilities. It then describes Eleanor and James Gibson's contextual theory of cognitive development and Piaget's theory of **sensorimotor intelligence**. From birth to age 2, infants learn about their environment by using their senses and motor skills.

Audio program 6, "First Words," is concerned with language development from birth until the first word is spoken. As explained by psycholinguist Jill de Villiers, around the world babies and parents move along similar paths as language emerges. In the program, these paths are illustrated by actual examples and the description of linguistic landmarks such as **crying, cooing, babbling**, and the first true word. Along the way, the listener discovers the importance of the biological clock in the maturation of language and the patterns of speech that adults use to promote linguistic development in children. This issue—the interaction between maturation and learning in cognitive development—is explored further in the textbook, where the theories of language development proposed by B. F. Skinner and Noam Chomsky are described. Skinner argues that language development is the product of conditioning, whereas Chomsky maintains that children have a biological predisposition to acquire language. Most developmental psychologists nevertheless view language development as a social, interactional process that reflects both nature (maturation) and nurture (conditioning).

As the program opens, we hear the voices of English- and Spanish-speaking parents reacting to a milestone in the lives of their children: their first word.

LESSON GOALS

By the end of this lesson you should be prepared to:

1. Explain the Gibsons' contextual view of perception, and discuss the idea of affordances.

2. Describe perceptual development, particularly in relation to cognitive maturity, during the first two years.

3. Outline and evaluate the theory of sensorimotor intelligence proposed by Piaget.

4. Describe language development during the first two years.

5. Contrast the theories of language development proposed by B. F. Skinner and Noam Chomsky, and explain current views on language learning.

Audio Assignment

Listen to the audio tape that accompanies Lesson 6: "First Words."

Write answers to the following questions. You may replay portions of the program if your memory needs to be refreshed. Answer guidelines may be found in the Lesson Guidelines section at the end of this chapter.

1. Outline the basic sequence and landmarks of language development from birth until the first word is spoken.

2. Identify the criteria used by developmental psychologists to determine whether an utterance represents the first actual word. What types of words are likely to be produced first?

3. Identify the characteristics of baby talk (Motherese), the special form of language that adults use to talk to infants.

4. Explain how parents use scaffolding to encourage conversation in their children.

Textbook Assignment

Read Chapter 6: "The First Two Years: Cognitive Development," pages 159–185 in *The Developing Person Through the Life Span, 5/e,* then work through the material that follows to review it. Complete the sentences and answer the questions. As you proceed, evaluate your performance for each secdtion by consulting the answers on page 79. Do not continue with the next section until you understand each answer. If you need to, review or reread the appropriate section in the textbook before continuing.

Perception and Cognition (pp. 159–164)

1. The first major theorist to realize that infants are active learners was _____ .

2. Much of the current research in perception and cognition has been inspired by the work of the Gibsons, who stress that perception is a(n) _____ (active/passive/automatic) cognitive phenomenon.

3. According to the Gibsons, any object in the environment offers diverse opportunities for interaction; this property of an object is called an

_____ .

4. Which of these an individual perceives in an object depends on the individual's

_____ _____ and

_____ _____ , on his

or her _____ _____ ,

and on his or her _____

_____ of what the object might be

used for.

5. Infants perceive the affordance of

_____ long before their manual dexterity has matured. The time it takes infants to grab objects successfully demonstrates that deliberate and thoughtful perception _____ (precedes/does not precede) the action.

List other affordances perceived by infants from a very early age.

6. A firm surface that appears to drop off is called a

_____ _____

Although perception of this drop off was once

linked to _____ maturity, later

research found that infants as young as

_____ are able to perceive the drop

off, as evidenced by changes in their

_____ _____ and their

wide open eyes.

7. Perception that is primed to focus on movement and change is called _____

_____ .

Give several examples of how infants use movement cues in perceiving objects.

8. A major cognitive accomplishment of infancy is the ability to understand that objects exist independently of _____ . This awareness is called _____ _____ .

9. To test for this awareness, Piaget devised a procedure to observe whether an infant will _____ for a hidden object. Using this test, Piaget concluded that this awareness does not develop until about _____ of age.

10. (Research Report) Using the habituation procedure, Renée Baillargeon has demonstrated that infants as young as _____ months have an awareness of object permanence that is concealed by the traditional Piagetian hidden-object tests.

Key Elements of Cognitive Growth (pp. 164–170)

11. From a very early age, infants coordinate and organize their perceptions into _____ . Researchers use the phenomenon of infant _____ to study these abilities.

12. Infants younger than 6 months can categorize objects according to their _____ ,

_____ , _____ ,

_____ , _____

_____ , and _____ . By the end of the first year, they can categorize

_____ , _____ , and

_____ , for example.

13. According to _____ , no one can remember anything that happened before the age of _____ . This hypothesized inability is called _____

_____ . Piaget _____ (agreed/disagreed) with this hypothesis.

14. Researchers have generally considered infants' long-term memory to be quite _____ (good/poor).

15. More recent studies demonstrate that babies have great difficulty storing new memories in their first _____ (how long?), but they can show that they remember when three conditions are met:

(a) _____

(b) _____

(c) _____

16. When these conditions are met, infants as young as _____ months "remembered" events from one week earlier or two weeks earlier, if they experienced a _____ prior to retesting.

17. The ability to remember and imitate behaviors that have been observed but never actually performed is called _____

_____ . This ability becomes apparent toward the _____ .

18. (A Life-Span View) Improvement in infant memory ability seems tied to _____ maturation and _____ development. Notable increases in memory capacity and duration occur at about _____ months, again at about _____ months, and again at age _____ . Research also demonstrates the importance of the _____ aspects of memory.

19. Another important cognitive accomplishment of infancy is the ability to recognize and associate

_____-_____-

_____ relations. Research using the _____ _____ procedure reveals that infants as young as

_____ months have a rudimentary understanding of such relations.

Piaget's Sensorimotor Intelligence (pp. 170–174)

20. A central concept in Piaget's theory of cognitive development is the notion of _____ intelligence.

21. When infants begin to explore the environment through sensory and motor skills, they are displaying what Piaget called _____ intelligence. In number, Piaget described _____ stages of development of this type of intelligence.

22. Sensorimotor intelligence begins with newborns' reflexes, such as _____ ,

_____ , _____ ,

and _____ . It lasts from birth to _____ of age.

23. Stage 2 begins when newborns show signs of _____ of their reflexes to the specifics of the environment. This is revealed in two ways: by _____ of new information into previously developed mental categories, or _____ ; and _____ of previous mental categories to incorporate new information.

Describe the development of the sucking reflex during stages one and two.

24. During stage three, which occurs between _____ and _____ months of age, infants repeat a specific action that has just elicited a pleasing response.

Describe a typical stage-three behavior.

25. In stage four, which lasts from _____ to _____ months of age, infants can better _____ events. At this stage, babies also engage in purposeful actions, or _____-_____ behavior.

26. During stage five, which lasts from _____ to _____ months, goal-directed activities become more expansive and creative.

Explain what Piaget meant when he described the stage-five infant as a "little scientist."

27. Stage six, which lasts from _____ to _____ months, is the stage of achieving new means by using _____ _____ .

28. One sign that children have reached stage six is their ability to enjoy a broader range of _____ activities.

Language Development (pp. 174–183)

29. Children the world over _____ (follow/do not follow) the same sequence of early language development. The timing of this sequence _____ (varies/does not vary).

30. Newborns show a preference for hearing _____ over other sounds.

31. By 4 months of age, most babies' verbal repertoire consists of _____ _____ .

32. At _____ months of age, babies begin to repeat certain syllables, a phenomenon referred to as _____ .

33. Deaf babies begin oral babbling _____ (earlier/later) than hearing babies do. Deaf babies may also babble

_____ , with this behavior emerging (earlier than/at the same time as/later than) hearing infants begin oral babbling.

34. The average baby speaks a few words at about _____ of age. When vocabulary reaches approximately 50 words, it suddenly begins to build rapidly, at a rate of _____ or more words a month.

35. Toddlers who primarily learn naming words first are called _____ , whereas those who acquire mainly words that can be used in social interaction are called _____ . Language acquisition is also shaped by our _____ , as revealed by the fact that North American infants are more _____ than Japanese infants.

36. One characteristic of infant speech is _____ , or overgeneralization, in which the infant applies a known word to a variety of objects and contexts. Initially, however, infants tend toward _____ of word meanings. Infants also might learn one name for something and refuse to use alternative names; this is called the _____ _____ .

37. Another characteristic is the use of the _____ , in which a single word expresses a complete thought.

38. Children begin to produce their first two-word sentences at about _____ months.

39. Reinforcement and other conditioning processes account for language development, according to the learning theory of _____ .

40. The theorist who stressed the infant's innate language abilities is _____ , who maintained that all children are born with a LAD, or _____ _____ _____ .

Summarize the conclusions of recent research regarding the theories of Skinner and Chomsky.

41. Adults talk to infants using a special form of language called _____ _____ .

(text and Changing Policy) Briefly describe the type of speech adults use with infants.

42. Four ways that adults support infants in their acquisition of language are: (a) _____ _____ ; (b) _____ _____ ; (c) _____ _____ ; and (d) _____ _____ .

Testing Yourself

After you have completed the audio and text review questions, see how well you do on the following quiz. Correct answers, with text and audio references, may be found at the end of this chapter.

1. Translated literally, the word *infant* means:
   a. little scientist.
   b. not speaking.
   c. innocent one.
   d. explorer.

2. Between 2 and 4 months of age children begin making a pleasant, relaxing speech sound called:
   a. babbling.
   b. cooing.
   c. scaffolding.
   d. baby talk.

3. At about 6 months of age babies begin to repetitively utter certain syllables; they do this more for experimentation than for socializing. This stage of language development is called:
   a. babbling.
   b. cooing.
   c. scaffolding.
   d. baby talk.

4. In order to qualify as a word, a sound must:
   a. serve as a symbol for something.
   b. be used consistently in a number of circumstances.
   c. resemble an adult word.
   d. possess all of the above characteristics.

5. When adults converse with children they usually do all of the following *except*:
   a. exaggerate their intonation.
   b. raise the pitch of their voices.
   c. use shorter sentences.
   d. speak only in the past tense.

6. In general terms, the Gibsons' concept of affordances emphasizes the idea that the individual perceives an object in terms of its:
   a. economic importance.
   b. physical qualities.
   c. function or use to the individual.
   d. role in the larger culture or environment.

7. According to Piaget, when a baby repeats an action that has just triggered a pleasing response from his or her caregiver, a stage _____ behavior has occurred.
   a. one
   b. two
   c. three
   d. six

8. Sensorimotor intelligence begins with a baby's first:
   a. attempt to crawl.
   b. reflex actions.
   c. auditory perception.
   d. adaptation of a reflex.

9. Piaget and the Gibsons would most likely agree that:
   a. perception is largely automatic.
   b. language development is biologically predisposed in children.
   c. learning and perception are active cognitive processes.
   d. it is unwise to "push" children too hard academically.

10. By the end of the first year, infants usually learn how to:
    a. accomplish simple goals.
    b. manipulate various symbols.
    c. solve complex problems.
    d. pretend.

11. When an infant begins to understand that objects exist even when they are out of sight, she or he has begun to understand the concept of object:
    a. displacement.
    b. importance.
    c. permanence.
    d. location.

12. Today, most cognitive psychologists view language acquisition as:
    a. primarily the result of imitation of adult speech.
    b. a behavior that is determined primarily by biological maturation.
    c. a behavior determined entirely by learning.
    d. determined by both biological maturation and learning.

13. Despite cultural differences, children all over the world attain very similar language skills:
    a. according to ethnically specific timetables.
    b. in the same sequence according to a variable timetable.
    c. according to culturally specific timetables.
    d. according to timetables that vary from child to child.

14. The average baby speaks a few words at about:
    a. 6 months.
    b. 9 months.
    c. 12 months.
    d. 24 months.

15. A single word used by toddlers to express a complete thought is:
    a. a holophrase.
    b. baby talk.
    c. an overextension.
    d. an underextension.

16. Which of the following theorists would most likely agree that the interactive, social context of early language development is of paramount importance?
    a. B. F. Skinner
    b. Noam Chomsky
    c. Lev Vygotsky
    d. Eleanor Gibson

17. A distinctive form of language, with a particular pitch, structure, etc., that adults use in talking to infants is called:
    a. a holophrase.
    b. the LAD.
    c. baby talk.
    d. conversation.

18. At 8 months, infants can categorize objects on the basis of
    a. angularity.
    b. shape.
    c. density.
    d. all of the above.

19. By what age can most infants properly interpret the cause-and-effect relations of the launching event experiment?
    a. 5 months
    b. 6 months
    c. 10 months
    d. 12 months

20. A toddler who taps on the computer's keyboard after observing her mother sending e-mail is demonstrating:
    a. assimilation.
    b. accommodation.
    c. deferred imitation.
    d. dynamic perception.

NAME _____   INSTRUCTOR _____

LESSON 6: BABY TALK

Exercise

To further your understanding of the nature and significance of **baby talk**, make arrangements to listen to an adult conversing with an infant or toddler for ten to fifteen minutes. Your subjects may be family members, other relatives, or friends. The conversation need not be structured in any particular way. The adult might read to the child, play with a favorite toy, or simply carry on a conversation with the child. It is important that you not give the adult clues as to what speech patterns you are looking for. Ask your subject to relax, be candid, and enjoy interacting with the child. If you wish, you might even record the conversation to allow for a more thorough analysis later. After listening to the conversation, answer the questions that follow and hand the completed exercise in to your instructor.

1. Describe the participants and setting that you chose for the baby-talk conversation.

2. Did you encounter any difficulties in completing the exercise (e.g., the adult was nervous; the child did not talk)?

3. Did the adult use baby talk with the child? What aspects of the adult's speech (e.g., intonation, pitch, vocabulary) changed during the conversation with the child?

4. Were there any particular characteristics of the adult's speech (e.g., repetitiveness, exaggerated intonation) that the child seemed particularly responsive to?

5. Based on his or her age and vocalizations, what stage of language development would you say the infant or toddler is in (e.g., cooing, babbling, one-word stage)? If you wish, give examples of the child's utterances that support your assessment.

LESSON GUIDELINES

Audio Question Guidelines

1. Compared with that of other species, human hearing—even for subtle differences in speech sounds—is very sensitive at birth, which contributes to language development.

   Cries are the first speech productions on the way to words.

   Between 2 and 4 months, **cooing** begins. Cooing is a pleasant and relaxing sound with an important social function: it attracts the attention of caregivers.

   At about 6 months infants begin to mix consonants with cooing. As they play with sound, they produce utterances such as "ba, ba, ba, ba," signaling their entrance into the stage of **babbling**. Babbling is not as social as cooing, but represents experimentation with the sounds of language.

   Infants below the age of about 8 months babble in very similar ways, so that the babbling of children from around the world is indistinguishable. At about 10 months babbling begins to take on the characteristics of the language the child will ultimately learn.

   The first true word usually comes at about 12 months of age, although there is wide, and normal, variation in that age.

2. The first criterion is that the sound must be a symbol referring to an object or an event.

   Second, the sound must be used consistently in a number of different circumstances.

   Third, the sound must resemble an adult word.

   The first words are likely to refer to something that moves, something the baby controls, and something that is very interesting. Examples are words for toys, foods, clothing, mothers, fathers, siblings, and pets.

3. **Baby talk** differs from adult speech in several ways: it is distinct in pitch (higher), intonation (more exaggerated and more low-to-high fluctuations), vocabulary (simpler and more concrete), and sentence length (shorter).

   Baby talk is also more repetitive and uses more questions and fewer past tenses, pronouns, and complex sentences.

   An intriguing fact is that people of all ages, including nonparents, use baby talk when conversing with infants.

   In many of the world's cultures, baby words for mother and father—such as "mama" and "dada"—are just the sort of easy-to-produce, repeated syllables that often are a child's first words.

4. **Scaffolding** refers to the tendency of parents and other adults to try to support the young child's conversation. In reading a book, for example, the parent might first read the entire story slowly and with exaggerated intonation to give the child time to process the information. The second time the story is read, the parent might pause at key points and wait for the child to respond in some way. Gradually, the parent removes more and more of the support, or scaffolding, so that the child's role in the conversation becomes more extensive, and precise.

Textbook Question Answers

1. Piaget
2. active
3. affordance
4. past experiences; developmental level; present needs; sensory awareness
5. graspability; precedes

From a very early age, infants understand which objects afford digestibility and suckability, which afford noisemaking, which afford movability, and so forth.

6. visual cliff; visual; 3 months; heart rate
7. dynamic perception

Infants use movement cues to discern not only the boundaries of objects but also their rigidity, wholeness, shape, and size. They even form expectations of the path that a moving object will follow.

8. one's perception of them even when they are moved out of sight; object permanence
9. search; 8 months
10. $4\frac{1}{2}$
11. categories; habituation
12. angularity; shape; color; density; relative size; number (up to 3 objects); faces; animals; birds
13. Freud; 2 years; infantile amnesia; agreed
14. poor
15. 6 months; (a) real-life situations are used; (b) motivation is high; (c) special measures aid memory retrieval
16. 3 months; reminder session
17. deferred imitation; end of the first year
18. brain; language; 8; 18; 5; social

19. cause-and-effect; launching event; 6

20. active

21. sensorimotor; 6

22. sucking; grasping; looking; listening; 1 month

23. adaptation; assimilation; schemas; accommodation

Stage-one infants suck everything that touches their lips. At about 1 month, they start to adapt their sucking to specific objects. By 3 months, they have organized the world into objects to be sucked for nourishment, objects to be sucked for pleasure, and objects not to be sucked at all.

24. 4; 8

A stage-three infant may squeeze a duck, hear a quack, and squeeze the duck again.

25. 8; 12; anticipate; goal-directed

26. 12; 18

Having discovered some action or set of actions that is possible with a given object, stage-five "little scientists" seem to ask, "What else can I do with this?"

27. 18; 24; mental combinations

28. pretend

29. follow; varies

30. speech

31. squeals, growls, grunts, croons, and yells, as well as some speechlike sounds

32. 6 or 7; babbling;

33. later; manually; at the same time as

34. 1 year; 100

35. referential; expressive; culture; referential

36. overextension; underextension; mutual exclusivity bias

37. holophrase

38. 21

39. B. F. Skinner

40. Noam Chomsky; language acquisition device

Recent research has suggested that both Skinner's and Chomsky's theories have some validity but that both miss the mark. Developmentalists today believe that language acquisition is an interactional process between the infant's genetic predisposition and the communication that occurs in the caregiver-child relationship.

41. baby talk

Baby talk is higher in pitch; has a characteristically low-to-high intonation pattern; uses simpler and more concrete vocabulary and shorter sentence length; and employs more questions, commands, and repetitions, and fewer past tenses, pronouns, and complex sentences.

42. (a) holding prelinguistic "conversations" with the infant; (b) engaging in baby talk; (c) persistently naming objects and events that capture the child's attention; and (d) expanding the child's sounds and words into meaningful communications

Answers to Testing Yourself

1. **b.** is the answer. Translated from its Latin roots, the word "infant" refers to someone who is "not yet speaking." (audio program)

2. **b.** is the answer. Cooing serves the very important social function of attracting the caregiver's attention. (audio program; textbook, p. 176)

3. **a.** is the answer. Babbling is sheer experimentation with the sounds of language. (audio program; textbook, p. 176)

4. **d.** is the answer. To qualify as an actual word, sounds must be symbols, resemble adult words, and be used consistently. (audio program)

5. **d.** is the answer. In speaking to children, adults generally confine their conversation to things in the "here and now." (audio program; textbook, p. 180)

6. **c.** is the answer. (textbook, p. 160)

7. **c.** is the answer. (textbook, p. 172)

8. **b.** is the answer. This was Piaget's most basic contribution to the study of infant cognition—that intelligence is revealed in behavior at every age. (textbook, p. 171)

9. **c.** is the answer. (textbook, pp. 160, 171)

   b. This is Chomsky's position.

   d. This issue was not discussed in the text.

10. **a.** is the answer. (textbook, p. 173)

    b. & c. These abilities are not acquired until children are much older.

    d. Pretending is associated with stage six (18 to 24 months).

11. **c.** is the answer. (textbook, pp. 163–164)

12. **d.** is the answer. (textbook, pp. 180–181)

13. **b.** is the answer. (textbook, p. 175)

    a., c., & d. Children the world over, and in every Piagetian stage, follow the same sequence, but the timing of their accomplishments may vary considerably.

14. c. is the answer. (textbook, p. 176)

15. a. is the answer. (textbook, p. 178)

b. Baby talk is the speech adults use with infants.

c. An overextension is a grammatical error in which a word is generalized to an inappropriate context.

e. An underextension is the use of a word to refer to a narrower category of objects or events than the term signifies.

16. c. is the answer. Vygotsky's concept of an "apprenticeship in thinking" is very much in keeping with the interactive, social nature of language development. (textbook, p. 182)

a. & b. Skinner and Chomsky both overlooked the social context of language development in their theories.

d. Gibson's research was not directly concerned with language development.

17. c. is the answer. (textbook, p. 180)

a. A holophrase is a single word uttered by a toddler to express a complete thought.

b. According to Noam Chomsky, the LAD, or lan-guage acquisition device, is an innate ability in humans to acquire language.

d. These characteristic differences in pitch and structure are precisely what distinguish baby talk from regular conversation.

18. d. is the answer. (textbook, p. 166)

19. c. is the answer. (textbook, p. 170)

20. c. is the answer (textbook, p. 168)

a. & b. In Piaget's theory, these refer to processes by which mental concepts incorporate new experiences (assimilation) or are modified in response to new experiences (accommodation).

d. Dynamic perception is perception that is primed to focus on movement and change.

Reference

de Villiers, Jill G., & de Villiers, Peter A. (1978). *Language acquisition.* Cambridge, MA: Harvard University Press.

A scholarly description of early language development by two eminent researchers.

The First Two Years: Psychosocial Development

AUDIO PROGRAM: Attachment: The Dance Begins

ORIENTATION

Lessons 5 and 6 of *Seasons of Life* examined biosocial and cognitive development during the first two years. Lesson 7, which is concerned with psychosocial development during infancy, explores the individual's emerging self-awareness, personality, emotional expression, and relationship to parents and society.

As discussed in Chapter 7 of *The Developing Person Through the Life Span*, 5/e, contemporary developmentalists have revised a number of the traditional views of psychosocial development. It was once believed, for example, that infants did not have any real emotions. Researchers now know, however, that in the very first days and weeks of life, infants express and sense many emotions, including fear, anger, happiness, and surprise.

In the traditional view of personality development, the infant was seen as a passive recipient of the personality created almost entirely by the actions of his or her parents. But it is now apparent that many personality dispositions are present in infants at birth, before parental influence is felt. In addition, active parent-infant interaction within a secure and nurturing environment is now viewed as a central factor in the child's psychosocial development.

Audio program 7, "Attachment: The Dance Begins," explores the who, when, where, and why of **attachment**—the affectional tie between infants and their primary caretakers. In infants the world over, attachment develops at about 7 months, when babies first become aware that other people stay in existence even when they're out of sight. Attachment helps ensure that the relatively helpless human infant receives the adult care it needs in order to survive.

What about infants who do not become securely attached? And what are the effects, for example, of adoption and day care on the development of attachment? Through the expert commentary of psychologists Michael Lamb, Janice Gibson, and Sheldon White, we explore these important issues in attachment—an intricate "interaction" between infant and caregiver that lays the foundation for psychosocial development throughout the subsequent seasons of life.

LESSON GOALS

By the end of this lesson you should be prepared to:

1. Describe the basic emotions expressed by infants during the first days and months.

2. Outline the main developments in the emotional life of the child between 6 months and 2 years.

3. Describe Freud's psychosexual stages of infant development and Erikson's psychosocial stages of development.

4. Discuss the origins of temperament and personality as an interaction of nature and nurture.

5. Discuss the significance of parent-infant interaction, particularly as it promotes or hinders attachment, in the infant's psychosocial development.

Audio Assignment

Listen to the audio tape that accompanies Lesson 7: "Attachment: The Dance Begins."

Write answers to the following questions. You may replay portions of the program if you need to refresh your memory. Answer guidelines may be found in the Lesson Guidelines sections at the end of this chapter.

1. Define attachment, outline its development, and explain why experts believe it to be a biologically determined event.

2. Discuss the impact of early mother-infant contact, adoption, and day care on attachment.

3. Discuss the immediate and long-range impact on infants of secure and insecure attachment.

Textbook Assignment

Read Chapter 7: "The First Two Years: Psychosocial Development," pages 187–214 in *The Developing Person Through the Life Span, 5/e,* then work through the material that follows to review it. Complete the sentences and answer the questions. As you proceed, evaluate your performance for each secdtion by consulting the answers on page 91. Do not continue with the next section until you understand each answer. If you need to, review or reread the appropriate section in the textbook before continuing.

1. Developmentalists believe that infants
   _____ (are/are not) innately predisposed to sociability.

Early Emotions (pp. 187–192)

2. The first emotion that can be reliably discerned in infants is _____ . Other early infant emotions include _____ ,
   _____ , and _____ .

3. The infant's smile in response to a human face or voice, which is called a _____ , begins to appear at about _____ of age. Full smiles are easy to elicit at _____ months.

4. Infant emotions become more differentiated and distinct sometime between _____ and _____ months of age. Infants begin to express anger by about _____ months. At this age, individual differences in the _____ and _____ with which emotions occur are also apparent.

5. Three universals that make the emotions of the older baby more selective and diverse are _____ maturation, growing _____ skills, and more varied _____ .

6. Stranger _____ is first noticeable at about _____ of age.

7. An infant's fear of being left by the mother or other caregiver, called _____ _____ , emerges at about _____ months, peaks at about _____ months, and then gradually subsides. Whether separation distresses an infant depends on such factors as _____ .

8. As early as _____ months of age, infants associate _____ meanings with specific _____ expressions and with different tones of voice. For example, infants look to trusted adults for emotional cues in uncertain situations; this is called _____ _____ . This becomes increasingly important as the infant becomes more _____ .

9. Infants use their fathers for social reference _____ (less than/about the same as/more than) their mothers. Fathers tend to be more _____ , and mothers are more _____ .

Briefly contrast how mothers and fathers tend to play with their infants.

10. The emerging sense of "me and mine" is part of what psychologists call _____ . This makes possible many new self-conscious emotions, including _____ , _____ , _____ , and _____ . This awareness emerges between _____ and _____ months.

Briefly describe the nature and findings of the classic rouge-and-mirror experiment on self-awareness in infants.

11. Developing self-awareness also enhances the toddler's _____ reactions and emotional responses such as _____ . Furthermore, it allows the child to react to his or her misdeeds with _____ at going against another's wishes.

The Origins of Personality (pp. 193–201)

12. Personality is defined as _____ _____ .

13. An early prevailing view among psychologists was that the individual's personality was permanently molded by the actions of his or her _____ . Two versions of this theory were the _____ and _____ theories.

14. According to early learning theory, personality is molded through the processes of _____ and _____ of the child's various behaviors. A strong proponent of this position was _____ .

15. Later theorists incorporated the role of _____ learning, that is, infants' tendency to _____ the personality traits of their parents. This form of learning is strengthened by _____ _____ .

Briefly explain how the kinds of signals caregivers send to toddlers influence their overall emotionality.

16. According to Freud, the experiences of the first _____ years of life and the child's relationship with his or her _____ were decisive in personality formation.

17. In Freud's theory, development begins with the _____ stage, so named because the _____ is the infant's prime source of gratification and pleasure.

18. According to Freud, in the second year the prime focus of gratification comes from stimulation and control of the bowels. Freud referred to this period as the _____ stage. This stage represents a shift in the way the infant interacts with others, from the more _____ , _____ mode of orality to the more _____ , _____ mode of anality.

Describe Freud's ideas on the importance of early oral experiences to later personality development.

19. Research has shown that the parents' overall pattern of _____ is more important to the child's emotional development than the particulars of feeding and weaning or toilet training.

20. The theorist who believed that development occurs through a series of psychosocial crises is _____ . According to his theory, the crisis of infancy is one of

    _____ ,

    whereas the crisis of toddlerhood is one of

    _____ .

    He maintained that experiences later in life _____ (can alter/have little impact on) the effects of early experiences on personality development.

21. The traditional views of personality emphasize the importance of early _____ , particularly that provided by a child's

    _____ .

22. (Changing Policy) According to Jay Belsky, extended infant day care _____ (is/is not) likely to result in negative developmental outcomes. Belsky admits, however—and other research has convincingly demonstrated— that when preschoolers experience early and extended amounts of high-quality day care, they show more _____ (positive/negative) outcomes than children without such experience.

23. (Changing Policy) Researchers have identified four factors that seem essential to high-quality day care:

    a. _____

    b. _____

    c. _____

    d. _____

24. (Changing Policy) A large-scale study of day care in the United States found that infants were likely to become insecurely attached only under three circumstances:

    a. _____

b. _____

c. _____

25. A person's inherent, relatively consistent, basic dispositions define his or her _____ . This overall makeup, which _____ (is/is not) evident at birth, begins in the _____ codes that guide the development of the brain and is affected by many prenatal experiences, including _____ _____ . However, as the person develops, the _____ _____ and the individual's _____ increasingly influence the nature and expression of this trait. Thus, this makeup is _____ .

26. (Research Report) List the nine temperamental characteristics measured in the NYLS study:

    _____

    _____

27. (Research Report) Most young infants can be described as one of three types: _____ ,

    _____   _____

    _____   _____

    or _____ .

28. (Research Report) The "big five" dimensions of personality are _____ ,

    _____ , _____ ,

    _____ , and _____ .

29. (Research Report) Temperament is linked to _____ . This means that parents _____ (can/cannot) be blamed, or credited, for all their infants' actions.

(Research Report) Describe two ways in which the environment can influence a child's temperamental characteristics.

Interaction Again (pp. 202–213)

30. Although infants are social from birth, they are not necessarily socially _____ .

31. Infants under 3 months of age often become upset for reasons that have little to do with the _____ they receive. At this age, _____ (boys/girls) tend to be fussier than _____ (boys/girls).

32. Babies begin to respond especially to their primary caregivers by _____ months of age. At this time, caregivers begin to initiate focused episodes of _____-_____-_____ play.

33. The coordinated interaction of response between infant and caregiver is called _____ . Partly through this interaction, infants learn to _____ and _____ emotions.

Describe the social play behaviors of adults with infants.

34. Episodes of face-to-face play _____ (are/are not) a universal feature of early interaction with infants.

35. Cultural variations in the _____ and _____ of social play, as well as the _____ of the adults who initiate face-to-face episodes, are common.

36. (In Person) The signs of dyssynchrony include _____ _____ . The ease of synchrony is affected not only by the caregiver's personality but also by the infant's _____ and _____ .

37. The emotional bond that develops between parents and infants is called _____ .

38. Approaching, following, and climbing onto the caregiver's lap are signs of _____-_____ behaviors, while clinging and resisting being put down are signs of _____-_____ behaviors.

39. An infant who derives comfort and confidence from the secure base provided by the caregiver is displaying _____ _____ . By contrast, _____ _____ is characterized by an infant's fear, anger, or seeming indifference to the caregiver.

40. The procedure developed by Ainsworth to measure attachment is called the _____ _____ . Approximately _____ (what proportion?) of all normal infants tested with this procedure demonstrate secure attachment.

(text and Table 7.1) Briefly describe three types of insecure attachment.

41. Among the features of caregiving that affect the quality of attachment are the following:
    a. _____
    b. _____
    c. _____

42. Attachment may also be affected by the broader family context, including the quality of the _____'s involvement in child care, the _____ _____ and the _____ _____ _____ . It is also affected by _____ and by the infant's _____ .

43. Most infants _____ (do/
do not) show signs of attachment to other caregivers, such as fathers, siblings, and day-care
workers.

44. By itself, a secure or insecure attachment in
infancy _____ (determines/ does
not determine) a child's later social relationships.

45. When a child's attachment is insecure, the parents _____ (are/are not) always to
blame. Recent research studies have found that
the child's temperament has a _____
(smaller/greater) impact on attachment than the
parent's caregiving pattern.

46. (Research Report) Mary Main has found that
adults can be classified into one of four categories
of attachment: _____ adults, who
value attachment relationships but can discuss
them objectively; _____
adults, who devalue attachment;
_____ adults, who dwell on past
relationships; and _____
adults, who have not yet reconciled their past
experiences with the present.

47. (Research Report) Autonomous mothers tend to
have infants who are _____
attached, dismissing mothers tend to have
_____ babies, and preoccupied
mothers tend to have _____
infants. A recent study found that mothers who
describe their own past attachment as
_____ tend to express more joy in
their infants, while mothers who are
_____ of their past relationship tend
to show anger toward their infants.

(Research Report) State several possible reasons for
the link between adult and infant attachment.

Testing Yourself

After you have completed the audio and text review
questions, see how well you do on the following quiz.
Correct answers, with text and audio references, may
be found at the end of this chapter.

1. Attachment between infant and primary caregiver typically happens at about what age?
   a. 1 or 2 months
   b. 3 or 4 months
   c. 6 or 7 months
   d. 10 or 11 months

2. Experts believe that the emergence of attachment
in infants is:
   a. biologically based and linked to the cognitive
ability to represent other individuals.
   b. a learned behavior elicited by responsible
caregiving.
   c. largely dependent upon early bonding
between mother and infant.
   d. unpredictable and of relative unimportance in
later psychosocial development.

3. Infants placed for adoption after 6 months of age:
   a. never form secure attachments.
   b. can still become securely attached to adoptive
parents.
   c. are more likely to be abused than infants
adopted at an earlier age.
   d. gain weight more slowly than infants adopted
at an earlier age.

4. Most infants who are regularly placed in day
care:
   a. develop attachments to day-care workers
rather than parents.
   b. become insecurely attached, out of confusion
over their primary caregivers.
   c. show signs of extreme anxiety when tested in
the Strange Situation.
   d. form secure attachments to their parents.

5. Stuffed animals, favorite blankets, and other
objects that children keep near them when apart
from their primary caregivers are called:
   a. security objects.
   b. transitional objects.
   c. vicarious parents.
   d. symbolic pacifiers.

6. One of the first emotions that can be discerned in
infancy is:
   a. shame.   c. guilt.
   b. distress.   d. pride.

7. The social smile begins to appear:
   a. at about 6 weeks.
   b. at about 8 months.
   c. after stranger wariness has been overcome.
   d. after the infant has achieved a sense of self.

8. An infant's fear of being left by the mother or other caregiver, called _____ , peaks at about _____ .
   a. separation anxiety; 14 months
   b. stranger wariness; 8 months
   c. separation anxiety; 8 months
   d. stranger wariness; 14 months

9. Social referencing refers to:
   a. parenting skills that change over time.
   b. changes in community values regarding, for example, the acceptability of using physical punishment with small children.
   c. the support network for new parents provided by extended family members.
   d. the infant response of looking to trusted adults for emotional cues in uncertain situations.

10. (Research Report) The "big five" personality dimensions are:
    a. emotional stability, openness, introversion, sociability, locus of control
    b. neuroticism, extroversion, openness, emotional stability, sensitivity
    c. agreeableness, conscientiousness, neuroticism, openness, extroversion
    d. neuroticism, gregariousness, extroversion, impulsiveness, sensitivity

11. Psychologists who favored the _____ perspective believed that the personality of the child was virtually "created" through reinforcement and punishment.
    a. psychoanalytic   c. psychosocial
    b. learning   d. epigenetic

12. Freud's oral stage corresponds to Erikson's crisis of:
    a. orality versus anality.
    b. trust versus mistrust.
    c. autonomy versus shame and doubt.
    d. secure versus insecure attachment.

13. Erikson felt that the development of a sense of trust in early infancy depends on the quality of the:
    a. infant's food.
    b. child's genetic inheritance.
    c. maternal relationship.
    d. introduction of toilet training.

14. Research studies demonstrate that the _____ is more influential than the _____ in determining the parent-child connection.
    a. parent's caregiving pattern; child's temperament
    b. child's temperament; parent's caregiving pattern
    c. child's gender; child's age
    d. parent's age; child's temperament

15. (Research Report) "Easy," "slow to warm up," and "difficult" are descriptions of different:
    a. forms of attachment.
    b. types of temperament.
    c. types of parenting.
    d. toddler responses to the Strange Situation.

16. The more physical play of fathers probably helps the children master motor skills and may contribute to the:
    a. infant's self-awareness.
    b. growth of the infant's social skills and emotional expression.
    c. tendency of the infant to become securely attached.
    d. infant's fear of strangers and separation anxiety.

17. *Synchrony* is a term that describes:
    a. the carefully coordinated interaction between parent and infant.
    b. a mismatch of the temperaments of parent and infant.
    c. a research technique involving videotapes.
    d. the concurrent evolution of different species.

18. The emotional tie that develops between an infant and his or her primary caregiver is called:
    a. self-awareness.   c. affiliation.
    b. synchrony.   d. attachment.

19. An important effect of secure attachment is the promotion of:
    a. self-awareness.
    b. curiosity and self-directed behavior.
    c. dependency.
    d. all of the above.

20. The sight of almost any human face is most likely to produce a smile in a _____-month-old.
    a. 3   c. 9
    b. 6   d. 12

LESSON 7: ATTACHMENT AND THE STRANGE SITUATION

Exercise

About 7 months after birth—around the time that children develop the ability to represent another person cognitively—infants develop an enduring affectional **attachment** to their primary caregivers.

Attachment can be measured in many ways. Infants express attachment by "proximity-seeking" behaviors, such as approaching, following, and clinging; and "contact-seeking" behaviors, such as crying, smiling, and calling. Parents express their attachment more by eye contact than by physical contact, and by reacting to their child's vocalizations, expressions, and gestures.

On the basis of many naturalistic observations, Mary Ainsworth developed a laboratory procedure in which the infant's reactions to a novel situation and the comings and goings of its caregiver indicate the security of the child's attachment. In this test (called the **Strange Situation**), which is conducted in a well-equipped playroom full of toys, most infants demonstrate **secure attachment**. The presence of their mother gives them the sense of security needed to express their natural curiosity and explore the new room. If their mother attempts to leave the room, securely attached infants will usually stop playing, protest verbally, and demonstrate contact-seeking behaviors.

Approximately one-third of infants show **insecure attachment** in this test situation, clinging nervously to their mother and being unwilling to explore even while she remains in the room. Others seem aloof and engage in little or no interaction with their mothers.

To better understand how attachment is measured, arrange to observe a 1- or 2-year-old and his or her caregiver in a play setting outside the child's home. Ideally, ask a relative or friend and their child to participate. The play setting could be in your home, at a local playground, or at any other mutually agreeable location. If you do not know someone with a young child, you can complete this exercise by visiting a playground or day-care center.

Before your scheduled observation period, read through the questions that follow so that you will know what behaviors to watch for. Observe your participants for 10 to 15 minutes of unstructured play. If possible, during the observation period, ask the adult to make a move as if he or she were going to leave. Observe the child's reaction. After the observation period, answer the questions and hand the completed exercise in to your instructor.

1. Describe the participants and setting that you chose for the attachment observation.

2. Did you encounter any difficulties in completing this exercise?

3. What signs of attachment did you observe in the child's behavior (e.g., contact-seeking, proximity-seeking)?

4. What signs of attachment did you observe in the adult's behavior (e.g., eye contact, responsiveness to child's behavior)?

5. If your observation included a move by the adult to leave the room, describe the child's reactions.

6. On the basis of the material covered in this lesson—and your brief observation—would you say that the child you observed was securely attached or insecurely attached? Give examples of the child's behavior that support your conclusion.

LESSON GOALS

Audio Question Guidelines

1. **Attachment** refers to the process by which infants develop a lasting affectional tie with their primary caregiver. Attachment goes two ways, from parent to child and from child to parent.

   From the parent's point of view, the bonding that leads to attachment begins during pregnancy, includes the special memories of birth, and continues to develop indefinitely.

   Babies give their first **social smiles** at about 4 to 6 weeks of age, which clearly contributes to attachment with the caregiver.

   Attachment emerges in children the world over at about 7 months of age. This regularity implies that it is a biologically based event.

   Attachment ensures that the relatively immature and helpless human newborn will receive the adult help it needs in order to survive.

   The signs of attachment to a particular person are clear. The baby turns to that person when distressed and protests when that person leaves. Babies may also cry when strangers appear.

2. There is no good evidence that early mother-infant contact has a major impact on attachment. In most cases, researchers report no reduction in the quality of the relationship formed between mothers and babies when contact in the first few weeks of life does not take place.

   Because babies form their first attachment at about 7 months of age, it is somewhat easier to place a child for adoption before that time. A child placed with adoptive parents after that age may have to go through a process of grieving the loss of an earlier attachment figure before investing emotionally in a new one.

   In most circumstances, babies form more than one attachment in the course of growing up.

   Approximately two-thirds of babies in this country form secure attachments to their mothers whether or not they are in regular day care. An important variable in day care is the quality of care that the child receives and the extent to which it matches the style of the parents.

   Because their children may develop attachments to day-care workers, day care may be a more difficult adjustment for parents than it is for children.

3. Three-year-old children who were **securely attached** at one year are more mature and significantly more independent, self-confident, cooperative, and sociable than those who were **insecurely attached**.

   Securely attached children are more likely to be persistent and resilient in challenging situations.

   The developmental advantages of securely attached children seem to continue to age 5 or 6, when children start school. Most likely, the reason is that their home has been consistently nurturant.

Textbook Question Answers

1. are
2. distress; sadness; interest; pleasure
3. social smile; 6 weeks; 5
4. 6; 9; 7; intensity; speed
5. physical; cognitive; experiences
6. wariness; 6 months
7. separation anxiety; 8 or 9; 14; the baby's prior experiences with separation and the manner in which the caregiver departs
8. 5; emotional; facial; social referencing; mobile
9. about the same as; encouraging; protective

Fathers' play is more noisy, emotional, boisterous, physical, and idiosyncratic. Mothers are more likely to caress, sing soothingly, and to combine play with caretaking activities.

10. self-awareness; embarrassment; guilt; shame; pride; 9; 15

In the classic self-awareness experiment, babies look in a mirror after a dot of rouge is put on their nose. If the babies react to the mirror image by touching their nose, it is clear they know they are seeing their own face. Most babies demonstrate this self-awareness between 15 and 24 months of age.

11. self-critical; shame; guilt
12. the emotions, behaviors, and attitudes that make an individual unique
13. parents; learning; psychoanalytic
14. reinforcement; punishment; John Watson
15. social; imitate; social referencing

If toddlers receive more signals of interest and encouragement than of fear and prohibition as they explore, they are likely to be friendlier and less aggressive. If an infant or toddler sees few signals of any kind, the child becomes relatively passive and emotionless.

16. 4; mother

17. oral; mouth

18. anal; passive; dependent; active; controlling

Freud believed that the oral and anal stages are fraught with potential conflict that can have long-term consequences for the infant. If nursing is a hurried or tense event, for example, the child may become fixated at the oral stage, excessively eating, drinking, smoking, or talking in quest of oral satisfaction.

19. warmth and sensitivity or coldness and domination

20. Erikson; trust versus mistrust; autonomy versus shame and doubt; can alter

21. nurture; mother

22. is; positive

23. (a) adequate attention to each child; (b) encouragement of sensorimotor exploration and language development; (c) attention to health and safety; (d) well-trained and professional caregivers.

24. (a) if their mothers were insensitive; (b) if the day-care quality was poor, (c) if they were in day care more than 20 hours per week

25. temperament; is; genetic; the nutrition and health of the mother; social context; experiences; epigenetic

26. activity level; rhythmicity; approach-withdrawal; adaptability; intensity of reaction; threshold of responsiveness; quality of mood; distractibility; attention span

27. easy; slow to warm up; difficult

28. extroversion; agreeableness; conscientiousness; neuroticism; openness

29. biological and neurological patterns that appear in the first month of life; cannot

One way is through the "goodness of fit" between the child's temperamental patterns and the demands of the home environment. Parents' expectations also can influence temperament.

30. competent

31. care; boys; girls

32. 2 to 3; face-to-face

33. synchrony; express; read

Adults tend to open their eyes and mouths wide in exaggerated expressions, make rapid clucking noises or repeated one-syllable sounds, raise and lower the pitch of their voice, change the pace of their movements, and imitate the infant's actions, for example.

34. are

35. frequency; duration; goals

36. the baby's averted eyes, stiffening or abrupt shifting of the body, and/or an unhappy noise; personality; predispositions

37. attachment

38. proximity-seeking; contact-maintaining

39. secure attachment; insecure attachment

40. Strange Situation; two-thirds

Some infants are avoidant: They engage in little interaction with their mother before and after her departure. Others are anxious and resistant: They cling nervously to their mother, are unwilling to explore, cry loudly when she leaves, and refuse to be comforted when she returns. Others are disorganized and/or disoriented: They show an inconsistent mixture of behavior toward the mother.

41. a. general sensitivity to the infant's needs

    b. responsiveness to the infant's specific signals

    c. talking and playing with the infant in ways that actively encourage growth and development

42. father; marital relationship; overall social context; changes in family circumstances; temperament

43. do

44. does not determine

45. are not; greater

46. autonomous; dismissing; preoccupied; unresolved

47. securely; avoidant; resistant; autonomous; dismissing

(a) Parents who value attachment may be more sensitive to their offspring and inspire secure attachment as a result; (b) inherited temperament may predispose a certain attachment pattern across most relationships; (c) the nature of parents' attachment with their children may influence their memories of, and attitudes about, other attachments; (d) some cultural contexts may encourage attachments while others do not; (e) life experiences after infancy may have an impact.

Answers to Testing Yourself

1. **c.** is the answer. In children throughout the world, attachment emerges at 6 or 7 months. (audio program)

2. **a.** is the answer. Attachment emerges at about the same age that infants develop the cognitive abili-

ty to maintain the image of another person in their minds. (audio program)

3. **b.** is the answer. Infants who are placed for adoption after the age of 6 months may first grieve the loss of an earlier attachment, but they can still develop new secure attachments. (audio program)

4. **d.** is the answer. Infants placed regularly in day care may develop attachments to day-care workers, but they still become attached to their parents. (audio program)

5. **b.** is the answer. Transitional objects help fill an emotional need in the time between when a child is physically near the parent and when he or she can be away from the parent completely. (audio program)

6. **b.** is the answer. (textbook, p. 187)

   a., c., & d. These emotions emerge later in infancy, at about the same time as self-awareness emerges.

7. **a.** is the answer. (textbook, p. 188)

8. **a.** is the answer. (textbook, p. 188)

   b. & d. This fear, which is also called fear of strangers, peaks by 10 to 14 months.

9. **d.** is the answer. (textbook, p. 189)

10. **c.** is the answer. (textbook, pp. 200–201)

11. **b.** is the answer. (textbook, p. 193)

   a. Reinforcement and punishment have no place in the psychoanalytic perspective.

   c. This is Erikson's theory, which sees development as occurring through a series of basic crises.

   d. This perspective analyzes how genes and environment contribute to development.

12. **b.** is the answer. (textbook, pp. 194, 195)

   a. Orality and anality refer to personality traits that result from fixation in the oral and anal stages, respectively.

   c. According to Erikson, this is the crisis of toddlerhood, which corresponds to Freud's anal stage.

   d. This is not a developmental crisis in Erikson's theory.

13. **c.** is the answer. (textbook, p. 195)

14. **b.** is the answer. (textbook, p. 211)

   c. & d. Neither gender nor age (of child or parent) was discussed as a factor in attachment.

15. **b.** is the answer. (textbook, p. 200)

   a. "Secure" and "insecure" are different forms of attachment.

   c. The chapter does not describe different types of parenting.

   d. The Strange Situation is a test of attachment, rather than of temperament.

16. **b.** is the answer. (textbook, p. 190)

17. **a.** is the answer. (textbook, p. 203)

18. **d.** is the answer. (textbook, p. 206)

   a. Self-awareness refers to the infant's developing sense of "me and mine."

   b. Synchrony describes the coordinated interaction between infant and caregiver.

   c. Affiliation describes the tendency of people at any age to seek the companionship of others.

19. **b.** is the answer. (textbook, p. 210)

   a. The text does not link self-awareness to secure attachment.

   c. On the contrary, secure attachment promotes *independence* in infants and children.

20. **a.** is the answer. (textbook, p. 188)

   b., c., & d. As infants become older, they smile more selectively.

Reference

Sroufe, L. A., Marshall, M. E., and Bronfenbrenner, U. (eds.) *Child Development: Its Nature and Course* (1995). New York: McGraw-Hill.

Professor Sroufe discusses the importance of attachment in psychosocial development.

The Play Years: Biosocial Development

ORIENTATION

Lesson 8 is the first of a three-lesson unit that describes the developing person from 2 to 6 years in terms of biosocial, cognitive, and psychosocial development. Lesson 8 examines biosocial development during the play years.

Children grow steadily taller and slimmer during the preschool years, with their genetic background and nutrition being responsible for most of the variation seen in children from various parts of the world. The most significant aspect of growth is the continued maturation of the nervous system and the refinement of the visual, muscular, and cognitive skills that will be necessary for the child to function in school. The brain becomes more specialized as it matures, with the left side usually becoming the center for speech, and the right the center for visual, spatial, and artistic skills.

The textbook also discusses these refinements in physical development. In addition, it includes a thorough discussion of a tragedy in child development: child abuse and neglect, including the prevalence of maltreatment, its causes, consequences, and treatment.

Play is especially appropriate for the extended period of childhood that has been programmed into the biological clock. Audio program 8, " 'How To' Time," explores the evolutionary origins of this period and the use to which humans have put it.

The human biological clock delays the onset of reproductive maturity and gives children time to acquire what Erik Erikson referred to as a sense of industry. Childhood is the time to pretend, to play, and to learn how to do things. And herein lies the key to our extended childhood. More than any other species, we humans are dependent upon complex, learned behavior for our survival. Through the expert commentary of pediatrician Howard Weinblatt,

endocrinologist Inese Beitins, anthropologist Barry Bogin, and evolutionary biologist Stephen Jay Gould, the significance of "how to" time is explored.

The program opens with the voice of a girl explaining how to ride a tricycle, a skill rarely used by adults but never forgotten.

LESSON GOALS

By the end of this lesson you should be prepared to:

1. Describe normal physical growth during the play years, and account for variations in height and weight.

2. Discuss brain growth and development, its effect on development during the play years, and the development of school readiness.

3. Outline the development of gross and fine motor skills during early childhood, and describe activities that foster these skills.

4. Discuss the significance of the extended period of human childhood and the importance of play in development.

5. Discuss various issues concerning child maltreatment, including its prevalence, causes, consequences, treatment, and prevention.

Audio Assignment

Listen to the audio tape that accompanies Lesson 8: " 'How To' Time."

Write answers to the following questions. You may replay portions of the program if you need to refresh your memory. Answer guidelines may be found in the Lesson Guidelines section at the end of this chapter.

1. Outline the biological clock's hormonal program for the timing of sexual maturity.

2. Cite two possible evolutionary explanations for the extended period of childhood in humans.

3. Explain the "down-and-out" principle of physical development.

Textbook Assignment

Read Chapter 8: "The Play Years: Biosocial Development," pages 219–243 in *The Developing Person Through the Life Span, 5/e*, then work through the material that follows to review it. Complete the sentences and answer the questions. As you proceed, evaluate your performance for each secdtion by consulting the answers on page 103. Do not continue with the next section until you understand each answer. If you need to, review or reread the appropriate section in the textbook before continuing.

Size and Shape (pp. 219–220)

1. During the preschool years, from age _____ to _____ , children add almost _____ in height and gain about _____ in weight per year. By age 6, the average child in a developed nation weighs about _____ and measures _____ in height.

2. The range of normal physical development is quite _____ (narrow/broad).

3. Of the many factors that influence height and weight, the most influential are the child's

_____ _____ ,

_____ _____ ,

and _____ .

4. The dramatic differences between physical development in developed and underdeveloped nations are largely due to differences in the average child's _____ .

5. In multiethnic countries, children of _____ descent tend to be tallest, followed by _____ , then _____ , and then _____ . The impact of _____ patterns on physical development can be seen in families in South Asia and the Indian subcontinent, where _____ (which gender?) are more highly valued and consequently better fed than the other sex when food is scarce.

6. (Research Report) During the preschool years, annual height and weight gain is much _____ (greater/less) than during infancy. This means that children need _____ (fewer/more) calories per pound during this period.

7. (Research Report) The most prevalent nutritional problem in developed countries during the preschool years is _____ _____ _____ , the chief symptom of which is _____ _____ . This problem stems from a diet deficient in _____ _____ . This problem is _____ (more/ less) common among low-income families than among others.

8. (Research Report) An additional problem for American children is that they, like most American adults, consume too much

_____ and too much

_____ .

Brain Growth and Development (pp. 221–227)

9. By age 5, the brain has attained about
_____ percent of its adult weight;
by age 7 it is _____ . In contrast,
total body weight of the average 7-year-old is
about _____ percent of that of the
average adult.

10. Part of the brain's increase in size during childhood is due to the continued proliferation of
_____ pathways and the ongoing
process of _____ . In addition, there
is notable expansion of brain areas dedicated to
_____ and _____ , the
_____ , and _____
processes. This helps children to develop
_____ reactions to stimuli and to be
able to control their reactions.

11. The band of nerve fibers that connects the right
and left sides of the brain, called the

_____ _____ ,

becomes thicker due to _____
growth and _____ . This helps children better coordinate functions that involve

_____ .

12. In all but the most disease-ridden or war-torn
countries of the world, the leading cause of childhood death is _____ .

13. The accident risk for particular children depends
on several factors, including their

_____ , _____
_____ , and _____ .

14. Injuries and accidental deaths are
_____ (more/less) frequent among
boys than girls.

15. The clearest risk factor in accident rates is
_____ _____ , with
_____ (high/low)-status children
being three times more likely than other children
to die an accidental death.. The impact of this factor is greatest during _____

_____ , when
_____ immaturity makes children
least able to understand danger.

16. (Changing Policy) Instead of "accident prevention," many experts speak of _____
_____ , an approach based on the
belief that most accidents _____
(are/are not) preventable.

17. (Changing Policy) Safety laws that include penalties for noncompliance seem to be even
_____ (less/more) effective than
educational measures in reducing injury rates.

18. (Changing Policy) The accidental death rate for
American children between the ages of 1 and 5
has _____ (increased/ decreased)
between 1980 and 1996.

19. Throughout the preschool years, the visual pathways of the brain that are associated with control
of _____ _____ and
_____ undergo considerable
growth. This, along with improved
_____ between the left and right
sides of the brain, enhances children's
_____-_____
coordination.

20. Brain growth during childhood
_____ (is/is not) necessarily linear,
sometimes occurring in _____
and _____ .

21. Development of the corpus callosum and the
frontal lobes of the brain as well as other qualitative changes in the brain at around age 5 facilitates formal schooling, because children are now
able to begin forming links between
_____ and _____

_____ .

Mastering Motor Skills (pp. 227–230)

22. Large body movements such as running, climbing, jumping, and throwing are called
_____ _____ skills.
These skills, which improve dramatically during
the preschool years, require guided
_____ , as well as a certain level of

_____ _____ . Most children learn these skills _____ (by themselves/from parents).

23. Skills that involve small body movements, such as pouring liquids and cutting food, are called _____ _____ skills. Preschoolers have greater difficulty with these skills primarily because they have not developed the _____ control, patience, or _____ needed—in part because the _____ of the central nervous system is not complete.

24. (In person) Many developmentalists believe that _____ is a form of play that enhances the child's sense of accomplishment. This form of play also provides a testing ground for another important skill, _____ . Mastery of this skill is related to overall _____ growth.

Child Maltreatment (pp. 230–242)

25. Until a few decades ago, the concept of child maltreatment was mostly limited to obvious _____ assault, which was thought to be the outburst of a mentally disturbed person. Today, it is known that most perpetrators of maltreatment _____ (are/are not) mentally ill.

26. Intentional harm to, or avoidable endangerment of, someone under age 18 defines child _____ . Actions that are deliberately harmful to a child's well-being are classified as _____ . A failure to act appropriately to meet a child's basic needs is classified as _____ .

27. Ideas about what constitutes child maltreatment vary with _____ and _____ norms.

28. Before a particular practice can be considered abusive, _____ and _____ _____ must be taken into account.

29. Two aspects of the overall context that seem universally conducive to maltreatment are

_____ and _____ . _____

Describe some of the deficits of children who have been maltreated.

30. (A Life-Span View) The phenomenon of maltreated children growing up to become abusive or neglectful parents themselves is called _____ _____ . A widely held misconception is that this phenomenon _____ (is/is not) avoidable.

31. (A Life-Span View) Approximately _____ percent of abused children actually become abusive parents.

32. New laws requiring teachers, social workers, and other professionals to report possible maltreatment _____ (have/have not) resulted in increased reporting. Out of their concern that reporting does not create enough protection for a maltreated child, some experts advocate a policy of _____ _____ . This policy separates high-risk cases that may require complete investigation and _____ of the child from low-risk cases that may require some sort of _____ measure.

33. Some children are officially removed from their parents and placed in a _____ _____ arrangement with another adult or family who is paid to nurture them.

34. The process of finding a long-term solution to the care of a child who has been abused is called _____ _____ .

35. The average length of stay in foster care in the United States has _____ (increased/decreased), and the number of chil-

dren needing foster placement has

_____ (increased/decreased).

36. In another type of foster care, called

_____ _____ , a rela-

tive of the maltreated child becomes the

approved caregiver. A final option is

_____ , which is ideal when fami-

lies are _____ and children are

_____ .

37. Public policy measures and other efforts designed to prevent maltreatment from ever occurring are called _____ _____ .

An approach that focuses on spotting and treating the first symptoms of maltreatment is called _____ _____ . A specific example of this approach occurs in countries such as England and New Zealand, where _____ _____ of families with young infants is routinely practiced.

Last ditch measures such as removing a child from an abusive home, jailing the perpetrator, and so forth constitute _____

_____ .

Testing Yourself

After you have completed the audio and text review questions, see how well you do on the following quiz. Correct answers, with text and audio references, may be found at the end of this chapter.

1. The primary sex hormones are _____ in females and _____ in males.
   a. testosterone; estrogen
   b. estrogen; testosterone
   c. adrenaline; noradrenaline
   d. progesterone; testosterone

2. Which of the following most accurately describes how the levels of sex hormones change from birth to puberty?
   a. In both males and females, levels of sex hormones increase from birth until puberty.
   b. In males only, levels of sex hormones increase from birth until puberty.
   c. In females only, levels of sex hormones increase from birth until puberty.
   d. In both males and females, levels of sex hormones are very high at birth, drop at about 18 months, and become high again at puberty.

3. Anthropologists have proposed that an extended period of childhood evolved in humans because:
   a. humans need this time to learn the many complex behaviors critical for survival.
   b. babysitting by older children conferred such an advantage on humans that our biological clock evolved to keep childhood as lengthy as possible.
   c. both a. and b. are true.
   d. none of the above is true.

4. The "down-and-out" principle of development would explain why:
   a. reproductive maturity does not occur until puberty.
   b. babies can sit up before their color vision is mature.
   c. babies can sit up before they can stand.
   d. physical development is more rapid in girls than in boys.

5. According to developmental psychologists, the play of "how to" time is an important way in which children:
   a. perfect motor skills.
   b. develop a sense of being useful and competent.
   c. develop what Erikson referred to as a sense of industry.
   d. do all of the above.

6. (Research Report) During the preschool years, the most common nutritional problem in developed countries is:
   a. serious malnutrition.
   b. excessive intake of sweets.
   c. iron deficiency anemia.
   d. excessive caloric intake.

7. The brain center for speech is usually located in the:
   a. right brain.
   b. left brain.
   c. corpus callosum.
   d. space just below the right ear.

8. Which of the following is an example of tertiary prevention of child maltreatment?
   a. removing a child from an abusive home
   b. home visitation of families with infants by health professionals
   c. new laws establishing stiff penalties for child maltreatment
   d. public-policy measures aimed at creating stable neighborhoods

9. (Changing Policy) Which of the following is *not* true regarding injury control?
    a. Broad-based television announcements do not have a direct impact on children's risk taking.
    b. Unless parents become involved, classroom safety education has little effect on children's actual behavior.
    c. Safety laws that include penalties are more effective than educational measures.
    d. Accidental deaths of 1- to 5-year-olds have held steady in the United States over the past two decades.

10. (Research Report) Like most Americans, children tend to have too much _____ in their diet.
    a. iron
    b. fat
    c. sugar
    d. b. and c.

11. Skills that involve large body movements, such as running and jumping, are called:
    a. activity-level skills.
    b. fine motor skills.
    c. gross motor skills.
    d. left-brain skills.

12. The brain's ongoing myelination during childhood helps children:
    a. control their actions more precisely.
    b. react more quickly to stimuli.
    c. focus more easily on printed letters.
    d. do all of the above.

13. The leading cause of death in childhood is:
    a. accidents.
    b. untreated diabetes.
    c. malnutrition.
    d. iron deficiency anemia.

14. At age 6, the proportions of a child's body:
    a. still retain the "top-heavy" look of infancy.
    b. are more adultlike in girls than in boys.
    c. are not very different from those of an adult.
    d. are influenced more by heredity than by health care or nutrition.

15. Which of the following factors is *most* responsible for differences in height and weight between children in developed and developing countries?
    a. the child's genetic background
    b. health care
    c. nutrition
    d. age of weaning

16. In which of the following age periods is serious malnutrition *least* likely to occur?
    a. infancy
    b. early childhood
    c. adolescence
    d. Serious malnutrition is equally likely in each of these age groups.

17. The relationship between accident rate and SES can be described as:
    a. a positive correlation.
    b. a negative correlation.
    c. curvilinear.
    d. no correlation.

18. Which of the following is true of the corpus callosum?
    a. It enables short-term memory.
    b. It connects the two halves of the brain.
    c. It must be fully myelinated before gross motor skills can be acquired.
    d. All of the above are correct.

19. Eye–hand coordination improves during the play years, in part because:
    a. the brain areas associated with this ability become more fully myelinated.
    b. the corpus callosum begins to function.
    c. fine motor skills have matured by age 2.
    d. gross motor skills have matured by age 2.

20. Adoption is most likely to be successful as an intervention for maltreatment when:
    a. children are young and biological families are inadequate.
    b. efforts at tertiary prevention have already failed.
    c. children have endured years of maltreatment in their biological family.
    d. foster care and kinship care have failed.

NAME _____   INSTRUCTOR _____

LESSON 8: PLAY SPACES AND PLAYGROUNDS

Exercise

A major theme of this lesson is that "play is the work of childhood." According to most developmental psychologists, both work and play are important activities at every stage of life. But the line between play and work is not clear-cut, especially in the play years. Rather than thinking about the two as opposites, many developmentalists argue that it is more profitable to think of them as endpoints along a continuum, from the most whimsical, spontaneous, nonproductive play on the one side, to the most deliberate, planned, productive work on the other.

Developmental psychologists view play as the major means through which physical, cognitive, and social skills are mastered. Unfortunately, many adults are so imbued with the work ethic that they tend to denigrate children's play. Some even punish their children for "horsing around," criticize nursery school teachers for letting children play "too much," or schedule their children's lives so heavily with lessons, homework, and chores that there is little time left for play.

Every age has its own special forms of play. Play that captures the pleasures of using the senses and motor abilities is called **sensorimotor play**. Associated most closely with infants, this type of play actually continues throughout childhood. Much of the physical play of childhood is **mastery play**, which refers to play that helps children to master new skills. This type of play is most obvious when physical skills are involved, but increasingly comes to include intellectual skills as children grow older. A third type of play is the **rough-and-tumble** wrestling, chasing, and hitting that occur purely in fun, with no intent to harm.

Young children need safe, adequate play space and the opportunity to play with children their own age. To increase your awareness of the play and play needs of children in your neighborhood, the exercise for Lesson 8 asks you to locate and observe play spaces within walking distance of your home. If there are none, what alternatives exist for preschoolers in your neighborhood? For example, do they play in backyards? Or are most preschoolers enrolled in nursery schools that have their own play spaces? Once you have answered the following questions, hand the completed exercise in to your instructor.

1. Describe a public or school playground within walking distance of your home. List the play equipment provided that is designed to be used by younger children (especially preschoolers).

2. Describe the population of children who visit the playground. (For example, are the children of different ages, or ethnic or racial backgrounds?)

3. Spend some time, if you can, observing the way in which preschoolers play. What types of play can you identify? Give several examples of each type.

4. If you can, observe the way in which preschoolers attempt to master the larger, more exciting structures on the playground. For example, observe their uses of the jungle gym, slide, or "big" swings. How do parents or caregivers respond to the exploration and risk-taking of their preschoolers? Identify differences in parenting styles you have seen.

LESSON GUIDELINES

Audio Question Guidelines

1. The biological clock is a metaphor for the body's mechanisms for the timing of physical development.

   Hormones are chemical messengers secreted into the bloodstream by glands and have a variety of effects on the body. **Sex hormones**, such as **estrogen** in females and **testosterone** in males, are responsible for triggering development of the reproductive system.

   By the end of the third month of prenatal development, the human fetus has sex organs and is producing sex hormones. At birth, sex hormones are present in a baby's bloodstream at levels equivalent to those at puberty.

   At about 18 months of age, the high levels of sex hormones drop and remain at a very low level until puberty, when there is another surge and reproductive maturity is attained.

2. Anthropologists have suggested that one reason humans have a much longer childhood than other animals (and that the development of their reproductive system is delayed) is to provide an opportunity for children to learn the many complex behaviors that gave our species its great cognitive capacity. This explanation is supported by the fact that our species' survival depends to a much greater extent on learned behavior than does that of any other species.

   Another possible explanation is that an extended childhood allows older children to take care of younger children. In hunting-and-gathering societies throughout the world, the prime job of children is to take care of younger children. In animal societies, by contrast, the mother must care for the young herself and is therefore limited in her capacity to produce more offspring.

3. The **"down-and-out" principle** of development is that maturation begins with the head and brain and works its way down the spine and out to the extremities. In the textbook (page 99), this pattern is referred to as cephalo-caudal (head to tail) and proximo-distal (near to far, or inside out) development.

   The down-and-out principle explains why babies are able to lift their heads before they can sit up, and can sit before they are able to stand. It also explains the normal progression of gross-motor-skill development. For example, younger children throw balls with their entire arms. Older children are able to control a throw more precisely by adding, successively, motion of the wrist, hand, and fingers.

Textbook Question Answers

1. 2; 6; 3 inches (7 centimeters); 4 $1/2$ pounds (2 kilograms); 46 pounds (21 kilograms); 46 inches (117 centimeters)
2. broad
3. genetic background; health care; nutrition
4. nutrition
5. African; Europeans; Asians; Latinos; cultural; boys
6. less; fewer
7. iron deficiency anemia; chronic fatigue; quality meats, whole grains, eggs, and dark green vegetables; more
8. sugar; fat
9. 90; full-grown; 33
10. communication; myelination; control; coordination; emotions; thinking; quicker
11. corpus callosum; dendrite; myelination; both sides of the brain and body
12. accidents
13. sex; socioeconomic status; neighborhood
14. more
15. socioeconomic status (SES); low; infancy and the play years; brain
16. injury control; are
17. more
18. decreased
19. eye movements; focusing; communication; eye–hand
20. is not; spurts; plateaus
21. spoken; written language
22. gross motor; practice; brain maturation; by themselves
23. fine motor; muscular; judgment; myelination
24. drawing; self-correction; intellectual
25. physical; are not
26. maltreatment; abuse; neglect
27. historical; cultural
28. customs; community standards
29. poverty; social isolation

Compared to well-cared-for children, chronically abused and neglected children are slower to talk, underweight, less able to concentrate, and behind in school. They also tend to regard others as hostile and exploitative, and so are less friendly, more aggressive, and more isolated than other children. As adolescents and adults, they often engage in self-destructive and/or other destructive behaviors.

30. intergenerational transmission; is not

31. 30–40

32. have; differential response; removal; supportive

33. foster care

34. permanency planning

35. decreased; increased

36. kinship care; adoption; inadequate; young

37. primary prevention; secondary prevention; home visitation; tertiary prevention

Answers to Testing Yourself

1. **b.** is the answer. Estrogen is the primary female sex hormone; testosterone, the primary male hormone. (audio program)

2. **d.** is the answer. At birth, the level of sex hormones in both sexes is as high as it will be at puberty. In the years in between, however, levels drop precipitously. (audio program)

3. **c.** is the answer. Anthropologists believe that the benefits of both learning and babysitting resulted in the evolution of an extended childhood in humans. (audio program)

4. **c.** is the answer. The muscles that permit sitting develop before those that permit standing, following the head-down principle of development. (audio program)

5. **d.** is the answer. Play is the "work" of childhood. (audio program)

6. **c.** is the answer. (textbook, p. 220)
   a. Serious malnutrition is much more likely to occur in infancy or in adolescence than in early childhood.
   b. Although an important health problem, eating too much candy or other sweets is not as serious as iron deficiency anemia.
   d. Since growth is slower during the preschool years, children need fewer calories per pound during this period.

7. **b.** is the answer. (textbook, p. 227)
   a. & d. The right brain is the location of areas associated with recognition of visual configurations.
   c. The corpus callosum helps integrate the functioning of the two halves of the brain; it does not contain areas specialized for particular skills.

8. **a.** is the answer. (textbook, p. 241)
   b. This is an example of secondary prevention.
   c. & d. These are examples of primary prevention.

9. **d.** is the answer. Accident rates have *decreased* during this time period. (textbook, p. 225)

10. **d.** is the answer. (textbook, p. 220)

11. **c.** is the answer. (textbook, p. 227)

12. **d.** is the answer. (textbook, pp. 222, 226)

13. **a.** is the answer. (textbook, p. 223)

14. **c.** is the answer. (textbook, p. 219)
    b. The proportions are more adultlike in both girls and boys.
    d. Nutrition is a bigger factor in growth at this age than either heredity or health care.

15. **c.** is the answer. (textbook, p. 220)

16. **b.** is the answer. (textbook, p. 220)

17. **b.** is the answer. Children with *lower* SES have *higher* accident rates. (textbook, p. 226)

18. **b.** is the answer. (textbook, p. 223)
    a. The corpus callosum is not directly involved in memory.
    c. Myelination of the central nervous system is important to the mastery of *fine* motor skills.

19. **a.** is the answer. (textbook, p. 226)
    b. The corpus callosum begins to function long before the play years.
    c. & d. Neither fine nor gross motor skills have fully matured by age 2.

20. **a.** is the answer. (textbook, p. 239)
    b. Removing a child from an abusive home is itself a form of tertiary prevention.
    c. Such children tend to fare better in group homes.
    d. Although adoption is the final option, children who have been unable to thrive in foster care or kinship care will probably not thrive in an adoptive home either.

References

Erikson, Erik. (1977). *Toys and reasons: Stages in the ritualization of experience*. New York: Norton.

Smith, Peter K. (1984). *Play in animals and humans*. Oxford: Basil Blackwell.

These two books discuss play as an essential part of the lives of children. Smith's book is a collection of fourteen articles on topics such as imaginary playmates and the costs and benefits of play.

The Play Years: Cognitive Development

AUDIO PROGRAM: Then Sentences

ORIENTATION

Each season of life has its particular perspective on the world. At no age is this more apparent than during the play years. Young children think and speak very differently from older children and adults. In countless everyday instances, as well as in the findings of numerous research studies, preschoolers reveal themselves to be remarkably thoughtful, insightful, and perceptive thinkers whose grasp of the causes of everyday events, memory of the past, and mastery of language is sometimes astounding.

In addition to exploring these cognitive and linguistic changes that occur in children between the ages of 2 and 6, Chapter 9 of the textbook takes a look at preschool education. In the past, most children remained home until about 6, but today most begin their schooling at an earlier age. How are today's children affected by their preschool experiences?

Audio program 9, "Then Sentences," picks up where program 6, "First Words," left off in describing the path children follow in acquiring language. With the expert commentary of psycholinguist Jill de Villiers, the audio program examines how children come to produce their first primitive sentences and then move on to produce more complex, grammatically correct speech.

The journey from cries to words to articulate speech is an intricate one unique to human beings. The similar developmental course of children the world over points to the importance of the biological clock in language development. The grammatical errors, abbreviations, and overextensions of rules in children's speech suggest that humans have a natural propensity to acquire language and that children master its complicated rules by actively experimenting with them, rather than merely by imitating the speech that they hear.

As the program opens, we hear audio snapshots of one child at three different ages. The snapshots reveal the remarkable transition from words to sentences.

LESSON GOALS

By the end of this lesson you should be prepared to:

1. Describe and discuss the major characteristics of preoperational thought, according to Piaget.

2. Discuss Vygotsky's views on cognitive development, focusing on the concept of guided participation.

3. Discuss young children's memory abilities and limitations.

4. Outline the main accomplishments and limitations of language development during the play years.

5. Discuss why the play years are a prime period for learning, and identify the kinds of experiences that best foster cognitive development during early childhood.

Audio Assignment

Listen to the audio tape that accompanies Lesson 9: "Then Sentences."

Write answers to the following questions. You may replay portions of the program if you need to refresh your memory. Answer guidelines may be found in the Lesson Guidelines section at the end of this chapter.

1. Outline the course of language development during the year after the child's production of his or her first word.

2. What evidence is there that the biological clock sets a common timetable for language development?

3. Describe the ways in which young children and adults speak to each other and how this interaction promotes the child's acquisition of the rules of language.

4. Compare and contrast the state of readiness of the auditory system, nervous system, and vocal tract for language acquisition during early childhood.

5. What evidence does the program present that humans have a natural propensity for learning sign language?

Textbook Assignment

Read Chapter 9: "The Play Years: Cognitive Development," pages 245–269 in *The Developing Person Through the Life Span, 5/e,* then work through the material that follows to review it. Complete the sentences and answer the questions. As you proceed, evaluate your performance for each secdtion by consulting the answers on page 113. Do not continue with the next section until you understand each answer. If you need to, review or reread the appropriate section in the textbook before continuing.

In Theory: How Young Children Think (pp. 245–253)

1. For many years, researchers maintained that young children's thinking abilities were sorely limited by their _____ .

2. According to Piaget, the most striking difference between cognition during infancy and the preschool years is _____

   _____ . He referred to cognitive development between the ages of 2 and 6 as _____ thought.

3. Young children's tendency to think about one aspect of a situation at a time is called

   _____ . One particular form of this characteristic is children's tendency to contemplate the world exclusively from their personal perspective, which is referred to as

   _____ . They also tend to focus on _____ to the exclusion of other attributes of objects and people.

4. Preschoolers' understanding of the world tends to be _____ (static/dynamic), which means that they tend to think of their world as

   _____ . A closely related characteristic is _____

   —the inability to recognize that reversing a process will restore the original conditions from which the process began.

5. The idea that amount is unaffected by changes in shape or configuration is called

   _____ . In the case of

   _____ _____

   _____ , preschoolers who are shown pairs of checkers in two even rows and who then observe one row being spaced out will say that the spaced-out row has more checkers.

6. The idea that children are "apprentices in thinking" emphasizes that children's intellectual growth is stimulated by their _____ _____ in _____ experiences of their environment. The critical element in this process is that the mentor and the child _____ to accomplish a task.

7. Much of the research from the sociocultural perspective on the young child's emerging cognition is inspired by the Russian psychologist _____ .

8. Unlike Piaget, this psychologist believed that cognitive growth is a _____ _____ more than a matter of individual discovery.

9. Vygotsky suggested that for each developing individual there is a _____ _____ _____ , a range of skills that the person can exercise with assistance but is not yet able to perform independently.

10. How and when new skills are developed depends, in part, on the willingness of tutors to _____ the child's participation in learning encounters.

11. Vygotsky believed that language is essential to the advancement of thinking in two crucial ways. The first is through the internal dialogue in which a person talks to himself or herself, called _____ _____ . In preschoolers, this dialogue is likely to be _____ (expressed silently/uttered aloud).

12. According to Vygotsky, another way language advances thinking is as the _____ of social interaction.

13. (Research Report) Piaget believed that it is _____ (possible/impossible) for preoperational children to grasp logical reasoning processes. It is now clear that with special training, preschoolers can succeed at some tests of _____ .

14. (Research Report) Vygotsky would have placed the blame for preschoolers' difficulty mastering conservation squarely in the child's _____ context. According to his view, the presence of a _____ adult, who uses an _____ game to measure this ability, can elicit such thinking years before age 6. However, a responsive adult _____ (is/is not) always available, and children _____ (are/are not) always interested in learning what adults want to teach.

In Fact: What Children Think (pp. 253–259)

15. Preschoolers are notorious for having a poor _____ . This shortcoming is due to the fact that they have not yet acquired skills for deliberate _____ and efficient _____ of information.

16. One way in which preschoolers are quite capable of storing in mind a representation of past events is by retaining _____ of familiar, recurrent past experiences. These devices reflect an awareness of the correct _____ and causal _____ of remembered events.

17. A study compared preschoolers' memory of Disney World in response to a series of focused questions. The results showed that age _____ (did/did not) significantly affect the amount of information the children remembered when they were asked specific questions.

18. The "Disney World" study strongly suggests that even very young preschoolers can recall a great deal of information when they are given appropriate cues, such as _____ and when the material is _____ to them.

19. (Changing Policy) Until quite recently, young children in most countries _____ (were/were not) prohibited from providing courtroom testimony.

20. (Changing Policy) Research has found that, particularly for young children, the _____ context in which children considered to be eyewitnesses are questioned is an important factor in the accuracy of their memory. Specifically, the _____ of the child to the questioner, the _____ of the questioner, and the _____ of the interview have a substantial influence on the child's testimony.

21. (Changing Policy) Research demonstrates that the great majority of children when questioned as eyewitnesses _____ (resist/fail to resist) suggestive questioning.

22. As a result of their experiences with others, young children acquire a _____

    _____ _____

    that reflects their developing concepts about human mental processes.

Describe the young child's theory of mind by age 3 or 4.

23. Most 3-year-olds _____ (have/do not have) difficulty realizing that a belief can be false.

24. Research studies reveal that theory-of-mind development depends as much on general _____ ability as it does on

    _____ _____ . A third helpful factor is having at least one

    _____ .

    Finally, _____ may be a factor.

Language (pp. 259–264)

25. During the preschool years, a dramatic increase in language occurs, with _____ increasing exponentially.

26. Through the process called _____

    _____ preschoolers often learn words after only one or two hearings.

27. Abstract nouns, metaphors, and analogies are _____ (more/no more) difficult for preschoolers to understand.

28. Because preschool children tend to think in absolute terms, they have difficulty with words that express _____ , as well as words expressing relativities of _____ and _____ .

29. The structures, techniques, and rules that a language uses to communicate meaning define its _____ . By age _____ , children typically demonstrate extensive understanding of this aspect of language.

30. Children's understanding of grammar is also facilitated by _____ and by _____ .

31. Most North American children have trouble with the _____ voice. Rather than brain maturation, as researchers once believed, it is _____ that is responsible for this limitation.

32. Preschoolers' tendency to apply rules of grammar when they should not is called

    _____ .

Give several examples of this tendency.

33. During the preschool years, children are able to comprehend _____ (more/less) complex grammar and vocabulary than they can produce.

Preschool Education (pp. 264–268)

List several characteristics of a high-quality preschool program.

34. Japanese culture places great emphasis on

_____ _____ and

_____ . Reflecting this emphasis, Japanese preschools provide training in the behavior and attitudes appropriate for

_____ _____ . In contrast, preschools in the United States are often designed to foster _____

and _____ .

35. In 1965, _____ _____

_____ was inaugurated to give low-income children some form of compensatory education during the preschool years. Longitudinal research found that, as they made their way through elementary school, graduates of this program scored _____ (higher/no higher) on achievement tests and had more positive school report cards than their non–Headstart counterparts.

Testing Yourself

After you have completed the audio and text review questions, see how well you do on the following quiz. Correct answers, with text and audio references, may be found at the end of this chapter.

1. Concerning the acquisition of language during early childhood, which of the following is true?
   a. The first true sentences do not occur until about age 3.
   b. Children's two-word sentences show a lack of knowledge of grammatical rules.
   c. Grammatical rules are evident even in the first two-word sentences of children.
   d. In acquiring language, children merely imitate the speech they hear.

2. Young children's abbreviated "telegrams" show that:
   a. they do not yet possess a knowledge of grammar.
   b. they are actively experimenting with the rules of grammar.
   c. they are imitating the sloppy grammar of the adults they listen to.
   d. adults tend to rush the acquisition of language before children are truly ready.

3. In terms of a child's readiness for hearing and producing sentences, which is the correct order in which the three structures indicated mature?
   a. auditory system; nervous system; vocal tract
   b. nervous system; auditory system; vocal tract
   c. vocal tract; auditory system; nervous system
   d. auditory system; vocal tract; nervous system

4. Children usually produce their first two-word sentences at about age:
   a. 1 year.
   b. 1 1/2 or 2.
   c. 2 1/2 or 3.
   d. 3 1/2 or 4.

5. Concerning the acquisition of the rules of language, which of the following is true?
   a. Rule-learning is quicker with sign language than with spoken language.
   b. Children learn the rules of language without being explicitly taught.
   c. Two-word sentences appear at the same time in all the world's cultures.
   d. All of the above are true.

6. Piaget believed that children are in the preoperational stage from ages:
   a. 6 months to 1 year.
   b. 1 to 3 years.
   c. 2 to 6 years.
   d. 5 to 11 years.

7. Compared with children in other developed countries, _____ children in the United States attend preschool.
   a. fewer
   b. about the same number of
   c. a slightly higher percentage of
   d. a significantly higher percentage of

8. (Changing Policy) When questioned as eyewitnesses to an event, most young children:
   a. are unable to resist suggestive questioning.
   b. are able to resist suggestive questioning.
   c. provide very inaccurate answers.
   d. have reliable short-term memories, but very unreliable long-term memories.

9. The typical script of a 4-year-old:
   a. has a beginning and an end.
   b. fails to recognize the causal flow of events.
   c. pertains only to the most familiar routines.
   d. is very difficult to follow for most adults.

10. Preschoolers' poor performance on memory tests is primarily due to:
    a. their tendency to rely too extensively on scripts.
    b. their lack of efficient storage and retrieval skills.
    c. the incomplete myelination of cortical neurons.
    d. their short attention span.

11. The vocabulary of preschool children consists primarily of:
    a. metaphors.
    b. self-created words.
    c. abstract nouns.
    d. verbs and concrete nouns.

12. Preschoolers sometimes apply the rules of grammar even when they shouldn't. This tendency is called:
    a. overregularization.   c. practical usage.
    b. literal language.   d. single-mindedness.

13. The Russian psychologist Vygotsky emphasized that:
    a. language helps children form ideas.
    b. children form concepts first, then find words to express them.
    c. language and other cognitive developments are unrelated at this stage.
    d. preschoolers learn language only for egocentric purposes.

14. Private speech can be described as:
    a. a way of formulating ideas to oneself.
    b. fantasy.
    c. an early learning difficulty.
    d. the beginnings of deception.

15. The child who has not yet grasped the principle of conservation is likely to:
    a. insist that a tall, narrow glass contains more liquid than a short, wide glass, even though both glasses actually contain the same amount.
    b. be incapable of egocentric thought.
    c. be unable to reverse an event.
    d. do all of the above.

16. In later life, Head Start graduates showed:
    a. better report cards, but more behavioral problems.
    b. significantly higher IQ scores.
    c. higher scores on achievement tests.
    d. alienation from their original neighborhoods and families.

17. The best preschool programs are generally those that provide the greatest amount of:
    a. behavioral control.
    b. adult-child conversation.
    c. instruction in conservation and other logical principles.
    d. demonstration of toys by professionals.

18. Compared with their rate of speech development, children's understanding of language develops:
    a. more slowly.
    b. at about the same pace.
    c. more rapidly.
    d. more rapidly in some cultures than in others.

19. (Research Report) Relatively recent experiments have demonstrated that preschoolers *can* succeed at tests of conservation when:
    a. they are allowed to work cooperatively with other children.
    b. the test is presented as a competition.
    c. the children are informed that they are being observed by their parents.
    d. the test is presented in a simple, gamelike way.

20. Through the process called fast mapping, children:
    a. immediately assimilate new words by connecting them through their assumed meaning to categories of words they have already mastered.
    b. acquire the concept of conservation at an earlier age than Piaget believed.
    c. are able to move beyond egocentric thinking.
    d. become skilled in the practical use of language.

LESSON GUIDELINES

Audio Question Guidelines

1. The first word is usually said around the time of the first birthday, the first two-word sentence between 1 1/2 and 2 years.

   Two-word utterances are not always sentences, however. The words must appear in isolation, and then in combination with one another to produce different meanings in order to qualify as true sentences.

   Early sentences are in effect "telegrams," in that they omit articles, conjunctions, prepositions, and other parts of speech that are not essential to meaning.

   During the next year the child actively experiments with the grammatical rules of language. Vocabulary increases rapidly and the two-word sentences soon become three- and four-word sentences.

   The slow-to-develop vocal tract of humans results in the same accommodations to language in children throughout the world. These include reducing consonant clusters to a single consonant and a preference for certain kinds of pronunciations.

2. The fact that deaf and hearing children babble at about the same age suggests a maturational basis for language development.

   The evidence for a common biological timetable in the maturation of language also includes the fact that the stage of two-word sentences comes at about the same age in every culture.

   The slow maturation of the human vocal tract results in the same accommodations in language pronunciation in children of similar age throughout the world.

3. The two- and three-word "telegrams" of children during these years are abbreviations of adult speech in which articles, conjunctions, prepositions, and other unessential words are dropped.

   At the same time that children abbreviate their speech, adults often restate their ideas and expand them into complete, grammatically correct utterances. This process implicitly calls the child's attention to the rules of language and indicates that children are experimenting with language, rather than merely imitating it.

   Another illustration of the creative and experimental process of language learning comes from the **overextensions** of grammatical rules that are typical of children during this stage.

4. The auditory system is mature and ready for hearing at birth.

   Between 1 1/2 and 2 years of age the brain and nervous system reach a point of maturation that permits the combination of words into primitive sentences.

   The vocal tract lags behind the auditory system and nervous system in maturing. Until it matures, children are unable to articulate complex sounds.

5. The evidence that humans have a natural propensity for acquiring sign language includes the fact that although deaf and hearing children babble at about the same age, deaf children produce their first signs sooner than hearing children produce their first words. This developmental advantage is maintained when it comes to forming two-word or two-sign combinations.

Textbook Question Answers

1. self-absorption
2. symbolic thinking; preoperational
3. centration; egocentrism; appearances
4. static; unchanging; irreversibility
5. conservation; conservation of number
6. guided participation; social; interact
7. Lev Vygotsky
8. social activity
9. zone of proximal development
10. scaffold
11. private speech; uttered aloud
12. mediator
13. impossible; conservation
14. social; responsive; interactive; is not; are not
15. memory; storage; retrieval
16. scripts; sequence; flow
17. did not
18. photographs of their experiences; meaningful
19. were
20. social; relationship; age; atmosphere
21. resist
22. theory of mind

By age 3 or 4, young children distinguish between mental phenomena and the physical events to which they refer; they appreciate how mental states arise from experiences in the world; they understand that

---

mental phenomena are subjective; they recognize that people have differing opinions and preferences; they realize that beliefs and desires can form the basis for human action; and they realize that emotion arises not only from physical events but also from goals and expectations.

23. have

24. language; brain maturation; brother or sister; culture

25. vocabulary

26. fast mapping

27. more

28. comparisons; time; place

29. grammar; 3

30. hearing conversations at home that model good grammar; receiving helpful feedback about their language use

31. passive; context

32. overregularization

Many preschoolers overapply the rule of adding "s" to form the plural, as well as the rule of adding "ed" to form the past tense. Thus, preschoolers are likely to say "foots" and "snows," and that someone "broked" a toy.

33. more

High-quality preschools are characterized by (a) a low teacher-child ratio, (b) a staff with training and credentials in early-childhood education, (c) a curriculum geared toward cognitive development, and (d) an organization of space that facilitates creative and constructive play.

34. social consensus; conformity; group activity; self-confidence; self-reliance

35. Project Head Start; higher

Answers to Testing Yourself

1. **c.** is the answer. Even the two- and three-word "telegrams" of preschoolers show evidence of a rudimentary understanding of grammar. (audio program; textbook, pp. 262–263)

2. **b.** is the answer. Children master the rules of grammar by experimenting and testing hypotheses, often overextending rules and making errors that cannot be attributed to imitation. (audio program; textbook, pp. 262–263)

3. **a.** is the answer. The slow-to-mature vocal tract forces accommodations in pronunciation that are similar the world over. (audio program)

4. **b.** is the answer. Although there is wide variation in normal development, the first primitive sentences usually occur between 1 1/2 and 2 years of age. (audio program)

5. **d.** is the answer. All of these statements are true, indicating a common timetable in the maturation of language and the natural propensity of children for acquiring language, including sign language. (audio program)

6. **c.** is the answer. (textbook, p. 247)

7. **a.** is the answer. Unlike the U.S. government, the governments of many other developed countries sponsor preschool education. (textbook, p. 264)

8. **b.** is the answer. (textbook, p. 254)

   c. & d. Research demonstrates that even young children often have very accurate long-term recall.

9. **a.** is the answer. (textbook, p. 256)

   b. & d. Because preschoolers' scripts *do* recognize the causal flow of events, they are not hard to follow.

   c. Preschoolers use scripts not only when recounting familiar routines but also in pretend play.

10. **b.** is the answer. (textbook, p. 254)

    a. Scripts tend to *improve* preschoolers' memory.

    c. & d. Although true, neither of these is the *primary* reason for preschoolers' poor memory.

11. **d.** is the answer. (textbook, p. 262)

    a. & c. Preschoolers generally have great difficulty understanding, and therefore using, metaphors and abstract nouns.

    b. Other than the grammatical errors of overregularization, the text does not indicate that preschoolers use a significant number of self-created words.

12. **a.** is the answer. (textbook, p. 263)

    b. & d. These terms are not identified in the text and do not apply to the use of grammar.

    c. Practical usage, which also is not discussed in the text, refers to communication between one person and another in terms of the overall context in which language is used.

13. **a.** is the answer. (textbook, p. 252)

    b. This expresses the views of Piaget.

    c. Because he believed that language facilitates thinking, Vygotsky obviously felt that language and other cognitive developments are intimately related.

    d. Vygotsky did not hold this view.

14. **a.** is the answer. (textbook, p. 252)

15. a. is the answer. (textbook, pp. 247–248)

b., c., & d. Failure to conserve is the result of thinking that is centered on appearances. Egocentrism and irreversibility are also examples of centered thinking.

16. c. is the answer. (textbook, p. 267)

b. This is not discussed in the text. However, although there was a slight early IQ advantage in Head Start graduates, the difference disappeared by grade 3.

a. & d. There was no indication of greater behavioral problems or alienation in Head Start graduates.

17. b. is the answer. (textbook, p. 264)

18. c. is the answer. (textbook, p. 264)

19. d. is the answer. (textbook, p. 250)

20. a. is the answer. (textbook, pp. 259–260)

Reference

de Villiers, P. A. & de Villiers, J. G. (1992). Language development. In M. H. Bornstein & M. E. Lamb (Eds.) *Developmental psychology: An advanced textbook* (3rd ed.). Hillside, NJ: Erlbaum.

Professor de Villiers, who is heard on the audio program, discusses the process by which children master the grammatical rules of language.

The Play Years: Psychosocial Development

AUDIO PROGRAM: Because I Wear Dresses

ORIENTATION

As we learned in Lessons 8 and 9, the biosocial and cognitive development that occurs between the ages of 2 and 6 is extensive. Body proportions begin to resemble those of adults; language develops rapidly; and the capacity to use mental representation and symbols increases dramatically. Lesson 10 concludes the unit on the play years by exploring ways in which preschool children relate to others in their ever-widening social environment.

During the preschool years a child's self-confidence, social skills, and social roles become more fully developed. This growth coincides with the child's increased capacity for communication, imagination, and understanding of his or her social context. Chapter 10 of *The Developing Person Through the Life Span, 5/e,* explores the ways in which young children begin to relate to others in an ever-widening social environment. The chapter begins where social understanding begins, with the emergence of the sense of self. The next sections explore the origins of helpful, prosocial behaviors, as well as antisocial behaivors. The chapter concludes with a description of children's emerging gender identity.

Audio program 10, "Because I Wear Dresses," focuses on how children develop gender identity as boys or girls. Through the expert commentary of psychologists Michael Stevenson and Jacquelynne Eccles, we discover that by the time children begin elementary school they have developed a strong sense of their gender. During these years children segregate themselves according to sex and become quite stereotyped in their thinking and behavior regarding gender.

Are the psychological differences between males and females a result of our biology or are they something we learn? One way of looking at this question is to examine how gender differences change across the life span. According to psychologist David Gutmann, masculinity and femininity mean different things at different ages. Although gender differences in such characteristics as aggressiveness may have a biological basis, the difference may not be the same for the entire life cycle. Researchers are finding that men and women become more alike in their actions and attitudes as they get older.

Social guidelines for males and females may be blurred in old age, but if you ask children about gender differences, you are likely to hear the kind of answers that open this program.

LESSON GOALS

By the end of this lesson you should be prepared to:

1. Discuss the relationship between the child's developing sense of self and social awareness.

2. Discuss emotional development during early childhood, focusing on emotional regulation, and how it relates to attachment.

3. Differentiate four types of aggression during the play years and explain why certain types are more troubling to developentalists.

4. Describe the transformation of gender identity and gender-typed behavior over the life span.

5. Discuss how various modes of family interaction affect children's development.

Audio Assignment

Listen to the audio tape that accompanies Lesson 10: "Because I Wear Dresses."

Write answers to the following questions. You may replay portions of the program if you need to refresh your memory. Answer guidelines may be found in the Lesson Guidelines section at the end of this chapter.

1. Describe the development of gender identity in preschoolers.

2. Explain some of the gender differences that are usually apparent in the first ten years of life.

3. Explain how gender differences in aggression change over the life span.

Textbook Assignment

Read Chapter 10: "The Play Years: Psychosocial Development," pages 271–296 in *The Developing Person Through the Life Span, 5/e*, then work through the material that follows to review it. Complete the sentences and answer the questions. As you proceed, evaluate your performance for each secdtion by consulting the answers on page 129. Do not continue with the next section until you understand each answer. If you need to, review or reread the appropriate section in the textbook before continuing.

The Self and the Social World (pp. 271–277)

1. Between 3 and 6 years of age, according to Erikson, children are in the stage of

_____ _____

_____ .

2. The play years are filled with examples of the child's emerging _____ .

3. The growth of preschoolers' self-awareness is especially apparent in their _____ with others.

4. As their theory of mind expands, preschoolers become less _____ and more

_____ .

5. Psychologists emphasize the importance of children's developing a positive _____ .

Preschoolers typically form impressions of themselves that are quite _____ . One manifestation of this tendency is that preschoolers regularly _____ (overestimate/underestimate) their own abilities. Most preschoolers think of themselves as competent _____ (in all/only in certain) areas.

6. As they grow, preschoolers become _____ (more/less) concerned with how others evaluate their behavior.

7. (Changing Policy) Worldwide, the number of only children is _____ (increasing/decreasing). The largest average family size occurs _____ (in which country?). In most ways, only children fare _____ (as well as or better/ worse) than children with siblings. Only children are particularly likely to benefit _____ , becoming more _____ and more _____ . A potential problem for only children is in their development of _____ skills.

8. The most significant emotional development during early childhood is _____ _____ , which is the growing ability to direct or modify one's feelings in response to expectations from _____ . This ability develops partly as the result of _____ maturation and partly as a result of _____ .

9. The development of fears during the play years is _____ (common/rare). Some preschoolers develop strong irrational fears called _____ ; this is particularly likely if the child's _____ share these fears. During these years, the child's enhanced _____ contributes to an increase in _____ .

10. How children regulate their emotions reflects the results of past _____ . For example, children who respond unsympathetically to another child's distress may have

_____ _____ .

11. Another example of emotional regulation is appropriate expression of _____ . According to _____ , the ability to direct emotions is crucial to the development of _____ _____ .

Antisocial and Prosocial Behavior (pp. 277–287)

12. Sharing, cooperating, and sympathizing are examples of _____ . _____ These attitudes correlate with _____ _____ . As the capacity for self-control increases between 2 and 5 years, there is a decrease in _____ _____ _____ . Conversely, actions that are destructive or deliberately hurtful are called _____ _____ . Such actions are often predicted by a lack of _____ _____ .

13. The roots of aggression are a negative _____ and inadequate _____ _____ during the early preschool years.

14. Developmentalists distinguish three types of physical aggression: _____ , used to obtain or retain a toy or other object; _____ , used in angry retaliation against an intentional or accidental act committed by a peer; and _____ , used in an unprovoked attack on a peer.

15. The form of aggression that is most likely to increase from age 2 to 6 is _____ _____ . Of greater concern are _____ _____ , because it can indicate a lack of _____ _____ , and _____ _____ , which is most worrisome overall.

16. Social aggression that involves insults or social rejection is called _____ _____ .

Victims of this type of aggression are more commonly preschoolers who are _____ .

17. The type of physical play that mimics aggression is called _____ - _____ - _____ play. A distinctive feature of this form of play, which _____ (occurs only in some cultures/is universal), is the positive facial expression that characterizes the _____ _____ . Age differences are evident, because this type of play relies on the child's _____ _____ . Gender differences _____ (are/are not) evident in rough-and-tumble play.

18. In _____ play, children act out various roles and themes in stories of their own creation. The increase in this form of play is related to the development of the child's _____ _____ _____ and emotional regulation, as well as the development of _____ . _____ (Girls/Boys) tend to engage in this type of play more often than do _____ (girls/boys).

19. (A Life-Span View) A typical preschool child In the United States watches more than _____ hours of television per day. This amount _____ (is/is not) greater than any other age group.

(A Life-Span View) State several negative effects of television from a developmental perspective.

20. (A Life-Span View) Another criticism of television is that it encourages _____ _____ in young children, in part by _____ them to violence in real life. Children who watch large amounts of video violence are more likely than

others to be _____

_____ .

21. A significant influence on early psychosocial growth is the style of _____ that characterizes a child's family life.

22. The seminal research on parenting styles, which was conducted by _____ , found that parents varied in their _____ toward offspring, in their strategies for _____ , in how well they _____ , and in their expectations for _____ .

23. Parents who adopt the _____ style demand unquestioning obedience from their children. In this style of parenting, nurturance tends to be _____ (low/ high), maturity demands are _____ (low/high), and parent–child communication tends to be _____ (low/high).

24. Parents who adopt the _____ style make few demands on their children and are lax in discipline. Such parents _____ (are/are not very) nurturant, communicate _____ (well/poorly), and make _____ (few/extensive) maturity demands.

25. Parents who adopt the _____ style democratically set limits and enforce rules. Such parents make _____ (high/low) maturity demands, communicate _____ (well/poorly), and _____ (are/are not) nurturant.

26. Follow-up studies indicate that children raised by _____ parents are likely to be obedient but unhappy; those raised by _____ parents are likely to lack self-control; and those raised by _____ parents are more likely to be successful, happy with themselves, and generous with others. These advantages _____ (grow stronger/ weaken) over time.

27. An important factor in the effectiveness of parenting style is the child's _____ .

28. To be effective, punishment should be more _____ than _____ .

29. (Research Report) A 1994 study investigated the relationship between spanking and aggressive behavior in the child. Observers scored kindergartners for instances of aggressive behavior. Compared with children who were not spanked, those children who were spanked were more likely to engage in _____ aggression.

30. Japanese mothers tend to use _____ as disciplinary techniques more often than do North American mothers, who are more likely to encourage _____ expressions of all sorts in their children. Throughout the world, most parents _____ (believe/do not believe) that spanking is acceptable at times. Although spanking _____ (is/is not) effective, it may teach children to be more _____ .

Boy or Girl: So What? (pp. 287–295)

31. Social scientists distinguish between biological, or _____ differences between males and females, and cultural, or _____ differences in the _____ and behaviors of the two sexes.

32. True sex differences are _____ (more/less) apparent in childhood than in adulthood; _____ differentiation seems more significant to children than to adults.

33. By age _____ , children can consistently apply gender labels and have a rudimentary understanding of the permanence of their own gender. By age _____ , most children express stereotypic ideas of each sex. Such stereotyping _____ (does/does not) occur in children whose parents provide nontraditional gender role models. Awareness that sex is a fixed biological characteristic does not become solid until about age _____ .

34. Freud called the period from age 3 to 7 the _____ _____ . According to his view, boys in this stage develop sexual feelings about their _____

and become jealous of their _____ . Freud called this phenomenon the

_____ _____ .

35. In Freud's theory, preschool boys resolve their guilty feelings defensively through _____ with their father. Boys also develop, again in self-defense, a powerful conscience called the _____ .

36. According to Freud, during the phallic stage little girls may experience the _____ _____ , in which they want to get rid of their mother and become intimate with their father. Alternatively, they may become jealous of boys because they have a penis; this emotion Freud called _____

_____ .

37. According to learning theory, preschool children develop gender-role ideas by being _____ for behaviors deemed appropriate for their sex and _____ for behaviors deemed inappropriate.

38. Social learning theorists maintain that children learn gender-appropriate behavior by

_____ .

39. Cognitive theorists focus on children's _____ of male-female differences. When their experience is ambiguous, preschoolers search for the simple _____ they have formed regarding gender roles.

40. According to the _____ theory, gender education varies by region, socioeconomic status, and historical period. Gender distinctions are emphasized in many _____ cultures. This theory points out that children can maintain a balance of male and female characteristics, or _____ , only if their culture promotes that idea.

41. According to _____

_____ theory, gender attitudes and roles are the result of interaction between

_____ and _____

_____ .

42. One idea that has recently found greater acceptance is the idea that some gender differences are _____ rather than _____ based.

43. In some respects, the two sexes are different because there are subtle differences in _____ development. Describe several of these differences.

44. These differences probably _____ (are/are not) the result of any single gene. More likely, they result from the differing

_____ _____

that influence brain development.

Testing Yourself

After you have completed the audio and text review questions, see how well you do on the following quiz. Correct answers, with text and audio references, may be found at the end of this chapter.

1. Most children are able to use gender labels accurately by age:
   a. 1.
   b. 3.
   c. 5.
   d. 7.

2. Concerning gender roles during later life, David Gutmann believes that:
   a. gender roles are the same as those in earlier life.
   b. during middle and late adulthood, each sex moves toward a middle ground between the traditional gender roles.
   c. once the demands of parenting are removed, traditional gender roles are reestablished.
   d. gender roles are unrelated to cultural experiences.

3. The greater aggressiveness of boys compared to girls is:
   a. due to boys having a higher natural level of testosterone.
   b. found in virtually all known cultures.
   c. maintained throughout the life cycle.
   d. such that a. and b. are true.

4. Concerning children's concept of gender, which of the following statements is true?
   a. Until the age of 5 or so, children think that boys and girls can change gender as they get older.
   b. Children as young as 18 months have a clear understanding of the anatomical differences between girls and boys.
   c. Children are inaccurate in labeling others' gender until about age 5.
   d. All of the above are true.

5. Which of the following most accurately summarizes the audio program's explanation of the psychological differences between males and females?
   a. Most differences are biologically determined.
   b. Most differences are learned.
   c. Most differences are jointly determined by learning and biology.
   d. None of the above is true.

6. Preschool children have a clear (but not necessarily accurate) concept of self. Typically, the preschooler believes that she or he:
   a. owns all objects in sight.
   b. is great at almost everything.
   c. is much less competent than peers and older children.
   d. is more powerful than her or his parents.

7. According to Freud, the third stage of psychosexual development, during which the penis is the focus of psychological concern and pleasure, is the:
   a. oral stage.
   b. anal stage.
   c. phallic stage.
   d. latency period.

8. Because it helps children rehearse social roles, work out fears and fantasies, and learn cooperation, an important form of social play is:
   a. sociodramatic play.
   b. mastery play.
   c. rough-and-tumble play.
   d. sensorimotor play.

9. The three *basic* patterns of parenting described by Diana Baumrind are:
   a. hostile, loving, and harsh.
   b. authoritarian, permissive, and authoritative.
   c. positive, negative, and punishing.
   d. indulgent, neglecting, and traditional.

10. Authoritative parents are receptive and loving, but they also normally:
    a. set limits and enforce rules.
    b. have difficulty communicating.
    c. withhold praise and affection.
    d. encourage aggressive behavior.

11. Children who watch a lot of violent television:
    a. are more likely to be aggressive.
    b. become desensitized to violence.
    c. are less likely to attempt to mediate a quarrel between other children.
    d. have all of the above characteristics.

12. Between 2 and 6 years of age, the form of aggression that is most likely to increase is:
    a. reactive
    b. instrumental
    c. relational
    d. bullying

13. During the play years, a child's self-concept is defined largely by his or her:
    a. expanding range of skills and competencies.
    b. physical appearance.
    c. gender.
    d. relationship with family members.

14. Learning theorists emphasize the importance of _____ in the development of the preschool child.
    a. identification
    b. praise and blame
    c. initiative
    d. a theory of mind

15. Children apply gender labels and have definite ideas about how boys and girls behave as early as age:
    a. 3.
    b. 4.
    c. 5.
    d. 7.

16. Psychologist Daniel Goleman believes that emotional regulation is especially crucial to the preschooler's developing:
    a. sense of self.
    b. social awareness.
    c. emotional intelligence.
    d. sense of gender.

17. Six-year-old Leonardo has superior verbal ability rivaling that of most girls his age. Dr. Laurent believes this is due to the fact that although his sex is predisposed to slower language development, Leonardo's upbringing in a linguistically rich home enhanced his biological capabilities. Dr. Laurent is evidently a proponent of:
    a. cognitive theory.
    b. gender-schema theory.
    c. sociocultural theory.
    d. epigenetic systems theory.

18. (Changing Policy) Compared with children with siblings, only children are likely to:
    a. be less verbal.
    b. fare as well or better in most ways.
    c. have greater competence in social skills.
    d. be less creative.

19. Compared to Japanese mothers, North American mothers are more likely to:
    a. use reasoning to control their preschoolers' social behavior.
    b. use expressions of disappointment to control their preschoolers' social behavior.
    c. encourage emotional expressions of all sorts in their preschoolers.
    d. do all of the above.

20. When her friend hurts her feelings, Maya shouts that she is a "mean old stinker!" Maya's behavior is an example of:
    a. instrumental aggression.
    b. reactive aggression.
    c. bullying aggression.
    d. relational aggression.

LESSON 10 EXERCISE: GENDER-ROLE DEVELOPMENT

During the play years, children acquire not only their gender identities but also many masculine or feminine behaviors and attitudes. These behaviors and attitudes largely reflect gender roles. A role is a set of social expectations that prescribes how those who occupy the role should act.

To what extent is your own gender identity a reflection of the behaviors modeled by your parents? Have gender roles become less distinct in recent generations? Should parents encourage gender-stereotyped behaviors in their children? These are among the many controversial questions regarding gender roles that researchers today are grappling with.

The exercise for this lesson asks you to reflect on the kinds of gender models your parents provided and to ask a friend or relative who is presently in a different season of life to do the same. After you and your respondent have completed the Gender Role Quizzes on the next two pages, answer the questions that follow and hand the completed exercise (only) in to your instructor.

Gender Role Quiz: Respondent #1

For each question, check whether the behavior described was more typical of your mother or father as you were growing up.

	Mother	Father
1. When your family went out, who drove?		
2. Who filled out the income tax forms?		
3. Who wrote the "thank you" notes for gifts?		
4. Who was more likely to ask, "Where are my socks/stockings?"		
5. When the car needed to be repaired, who took it to the garage?		
6. Who did the laundry?		
7. Who dusted and vacuumed your house?		
8. When you had a fever, who knew where to find the thermometer?		
9. When the sink needed fixing, who knew where to find the pipe wrench?		
10. Who knew where the summer clothes were packed away?		
11. When you had guests for dinner, who made the drinks?		
12. Who watered the house plants?		
13. Who mowed the lawn?		
14. When you went on a trip, who packed the car?		

Source: Adapted from Doyle, J. A., & Paludi, M. A. (1995). *Sex and gender: The human experience* (3rd ed.). © 1995 WCB/McGraw-Hill. Used with permission of the McGraw-Hill Companies.

Gender Role Quiz: Respondent #2

For each question, check whether the behavior described was more typical of your mother or father as you were growing up.

	Mother	Father
1. When your family went out, who drove?		
2. Who filled out the income tax forms?		
3. Who wrote the "thank you" notes for gifts?		
4. Who was more likely to ask, "Where are my socks/stockings?"		
5. When the car needed to be repaired, who took it to the garage?		
6. Who did the laundry?		
7. Who dusted and vacuumed your house?		
8. When you had a fever, who knew where to find the thermometer?		
9. When the sink needed fixing, who knew where to find the pipe wrench?		
10. Who knew where the summer clothes were packed away?		
11. When you had guests for dinner, who made the drinks?		
12. Who watered the house plants?		
13. Who mowed the lawn?		
14. When you went on a trip, who packed the car?		

Sources: Adapted from Doyle, J. A., & Paludi, M. A. (1995). *Sex and gender: The human experience* (3rd ed.). © 1995 WCB/McGraw-Hill. Used with permission of the McGraw-Hill Companies.

NAME _____   INSTRUCTOR _____

LESSON 10: GENDER-ROLE DEVELOPMENT

Exercise

1. In what seasons of life were your quiz respondents?

2. **a.** Is there evidence of gender-stereotyped behaviors in the respondents' answers? Explain.

   b. Were items 1, 2, 4, 5, 9, 11, 13 and 15 checked as more typical of fathers?

   c. Were items 3, 6, 7, 8, 10, 12, and 14 checked as more typical of mothers?

   d. For each respondent, indicate the total number of responses (out of 15) that are *in agreement* with the traditional gender-role breakdown in this list.

	Younger Respondent	Older Respondent
Number of items in agreement with traditional gender roles (maximum = 15)		

   e. If there is a difference in responses given by your younger and older respondents, please explain the difference.

3. To what extent do you believe your own gender identity and gender-role development were influenced by the behaviors modeled by your parents? In what ways is your own behavior modeled after that of your same-sex parent? In what ways is it different?

4. To what extent is your concept of the ideal person of the opposite sex a reflection of the behaviors modeled by your opposite-sex parent? In what ways is it different?

5. In your estimation, should parents encourage or discourage traditional gender-role development in their children? Please explain your reasoning.

LESSON GUIDELINES

Audio Question Guidelines

1. It is likely that children begin to recognize the categories of male and female as early as 18 months of age.

   Most 2-year-olds know whether they are boys or girls, but they have not yet mastered **gender constancy**. They may think that their sex can change when they grow older or wear different clothes.

   Before the age of 5, most children do not understand the anatomical differences between boys and girls. Instead, they are likely to identify the sexes on the basis of hair length, clothing, or whether a person cooks or goes to work.

   By the time children start school they have developed a very strong sense of their own **gender identity**, and they know that it will remain constant.

2. Although both biology and environment contribute to differences between the sexes, these differences are slight. There is more variation between individuals *of the same sex* than there is between the sexes.

   As infants, boys are more likely than girls to have been born prematurely, to suffer from birth trauma, to show delayed development, and to be subject to colic and nonrhythmic behaviors that make them somewhat harder to deal with.

   Male infants tend to be less easily cuddled, more resistant to being wrapped up, and more active.

   Perhaps as a consequence of their exposure to higher prenatal levels of testosterone, boys are more likely than girls to get into aggressive encounters.

   From very early on, girls may be more sensitive than boys to faces and to language cues.

   Boys and girls may also develop different play styles as they go through childhood, with a greater emphasis on competition in boys' games and a greater emphasis on cooperation in girls' games.

3. In nearly every known culture, boys play more aggressively than girls. Boys also have higher levels of testosterone, a hormone linked to aggressiveness.

   David Gutmann believes that males evolved into the more aggressive sex because from the standpoint of species survival, men are more expendable than women. Gutmann also believes that women are responsible for instilling in their children a sense of basic trust—a task facilitated by reduced levels of aggression.

As men and women get beyond what Gutmann calls the "chronic emergency of parenting," changes in their dispositions become evident. In men, there is an ebbing away of aggressiveness and a flowing in of affiliative and nurturant qualities.

In women the reverse occurs. Freed of the responsibility for their children's emotional security, women's natural aggressiveness begins to surface. The net result of these changes is that the two sexes become more alike in later life.

Textbook Question Answers

1. initiative versus guilt
2. self-definition
3. negotiations
4. stubborn (or demanding); compromising
5. self concept; optimistic; overestimate; in all
6. more
7. increasing; Africa; as well as or better; intellectually; verbal; creative; social
8. emotional regulation; society; neurological; learning
9. common; phobias; parents; imagination; nightmares
10. caregiving; insecure attachments
11. friendliness; Daniel Goleman; emotional intelligence
12. prosocial behavior; the making of new friends; violent temper tantrums, uncontrollable crying, and terrifying phobias; antisocial behavior; emotional regulation
13. self-concept; emotional regulation
14. instrumental; reactive; bullying
15. instrumental aggression; reactive aggression; emotional regulation; bullying aggression
16. relational aggression; less prosocial and less likely to have friends
17. rough-and-tumble; is universal; play face; social experience; are
18. sociodramatic; theory of mind; self-understanding; Girls; boys
19. 3; is

Television takes away from active, interactive, and imaginative play; exposes children to faulty nutritional messages and sexist, racist, and ageist stereotypes; undermines sympathy for emotional pain; and undercuts values that lead to prosocial activity.

20. physical aggression; desensitizing; bullies, to retaliate physically, to be passive victims, and to be onlookers rather than mediators when other children fight
21. parenting
22. Baumrind; nurturance; discipline; communicate; maturity
23. authoritarian; low; high; low
24. permissive; are; well; few
25. authoritative; high; well; are
26. authoritarian; permissive; authoritative; grow stronger
27. temperament
28. proactive; punitive
29. reactive
30. reasoning; emotional; believe; is; aggressive
31. sex; gender; roles
32. less; gender
33. 2; 6; does; 8
34. phallic stage; mother; father; Oedipus complex
35. identification; superego
36. Electra complex; penis envy
37. reinforced; punished
38. observing and interacting with other people
39. understanding; script
40. sociocultural; traditional; androgyny
41. epigenetic systems; genes; early experience
42. biologically; culturally
43. brain

In females, the corpus callosum is thicker, and overall brain maturation occurs more quickly. In males, right-hemisphere activity and dendrite formation tend to be more pronounced.

44. are not; sex hormones

Answers to Testing Yourself

1. **b.** is the answer. Between 2 and 3 years of age, children become very accurate at labeling others as "he" and "she." (audio program; textbook, pp. 287–288)
2. **b.** is the answer. David Gutmann believes that gender roles become less distinct as we grow older. (audio program)
3. **d.** is the answer. Boys have a greater natural endowment of testosterone and are more aggressive in virtually all cultures. (audio program)
4. **a.** is the answer. Before age 5, many children

think their gender may change as they get older. (audio program)

5. **c.** is the answer. (audio program)
6. **b.** is the answer. (textbook, pp. 272–273)
7. **c.** is the answer. (textbook, p. 289)

   a. & b. In Freud's theory, the oral and anal stages are associated with infant and early childhood development, respectively.

   d. In Freud's theory, the latency period is associated with development during the school years.

8. **a.** is the answer. (textbook, p. 280)

   b. & d. These two types of play are not discussed in this chapter. Mastery play is play that helps children develop new physical and intellectual skills. Sensorimotor play captures the pleasures of using the senses and motor skills.

   c. Rough-and-tumble play is physical play that mimics aggression.

9. **b.** is the answer. (textbook, p. 283)

   d. Traditional is a variation of the basic styles uncovered by later research. Indulgent and neglecting are not discussed in the text.

10. **a.** is the answer. (textbook, p. 283)

    b. & c. Authoritative parents communicate very well and are quite affectionate.

    d. This is not typical of authoritative parents.

11. **d.** is the answer. (textbook, p. 281)
12. **b.** is the answer. (textbook, p. 278)
13. **a.** is the answer. (textbook, p. 272)
14. **b.** is the answer. (textbook, p. 290)

    a. This is the focus of Freud's phallic stage.

    c. This is the focus of Erikson's psychosocial theory.

    d. This is the focus of cognitive theorists.

15. **a.** is the answer. (textbook, p. 288)
16. **c.** is the answer. (textbook, p. 277)
17. **d.** is the answer. In accounting for Leonardo's verbal ability, Dr. Laurent alludes to both genetic and environmental factors, a dead-giveaway for epigenetic systems theory. (textbook, p. 294)

    a., b., & c. These theories do not address biological or genetic influences on development.

18. **b.** is the answer. (textbook, p. 274)

    a. & d. Only children often benefit intellectually, becoming more verbal and more creative.

    c. Because only children may miss out on the benefits of social play, they may be weaker in their social skills.

19. **c.** is the answer. (textbook, p. 286)

　a., **& b.** These strategies are more typical of Japanese mothers.

20. **d.** is the answer. (textbook, p. 278)

Reference

Doyle, J. A., & Paludi, M. A. (1995). *Sex and gender: The human experience* (3rd ed.). New York: McGraw-Hill.

　Doyle's book discusses many controversial issues in the development of gender roles and gender identity.

The School Years: Biosocial Development

AUDIO PROGRAM: Everything Is Harder

ORIENTATION

For most boys and girls, the years of middle childhood are a time when physical growth is smooth and uneventful. Body maturation coupled with sufficient practice enables school-age children to master many motor skills. Chapter 11 of *The Developing Person Through the Life Span, 5/e,* outlines biosocial development during the school years, noting that boys and girls have about the same physical skills in this season of life. Although malnutrition limits the growth of children in some regions of the world, most of the variations in physical development in developed countries are due to heredity. Diet does exert its influence, however, by interacting with heredity, activity level, and other factors to promote **obesity**—a serious growth problem in American children during the school years.

The text also examines the development and measurement of intellectual skills as well as the experiences of children with special needs, such as autistic children, children with learning disabilities, and those diagnosed as having attention-deficit hyperactivity disorder. The causes of and treatments for these problems are discussed, with emphasis placed on insights arising from the new **developmental psychopathology** perspective.

Audio program 11, "Everything Is Harder," introduces Sean Miller and Jenny Hamburg, each of whom is disabled by **cerebral palsy**. Through their stories, illuminated by the expert commentary of physical rehabilitation specialist Dr. Virginia Nelson, we discover that when physical development does not go as expected, everything is "off-time" and harder for all concerned. For **disabled** children, **handicapped** by the world around them, nothing—from getting around to meeting the ordinary developmental tasks of life—comes smoothly or easily.

LESSON GOALS

By the end of this lesson you should be prepared to:

1. Describe patterns of normal physical growth and development during middle childhood, and account for the usual variations among children.

2. Identify the causes of obesity, and describe methods for preventing and treating childhood obesity.

3. Describe motor-skill development during the school years, focusing on variations due to gender, culture, and genetics.

4. Explain how achievement and aptitude tests are used in evaluating individual differences in cognitive growth, and discuss why use of such tests is controversial.

5. Discuss the diagnosis and possible causes and treatment of specific learning disabilities, as well as autism and attention-deficit hyperactivity disorders.

Audio Assignment

Listen to the audio tape that accompanies Lesson 11: "Everything Is Harder: Children with Disabilities."

Write answers to the following questions. You may replay portions of the program if you need to refresh your memory. Answer guidelines may be found in the Lesson Guidelines section at the end of this chapter.

1. Identify the causes and characteristics of cerebral palsy.

2. Differentiate physical disabilities from social handicaps and cite several reasons that development is harder for disabled children.

Textbook Assignment

Read Chapter 11: "The School Years: Biosocial Development," pages 301–325 in *The Developing Person Through the Life Span, 5/e*, then work through the material that follows to review it. Complete the sentences and answer the questions. As you proceed, evaluate your performance for each secdtion by consulting the answers on page 141. Do not continue with the next section until you understand each answer. If you need to, review or reread the appropriate section in the textbook before continuing.

1. Compared with biosocial development during other periods of the life span, biosocial development during middle childhood is _____ (relatively smooth/often fraught with problems). For example, disease and death during these years are _____ (more common/rarer) than during any other period. For another, sex differences in physical development and ability are _____ (very great/minimal).

Size and Shape (pp. 301–306)

2. Children grow _____ (faster/more slowly) during middle childhood than they did earlier or than they will in adolescence. The typical child gains about _____ pounds and _____ inches per year.

Describe several other features of physical development during the school years.

3. In some undeveloped countries, most of the variation in children's height and weight is caused by differences in _____ . In developed countries, most children grow as tall as their _____ allow.

4. The precise point at which a child is considered obese depends on _____ _____ , on the proportion of _____ to _____ , and on _____ _____ .

5. One measure of obesity is the _____ _____ _____ , which is the child's weight in _____ divided by the square of the _____ in meters. At age 6, obesity begins at a value of _____ on this index. At age 10, obesity begins at a value of _____ .

6. Experts estimate that between _____ and _____ percent of American children are obese.

7. Two physical problems associated with childhood obesity are _____ and _____ problems.

(Research Report) Identify several inherited characteristics that might contribute to obesity.

8. (Research Report) Inactive people burn _____ (more/fewer) calories and are _____ (no more/more) likely to be obese than active people.

9. (Research Report) Excessive television-watching by children _____ (is/is not) directly correlated with obesity. When children watch TV, their metabolism _____ (slows down/speeds up).

(Research Report) Identify three factors that make television-watching fattening.

10. (Research Report) American children whose parents were immigrants from developing countries are _____ (more/less) likely to be overweight. This demonstrates the importance of another factor in obesity: _____

_____ .

11. (Research Report) The onset of childhood obesity _____ (is/is not) commonly associated with a traumatic experience.

12. (Research Report) Fasting and/or repeated dieting _____ (lowers/raises) the rate of metabolism. For this reason, after a certain amount of weight loss, additional pounds become _____ (more/less) difficult to lose.

13. (Research Report) Strenuous dieting during childhood _____ (is/is not) potentially dangerous.

14. The best way to get children to lose weight is to increase their _____

_____ . Developmentalists agree that treating obesity early in life _____ (is/is not) very important in ensuring the child's overall health later in life.

15. (Changing Policy) A chronic inflammatory disorder of the airways is called _____ . This health problem is becoming increasingly prevalent in _____ nations. It usually disappears by _____

_____ . Crucial in the epidemiology of this disorder are _____ factors.

16. (Changing Policy) Among the aspects of modern life that contribute to asthma are _____

_____

_____ .

(Changing Policy) List three environmental factors that are implicated in asthma.

Skill Development (pp. 306–313)

17. Children become more skilled at controlling their bodies during the school years, in part because they _____ .

18. The length of time it takes a person to respond to a particular stimulus is called _____

_____ . A key factor in this motor skill is _____ _____ .

19. Other important abilities that continue to develop during the school years are _____-

_____ _____ , balance, and judgment of _____ .

20. Because during the school years boys have greater _____-_____ strength than girls, they tend to have an advantage in sports such as _____ , whereas girls have an advantage in sports such as

_____ .

21. For most physical activities during middle childhood, biological sex differences are _____ , with expertise depending on three elements: _____ ,

_____ , and _____ . The development of specific motor skills also depends on _____

_____ and _____ .

22. Many of the sports that adults value _____ (are/are not) well suited for children.

23. Due to _____ differences, some children are simply more gifted in developing specific motor skills.

24. Motor habits that rely on coordinating both sides of the body improve because the _____

_____ between the brain's hemispheres continues to mature. Animal research also demonstrates that brain development is stimulated through _____ . In addition, _____ play may help boys overcome their tendencies toward _____ because it helps with regulation in the _____ _____ of the brain.

25. Tests that are designed to measure what a child has learned are called _____ tests. Tests that are designed to measure learning potential are called _____ tests.

26. The most commonly used aptitude tests are _____ _____ . In the original version of the most commonly used test of this type, a person's score was calculated as a _____ (the child's _____ divided by the child's _____ _____ and multiplied by 100 to determine his or her _____).

27. Two highly regarded IQ tests are the _____-_____ and the _____ .

28. (Figure 11.4) On current tests, 70 percent of all children score somewhere between _____ and _____ . Children who score above _____ are considered gifted, whereas those who score in the _____-_____ range are considered to be slow learners.

29. Testing is controversial in part because a child's test performance can be affected by nonacademic factors, such as _____ .

30. IQ scores may seriously underestimate the intellectual potential of a _____ child or overestimate that of a child from an _____ background.

31. (A Life-Span View) Robert Sternberg believes that there are three distinct types of intelligence: _____ , _____ , and _____ . Similarly, Howard Gardner

describes _____ (how many?) distinct intelligences.

Children with Special Needs (pp. 313–323)

32. Among the psychological disorders that impair the development of children with special needs are _____ _____ .

33. The field of study that is concerned with childhood psychological disorders is _____ _____ .

34. This perspective has made diagnosticians much more aware of the _____ _____ of childhood problems. This awareness is reflected in the official diagnostic guide of the American Psychiatric Association, which is the _____ _____ .

35. One of the most severe disturbances of early childhood is _____ , a term that Leo Kanner first used to describe children who are _____ .

36. Children who have autistic symptoms that are less severe than those in the classic syndrome are sometimes diagnosed with _____ _____ .

37. Autism is more common in _____ (boys/girls).

38. In early childhood autism, severe deficiencies appear in three areas: _____ _____ , _____ _____ , and _____ _____ . The first two deficiencies are usually apparent during _____ .

39. Some autistic children engage in a type of speech called _____ , in which they repeat, word for word, things they have heard.

40. The unusual play patterns of autistic children are characterized by repetitive _____ and an absence of spontaneous _____ play.

41. The most devastating problem of autistic children often proves to be the lack of _____ _____ . Autistic children appear to lack a _____ _____ _____ .

42. Unaffected by others' opinions, autistic children also lack _____ _____ .

43. Some children have difficulty in school due to an overall slowness in development; that is, they suffer _____ _____ . If that difficulty _____ (is/is not) attributable to an overall intellectual slowness, a physical handicap, a severely stressful situation, or a lack of basic education, the child is said to have a _____ _____ .

44. A disability in reading is called _____ ; in math, it is called _____ . Other specific academic subjects that may show a learning disability are _____ and _____ .

45. A disability that manifests itself in a difficulty in concentrating for more than a few moments and a need to be active, often accompanied by excitability and impulsivity, is called _____-_____ _____ _____ . The crucial problem in these conditions seems to be a neurological difficulty in paying _____ .

46. Researchers have identified several factors that may contribute to ADHD. These include _____ _____ , prenatal damage from _____ , and postnatal damage, such as from _____ _____ .

47. Children with attention-deficit disorder without hyperactivity appear to be prone to _____ and _____ .

48. Many children with ADHD are prone to _____ , a fact that has led some researchers to propose a subtype of the disorder called _____ _____ . Such children also are at risk for developing _____ and _____ disorders.

49. Developmental and contextual variations in ADHD help explain _____ differences in the frequency of this disorder. For example, children in _____ _____ are less likely to be diagnosed as having ADHD than U.S. children, but they are more likely to be diagnosed with _____ _____ .

50. Children with ADHD _____ (do/do not) tend to have continuing problems as adults.

51. In childhood, the most effective forms of treatment for ADHD are _____ , _____ therapy, and changes in the _____ .

52. Certain drugs that stimulate adults, such as _____ and _____ , have a reverse effect on many hyperactive children.

53. Teacher behavior that is too _____ or too _____ tends to exacerbate ADHD.

54. (In-Person) The training approach in which learning-disabled children are not separated into special classes is called _____ . More recently, some schools have developed a _____ _____ , in which such children spend part of each day with a teaching specialist. In the most recent approach, called _____ , learning-disabled children receive targeted help within the setting of a regular classroom.

Testing Yourself

After you have completed the audio and text review questions, see how well you do on the following quiz. Correct answers, with text and audio references, may be found at the end of this chapter.

1. A movement disorder that results from brain injury occurring at birth is called:
   a. epilepsy.
   b. Huntington's disease.
   c. Parkinson's disease.
   d. cerebral palsy.

2. According to experts in the audio program, disabilities are _____ imposed and handicaps are _____ imposed.
   a. physically; socially
   b. socially; physically
   c. physically; physically
   d. socially; socially

3. Which of the following was *not* cited in the program as a developmental obstacle faced by disabled children and their parents?
   a. There are few good role models with physical disabilities.
   b. Because many things take more time, difficult choices between activities must sometimes be made.
   c. Parents of disabled children experience many stresses that other parents do not.
   d. Counselors of disabled children are unwilling to let them make their own choices.

4. According to the experts heard in the audio program, the most difficult season of life for a disabled person is likely to be:
   a. early childhood.
   b. early adolescence.
   c. early adulthood.
   d. all seasons of life.

5. As children move into middle childhood:
   a. the rate of accidental death increases.
   b. sexual urges intensify.
   c. the rate of weight gain increases.
   d. biological growth slows and steadies.

6. During middle childhood:
   a. girls are usually stronger than boys.
   b. boys have greater physical flexibility than girls.
   c. boys have greater upper-arm strength than girls.
   d. the development of motor skills slows drastically.

7. (Research Report) To help obese children, nutritionists usually recommend:
   a. strenuous dieting to counteract early overfeeding.
   b. the use of amphetamines and other drugs.
   c. more exercise, stabilization of weight, and time to "grow out" of the fat.
   d. no specific actions.

8. A factor that is *not* primary in the development of motor skills during middle childhood is:
   a. practice.   c. brain maturation.
   b. gender.   d. age.

9. Dyslexia is a learning disability that affects the ability to:
   a. do math.   c. write.
   b. read.   d. speak.

10. (Research Report) In relation to weight in later life, childhood obesity is:
    a. not an accurate predictor of adolescent or adult weight.
    b. predictive of adolescent but not adult weight.
    c. predictive of adult but not adolescent weight.
    d. predictive of both adolescent and adult weight.

11. The developmental psychopathology perspective is characterized by its:
    a. contextual approach.
    b. emphasis on individual therapy.
    c. emphasis on the cognitive domain of development.
    d. concern with all of the above.

12. The time—usually measured in fractions of a second—it takes for a person to respond to a particular stimulus is called:
    a. the interstimulus interval.
    b. reaction time.
    c. the stimulus-response interval.
    d. response latency.

13. Researchers have suggested that excessive television-watching is a possible cause of childhood obesity because:
    a. TV bombards children with persuasive junk food commercials.
    b. children often snack while watching TV.
    c. body metabolism slows while watching TV.
    d. of all the above reasons.

14. The underlying problem in attention-deficit hyperactivity disorder appears to be:
    a. low overall intelligence.
    b. a neurological difficulty in paying attention.
    c. a learning disability in a specific academic skill.
    d. the existence of a conduct disorder.

15. Teacher behavior that seems to aggravate or increase problems in children with attention-deficit hyperactivity disorder tends to be:
    a. too rigid.
    b. too permissive.
    c. too rigid or permissive.
    d. none of the above.

16. In developed countries, most of the variation in children's size and shape can be attributed to:
    a. the amount of daily exercise.
    b. nutrition.
    c. genes.
    d. the interaction of the above factors.

17. Autistic children generally have severe deficiencies in all but which of the following?
    a. social skills
    b. imaginative play
    c. echolalia
    d. communication ability

18. (Changing Policy) Although asthma has genetic origins, several environmental factors contribute to its onset, including:
    a. urbanization.
    b. airtight windows.
    c. dogs and cats living inside the house.
    d. all of the above.

19. Psychoactive drugs are most effective in treating attention-deficit hyperactivity disorder when they are administered:
    a. before the diagnosis becomes certain.
    b. for several years after the basic problem has abated.
    c. as part of the labeling process.
    d. with psychological support or therapy.

20. Tests that measure a child's potential to learn a new subject are called _____ tests.
    a. aptitude
    b. achievement
    c. vocational
    d. intelligence

21. In the earliest aptitude tests, a child's score was calculated by dividing the child's _____ age by his or her _____ age to find the _____ quotient.
    a. mental; chronological; intelligence
    b. chronological; mental; intelligence
    c. intelligence; chronological; mental
    d. intelligence; mental; chronological

LESSON GUIDELINES

Audio Question Guidelines

1. **Cerebral palsy** is a movement disorder that results from a brain injury, usually one that occurs at birth.

   Although the most obvious symptom of cerebral palsy is the person's inability to move body parts the way he or she normally would, other associated symptoms may occur. These include seizures, mental retardation, and hearing and vision problems.

   Unlike many disorders, cerebral palsy is nonprogressive—it does not become worse as the person gets older.

2. **Disabilities** are the result of injury or heredity. **Handicaps** are imposed by society. Social handicaps, such as an environmental obstacle that prevents wheelchair access to a building or attitudes that are prejudicial, are, in many cases, more disabling than physical disabilities.

   Development is harder for children with disabilities for many reasons. One is the additional stresses the disability places on parents and other family members.

   Another obstacle to development is the lack of good role models for disabled children.

   Children with disabilities may need greater self-confidence, self-esteem, and "stick-to-itiveness" than normal children simply because most things are more difficult and take longer.

   Social attitudes often become obstacles for disabled individuals, particularly during adolescence when they want to be like everyone else and discover they are not.

Textbook Question Answers

1. relatively smooth; rarer; minimal
2. more slowly; 5; 2 1/2

During the school years, children generally become slimmer, muscles become stronger, and lung capacity increases.

3. nutrition; genes
4. body type; fat; muscle; cultural standards
5. body mass index (BMI); kilograms; height; 19; 24
6. 20; 30
7. orthopedic; respiratory

Body type, including the amount and distribution of fat, as well as height and bone structure; individual differences in metabolic rate; and activity level are all influenced by heredity and can contribute to obesity.

8. fewer; more
9. is; slows down

While watching television, children (a) are bombarded with commercials for junk food, (b) consume many snacks, and (c) burn fewer calories than they would if they were actively playing.

10. more; cultural attitudes toward food
11. is
12. lowers; more
13. is
14. physical activity; is
15. asthma; developed; late adolescence; environmental
16. carpeted floors, more bedding, dogs and cats living inside the house, airtight windows, less outdoor play, crowded living conditions

The rate of asthma has at least doubled since 1980 in virtually every developed nation. Asthma patients tend to be those least susceptible to other childhood illnesses. Asthma is at least 10 times more common in urban areas than in rural areas.

17. grow slowly
18. reaction time; brain maturation
19. hand-eye coordination; movement
20. upper-arm; baseball; gymnastics
21. minimal; motivation; guidance; practice; national policy; genetics
22. are not
23. hereditary
24. corpus callosum; play; rough-and-tumble; hyperactivity and learning disabilities; frontal lobes
25. achievement; aptitude
26. intelligence tests; quotient; mental age; chronological age; IQ
27. Stanford-Binet; Wechsler
28. 85; 115; 130; 70–85
29. the capacity to pay attention and concentrate, emotional stress, health, language difficulties, and test-taking anxiety
30. disadvantaged; advantaged
31. academic; creative; practical; seven
32. aggression, anxiety, autism, conduct disorder, depression, developmental delay, hyperactivity, learning disabilities, mutism, and mental slowness
33. developmental psychopathology
34. social context; *Diagnostic and Statistical Manual of Mental Disorders* (DSM-IV)
35. autism; self-absorbed
36. Asperger syndrome

37. boys
38. communication ability; social skills; imaginative play; infancy
39. echolalia
40. rituals; imaginative
41. social understanding; theory of mind
42. emotional regulation
43. mental retardation; is not; learning disability
44. dyslexia; dyscalcula; spelling; handwriting
45. attention-deficit hyperactivity disorder; attention
46. genetic inheritance; teratogens; lead poisoning or repeated blows to the head
47. anxiety; depression
48. aggression; attention-deficit hyperactivity disorder with aggression (ADHDA); oppositional; conduct
49. cultural; Britain; conduct disorder
50. do
51. medication; psychological; family and school environment
52. amphetamines; methylphenidate (Ritalin)
53. rigid; permissive
54. mainstreaming; resource room; inclusion

Answers to Testing Yourself

1. **d.** is the answer. (audio program)
2. **a.** is the answer. Social handicaps are often more disabling than physical difficulties. (audio program)
3. **d.** is the answer. Rehabilitation specialist Virginia Nelson encourages her clients to make their own decisions with regard to walking and driving, for example. (audio program)
4. **b.** is the answer. Because of the particular pressures of adolescence—such as wanting to be like everyone else—this may be the most difficult season for the disabled person. (audio program)
5. **d.** is the answer. (textbook, p. 301)
6. **c.** is the answer. (textbook, p. 308)

    a. Especially in forearm strength, boys are usually stronger than girls during middle childhood.

    b. During middle childhood, girls usually have greater overall flexibility than boys.

    d. Motor-skill development improves greatly during middle childhood.
7. **c.** is the answer. (textbook, p. 305)

    a. Strenuous dieting can be physically harmful and often makes children irritable, listless, and even sick—adding to the psychological problems of the obese child.

b. Although not specifically mentioned in the box, the use of amphetamines to control weight is not recommended at any age.

8. **b.** Boys and girls are just about equal in physical abilities during the school years. (ptextbook, p. 307–308)
9. **b.** is the answer. (textbook, p. 317)

    a. This is dyscalcula.

    c. & d. The text does not give labels for learning disabilities in writing or speaking.
10. **d.** is the answer. (textbook, p. 305)
11. **a.** is the answer. (textbook, p. 314)

    b. & c. Because of its contextual approach, developmental psychopathology emphasizes *group* therapy and *all* domains of development.
12. **b.** is the answer. (textbook, p. 307)
13. **d.** is the answer. (textbook, p. 304)
14. **b.** is the answer. (textbook, pp. 319–320)
15. **c.** is the answer. (textbook, p. 321)
16. **c.** is the answer. (textbook, p. 302)

    a. The amount of daily exercise a child receives is an important factor in his or her tendency toward obesity; exercise, however, does not explain most of the variation in childhood physique.

    b. In some parts of the world malnutrition accounts for most of the variation in physique; this is not true of developed countries, where most children get enough food to grow as tall as their genes allow.
17. **c.** is the answer. Echolalia *is* a type of communication difficulty. (textbook, p. 316)
18. **d.** is the answer. (textbook, p. 306)
19. **d.** is the answer. (textbook, pp. 320–321)
20. **a.** is the answer. (textbook, p. 310)

    b. Achievement tests measure what has already been learned.

    c. Vocational tests, which, as their name implies, measure what a person has learned about a particular trade, are achievement tests.

    d. Intelligence tests measure general aptitude, rather than aptitude for a specific subject.
21. **a.** is the answer. (textbook, pp. 310–311)

Reference

Accardo, P. J., Blondis, T. A., & Whitman, B. Y. (1991). *Attention deficit disorders and hyperactivity in children.* New York: Marcel Dekker.

> Various chapters in this book discuss the nature, causes, and treatment of this puzzling childhood disorder.

The School Years: Cognitive Development

AUDIO PROGRAM: Piaget and the Age of Reason

ORIENTATION

Cognitive development between the ages of 6 and 11 is impressive, as attested to by children's reasoning strategies, mastery of school-related skills, and use of language. Lesson 12 explores these changes and their significance to the developing person.

Chapter 12 of the textbook begins with a description of changes in the child's selective attention, processing speed and capacity, memory strategies, knowledge base, and problem-solving strategies. The next section discusses Piaget's view of the child's cognitive development, which involves a growing ability to use logic and reasoning.

The following section looks at language learning in the school years. During this time, children develop a more analytic understanding of words and show a marked improvement in pragmatic skills, such as changing from one form of speech to another when the situation demands. It also discusses the difficulties and values of bilingual education, and cultural variations in schooling.

The final section describes innovative new teaching methods, which emphasize active rather than passive learning and are derived from the developmental theories of Piaget, Vygotsky, and others. The chapter concludes by examining measures of cognitive growth and variations in cultural standards.

Audio program 12, "Piaget and the Age of Reason," focuses on a description and critique of Piaget's stages of preoperational and concrete operational thought. Piaget's famous **conservation** experiments are illustrated with children of several ages, and expert commentary is provided by psychologist David Elkind. Several landmarks of the transition from preoperational to concrete operational thought are illustrated, including the disappearance of **egocentric** thinking, and the emergence of abilities to

classify, deal with rules, consider two dimensions at once, and take another's perspective. Professor Elkind also discusses the contemporary concept of the **competent child** and why the efforts of many modern parents to accelerate cognitive development in their children may be futile.

As the program opens we hear the voices of two children—one who has not yet attained what philosophers once called "The Age of Reason," and one who has.

LESSON GOALS

By the end of this lesson you should be prepared to:

1. Describe the components of the information-processing system, noting how they interact.
2. Discuss advances in selective attention, metacognition, and processing speed during middle childhood.
3. Discuss the logical structures of concrete operational thought, according to Piaget.
4. Describe how children's language abilities change between the ages of 7 and 11.
5. Discuss variations in the schooling of children, focusing on the impact of cultural needs and standards for how schoolchildren spend their time.

Audio Assignment

Listen to the audio tape that accompanies Lesson 12: "Piaget and the Age of Reason."

Write answers to the following questions. You may replay portions of the program if you need to refresh your memory. Answer guidelines may be found in the Lesson Guidelines section at the end of this chapter.

1. Identify and describe the major characteristics of preoperational thinking.

2. Explain the conservation-of-liquid task and identify the cognitive abilities that enable children to succeed in this task.

3. Identify the cognitive gains that come with concrete operational thought. In what ways is thinking still limited among children in this stage?

4. Discuss some of the psychological and social effects of preoperational and concrete operational thought on children.

5. Discuss how some of Piaget's ideas have been modified recently and how the social revolutions of the past 25 years have changed parents' expectations of children.

Textbook Assignment

Read Chapter 12: "The School Years: Cognitive Development," pages 327–353 in *The Developing Person Through the Life Span, 5/e,* then work through the material that follows to review it. Complete the sentences and answer the questions. As you proceed, evaluate your performance for each secdtion by consulting the answers on page 153. Do not continue with the next section until you understand each answer. If you need to, review or reread the appropriate section in the textbook before continuing.

Remembering, Knowing, and Processing (pp. 327–332)

1. During middle childhood, children not only know more but also are more resourceful in using their cognitive resources in _____ _____ . In the words of John Flavell, they have acquired a sense of "the _____ of thinking."

2. The idea that the advances in thinking that accompany middle childhood occur because of basic changes in how children _____ and _____ data is central to the _____-_____ theory.

3. Incoming stimulus information is held for a split second in the _____ _____ , after which most of it is lost.

4. Meaningful material is transferred into _____ _____ , which is sometimes called _____-_____ _____ . This part of memory handles mental activity that is _____ .

5. The part of memory that stores information for days, months, or years is _____- _____ _____ .

6. The part of the information-processing system that regulates the analysis and flow of information is the _____ _____ .

7. The ability to use _____ _____—to screen out distractors and concentrate on relevant information—improves steadily during the school years.

8. (A Life-Span View) Children in the school years are better learners and problem solvers than younger children are, because they have faster

   _____ _____ ,

   and they have a larger

   _____ _____ .

9. (A Life-Span View) One reason for the cognitive advances of middle childhood is

   _____ maturation, especially the

   _____ of nerve pathways and the

   development of the _____

   _____ .

10. (A Life-Span View) Processing capacity also becomes more efficient through

    _____ , as familiar mental activities

    become routine.

11. (A Life-Span View) Memory ability improves during middle childhood in part because of the child's expanded _____

    _____ .

12. (A Life-Span View) Research suggests that high-IQ children _____ (are/are not) always more cognitively competent than low-IQ children, and that a larger _____

    _____ may be sufficient to overcome slower thinking.

13. The ability to evaluate a cognitive task to determine what to do—and to monitor one's performance—is called _____ . When such efforts involve memory techniques, they are called _____ _____ .

List some indicators of this developmental change during the school years.

Stages of Thinking (pp. 332–341)

14. The information-processing perspective sees cognitive development as occurring in

    _____ _____ . In contrast, Jean Piaget sees cognitive development as occurring in _____ .

15. The rapid change in intellectual competence that many children experience during middle childhood is known as the _____-

    _____-_____

    _____ . As a result, older children are more logical thinkers who seek explanations that are _____ , _____ ,

    and _____ .

16. According to Piaget, between ages 7 and 11 children are in the stage of _____

    _____ _____ .

17. The logical principle that certain characteristics of an object remain the same even when other characteristics change is _____ . The idea that a transformation process can be reversed to restore the original condition is

    _____ .

18. Many concrete operations underlie the basic ideas of elementary-school _____ and _____ ; they are also relevant to everyday _____
    problem solving.

19. The theorist who has extensively studied moral development by presenting subjects with stories that pose ethical dilemmas is

    _____ . According to his theory, the three levels of moral reasoning are

    _____ , _____ , and

    _____ .

20. (Table 12.2) In preconventional reasoning, emphasis is on getting _____ and avoiding _____ . "Might makes right" describes stage _____ (1/2), whereas "look out for number one" describes stage _____ (1/2).

21. (Table 12.2) In conventional reasoning, emphasis is on _____ _____ ,

such as being a dutiful citizen, in stage
_____ (3/4), or winning approval
from others, in stage _____ (3/4).

22. (Table 12.2) In postconventional reasoning,
emphasis is on _____ .
_____ , such as _____
_____ (stage 5) and _____
_____ _____ (stage 6).

23. Although moral values begin to develop by age
_____ , childhood is the time when
moral values are _____ .

24. One criticism of Kohlberg's theory was that his
dilemmas were too _____ and
_____ . A second is that the later
stages reflect values associated with
_____ , _____ cul-
tures.

25. Carol Gilligan believes that females develop a
_____ _____
_____ , based on concern for the
well-being of others, more than a
_____ _____
_____ based on depersonalized
standards of right and wrong.

26. Most researchers believe that abstract reasoning
about hypothetical moral dilemmas
_____ (is/is not) the only way to
measure moral judgment.

27. Recent studies have found that cognitive development is _____ (less/more) erratic
than Piaget's descriptions would suggest.
Cognitive development seems to be more affected
by _____ factors than Piaget's
descriptions imply.

Learning and Schooling (pp. 341–352)

28. There _____ (is/is not) universal
agreement on how best to educate schoolchildren.

29. Historically, _____ (boys/girls) and
wealthier children have been most likely to be
formally taught and to have the greatest educational demands placed upon them.

30. Teaching techniques vary from the
_____ _____
method to _____
_____ , in which students are
encouraged to interact and make use of all classroom resources.

31. (Changing Policy) Worldwide, teachers have
become more _____ of children's
efforts. Although the specific styles and methods
of education will vary, depending on
_____ _____ and
_____ _____ ,
any developmental approach attempts to engage
every student in an _____ learning
process. A new approach in math replaces rote
learning with _____-
_____ materials and active discussion, promoting a problem-solving approach to
learning.

32. One of the most important skills for children to
learn in school is _____ .

33. Schoolchildren's love of words is evident in their
_____ , secret _____ ,
and _____ that they create.

34. Children become more _____ and
_____ in their processing of vocabulary and are better able to define words by analyzing their _____ to other words.

35. Changing from one form of speech to another is
called _____-_____ .
The _____ _____ ,
which children use in situations such as the classroom, is characterized by extensive
_____ , complex _____ ,
and lengthy _____ . With their
friends, children tend to use the _____
_____ , which
has a more limited use of vocabulary and syntax
and relies more on _____ and
_____ to convey meaning.

36. Compared with the formal code, which is con-
text-_____ (free/bound), the informal
code is context-_____ (free/bound).

While adults often stress the importance of mastery of the formal code, the informal code is also evidence of the child's _____ .

37. Cognitively and linguistically, it is a(n) _____ (advantage/disadvantage) for children to learn more than one language.

38. The approach to bilingual education in which the child's instruction occurs entirely in the second language is called _____ . In _____ _____ programs, the child is taught first in his or her native language, until the second language is taught as a "foreign" language.

39. In ESL, or _____ programs, children must master the basics of English before joining regular classes with other children. In contrast, _____ _____ requires that teachers instruct children in both their native language as well as in English. An approach to teaching a second language that recognizes the importance of nonnative cultural strategies in learning is called _____- _____ _____ .

40. Immersion programs have been successful in _____ , with English-speaking children who were initially placed in French-only classrooms. In Guatemala, however, _____ _____ (which strategy?) seems to work best in teaching children a second language. Immersion tends to fail if the child feels _____ , _____ , or _____ _____ .

41. The crucial difference between success and failure in second-language learning rests with _____ _____ , who indicate to the children whether learning a second language is really valued.

42. Ideally, children learn a first and second spoken language best under age _____ .

43. The best teachers of a second language are _____ .

44. (Table 12.3) Compared to their counterparts in 1981, schoolchildren in the United States in 1997 spend more time _____ _____ , and less time _____ _____ . This shift is a result of the perception that the superior academic performance of children from _____ is due to this distribution of activities and time.

Testing Yourself

After you have completed the audio and text review questions, see how well you do on the following quiz. Correct answers, with text and audio references, may be found at the end of this chapter.

1. The kind of thinking that does not allow one to see the world from another's point of view is called:
   a. centration.
   b. egocentrism.
   c. concrete operations.
   d. preoperational thought.

2. Although Piaget believed that children could not take another's point of view before the age of _____ , some contemporary researchers believe that children as young as age _____ can grasp this concept.
   a. 4; 2
   b. 9; 5
   c. 6; 4
   d. 7; 3

3. Preoperational children lack the concept of conservation because they fail to realize that:
   a. a change in one dimension of an object brings about a change in another dimension, too.
   b. matter can neither be created nor destroyed.
   c. rules are not immutable and can be modified.
   d. a transformation can be reversed to restore the original form.

4. The principle that properties such as volume, number, and area remain the same despite changes in the appearance of objects is called:
   a. constancy.
   b. reversibility.
   c. conservation.
   d. reciprocity.

5. Current research on cognitive development indicates that:
   a. Piaget's theory is applicable only to upper-class children.
   b. Piaget overlooked the importance of social development on cognition.
   c. certain cognitive abilities may be acquired at an earlier age than Piaget believed.
   d. Piaget may have overestimated the competence of young children.

6. According to Piaget, the stage of cognitive development in which a person understands specific logical ideas and can apply them to concrete problems is called:
   a. preoperational thought.
   b. operational thought.
   c. concrete operational thought.
   d. formal operational thought.

7. The "5-to-7 shift" refers to the rapid change in _____ that children experience between ages 5 and 7.
   a. social competence
   b. moral reasoning
   c. friendship networks
   d. every domain of thinking

8. The idea that an object that has been transformed in some way can be restored to its original form by undoing the process is:
   a. identity.   c. total immersion.
   b. reversibility.   d. automatization.

9. Information-processing theorists contend that major advances in cognitive development occur during the school years because:
   a. the child's mind becomes more like a computer as he or she matures.
   b. children become better able to process and analyze information.
   c. most mental activities become automatic by the time a child is about 13 years old.
   d. the major improvements in reasoning that occur during the school years involve increased long-term memory capacity.

10. The ability to filter out distractions and concentrate on relevant details is called:
    a. metacognition.
    b. information processing.
    c. selective attention.
    d. decentering.

11. Concrete operational thought is Piaget's term for the school-age child's ability to:
    a. reason logically about things and events he or she perceives.
    b. think about thinking.
    c. understand that certain characteristics of an object remain the same when other characteristics are changed.
    d. understand that moral principles may supercede the standards of society.

12. The term for the ability to monitor one's cognitive performance—to think about thinking—is:
    a. pragmatics.
    b. information processing.
    c. selective attention.
    d. metacognition.

13. Long-term memory is _____ permanent and _____ limited than working memory.
    a. more; less
    b. less; more
    c. more; more
    d. less; less

14. In making moral choices, according to Gilligan, females are more likely than males to:
    a. score at a higher level in Kohlberg's system.
    b. emphasize the needs of others.
    c. judge right and wrong in absolute terms.
    d. formulate abstract principles.

15. During middle childhood, children become more analytical and logical in their understanding of words. This means that they:
    a. learn more words per year than they did during the play years.
    b. can first learn a second language.
    c. no longer engage in verbal play.
    d. become much more "teachable."

16. The formal code that children use in the classroom is characterized by:
    a. limited use of vocabulary and syntax.
    b. context-bound grammar.
    c. extensive use of gestures and intonation to convey meaning.
    d. extensive vocabulary, complex syntax, and lengthy sentences.

17. Which of the following is *not* an approach used in the United States to avoid the shock of complete immersion in the teaching of English?
    a. reverse immersion
    b. English as a second language
    c. bilingual education
    d. bilingual-bicultural education

18. Information-processing theorists see cognitive development as occurring in _____ , and Jean Piaget sees cognitive development as occurring in _____ .
    a. stages; small steps
    b. small steps; stages
    c. unpredictable ways; predictable ways
    d. predictable ways; unpredictable ways

19. Historically, boys and wealthier children were more likely to be formally taught and to have greater educational demands placed on them than girls or poor children. Today, this inequality:
    a. can be found only in developing countries.
    b. has largely disappeared.
    c. persists, even in developed countries.
    d. has been eliminated for girls but not for poor children.

20. Of the following, which was not identified as an important factor in the difference between success and failure in second-language learning?
    a. the age of the child
    b. the attitudes of the parents
    c. community values regarding second language learning
    d. the difficulty of the language

NAME _____   INSTRUCTOR _____

LESSON 12: PREOPERATIONAL AND CONCRETE OPERATIONAL THOUGHT

Exercise

According to Piaget, preoperational and concrete operational children think about the world in very different ways. The **preoperational** child (4- to 5-year-old) sees the world from his or her own perspective (**egocentrism**), and has not yet mastered the principle of **conservation**: the idea that properties such as mass, volume, and number remain the same despite changes in appearance. The **concrete operational** child (6- to 11-year-old) is less egocentric and demonstrates mastery of logical thought, including conservation, with tangible objects.

These Piagetian concepts can be demonstrated if you know a 4- or 5-year-old and a 7- or 8-year-old—perhaps the children of relatives, friends, or neighbors—who are willing to participate. First try several of the conservation tasks described in the audio program and in the text (p. 232). Choose from the tests for the conservation of liquid, number, matter, length, volume, and area.

Then probe your subjects' ability to take another person's point of view. Asked why the sun shines, the preoperational child might answer, "So that I can see." Try asking your subjects the following questions and any others that you can think of. Why does the sun shine? Why is there snow? Why does it rain? Also have your subjects shut their eyes, then ask if they think that you can still see them. The preoperational child is likely to say no. As Professor Kotre did in the program, inquire how many brothers and sisters each child has. Follow up by asking how many children her or his parents have. The preoperational child is likely to know the number of siblings but not the number of children his or her parents have.

After you have conducted your tests, answer the questions that follow and hand the completed exercise in to your instructor.

1. Describe the participants (ages, sex, relationship to you) and setting that you chose for the interview.

2. Briefly describe each child's response to the conservation test you attempted.

   a. Conservation of _____

   Younger child's response

   Older child's response

    b. Conservation of _____

       Younger child's response

       Older child's response

    c. Conservation of _____

       Younger child's response

       Older child's response

3. Briefly describe each child's response to the test of egocentric thought. Was egocentric thinking evident in any of the answers given? If so, give examples.

       Younger child's response

       Older child's response

4. Do your subjects' ages and test responses support Piaget's stage theory of cognitive development? Why or why not?

LESSON GUIDELINES

Audio Question Guidelines

1. Preoperational children possess the notion of **phenomenalistic causality**, mistakenly believing that two things that happen together are related causally.

   Preoperational thought is also **egocentric**, making it difficult for young children to take the perspective of someone else. Egocentrism is lost gradually as the preschooler learns to keep track of two dimensions at once.

2. **Conservation** refers to the principle that an entity remains the same despite changes in its appearance. Preoperational children fail tests for conservation of volume, number, and area.

   In the test for conservation of volume, for example, the same amount of water is poured into a short fat glass and a tall skinny glass. Failing to conserve, the preoperational child judges that the tall skinny glass contains more water.

   The failure to conserve is due to the child's failure to realize that a change in one dimension of an object brings about a change in another dimension too. Preoperational children **center** their attention on the height of the water and forget about the width of the glass.

   Children who are able to conserve take both dimensions into consideration. They have entered the stage of **concrete operations**.

3. Around the age of 6 or 7 children enter the stage of concrete operations. Now, logical operations—the workings of reason—are evident in their handling of concrete objects.

   The newly found abilities include mastery of conservation and the emergence of **classification**, which is the ability to sort objects into categories and subcategories.

   The logic of **concrete operational thinking** means that children are also able to deal with rules. Rule-regulated thinking is evident in children's symbolic play and in the typical school curriculum (math rules, reading rules, science rules, etc.).

   Another characteristic of concrete operational thinking is the loss of egocentrism.

   Although children are able to think logically, this is true only for tangible objects. They are not yet capable of reasoning in the abstract.

4. Preoperational children's notion of cause and effect and their egocentrism have profound psy-chological effects. Their concepts of birth and death, for example, reflect the absence of any biological awareness of where babies come from or of the finality of death. Their sense that co-occurring events cause one another may lead them to believe that some particular act of theirs may have been the cause of their parents' divorce.

   There are many social ramifications to the attainment of concrete operations, including the newly found concern with rules in symbolic play and games, and the emerging ability to take the perspective of another person.

5. Although Piaget believed that children acquire the ability to perform concrete operations around 6 or 7, contemporary researchers have found otherwise. When experiments on conservation, classification, and egocentrism are simplified, younger children are often able to respond correctly.

   Other research has shown that the transition from preoperational thought to concrete operational thought is not as sudden or abrupt as Piaget believed.

   Professor Elkind notes that society's concept of the child is constructed to meet the needs of adults. During the past few decades, as adults have become more "liberated," the concept of the **competent child** has emerged. Many parents have responded by trying too hard to hurry their children's development.

   Professor Elkind notes that there is no evidence that the stages of cognitive development can be accelerated, and that indeed it may be a mistake to hurry children along the path of development.

Textbook Question Answers

1. problem solving; game
2. process; analyze; information-processing
3. sensory register
4. working memory; short-term memory; conscious
5. long-term memory
6. control processes
7. selective attention
8. processing speed; processing capacity
9. neurological; myelination; frontal cortex
10. automatization
11. knowledge base
12. are not; knowledge base
13. metacognition; cognitive strategies

School-age children's better use of cognitive strategies

derives from metacognitive growth. Furthermore, they know how to identify challenging tasks and devote greater effort to them; they also know how to evaluate their learning progress and how to distinguish fantasy from reality. In short, they approach cognitive tasks in a more strategic and analytic manner.

14. small steps; stages

15. 5-to-7 shift; rational; consistent; generalizable

16. concrete operational thought

17. identity; reversibility

18. math; science; social

19. Kohlberg; preconventional; conventional; postconventional

20. rewards; punishments; 1; 2

21. social rules; 4; 3

22. moral principles; social contracts; universal ethical principles

23. 2; taught

24. narrow; restricted; liberal Western

25. morality of care; morality of justice

26. is not

27. more; sociocultural

28. is not

29. boys

30. strict lecture; open education

31. encouraging; teacher personality; cultural assumptions; interactive; hands-on

32. communication

33. poems; languages; jokes

34. logical; analytical; connections

35. code-switching; formal code; vocabulary; syntax; sentences; informal code; gestures; intonation

36. free; bound; ability

37. advantage

38. immersion; reverse immersion

39. English as a second language; bilingual education; bilingual-bicultural education

40. Canada; reverse immersion; shy; stupid; socially isolated

41. the attitudes of parents, teachers, and the community

42. 5

43. peers

44. in school, playing sports, studying, doing art, reading; being outdoors, playing, watching TV; Asia

Answers to Testing Yourself

1. **b.** is the answer. "Egocentrism" is self-defining. Thought is centered (centrism) on the self, or ego. (audio program)

2. **d.** is the answer. When Piaget's original experiments are simplified, younger children are remarkably successful at them. (audio program)

3. **a.** is the answer. In the conservation of liquid experiment, younger children center their attention on the height of the water and do not consider the width of the glass. (audio program)

4. **c.** is the answer. Attainment of conservation marks the transition from preoperational to concrete operational thinking. (audio program)

5. **c.** is the answer. Using simpler tasks for measuring conservation, classification, and egocentrism, researchers have found that younger children are able to respond correctly. (audio program)

6. **c.** is the answer. (textbook, p. 332)

   a. Preoperational thought is "pre-logical" thinking.

   b. There is no such stage in Piaget's theory.

   d. Formal operational thought extends logical reasoning to abstract problems.

7. **d.** is the answer. (textbook, p. 332)

8. **b.** is the answer. (textbook, p. 334)

   a. This is the concept that certain characteristics of an object remain the same even when other characteristics change.

   c. This is a form of bilingual education in which the child is taught totally in his or her nonnative language.

   d. This is the process by which familiar mental activities become routine and automatic.

9. **b.** is the answer. (textbook, p. 327)

   a. Information-processing theorists use the mind-computer metaphor at every age.

   c. Although increasing automatization is an important aspect of development, the information-processing perspective does not suggest that most mental activities become automatic by age 13.

   d. Most of the important changes in reasoning that occur during the school years are due to the improved processing capacity of the person's *working memory.*

10. **c.** is the answer. (textbook, p. 329)

    a. This is the ability to evaluate a cognitive task and to monitor one's performance on it.

    b. Information processing is a perspective on cognitive development that focuses on how the mind analyzes, stores, retrieves, and reasons about information.

d. Decentering, which refers to the school-age child's ability to consider more than one aspect of a problem simultaneously, is not discussed in this chapter.

11. a. is the answer. (textbook, p. 332)

b. This refers to metacognition.

c. This refers to Piaget's concept of identity.

d. This is characteristic of Kohlberg's postconventional moral reasoning.

12. d. is the answer. (textbook, p. 330)

a. Pragmatics refers to the practical use of language to communicate with others.

b. The information-processing perspective views the mind as being like a computer.

c. This is the ability to screen out distractions in order to focus on important information.

13. a. is the answer. (textbook, p. 328)

14. b. is the answer. (textbook, pp. 337–338)

15. d. is the answer. (textbook, p. 343)

a. In fact, vocabulary growth is less explosive than in earlier years.

b. Second language learning proceeds most smoothly when it begins at a younger age.

c. This is "prime time" for verbal play, as evidenced in the jokes and poems children create during the school years.

16. d. is the answer. (textbook, p. 345)

a., b., & c. These are characteristic of the informal code that children use with friends in other settings.

17. a. is the answer. (textbook, p. 348)

18. b. is the answer. (textbook, p. 332)

c. & d. Both theorists view cognitive development as being at least somewhat predictable.

19. c. is the answer. (textbook, p. 341)

20. d. is the answer. (textbook, pp. 348)

References

Elkind, David. (1974). *Children and adolescents: Interpretive essays on Jean Piaget.* New York: Oxford University Press.

Elkind, David. (1981). *The hurried child: Growing up too fast too soon.* Reading, MA: Addison-Wesley.

Professor Elkind presents an illuminating discussion of Piaget's theory of cognitive development and elaborates on an issue introduced in the audio program: Do adults do children a disservice by attempting to accelerate their cognitive development?

The School Years: Psychosocial Development

AUDIO PROGRAM: The First Day

ORIENTATION

This lesson on psychosocial development brings to a close the unit on the school years. Lessons 11 and 12 noted that from ages 6 to 11 children become stronger and more competent as they master the biosocial and cognitive skills important in their cultures. Their psychosocial development during these years is no less impressive.

As described in Chapter 13 of *The Developing Person Through the Life Span, 5/e,* the major theories of development emphasize similar characteristics in describing the school-age child. They portray an individual who is much more independent, capable, and open to the challenges of the world.

Although the expanded social world of children in the school years is full of opportunities for growth, it also presents challenges and potential problems. Chapter 13 discusses the impact of bullying, peer rejection, and living in a family that is angry, impoverished, or unstable on children's psychosocial development. Most children, however, are sufficiently resilient and resourceful to cope with the stresses they may face during middle childhood. The emotional stability of parents and the amount of attention each child receives are significant factors in their healthy adjustment to environmental stress.

Audio program 13, "The First Day," focuses on the universal experience of children taking their first step onto a new stage of life: a stage where the world outside the family becomes very important. As children begin school, they confront a much more complex social world than they have previously experienced. It is a world with a new authority figure: the teacher. It is also a world with a large number of peers who provide opportunities for conversation, play, exploration, and the shared joy of friendship. Through the expert commentary of psychologists Steven Asher and Sheldon White, we discover both the problems and the promise of this world of school

and friends and its landmark status in the life story of the developing person.

As the program opens, the host speaks with 5-year-old Hannah who, like the main character in her favorite book, is about to embark on a journey beyond the security of home and family. In Hannah's case, the journey into the world of school and friends begins with her first day of kindergarten.

LESSON GOALS

By the end of this lesson you should be prepared to:

1. Identify the common themes or emphases of different theoretical views of the psychosocial development of school-age children.

2. Define social cognition, and explain how children's theory of mind and emotional understanding evolve during middle childhood.

3. Discuss the impact that peers have on psychosocial development during middle childhood, focusing on how friendship circles change and on the plight of rejected children.

4. Identify the various ways in which functional families nurture school-age children, and contrast the styles of open and closed families.

5. Describe the problems that may cause stress in middle childhood and factors that help to alleviate the effects of stress.

Audio Assignment

Listen to the audio tape that accompanies Lesson 13: "The First Day."

Write answers to the following questions. You may replay portions of the program if you need to refresh your memory. Answer guidelines may be found in the Lesson Guidelines section at the end of this chapter.

1. Summarize the cognitive and social skills of the 5- to 7-year-old child that make possible the important transition that takes place at this age.

2. Discuss the important role that friends play in the psychosocial development of school-age children.

3. (Audio and A Closer Look) Discuss the plight of the rejected child during the school years.

Textbook Assignment

Read Chapter 13: "The School years: Psychosocial Development," pages 335–376 in *The Developing Person Through the Life Span, 5/e*, then work through the material that follows to review it. Complete the sentences and answer the questions. As you proceed, evaluate your performance for each secdtion by consulting the answers on page 165. Do not continue with the next section until you understand each answer. If you need to, review or reread the appropriate section in the textbook before continuing.

An Expanding Social World (pp. 355–357)

1. Freud describes middle childhood as the period of _____ , when emotional drives are _____ , psychosexual needs are _____ , and unconscious conflicts are _____ .

2. According to Erikson, the crisis of middle childhood is _____ _____ _____ .

3. Developmentalists influenced by learning theory are more concerned with children's _____ of new cognitive abilities; those influenced by the cognitive perspective focus on _____ ; and the sociocultural perspective emphasizes _____ _____ .

Briefly describe the epigenetic systems perspective on the school-age child's new independence.

4. School-age children advance in their understanding of other people and groups; that is, they advance in _____ _____ . At this time, the preschooler's one-step theory of mind begins to evolve into a complex, _____ view of others.

5. In the beginning of the school years children often explain their actions by focusing on the immediate _____ ; a few years later, they more readily relate their actions to their _____ and _____ _____ .

6. In experiments on children's social cognition, older children are more likely to understand the _____ and origin of various behaviors.

7. Another example of children's advancing social cognition is that, as compared with younger children, older children are more likely to focus on _____ (physical characteristics/personality traits) when asked to describe other children.

8. During the school years, children are able to mentally _____ themselves to keep from getting bored, and they can mask or _____ inborn tendencies. As a result of their new social cognition, children can better manage their own _____ .

The Peer Group (pp. 357–366)

9. A peer group is defined as _____
    _____ .

10. (In Person) As their self-understanding sharpens,
    children gradually become _____
    (more/less) self-critical, and their self-esteem
    _____ (rises/dips). One reason is
    that they more often evaluate themselves through
    _____ _____ . As they
    mature, children are also _____
    (more/less) likely to feel personally to blame for
    their shortcomings.

11. Although working parents tend to worry about
    their children's after-school supervision, children
    tend to be more concerned about breakdowns in
    their _____ _____ and
    their parents' _____
    _____ .

12. Some social scientists call the peer group's sub-
    culture the _____
    _____ _____ , high-
    lighting the distinctions between children's
    groups and the general culture.

Identify several distinguishing features of this subculture.

13. Having a personal friend is _____
    (more/less) important to children than accep-
    tance by the peer group.

14. Friendships during middle childhood become
    more _____ and _____ .
    As a result, older children _____
    (change/do not change) friends as often and find
    it _____ (easier/harder) to make
    new friends.

15. Middle schoolers tend to choose best friends
    whose _____ , _____ ,
    and _____ are similar to their own.
    Generally, having a best friend who is not the

same _____ or _____
correlates with being _____ by
one's classmates.

16. Friendship groups typically become
    _____ (larger/smaller) and
    _____ (more/less) rigid during the
    school years. This trend _____ (is/is
    not) followed by both sexes.

17. In their friendship networks, boys tend to empha-
    size group _____ and
    _____ , while girls form
    _____ and more _____
    networks.

18. Children who are actively rejected tend to be
    either _____-_____ or
    _____-_____ .
    Children in the latter group are typically
    _____ , anxious, and unhappy; low
    in _____ ; and particularly vulnera-
    ble to _____ . Those in the former
    group tend to be _____
    and immature in their _____
    _____ . As rejected children get
    older, their problems _____
    (diminish/get worse).

Give an example of the immaturity of rejected children.

19. A key aspect in the definition of bullying is that
    harmful attacks are _____ .

20. One factor in bullying is that both boys and girls
    are restricted by overly rigid _____
    _____ , that encourage boys to
    _____ if they are victimized, while
    girls are expected _____
    _____ .

21. (text and Research Report) Bullying during mid-
    dle childhood _____ (is/is not) uni-
    versal. An effective intervention in controlling
    bullying is to change the _____

_____ within the school so that bully-victim cycles are not allowed to persist.

Describe the effects of bullying on children.

22. Contrary to the public perception, bullies usually are not _____ or _____ at the peak of their bullying.

23. Children who regularly victimize other children often become _____ later on.

Coping with Problems (pp. 366–375)

24. Between ages 7 and 11 the overall frequency of various psychological problems _____ (increases/decreases), while the number of evident competencies _____ (increases/decreases).

25. Two factors that combine to buffer school-age children against the stresses they encounter are the development of _____ _____ and an expanding _____ _____ .

26. *Family function* refers to how well the family _____ _____ .

27. A functional family nurtures school-age children by meeting their basic _____ , by encouraging _____ , fostering the development of _____ , nurturing peer _____ , and by providing _____ and _____ .

28. Families with an _____ style encourage contributions from every family member; in those with a _____ style, one parent, usually the _____ , sets strict guidelines and rules.

29. Family structure is defined as the _____ _____ .

30. Children can thrive _____ (only in certain family structures/in almost any family structure).

31. (A Life-Span View) The disruption surrounding divorce almost always adversely affects children for at least _____ . Children younger than age _____ and older than _____ seem to cope better overall. Divorce may be hardest of all on children at the _____ of middle childhood

32. (A Life-Span View) Divorce jeopardizes both the _____ and _____ of a well-functioning family.

Identify several circumstances under which divorce may not harm the children.

33. (A Life-Span View) Custody means having _____ responsibility for children. Although _____ _____ is theoretically the best decision following a divorce, in practice this often is not the case. Developmental research reveals that _____ (mothers/fathers/neither parent) tend(s) to function better as the custodial parent.

(A Life-Span View) Give several reasons that children whose fathers have custody may fare better than children whose mothers have custody.

34. The impact of a given stress on a child (such as divorce) depends on three factors:

a. _____

b. _____

c. _____

35. (Changing Policy) On the whole, homeless children are even more disadvantaged than their peers of equal SES, with the result that many suffer from a loss of faith in life's possibilities and

_____ _____ .

36. One reason that competence can compensate for life stresses is that if children feel confident, their _____ benefits, and they are better able to put the rest of their life in perspective. This explains why older children tend to be _____ (more/less) vulnerable to life stresses than are children who are just beginning middle childhood.

37. Another element that helps children deal with problems is the _____ _____ they receive.

38. A child who is at risk because of poor parenting, difficult temperament, or poverty _____ (probably will/probably won't) still be at risk as an adolescent.

39. During middle childhood, there are typically _____ (fewer/more) sources of social support. This can be obtained from grandparents or siblings, for example, or from _____ and _____ . In addition, _____ can also be psychologically protective for children in difficult circumstances.

40. Most children _____ (do/do not) have an idyllic childhood. Such a childhood _____ (is/is not) necessary for healthy development.

Testing Yourself

After you have completed the audio and text review questions, see how well you do on the following quiz. Correct answers, with text and audio references, may be found at the end of this chapter.

1. By age 5, the preschooler's brain has attained approximately _____ percent of its eventual adult size.
   a. 65
   b. 75
   c. 85
   d. 90

2. The transition from the family environment of a young child into the broader world beyond the immediate family:
   a. occurs in children between 5 and 7 years of age throughout the world.
   b. is characteristic only of well-educated, pluralistic societies.
   c. occurs at different ages in different societies.
   d. reflects a relatively recent setting of the social clock.

3. The "vision quest" refers to:
   a. a Native American rite of passage in which young children make a journey to seek their totemic animal.
   b. a friendship game played by children the world over.
   c. the efforts of rejected children to make friends.
   d. the developmental process by which school-age children attain a sense of industry.

4. Social cognition is defined as:
   a. a person's awareness and understanding of human personality, motives, emotions, and interactions.
   b. the ability to form friendships easily.
   c. a person's skill in persuading others to go along with his or her wishes.
   d. the ability to learn by watching another person.

5. A common thread running through the five major developmental theories is that cultures throughout history have selected age 6 as the time for:
   a. a period of latency.
   b. the emergence of a theory of mind.
   c. more independence and responsibility.
   d. intellectual curiosity.

6. The best strategy for helping children who are at risk of developing serious psychological problems because of multiple stresses would be to:
   a. obtain assistance from a psychiatrist.
   b. increase the child's competencies or social supports.
   c. change the household situation.
   d. reduce the peer group's influence.

7. Considering different family styles, which would be best for a child?
   a. an open family in which every member contributes
   b. a closed family in which strict guidelines and rules are set
   c. a flexible family style that balances the family's nurturance and the child's need for independence.
   d. none of the above.

8. Compared with preschoolers, older children are more likely to blame:
   a. failure on bad luck.
   b. teachers and other authority figures.
   c. their parents for their problems.
   d. themselves for their shortcomings.

9. As rejected children get older:
   a. their problems often get worse.
   b. their problems usually decrease.
   c. their friendship circles typically become larger.
   d. the importance of the peer group to their self-esteem grows weaker.

10. Compared with average or popular children, rejected children tend to be:
    a. brighter and more competitive.
    b. affluent and "stuck-up."
    c. economically disadvantaged.
    d. socially immature.

11. Compared to middle school girls, middle school boys are more likely to emphasize _____ in their friendship networks.
    a. fewer but closer friends
    b. group identity and loyalty
    c. having one, and only one, best friend on whom they depend
    d. friendships with others who are not the same age or sex

12. (A Life-Span View) Divorce may not be harmful to the child if the:
    a. family income remains stable.
    b. mother has custody of the children.
    c. father does not interfere with the mother's caregiving.
    d. the parents of the child's friends are also divorced.

13. Older schoolchildren tend to be _____ vulnerable to the stresses of life than children who are just beginning middle childhood because they _____ .
    a. more; tend to overpersonalize their problems
    b. less; have better developed coping skills
    c. more; are more likely to compare their well-being with that of their peers
    d. less; are less egocentric

14. Between the ages of 7 and 11, the overall frequency of various psychological problems:
    a. increases in both boys and girls.
    b. decreases in both boys and girls.
    c. increases in boys and decreases in girls.
    d. decreases in boys and increases in girls.

15. Bullying during middle childhood:
    a. occurs only in certain cultures.
    b. is more common in rural schools than in urban schools.
    c. seems to be universal.
    d. is rarely a major problem, since other children usually intervene to prevent it from getting out of hand.

16. During the school years, children become _____ selective about their friends, and their friendship groups become _____ .
    a. less; larger   c. more; larger
    b. less; smaller   d. more; smaller

17. Which of the following was *not* identified as a pivotal issue in determining whether divorce or some other problem will adversely affect a child during the school years?
    a. how many other stresses the child is already experiencing
    b. how many protective buffers are in place
    c. how much the stress affects the child's daily life
    d. the specific structure of the child's family

18. Erikson's crisis of the school years is that of:
    a. industry versus inferiority.
    b. acceptance versus rejection.
    c. initiative versus guilt.
    d. male versus female.

NAME _____   INSTRUCTOR _____

LESSON 13: SCHOOL-AGE FRIENDSHIPS

Exercise

A central theme of Lesson 13 is that middle childhood is a developmental period characterized by the child's growing inclusion in the social world beyond the family. This world is a complex social environment that includes a large number of peers at school and the shared joy of a smaller network of friends.

To help you apply the material from this lesson to your own life experiences, the exercise asks you to recall the social organization of your own elementary school days and to reflect on the importance of your own friendships. You may, of course, ask the questions of someone other than yourself.

After you have noted your responses, hand the completed exercise in to your instructor.

Think back to the social organization of your own elementary school days in answering the following questions.

1. Under what circumstances outside of school (e.g., birthday parties, outings, slumber parties, "sleep overs") did you and your friends get together?

2. Describe any social groups that formed on your street, in your apartment building, or around activities such as scouting, sports, lessons, or school activities.

3. Describe any special feelings that you have regarding the socializing you did as a child. For example, in what lasting ways did you benefit from the friendships you had in your school years?

4. Everyone experiences social rejection at one time or another. If you remember being teased, rejected, or called a derogatory name during grade school, describe your feelings about this experience. If you do not recall such an experience, describe someone you knew who suffered rejection, explain why he or she was rejected, and suggest how the person might have improved his or her popularity.

LESSON GUIDELINES

Audio Question Guidelines

1. In children between 5 and 7 years of age, the biological and social clocks are in sync, preparing the child to take his or her first step into the world of school and friends.

   By age 5 the brain has reached 90 percent of its eventual adult size, children have acquired the basic vocabulary and grammar of their language, and they are on the threshold of reaching the "age of reason."

   Socially, children are able to be away from their families for relatively long periods of time, and they are able to get along with other children, forming friendships, alliances, and other social groupings.

   Among some Native American tribes, children mark this transition with the "vision quest," a journey in which they go alone into the woods to search for a totem animal that will remain associated with them for the rest of their lives. As children become connected to nature, they also become connected to the world outside their families.

2. An important task that children face during the school years is making friends.

   As children grow older, their friendships become more important, more intense, and more intimate.

   School-age children become choosier about their friends and demand more of a smaller network of friends.

   The way that children think and talk about friendship changes as they get older. Younger children describe a friend in terms of the things they do together. Older children stress the importance of the help and emotional support their friends provide.

   Forming friendships can be very important to the child's psychological development. Children confide in their friends, and their friends help to reassure them about fears or feelings of inadequacy they might have.

   Friends offer comfort and security as children try a new task or approach a new situation.

   Children also learn new skills from their friends.

3. All children are rejected at some time.

   An estimated 5 to 15 percent of all schoolchildren experience serious difficulty in their peer relationships.

   Such children can be grouped into several categories: aggressive children; those who are shy, withdrawn, and have feelings that are easily hurt; and those who simply lack positive social skills.

   Rejected children typically are lonely and immature in social cognition, and have low self-esteem.

   Children who have poor peer relationships in elementary school run a higher risk of having problems coping later in life.

   Teaching rejected children social skills may help them to form stable friendships.

   Children should also be encouraged to develop their own interests and confidence apart from the social scene.

   Research has shown that children who improve their academic skills are likely to improve in self-esteem as well.

Textbook Question Answers

1. latency; quieter; repressed; submerged
2. industry versus inferiority
3. acquisition; self-understanding; social awareness

From an epigenetic systems perspective, the school-age child's independence is the result of the species' need to free parental efforts so that they may be focused on younger children and to accustom school-age children to their peers and the adults in the community.

4. social cognition; multifaceted
5. behavior; implications; possible consequences
6. motivation
7. personality traits
8. distract; alter; emotions
9. a group of individuals of similar age and social status who play, work, and learn together
10. more; dips; social comparison; more
11. peer relationships; fights or alcohol and cigarette use
12. society of children

The society of children typically has special norms, vocabulary, rituals, dress codes, and rules of behavior.

13. more
14. intense; intimate; do not change; harder
15. interests; values; backgrounds; age; sex; rejected
16. smaller; more; is
17. identity; loyalty; smaller; intimate

18. aggressive-rejected; withdrawn-rejected; lonely; self-esteem; bullying; impulsive; social cognition; get worse

Rejected children often misinterpret social situations—considering a compliment to be sarcastic, for example.

19. repeated

20. sex roles; become tough and not to ask for help; not to be physically assertive

21. is; social climate

The effects of bullying can be long-lasting. Bullied children are anxious, depressed, underachieving, and have lower self-esteem and painful memories.

22. insecure; lonely

23. violent criminals

24. decreases; increases

25. social cognition; social world

26. nurtures its children to develop their full potential

27. needs; learning; self-esteem; friendships; harmony; stability

28. open; closed; father

29. legal and genetic relationship between the adults and children in a household

30. in almost any family structure

31. a year or two; 2; 18; beginning or end

32. harmony; stability

Divorce may not harm children if the family income remains stable, if fights between the parents are few, and if caregiving by both parents is as good as or better than it was before the divorce.

33. caregiving; joint custody; neither parent

Children sometimes respond better to a man's authority than to a woman's. In addition, fathers who choose custody are those who are likely to be suited for it, whereas mothers typically have custody whether they prefer it or not. Father-only homes are, on average, more financially secure.

34. a. how many other stresses the child is already experiencing
    b. how much these stresses affect the child's daily life
    c. how many protective buffers and coping patterns are in place

35. clinical depression

36. self-esteem; less

37. social support

38. probably will

39. more; peers; pets; religion

40. do not; is not

Answers to Testing Yourself

1. **d.** is the answer. (audio program)

2. **a.** is the answer. The transition from immediate family to the larger social world is a universal phenomenon. (audio program)

3. **a.** is the answer. In the vision quest, young Native American children search for their totemic animal, marking their connection with nature and the larger world outside the family. (audio program)

4. **a.** is the answer. (textbook, p. 356)

5. **b.** is the answer. (textbook, p. 356)

6. **b.** is the answer. (textbook, p. 372)

7. **c.** is the answer. (textbook, p. 368)

8. **d.** is the answer. (textbook, pp. 356–357)
   a., b., & c. Compared with preschool children, schoolchildren are more self-critical, and their self-esteem dips, so they blame themselves.

9. **a.** is the answer. (textbook, p. 362)

10. **d.** is the answer. (textbook, p. 362)

11. **b.** is the answer. (textbook, p. 360)

12. **a.** is the answer. (textbook, p. 370)

13. **b.** is the answer. (textbook, p. 367)

14. **b.** is the answer. (textbook, p. 367)

15. **c.** is the answer. (textbook, p. 364)
    d. In fact, children rarely intervene, unless a best friend is involved.

16. **d.** is the answer. (textbook, p. 360)

17. **d.** is the answer. (textbook, p. 369)

18. **a.** is the answer. (textbook, p. 355)

Reference

Asher, Steven R., & Gottman, John M. (1981). *The development of children's friendships.* Cambridge, England: Cambridge University Press.

> Various issues in the importance of friendship to psychosocial development are discussed in this collection of articles edited by Professor Asher, who is heard in the audio program.

Adolescence: Biosocial Development

AUDIO PROGRAM: **Changing Bodies, Changing Selves**

ORIENTATION

For most people, adolescence is an eventful season that brings dramatic changes in the ticking of each of the three developmental clocks—biological, psychological, and social. Along with physical growth that occurs at a more rapid rate than at any time since early childhood, the changes associated with sexual maturation contribute a new dimension to the ways in which adolescents think about themselves and relate to others. Lesson 14, which focuses on the nature and consequences of biosocial development during adolescence, begins a three-lesson unit on development between the ages of 10 and 20—the season when young people cross the boundary between childhood and adulthood.

Chapter 14 of *The Developing Person Through the Life Span, 5/e* takes a detailed look at the physical metamorphosis adolescents experience in puberty, with emphasis on sexual maturation, nutrition, and the possible problems arising from dissatisfaction with one's appearance. The text also addresses two hazards that too often affect adolescence: sexual abuse, and the use of alcohol, tobacco, and other drugs.

In audio program 14, "Changing Bodies, Changing Selves," the mechanisms by which the biological clock programs puberty are discussed. In this century, children are entering puberty earlier and earlier. Around the age of 9 in girls and 10 in boys, puberty begins when the **pituitary gland** in the brain releases hormones that affect the ovaries in girls and the testes in boys. Dr. Inese Beitins, a pediatric endocrinologist, explains the intricate sequence of bodily changes triggered by this hormonal surge. In boys and girls, the sequences are nearly opposite,

with fertility arriving late in the pubertal cycle of girls and early in that of boys. The possible explanations for this sex difference are explored by anthropologists Jane Lancaster and Barry Bogin, and psychologist Laurence Steinberg. According to one view, the male-female difference was shaped by our evolutionary past, at a time when the biological and social clocks were in sync. Today, however, fertility often arrives a decade before society confers on the young person the status of adult, bringing with it a time when the biological clock says "ready," but the social clock says "wait."

For all of us, the changes of adolescence have a memorable and lifelong impact on our bodies and self-images. Perhaps we can recall the excitement and embarrassment of an event like the one that opens the program.

LESSON GOALS

By the end of this lesson you should be prepared to:

1. Outline the biological changes of puberty, and discuss the emotional and psychological impact of pubertal hormones.

2. Compare and contrast the development of the primary and secondary sex characteristics in adolescent males and females.

3. Discuss the evolutionary perspective on male-female differences in development during puberty.

4. Describe the possible problems faced by boys and girls during adolescence, including dissatisfaction with body image, sexual abuse, and drug use.

Audio Assignment

Listen to the audio tape that accompanies Lesson 14: "Changing Bodies, Changing Selves."

Write answers to the following questions. You may replay portions of the program if you need to refresh your memory. Answer guidelines may be found in the Lesson Guidelines section at the end of this chapter.

1. Outline what is known of the neural and hormonal mechanisms that govern the onset of puberty.

2. Explain why, according to some anthropologists, the biological clock programs fertility to arrive late in the pubertal sequence for girls, and early in the sequence for boys.

3. Contrast the effects of early and late maturation on boys and girls in today's society.

Textbook Assignment

Read Chapter 14: "Adolescence: Biosocial Development," pages 381–405 in *The Developing Person Through the Life Span, 5/e,* then work through the material that follows to review it. Complete the sentences and answer the questions. As you proceed, evaluate your performance for each secdtion by consulting the answers on page 177. Do not continue with the next section until you understand each answer. If you need to, review or reread the appropriate section in the textbook before continuing.

Puberty Begins (pp. 381–386)

1. The period of adolescence extends roughly from age _____ to _____ . The period of rapid physical growth and sexual maturation that ends childhood and brings the young person to adult size, shape, and sexual potential is called _____ .

   List, in order, the major physical changes of puberty in

   Girls: _____

   _____

   Boys: _____

   _____

2. Puberty begins when a hormonal signal from the _____ triggers hormone production in the _____

   _____ , which in turn triggers increased hormone production by the

   _____ _____

   and by the _____ , which include the _____ in males and the _____ in females.

3. The hormone _____ causes the gonads to dramatically increase production of sex hormones, especially _____ in girls and _____ in boys. This, in turn, triggers the hypothalamus and pituitary to increase production of _____ .

4. The increase in the hormone _____ is dramatic in boys and slight in girls, whereas the increase in the hormone _____ is marked in girls and slight in boys.

5. During puberty, hormonal levels have their greatest emotional impact _____ (directly/indirectly), via the _____ _____ of _____ _____ . That impact is powerfully influenced by the _____ and _____ of the adolescent's family, peer group, and culture.

6. Normal children begin to notice pubertal changes between the ages of _____ and _____ .

7. (A Life-Span View) Children under extreme stress grow more _____ , because stress reduces the production of _____

_____ .

8. (A Life-Span View) Longitudinal research suggests that family emotional distance and stress may _____ (accelerate/delay) the onset of puberty. Animal studies have revealed that this phenomenon occurs because stress causes an _____ (increase/decrease) in the production of _____ that initiate puberty. Despite this relationship, it is likely that puberty is triggered by the interaction of _____ and _____ factors.

9. The average American girl experiences her first menstrual period, called _____ , between ages _____ and

_____ .

10. Genes are an important factor in the timing of menarche, as demonstrated by the fact that _____ and _____

_____ reach menarche at very similar ages.

11. The average age of puberty _____ (varies/does not vary) from nation to nation and from ethnic group to ethnic group.

12. Stocky individuals tend to experience puberty _____ (earlier/later) than those with taller, thinner builds.

13. Menarche seems to be related to the accumulation of a certain amount of body _____ . Consequently, female dancers, runners, and other athletes menstruate _____ (earlier/later) than the average girl, whereas females who are relatively inactive menstruate _____ (earlier/later).

The Growth Spurt (pp. 386–390)

14. The first sign of the growth spurt is increased bone _____ , beginning at the tips of the extremities and working toward the center of the body. At the same time, children begin to _____ (gain/lose) weight at a relatively rapid rate.

15. The change in weight that typically occurs between 10 and 12 years of age is due primarily to the accumulation of body _____ . The amount of weight gain an individual experiences depends on several factors, including

_____ , _____ , _____ , and _____ .

16. During the growth spurt , a greater percentage of fat is retained by _____ (males/females), who naturally have a higher proportion of body fat in adulthood. The height spurt that soon follows _____ (does/does not) burn up some of the stored fat.

17. About a year after these height and weight changes occur, a period of _____ increase occurs, causing the pudginess and clumsiness of an earlier age to disappear. In boys, this increase is particularly notable in the _____ body.

18. Overall, between the ages of 10 and 14, the typical girl gains about _____ in weight and _____ in height; between the ages of 12 and 16, the typical boy gains about _____ in height and about _____ in weight.

19. The chronological age for the growth spurt _____ (varies/does not vary) from child to child.

20. As they mature, adolescent girls generally become increasingly _____ (satisfied/dissatisfied) with their bodies while boys become increasingly _____ (satisfied/dissatisfied).

21. One of the last parts of the body to grow into final form is the _____ .

22. The two halves of the body _____ (always/do not always) grow at the same rate.

23. Young people who experience puberty at the same time as their friends tend to view the experience more _____ (positively/ negatively) than those who experience it early or late.

24. For girls, _____ (early/late) maturation may be especially troublesome.

25. For boys, _____ (early/late) maturation is usually more difficult.

26. Internal organs also grow during puberty. The
_____ increase in size and capacity,
the _____ doubles in size, heart rate
_____ (increases/decreases), and
blood volume _____ (increases/
decreases). These changes increase the adolescent's physical _____ .

Explain why the physical demands placed on a
teenager, as in athletic training, should not be the
same as those for a young adult of similar height and
weight.

27. During puberty, one organ system, the
_____ system, decreases in size,
making teenagers _____
(more/less) susceptible to respiratory ailments.

28. The hormones of puberty also cause many relatively minor physical changes that can have significant emotional impact. These include
increased activity in _____ ,
_____ , and _____
glands.

29. Due to rapid physical growth, the adolescent
needs a higher daily intake of
_____ , _____ and
_____ . Specifically, the typical adolescent needs about 50 percent more of the minerals _____ , _____ , and
_____ during the growth spurt.

30. Some middle schoolers resort to self-destructive
behaviors, such as inducing _____
or using _____ to control their
weight.

31. Because of menstruation, adolescent females also
need additional _____ in their diets
and are more likely to suffer _____-
_____ _____ than any
other subgroup of the population.

Sexual Characteristics (pp. 390–396)

32. Changes in _____
_____ _____
involve the sex organs that are directly involved
in reproduction.

Describe the major changes in primary sex characteristics that occur in both sexes during puberty.

33. In girls, the event that is usually taken to indicate
sexual maturity is _____ . In boys,
the indicator of reproductive potential is the first
ejaculation of seminal fluid containing sperm,
which is called _____ .

34. (In Person) Attitudes toward menarche, menstruation, and spermarche _____
(have/have not) changed over the past two
decades, so that most young people
_____ (do/do not) face these events
with anxiety, embarrassment, or guilt.

35. Sexual features other than those associated with
reproduction are referred to as _____
_____ _____ .

Describe the major pubertal changes in the secondary
sex characteristics of both sexes.

36. Two secondary sex characteristics that are mistakenly considered signs of womanhood and
manliness, respectively, are _____
_____ and the growth of
_____ .

Breasts can be absent completely with no effect
on _____ , _____ , or
_____ .

37. (Research Report) Adolescents' mental conception of, and attitude toward, their physical appearance is referred to as their

_____ _____ .

(Research Report) Identify some common behaviors related to adolescents' preoccupation with their body image.

38. (Research Report) Adolescent girls with more body fat have fewer _____ or _____ than their thinner counterparts. Among adolescent boys, larger bodies correlate with greater _____ .

39. (Research Report) Media images reinforce the cultural ideal that American men should be _____ and _____ and that women should be _____ and _____ .

Health and Hazards (pp. 396–404)

40. The minor illnesses of childhood become _____ (less/more) common during adolescence, because of increased _____ at this age.

41 Any activity in which an adult uses a child for his or her own sexual stimulation or pleasure is considered _____

_____ _____ .

42. The damage done by sexual abuse depends on many factors, including how often it is _____ , how much it distorts _____ -_____ _____ , and how much it impairs normal _____ .

43. Sexualized adult–child interactions may escalate in late childhood or early adolescence, with onset typically between ages _____ and _____ .

44. Adolescents may react to maltreatment in ways that younger children rarely do, with _____ or by _____ .

45. Although _____ (boys/girls) are more often the victims of sexual abuse, the other sex is also often sexually abused. Molested boys often feel _____ and are likely to worry that they are _____ .

46. Although most abusers are _____ (male/female), about 20 percent of sexual abusers are of the other sex.

47. Drug _____ always harms physical and psychological development, whether or not it becomes _____ . Drug _____ may or may not be harmful, depending in part on the _____ of the person and the reason for the drug's use.

48. After a long period of _____ (decline/increase) during the 1980s, drug use by adolescents began to _____ (increase/decrease) in the 1990s.

(Changing Policy) Why do developmentalists urge teens to delay drug experimentation as long as possible?

(Changing Policy) List several measures that have proven to be at least partly effective in postponing and decreasing drug use.

49. (Changing Policy) An important social factor in adolescent drug use is _____ _____ . A study in Scotland found that parents of middle-school children were more worried about _____

_____ than about _____ ,
_____ , or _____
_____ . These concerns
_____ (matched/did not match) the
actual prevalence of these drug use categories in
their children.

50. (Changing Policy) In the United States, students
who participate in Project D.A.R.E are
_____ (less/no more) likely to
abstain from drugs during high school than those
who do not.

51. (Changing Policy) The likelihood of young people using drugs is also related to their
_____ about drugs use, which, in
turn, are affected by _____
_____ .

52. (Changing Policy) Antidrug attitudes softened
among adolescent Americans during the 1990s,
perhaps because each cohort goes through
_____ _____

53. Tobacco, alcohol, and marijuana may act as
_____ _____ , opening
the door not only to regular use of multiple drugs
but also to other destructive behaviors, such as
risky _____ , _____
from school, _____ behavior, poor
_____ _____ , and
_____ .

54. By decreasing food consumption and the absorp-
tion of nutrients, tobacco can limit the adolescent's _____ _____ .

55. Because alcohol loosens _____
and impairs _____ , even moderate
use can be destructive in adolescence. Teenagers
who drink regularly are more likely to be
_____ active, to engage in
_____ behaviors, to be excessively
absent from _____ , and more likely
to ride in a car with a driver who has been
_____ .

56. Marijuana _____ (slows/acceler-
ates) thinking processes, particularly those
related to _____ and
_____ reasoning.

Testing Yourself

After you have completed the audio and text review
questions, see how well you do on the following quiz.
Correct answers, with text and audio references, may
be found at the end of this chapter.

1. Which of the following is true regarding the pubertal sequence of physical changes in boys and
girls?
   a. For both boys and girls, fertility comes very
   early in the pubertal sequence.
   b. Fertility comes earlier in the pubertal sequence for girls than for boys.
   c. Fertility comes earlier in the pubertal sequence for boys than for girls.
   d. For both boys and girls, fertility comes very
   late in the pubertal sequence.

2. Compared to the turn of the century, today the
average age at which children enter puberty is:
   a. younger.
   b. older.
   c. no different.
   d. less predictable and more dependent on factors such as diet and exercise.

3. One evolutionary perspective on sex differences
in pubertal development holds that for our ancestors:
   a. males who retained boyish features for a
   while after they became fertile were more successful reproductively than those who did not.
   b. females who did not become fertile until after
   they were physically mature were more successful reproductively than those who became
   fertile earlier.
   c. the biological clock programmed fertility to
   occur at about the same time in males and
   females, with the bodily changes of puberty
   beginning about one year earlier in females.
   d. all of the above statements are true.

4. Regarding the effects of early and late maturation
on boys and girls, which of the following is *not*
true?
   a. Early maturation is usually easier for boys to
   manage than it is for girls.
   b. Late maturation is usually easier for girls to
   manage than it is for boys.
   c. Early-maturing girls may be drawn into older
   peer groups and may become involved in
   problem behaviors such as drug use and early
   sexual activity.
   d. Late-maturing boys do not "catch up" physically, or in terms of their self-images, for
   many years.

5. Which of the following most accurately describes the sequence of pubertal development in girls?
   a. breast buds and pubic hair; growth spurt in which fat is deposited on hips and buttocks; first menstrual period; ovulation
   b. growth spurt; breast buds and pubic hair; first menstrual period; ovulation
   c. first menstrual period; breast buds and pubic hair; growth spurt; ovulation
   d. breast buds and pubic hair; growth spurt; ovulation; first menstrual period

6. Although both sexes grow rapidly during adolescence, boys typically begin their accelerated growth about:
   a. a year or two later than girls.
   b. a year earlier than girls.
   c. the time they reach sexual maturity.
   d. the time facial hair appears.

7. The first readily observable sign of the onset of puberty is:
   a. the growth spurt.
   b. the appearance of facial, body, and pubic hair.
   c. a change in the shape of the eyes.
   d. a lengthening of the torso.

8. More than any other group in the population, adolescent girls are likely to have:
   a. asthma.
   b. acne.
   c. iron-deficiency anemia.
   d. testosterone deficiency.

9. More than half of all teenagers do not get enough of which nutrient in their diet?
   a. vitamin C
   b. magnesium
   c. iron
   d. calcium

10. For males, the secondary sex characteristic that usually occurs last is:
    a. breast enlargement.
    b. the appearance of facial hair.
    c. growth of the testes.
    d. the appearance of pubic hair.

11. For girls, the specific event that is taken to indicate fertility is _____ ; for boys, it is _____ .
    a. the growth of breast buds; voice deepening
    b. menarche; spermarche
    c. anovulation; the testosterone surge
    d. the growth spurt; pubic hair

12. The most significant hormonal changes of puberty include an increase of _____ in _____ and an increase of _____ in _____ .
    a. progesterone; boys; estrogen; girls
    b. estrogen; boys; testosterone; girls
    c. progesterone; girls; estrogen; boys
    d. estrogen; girls; testosterone; boys

13. (Research Report) In general, most adolescents are:
    a. overweight.
    b. satisfied with their appearance.
    c. dissatisfied with their appearance.
    d. unaffected by cultural attitudes about beauty.

14. Most developmentalists agree that puberty is triggered:
    a. by biogenetic factors.
    b. by psychosocial factors.
    c. by the interaction of biogenetic and psychosocial factors.
    d. in a manner that is almost completely unpredictable in any specific person.

15. The damage caused by sexual abuse depends on all of the following factors *except*:
    a. repeated incidence.
    b. the gender of the perpetrator.
    c. distorted adult-child relationships.
    d. impairment of the child's ability to develop normally.

16. Early physical growth and sexual maturation:
    a. tend to be equally difficult for girls and boys.
    b. tend to be more difficult for boys than for girls.
    c. tend to be more difficult for girls than for boys.
    d. are easier for both girls and boys than late maturation.

17. (Research Report) Developmentalists believe that teenagers' concern about their body image:
    a. should simply be ignored by parents as a passing phase.
    b. is a healthy sign that the developing person is beginning to assume responsibility for his or her own health.
    c. is a minor issue, since it tends to occur only in a small segment of the peer culture.
    d. should not be taken lightly.

18. Drug use by adolescents:
    a. peaked in the 1970s.
    b. peaked in the 1980s.
    c. has begun to increase in the 1990s.
    d. continues to decline in the 1990s.

19. (Changing Policy) A study in Scotland found that the parents of middle-school children were most concerned about their children's use of:
    a. illegal drugs.
    b. tobacco.
    c. glue and other sniffable solvents.
    d. alcohol.

NAME _____   INSTRUCTOR _____

LESSON 14: BODY IMAGES IN ADOLESCENCE

Exercise

A major theme of Lesson 14 is that the biosocial changes of puberty have a profound impact on our self-images. Most people are able to remember at least one event, attitude, misconception, or worry they experienced in connection with the biosocial changes of puberty: having had big feet; having been the first or the last to experience **menarche**; having been concerned about having a small penis or being oversexed; having worried about acne, or voice change.

The young people who have the most difficulty are those who must adjust to these changes earlier or later than the majority of their peers. Early or late maturation may be difficult because one of the things an adolescent does not want to do is stand out from the crowd in a way that is not admirable. Early-maturing girls who are taller and more developed are often teased about their bodies by boys and accused of being "boy crazy" by girls. Late-maturing boys may compensate for being physically outdistanced by peers by becoming the class "brain," clown, or trouble-maker.

Several studies have found that early-maturing girls and late-maturing boys may experience problems that reflect their difficulty in adjusting to their bodies. Early-maturing girls may be drawn to an older peer group and be more likely to engage in problem behaviors, such as drug use and early sexual activity. Follow-up studies of late-maturing boys during adulthood found that although most of them had reached average or above average height, some of the personality patterns of their adolescence persisted. Compared to early- or average-maturing boys, men who had been late-maturers tended to be less controlled and less responsible, and to harbor feelings of inferiority or rejection.

To help you recall your own adolescent preoccupation with appearance, the exercise for Lesson 14 asks you to respond to questions about your body image during your own adolescence. Once you have worked through the items, hand the completed exercise in to your instructor. If you prefer, you may base your answers to the questions on the experiences of a friend or relative.

Think back to your opinion about your physical appearance when you were in the eighth or ninth grade—when you were 14 or 15 years old.

1. What did you consider your "best feature"?

2. What did others (such as your parents) tell you was your "best feature"?

3. What did you consider your "worst feature"—the aspect of your appearance that you felt required the most care or upgrading?

4. Compared to your classmates and friends, were you an average-maturing, early-maturing, or late-maturing individual? What impact do you feel the timing of your puberty had on you at the time? What impact has it had on who you are today?

5. Do the ideas you had about your physical appearance at age 14 or 15 reflect your current body image? Why or why not (or to what extent)?

LESSON GUIDELINES

Audio Question Guidelines

1. The term **puberty** refers to the set of biological changes that occur at the start of adolescence and result in sexual maturity.

   Although infants have high levels of sex hormones, an unknown biological switch lowers the hormone level by the age of 2 and slows children's sexual development.

   At about the age of 9 in girls and 10 in boys, the **pituitary gland** in the brain releases hormones that affect the ovaries in girls and the testes in boys. In response, the ovaries and testes release sex hormones, and a year or so later the first outward signs of sexual maturation appear.

   In girls, the development of breast buds and pubic hair is followed by a **growth spurt**, in which fat is deposited on the hips and buttocks; by the first menstrual period; and finally, by **ovulation**—the release of the first egg.

   In boys, the normal sequence of events at puberty is nearly the reverse: First, the sex organs grow larger and pubic hair appears; followed by the first **ejaculation** of semen; then the growth spurt; and, finally, a lowering of the voice and appearance of facial hair.

2. Although girls start the sequence of puberty a year or so earlier than boys, both sexes become fertile at about the same time.

   Some anthropologists believe that puberty occurs earlier today than in previous eras because of the high fat and sugar levels in our diets.

   Other experts see the biological clock as being shaped by social needs. According to this view, early in human history, females who developed a mature appearance early in life, prior to their becoming fertile, may have had more opportunities to practice the various skills needed to take on the soon-to-be-attained social role of adult. Females who followed this growth pattern may have been more successful in having babies and rearing more of those babies to adulthood. In this way, the timing of the female pubertal sequence may have become coded into their biological clocks.

   In boys, according to this viewpoint, early development of the physical characteristics of stature, muscles, facial hair, and a deep voice, prior to their becoming fertile, might have been dangerous. If boys looked like men before they were fertile, they might have been perceived as competitors by older men. Such individuals would probably have been less successful reproductively, leading to the coding of mature appearance late in the pubertal sequence of boys' biological clocks.

3. The adolescents who have the most difficult time with puberty are early-maturing girls and late-maturing boys.

   Early-maturing girls are often teased and may suffer a loss of self-esteem.

   Early-maturing girls may be drawn into an older peer group and be more likely to engage in problem behavior, such as drinking, drug use, and early sexual activity.

   Late-maturing boys are at a disadvantage because, being smaller and less muscular, they tend to be less competitive at sports—the ticket to popularity for boys in most junior and senior high schools. This may have a continuing negative impact on the late-maturing boy's self-image.

Textbook Question Answers

1. 11; 20; puberty

   Girls: onset of breast growth, initial appearance of pubic hair, peak growth spurt, widening of the hips, first menstrual period, completion of pubic-hair growth, and final breast development

   Boys: initial appearance of pubic hair, growth of the testes, growth of the penis, first ejaculation, peak growth spurt, voice changes, beard development, and completion of pubic-hair growth

2. hypothalamus; pituitary gland; adrenal glands; gonads (sex glands); testes; ovaries

3. GnRH (gonad releasing hormone); estrogen; testosterone; GH (growth hormone)

4. testosterone; estrogen

5. indirectly; psychological impact; visible changes; values; expectations

6. 8; 14

7. slowly; growth hormones

8. accelerate; increase; hormones; biogenetic; psychosocial

9. menarche; 9; 18

10. sisters; monozygotic twins

11. varies

12. earlier

13. fat; later; earlier

14. length; gain

15. fat; gender; heredity; diet; exercise

16. females; does

17. muscle; upper

18. 38 pounds (17 kilograms); 9 5/8 inches (24 centimeters); 10 inches (25 centimeters); 42 pounds (19 kilograms)

19. varies

20. dissatisfied; satisfied

21. head

22. do not always

23. positively

24. early

25. late

26. lungs; heart; decreases; increases; endurance

The fact that the more visible spurts of weight and height precede the less visible ones of the muscles and organs means that athletic training and weight-lifting should be designed to match the young person's size of a year or so earlier.

27. lymphoid; less

28. oil; sweat; odor

29. calories; vitamins; minerals; calcium; iron; zinc

30. vomiting; laxatives

31. iron; iron-deficiency anemia

32. primary sex characteristics

Girls: growth of uterus and thickening of the vaginal lining

Boys: growth of testes and lengthening of penis; also scrotum enlarges and becomes pendulous

33. menarche; spermarche

34. have; do not

35. secondary sex characteristics

Males grow taller than females and become wider at the shoulders than at the hips. Females take on more fat all over and become wider at the hips, and their breasts begin to develop. About 65 percent of boys experience some temporary breast enlargement. As the larynx grows, the adolescent's voice (especially in boys) becomes lower. Head and body hair become coarser and darker in both sexes. Facial hair (especially in boys) begins to grow.

36. breast development; facial and body hair; conception; pregnancy; birth

37. body image

Many adolescents spend hours examining themselves in front of the mirror; some exercise or diet with obsessive intensity.

38. dates; boyfriends; aggression

39. tall; muscular; thin; shapely

40. less; immunity

41. childhood sexual abuse

42. repeated; adult–child relationships; development

43. 8; 12

44. self-destruction; counterattacking

45. girls; shame at being weak; homosexual

46. male

47. abuse; addictive; use; maturation

48. decline; increase

Delaying experimentation increases the adolescent's chances of becoming realistically informed about the risks of drug use and of developing the reasoning ability to limit or avoid the use of destructive drugs in dangerous circumstances.

The measures include health education classes that honestly portray the risk of drug use; increased punishment for store owners who sell alcohol or cigarettes to minors; raising the price of alcohol and cigarettes; enforcing drunk-driving laws; and teaching parents how to communicate with teenagers.

49. parental attitudes; illegal drugs; smoking; drinking; solvent sniffing; did not match

50. no more

51. attitudes; national and local policies, and personal experience

52. generational forgetting

53. gateway drugs; sex; alienation; antisocial; physical health; depression

54. growth spurt

55. inhibitions; judgment; sexually; antisocial; school; drinking

56. slows; memory; abstract

Answers to Testing Yourself

1. **c.** is the answer. Although pubertal changes begin a year earlier for girls than for boys, fertility occurs near the end of the sequence in girls and near the beginning of the sequence in boys. (audio program)

2. **a.** is the answer. For the past 100 years or so, each generation has experienced puberty at an earlier age than the preceding generation. (audio program)

3. **d.** is the answer. All of these are true according to the evolutionary perspective discussed in the program. (audio program)

4. **d.** is the answer. Late-maturing boys generally do catch up physically within a relatively short period of time. (audio program)

5. **a.** is the answer. (textbook, p. 381)

6. **a.** is the answer. (textbook, p. 384)

7. **a.** is the answer. (textbook, p. 386)

8. **c.** is the answer. This is because each menstrual period depletes some iron from the body. (textbook, p. 390)

9. **c.** is the answer. (textbook, p. 389)

10. **b.** is the answer. (textbook, p. 382)

11. **b.** is the answer. (textbook, p. 391)

12. **d.** is the answer. (textbook, p. 383)

13. **c.** is the answer. (textbook, p. 394)

   a. Although some adolescents become overweight, many diet and lose weight in an effort to attain a desired body image.

   d. On the contrary, cultural attitudes about beauty are an extremely influential factor in the formation of a teenager's body image.

14. **c.** is the answer. (textbook, p. 384)

15. **b.** is the answer. (textbook, p. 397)

16. **c.** is the answer. (textbook, p. 388)

17. **d.** is the answer. For most adolescents, *thinking* that they look terrible makes them feel terrible—even depressed. (textbook, p. 375)

18. **c.** is the answer. (textbook, p. 399)

19. **a.** is the answer. (textbook, p. 402)

Reference

Katchadourian, H. (1990). *Biological aspects of human sexuality*. New York: Harcourt Brace.

   A very readable and comprehensive description of the physical changes of puberty and the biological mechanisms by which they are programmed.

Adolescence: Cognitive Development

AUDIO PROGRAM: All Things Possible

ORIENTATION

Lesson 14 explored the biosocial changes that transform children into adolescents, giving them adult size, shape, and reproductive capacity. But equally important psychological and social changes occur during this sometimes tumultuous season. Lesson 15, which focuses on cognitive development, is the second of a three-lesson unit on adolescent development.

During adolescence, young people become increasingly able to speculate, hypothesize, and use logic. Unlike younger children, whose thinking is tied to **concrete operations**, adolescents with the ability to think in terms of formal operations are able to consider possibilities as well as reality. Not everyone reaches the stage of **formal operational** thought, however, as revealed in the discussion of adolescent egocentrism. Adolescents have difficulty thinking rationally about themselves and their immediate experiences.

The next section of the chaper addresses the question, "What kind of school best fosters adolescent intellectual growth?" Unfortunately, the rigid behavioral demands and intersified competition of most secondary schools do not provide a supportive learning environment for adolescents. The chapter concludes with an example of adolescent cognition at work: decision making in the area of sexual behavior.

Adolescent thinking has its limitations, however. As psychologist David Elkind notes in audio program 15, "All Things Possible," adolescents often create for themselves an **imaginary audience** and a **personal fable**, as they fantasize about how they appear to others, imagine their own lives as heroic, and feel that they are immune to danger.

The audio program also explores a new theory of intelligence proposed by psychologist Robert Sternberg. Professor Sternberg believes that **practical intelligence** reflects an ability to function effectively in everyday life. The emergence of practical intelligence may help adolescents to develop a more realistic picture of who they are.

Perhaps most significantly, the logical, idealistic, and egocentric thinking of adolescence represents a significant step in the process of creating a life story. Such is the view of psychologist Dan McAdams, who sees this season as a time when individuals begin to define that which makes them unique. As discussed in the audio program and in Chapter 16 of the textbook, Erik Erikson views adolescence as a time when young people struggle to form an **identity**. As they do, they create a background of ideology and write the first draft of their own life stories.

LESSON GOALS

By the end of this lesson you should be prepared to:

1. Describe the cognitive abilities of the typical adolescent.

2. Discuss adolescent egocentrism and the significance of adolescent thinking in the formation of identity and the process of creating a life story.

3. Evaluate the typical secondary school's ability to meet the cognitive needs of the typical adolescent.

4. Discuss the typical adolescent's inability to make major life decisions.

5. Explain how adolescent thinking contributes to adolescent pregnancy and sexually transmitted disease.

Audio Assignment

Listen to the audio tape that accompanies Lesson 15: "All Things Possible."

Write answers to the following questions. You may replay portions of the program if you need to refresh your memory. Answer guidelines may be found in the Lesson Guidelines section at the end of this chapter.

1. Explain how the development of formal operational thinking influences adolescents' attitudes toward family and society.

2. Compare and contrast formal operational thought with practical intelligence.

3. Discuss the significance of the imaginary audience and personal fable in the adolescent's formation of identity and creation of a life story.

Textbook Assignment

Read Chapter 15: "Adolescence: Cognitive Development," pages 407–433 in *The Developing Person Through the Life Span, 5/e*, then work through the material that follows to review it. Complete the sentences and answer the questions. As you proceed, evaluate your performance for each secdtion by consulting the answers on page 191. Do not continue with the next section until you understand each answer. If you need to, review or reread the appropriate section in the textbook before continuing.

Adolescent Thought (pp. 407–416)

1. The basic skills of thinking, learning, and remembering that advance during the school-age years _____ (continue to progress/stabilize) during adolescence.

2. Advances in _____ _____ improve concentration, while a growing _____ _____ and memory skills allow teens to connect new ideas to old ones, and strengthened _____ and _____ help them become better students.

3. Piaget's term for the fourth stage of cognitive development is _____ _____ thought. Other theorists may explain adolescent advances differently, but virtually all theorists agree that adolescent thought _____ (is/is not) qualitatively different from children's thought. For many developmentalists, the single most distinguishing feature of adolescent thought is the capacity to think in terms of _____ . One specific example of this type of thinking is the development of _____ thought.

4. Compared with younger individuals, adolescents have _____ (more/less) difficulty arguing against their personal beliefs and self-interest.

5. During the school years, children make great strides in _____ (inductive/deductive) reasoning.

6. During adolescence, they become more capable of _____ reasoning—that is, they can begin with a general _____ or _____ and draw logical _____ from it. This type of reasoning is a hallmark of formal operational thought.

7. (Research Report) In the developmental progression from inductive to deductive reasoning, some psychologists believe that adults can reach a less _____ stage following the formal operational stage.

8. Piaget devised a number of famous tasks involving _____ principles to study how children of various ages reasoned hypothetically and deductively.

Briefly describe how children reason differently about the "balance-beam" problem at ages 7, 10, and 13.

9. More recent research has shown that the growth of formal reasoning abilities _____ (always occurs/does not always occur) during adolescence and may be _____ (more/less) complete than Piaget and others believed it to be. Each individual's intellect, experience, talents, and interests _____ (do/do not) affect his or her thinking as much as the ability to reason formally. In addition, past _____ and _____ conditions also have an effect. A study of 13- to 15-year-olds in France found about _____ (what proportion?) at the concrete level, _____ at an intermediate level, and _____ at a formal level. Ten years later, these proportions _____ (had/had not) changed.

10. The adolescent's belief that he or she is uniquely significant and that the social world revolves around him or her is a psychological phenomenon called _____ _____ .

11. An adolescent's tendency to feel that he or she is somehow immune to the consequences of dangerous or illegal behavior is expressed in the _____ _____ .

12. An adolescent's tendency to imagine that her or his own life is unique, heroic, or even mythical, and that she or he is destined for great accomplishments, is expressed in the _____ _____ .

13. Adolescents, who believe that they are under constant scrutiny from nearly everyone, create for themselves an _____

_____ . Their acute self-consciousness reveals that young people are often not at ease with the broader _____

_____ .

14. Adolescent egocentrism enables them to reflect more thoughtfully on their lives but often at the cost of great _____ .

Schools, Learning, and the Adolescent Mind (pp. 416–422)

15. The best setting for personal growth, called the optimum _____–

_____ _____ ,

depends on several factors, including

_____

_____ .

16. The emergence of hypothetical, abstract thought makes adolescents _____ (more/less) interested in the opinions of others. At the same time, they are _____ (more/less) vulnerable to criticism than their behaviors imply. Instead of there being a good fit between adolescents' needs and the schools, there is often a _____

_____ .

Cite several ways in which educational settings tend *not* to be supportive of adolescents' self-confidence.

17. One outcome of the relatively common mismatch between student needs and the school environment is a widespread dip in academic _____ as young people enter middle school.

18. Educational goals _____ (vary/do not vary) by culture. Similarly, the goals of the American education system _____ (have/have not) changed

much over the centuries. Ethnic diversity and geographic differences in learning also are widespread and deep. One example is the widespread national variation in the _____ _____ completion rate.

19. One debate concerns the extent to which academic grades should be based solely on individual _____ _____ , with students _____ against each other from best in the class to worst. In such situations, many students, especially _____ and students from _____ backgrounds, find it psychologically safer not to work very hard.

20. One possible solution to the stress of individual competition is to encourage team projects and discussion groups, which allow students to succeed if they _____ . In this type of learning, the goal is to excel at the _____ , not necessarily to be better than one's classmates.

21. One benefit of cooperative learning is that it often provides students with their first exposure to people of different _____ , _____ , _____ , and _____ backgrounds.

22. Cooperative learning is _____ (more/less) likely to lead to rivalry among various ethnic, religious, and racial groups.

Adolescent Decision Making (pp. 422–432)

23. For most of the big decisions, such as whether and where to go to college or find a job, adolescents _____ (do/do not) play a major role in choosing.

24. (Changing Policy) Attitudes regarding after-school jobs _____ (vary/do not vary) from country to country.

25. (Changing Policy) In some nations, such as _____ , almost no adolescent is employed or even does significant chores at home. In many _____ countries, many older adolescents have jobs as part of their

school curriculum. Most parents in the United States _____ (approve/do not approve) of youth employment.

26. (Changing Policy) Perhaps because many of today's jobs for adolescents are not _____ , research finds that when adolescents are employed more than _____ hours a week, their grades suffer. As adults, those who were employed extensively as teenagers are more likely to use _____ and to feel _____ (more/less) connected to their families.

27. Generally, research reveals that adolescent beliefs, values, and reasoning processes _____ (do/do not) significantly affect their sexual behavior.

28. Diseases that are spread by sexual contact are called _____ _____ diseases. Among these are _____ _____ . Sexually active adolescents also risk exposure to the _____ virus.

29. Teenagers today have _____ (more/fewer) pregnancies than adults in their 20s and _____ (more/fewer) than teenagers did 35 years ago.

30. A major factor in the teen birth problem is that in 1960, most teenage mothers _____ (were/were not) married, _____ (wanted/did not want) their babies, and expected to be _____ . Today, most teenage mothers _____ (are/are not) married, and most _____ (wanted/did not want) to become pregnant.

Describe the likely consequences to all concerned of an American adolescent giving birth.

31. Most young people _____
(believe/do not believe) sex should occur within
the context of a committed, loving relationship.
This attitude _____
(varies/does not vary) from country to country.

32. Unfortunately, for many adolescents, high-risk
behaviors are a proven way to _____
_____ .

33. Ignorance about sex and unavailability of contraception _____ (do/do not) explain
the high rates of adolescent pregnancy and STDs.

34. Knowing facts about sex has so little effect on
adolescent sexual behavior, because they find it
difficult to envision all the _____
_____ ; instead,
they focus on _____ considerations
or difficulties.

35. The first step in encouraging adolescents to make
more rational decisions about their sexuality
requires adults to be more _____
in *their* thinking about adolescent sexuality.

36. Many school systems are revising their sex education programs to make them more
_____ and focused on
_____ _____ .

37. (A Life-Span View) Most parents _____
(are/are not) adequate sex educators for their
children. One reason is that many parents are too
_____ in beginning to discuss sexu-
al issues.

38. (A Life-Span View) One study found that mothers who were more religious, and more disap-
proving of teen sex, were _____
(less/more) likely to know when their children
were sexually active.

39. In the United States, the teenage birth rate
_____ (increased/declined)
between 1991 and 1997. At the same time, con-
dom use among _____
(males/females/both sexes) has
_____ (increased/decreased). This
latter change parallels a change in
_____ and _____
_____ .

Testing Yourself

After you have completed the audio and text review
questions, see how well you do on the following quiz.
Correct answers, with text and audio references, may
be found at the end of this chapter.

1. One distinguishing feature of adolescent thought
is the ability to think in terms of:
   a. concrete operations.
   b. sensory-motor schemas.
   c. "us" versus "them."
   d. possibility as well as reality.

2. The imaginary audience refers to:
   a. the concrete operational child's preoccupation
   with performing for everyone, including toys
   and imaginary people.
   b. the adolescent's fear of being spied on.
   c. the ability of adolescents to empathize with
   others by putting themselves in their shoes.
   d. the egocentric fantasy of adolescents that their
   behavior and appearance are constantly being
   monitored by others.

3. According to Piaget, the final stage of cognitive
development is that of:
   a. concrete operations.
   b. practical intelligence.
   c. formal operations.
   d. postformal operations.

4. A chief executive officer of a major company who
does poorly on standardized intelligence tests,
yet is very successful professionally, would probably be described by Robert Sternberg as possess-
ing considerable:
   a. practical intelligence.
   b. fluid intelligence.
   c. crystallized intelligence.
   d. egocentrism.

5. The personal fable refers to adolescents':
   a. preoccupation with what they perceive as
   faults in their appearance and personality.
   b. fantasy of being destined to live heroic lives of
   fame and fortune.
   c. belief that they are the center of attention
   everywhere they go.
   d. earliest memories and myths of their origin.

6. Many psychologists consider the distinguishing feature of adolescent thought to be the ability to think in terms of:
   a. moral issues.
   b. concrete operations.
   c. possibility, not just reality.
   d. logical principles.

7. Piaget's last stage of cognitive development is:
   a. formal operational thought.
   b. concrete operational thought.
   c. universal ethical principles.
   d. symbolic thought.

8. Advances in metamemory and metacognition deepen adolescents' abilities in:
   a. studying.
   b. the invincibility fable.
   c. the personal fable.
   d. adolescent egocentrism.

9. The adolescent who takes risks and feels immune to the laws of mortality is showing evidence of the:
   a. invincibility fable.   c. imaginary audience.
   b. personal fable.   d. death instinct.

10. Imaginary audiences, invincibility fables, and personal fables are expressions of adolescent:
    a. morality.   c. decision making.
    b. thinking games.   d. egocentrism.

11. The typical adolescent is:
    a. tough-minded.
    b. indifferent to public opinion.
    c. self-absorbed and hypersensitive to criticism.
    d. all of the above.

12. When adolescents enter secondary school, many:
    a. experience a drop in their academic self-confidence.
    b. are less motivated than they were in elementary school.
    c. are less conscientious than they were in elementary school.
    d. experience all of the above.

13. Over the past century, the goals of education in the United States have:
    a. not substantially changed.
    b. shifted from an emphasis on vocational training to scientific understanding.
    c. shifted from an emphasis on scientific understanding to vocational training.
    d. come more in line with the rest of the developed world.

14. Thinking that begins with a general premise and then draws logical conclusions from it is called:
    a. inductive reasoning.
    b. deductive reasoning.
    c. "the game of thinking."
    d. hypothetical reasoning.

15. Serious reflection on important issues is a wrenching process for many adolescents because of their newfound ability to reason:
    a. inductively.   c. hypothetically.
    b. deductively.   d. symbolically.

16. The main reason for high rates of STDs and pregnancy during adolescence is cognitive immaturity, as evidenced by:
    a. the decline of the "good girl" morality.
    b. increased sexual activity.
    c. the inability to think logically about the consequences of sexual activity.
    d. a lack of information about sexual matters.

17. Many adolescents seem to believe that *their* love-making will not lead to pregnancy. This belief is an expression of the:
    a. personal fable.   c. imaginary audience.
    b. invincibility fable.   d. "game of thinking."

18. (Changing Policy) A parent in which of the following countries is *least* likely to approve of her daughter's request to take a part-time job after school?
    a. the United States   c. Great Britain
    b. Germany   d. Japan

19. Many school systems have revised their sex education classes to be:
    a. more practical and focused on social interaction.
    b. based on scare tactics designed to discourage sexual activity.
    c. more dependent upon bringing the parents into the education process.
    d. changed in all of the above ways.

20. To estimate the risk of a behavior, such as unprotected sexual intercourse, it is most important that the adolescent be able to think clearly about:
    a. universal ethical principles.
    b. personal beliefs and self-interest.
    c. probability.
    d. peer pressure.

NAME _____   INSTRUCTOR _____

LESSON 15: LOGICAL VERSUS PRACTICAL INTELLIGENCE

Exercise

During adolescence, **formal operational thought**—including **scientific reasoning**, logical construction of arguments, and critical thought—becomes possible. Piaget's finding that adolescents are more logical and systematic than preadolescents has been replicated in experiments many times. But not all problems encountered by adolescents and adults require thinking at this level. Also, while many adolescents and adults are capable of thinking logically, they do not always do so. Indeed, older adults often find that a formal approach to solving problems is unsatisfactory and oversimplified.

One theme of this lesson is that a new kind of **practical intelligence** begins to emerge during late adolescence and early adulthood. This type of thinking is more applicable to everyday situations than formal thought. It recognizes that for many problems there may be no single correct answer, and that "logical" answers are often impractical. Some researchers believe that this new way of thinking reflects the greater cognitive maturity of adults in reconciling formal thought with the reality of their lives. If this is true, measuring adult intelligence by the same standards used to assess the "pure" logic of the adolescent is clearly inappropriate.

To stimulate your own thinking about the difference between formal thought and practical intelligence, consider the following problems. After you have answered the questions, hand the completed exercise in to your instructor.

1. In audio program 12, several children were presented with a Piagetian conservation-of-area task. Five "houses" were arranged in different ways on two "meadows." In one arrangement, representing a town, the houses were placed in a single group in one corner of the meadow. In another, representing the country, the houses were scattered about the meadow. Children were asked whether the spatial arrangement of the houses would affect the amount of grass each house's residents needed to mow. Would there be more grass to cut in the "town" or in the "country"?

   a. What is the *logically* correct answer to this question?

   b. What *practical* reasons might lead one to think differently about this question?

2. A woman threatens to leave her drunkard husband if he comes home drunk one more time. One week later, he comes home drunk. What should the woman do?

    a. What is the *logical* answer to this question?

    b. What is a more *practical* answer to this problem, and why?

3. Consider the following domestic scene:

    Downstairs, there are three rooms: the kitchen, the dining room, and the sitting room. The sitting room is in the front of the house, and the kitchen and dining room face onto the vegetable garden at the back of the house. The noise of the traffic is very disturbing in the front of the house. Mother is in the kitchen cooking and Grandfather is reading the paper in the sitting room. The children are at school and won't be home until tea time. Who is being disturbed by the traffic noise?*

    a. What is the *logical* answer to this question?

    b. What *practical* considerations might lead one to a different answer to this question?

4. Describe or create a "real-life" problem in which the logical answer may differ from a practical answer.

   a. State the problem.

   b. State the *logical* answer.

   c. State a *practical* answer that differs from the logical answer.

*The example is from Cohen, G. (1979). Language and comprehension in old age. *Cognitive Psychology, 11*, pp. 412–429. One practical consideration suggested by psychologist Gisela Labouvie-Vief is Grandfather's hearing ability.
Labouvie-Vief, G. (1985). Intelligence and cognition. In J. E. Birren and K. W. Schaie (Eds.), *Handbook of the psychology of aging* (2nd ed.). New York: Van Nostrand, pp. 500–530.

LESSON GUIDELINES

Audio Question Guidelines

1. The development of **formal operational thought** enables adolescents to move beyond the concrete operational world of "here and now" to a world of possibility, where abstract, logical, and scientific thinking becomes typical.

   Because they are able to speculate about possibilities, adolescents often think about ideal parents and an ideal society. This idealism may cause some teenagers to become dissatisfied with their present situation and want to change it. Adolescents are also able to imagine ideal mates, and so they are susceptible to "crushes."

2. Formal operational thought is hypothetical, logical, and abstract. This kind of thinking is emphasized by schools and teachers.

   According to Robert Sternberg, most of the everyday problems people face do not have clear correct or incorrect solutions that can be arrived at by using formal operational thinking.

   In addition to academic intelligence, a valuable kind of thinking that educators generally overlook is **practical intelligence**. This is the ability to adapt, shape, and select real-world environments. It represents an ability to function effectively in the everyday world.

   Many people who have relatively low scores on standardized tests of academic intelligence may nevertheless be very successful in careers in which practical intelligence is especially useful.

3. According to David Elkind, **adolescent egocentrism**, which is different from childhood egocentrism, leads young people to see themselves as being much more central to their social world than they really are. Adolescents often create an **imaginary audience** for themselves and fantasize about how others will react to their appearance and behavior.

   Egocentrism may also lead adolescents to develop their own **personal fable**, in which they imagine their lives as heroic or destined for fame and fortune, and an **invincibility fable**, in which they see themselves as immune to dangers.

   These cognitive tendencies prepare the way for the process of forming a life story. Through them the teenager begins to define how he or she is different from others, which leads to the formation of an **identity**. Over time, the early fantasies and fables become more realistic. The older adolescent develops a belief and value system that serves as an **ideological** background for his or her life story.

Textbook Question Answers

1. continue to progress
2. selective attention; knowledge base; metamemory; metacognition
3. formal operational; is; possibilities; hypothetical
4. less
5. inductive
6. deductive; premise; theory; conclusions
7. absolutist
8. scientific

Preschoolers have no understanding of how to solve the problem. By age 7, children understand balancing the weights but don't know that distance from the center is also a factor. By age 10, they understand the concepts but are unable to coordinate them. By ages 13 or 14, they are able to solve the problem.

9. does not always occur; less; do; education; historical; one-third; one-third; one-third; had
10. adolescent egocentrism
11. invincibility fable
12. personal fable
13. imaginary audience; social world
14. self-criticism
15. person–environment fit; the individual's developmental stage, cognitive strengths, and learning style as well as the traditions, educational objectives, and future needs of the society
16. more; more; volatile mismatch

Compared to elementary schools, most secondary schools have more rigid behavioral demands, intensified competition, more punitive grading practices, as well as less individualized attention and procedures.

17. achievement
18. vary; have; high school
19. test performance; ranked; girls; minority
20. cooperate; task
21. economic; ethnic; religious; racial
22. less
23. do not
24. vary
25. Japan; European; approve
26. meaningful; 15; drugs; less
27. do
28. sexually transmitted; gonorrhea, genital herpes, syphilis, and chlamydia; HIV
29. fewer; fewer

30. were; wanted; full-time homemakers; are not; did not want

For the mother, the consequences include interference with education and social, personal, and vocational growth; for the couple if they marry, greater risk of abuse, abandonment, or divorce; for the child, greater risk of prenatal and birth complications, of lower academic achievement, and, at adolescence, of drug abuse, delinquency, dropping out of school, and early parenthood.

31. believe; does not vary

32. gain status, bond with friends, and free emotions, at least for the moment

33. do not

34. possible alternatives (or consequences); immediate

35. rational

36. practical; social interaction

37. are not; late

38. less

39. declined; both sexes; increased; attitudes; sexual communication

Answers to Testing Yourself

1. **d.** is the answer. Before she or he attains formal operational thought, the child is limited to thinking about the concrete world of the here and now; the adolescent, by contrast, is capable of dealing with possibilities and with the future. (audio program; textbook, p. 408)

2. **d.** is the answer. The imaginary audience is an especially vivid expression of adolescent egocentrism. (audio program; textbook, p. 415)

3. **c.** is the answer. (audio program; textbook, p. 407)

4. **a.** is the answer. Practical intelligence is the ability to function effectively in the everyday world. (audio program)

5. **b.** is the answer. The personal fable is another manifestation of adolescent egocentrism. (audio program; textbook, p. 413)

6. **c.** is the answer. (textbook, p. 408)

   a. Although moral reasoning becomes much deeper during adolescence, it is not limited to this stage of development.

   b. & d. Concrete operational thought, which *is* logical, is the distinguishing feature of childhood thinking.

7. **a.** is the answer. (textbook, p. 407)

   b. In Piaget's theory, this stage precedes formal operational thought.

   c. & d. These are not stages in Piaget's theory.

8. **a.** is the answer. (textbook, p. 407)

   b., c., & d. These are examples of limited reasoning ability during adolescence.

9. **a.** is the answer. (textbook, p. 413)

   b. This refers to adolescents' tendency to imagine their own lives as unique, heroic, or even mythical.

   c. This refers to adolescents' tendency to fantasize about how others will react to their appearance and behavior.

   d. This is a concept in Freud's theory.

10. **d.** is the answer. These thought processes are manifestations of adolescents' tendency to see themselves as being much more central and important to the social scene than they really are. (textbook, p. 413)

11. **c.** is the answer. (textbook, p. 407)

12. **d.** is the answer. (textbook, pp. 416–417)

13. **b.** is the answer. (textbook, p. 418)

    d. Educational goals vary widely from nation to nation.

14. **b.** is the answer. (textbook, pp. 409–410)

    a. Inductive reasoning moves from specific facts to a general conclusion.

    b. & c. The "game of thinking," which is an example of hypothetical reasoning, involves the ability to think creatively about possibilities.

15. **c.** is the answer. (textbook, p. 409)

16. **c.** is the answer. (textbook, p. 428)

    a. The text does not suggest that declining moral standards are responsible for the increased rate of STDs.

    b. Although this may be true, in itself it is not necessarily a result of adolescent cognitive immaturity.

    d. Various studies have found that merely understanding the facts of sexuality does not correlate with more responsible and cautious sexual behavior.

17. **b.** is the answer. (textbook, pp. 413, 428)

    a. This refers to adolescents' tendency to imagine their own lives as unique, heroic, or even mythical.

    c. This refers to adolescents' tendency to fantasize about how others will react to their appearance and behavior.

d. This is the adolescent ability to suspend knowledge of reality in order to think playfully about possibilities.

18. **d.** is the answer. Japanese adolescents almost never work after school. (textbook, p. 423)

a. American parents generally approve of adolescent employment.

b. & c. Jobs are an important part of the school curriculum in many European countries.

19. **a.** is the answer. (textbook, p. 429)

b. Scare tactics were often a central feature of earlier sex education classes.

c. Generally speaking, parents are not effective sex educators.

20. **c.** is the answer. (textbook, p. 428)

Reference

Sternberg, R. J., & Wagner, R. K. (1994). *Mind in context: Interactionist perspectives on human intelligence.* Cambirdge, MA: Cambridge University Press.

In this highly readable book, Professor Sternberg develops his concept of practical intelligence and explains how people can improve their intellectual skills.

Adolescence: Psychosocial Development

AUDIO PROGRAM: Second Chances

ORIENTATION

As discussed in Lessons 14 and 15, the biosocial changes of adolescence transform the child's body into that of an adult, while the cognitive changes enable the young person to think logically and more practically. These changes set the stage for psychosocial development, which is the subject of Lesson 16.

According to Erik Erikson, adolescence brings the dawning of commitment to a personal **identity** and future, to other people, and to ideologies (see also Lesson 15). Friends, family, community, and culture are powerful social forces that act to help or hinder the adolescent's transition from childhood to adulthood.

Chapter 16 of *The Developing Person Through the Life Span, 5/e,* focuses on the adolescent's efforts toward **identity achievement**. The influences family, friends, and society have on psychosocial development are examined in detail, as are the normal difficulties and special problems of adolescence. These problems include suicide and minor lawbreaking.

Audio program 16, "Second Chances," examines the psychosocial challenges of adolescence, emphasizing the particular vulnerability of today's teenagers. This vulnerability is dramatically illustrated by the stories of two teenage "casualties." Although Valerie and Tony have troubled beginnings, both teenagers were afforded "second chances" and seem to be taking advantage of them.

While many of today's teenagers are visibly damaged by the problems of this tumultuous season, the image of the troubled adolescent as irretrievable is not accurate. Through the expert commentary of psychologists Ruby Takanishi and Richard Jessor, we discover that although peer group pressure is often the initial trigger for problem behaviors in adolescence, the socializing role of peers has many potentially positive effects—in particular, peers facilitate identity formation, independence, and the development of

social skills that help the young person eventually attain adult status and maturity.

As adolescents forge an identity and attempt to make wise choices about the future, their social context encourages some paths to identity and forecloses others. The result of this interaction will be, in the ideal case, young people who are sure of themselves and are able to pass through these vulnerable years of adolescence successfully.

LESSON GOALS

By the end of this lesson you should be prepared to:

1. Describe the development of identity during adolescence, focusing on four identity statuses.

2. Discuss parental influence on identity formation, including the effect of parent–adolescent conflict and other aspects of family functioning.

3. Discuss the constructive functions of peer relationships and close friendships during adolescence.

4. Discuss adolescent suicide, noting its incidence and prevalence, contributing factors, warning signs, and gender and national variations.

5. Discuss delinquency among adolescents today, noting its prevalence, significance for later development, and best approaches for prevention or treatment.

Audio Assignment

Listen to the audio tape that accompanies Lesson 16: "Second Chances."

Write answers to the following questions. You may replay portions of the program if you need to refresh your memory. Answer guidelines can be found in the Lesson Guidelines section at the end of this chapter.

1. Explain why early adolescence is considered a period of particular vulnerability for young people today.

2. Discuss the issue of retrievability in adolescence and who is most likely to receive a "second chance."

3. Identify and explain the kinds of interventions that have helped adolescents take advantage of such second chances.

Textbook Assignment

Read Chapter 16: "Adolescence: Psychosocial Development," pages 435–460 in *The Developing Person Through the Life Span, 5/e*, then work through the material that follows to review it. Complete the sentences and answer the questions. As you proceed, evaluate your performance for each secdtion by consulting the answers on page 203. Do not continue with the next section until you understand each answer. If you need to, review or reread the appropriate section in the textbook before continuing.

The Self and Identity (pp. 435–439, 440)

1. The momentous changes that occur during the teen years challenge adolescents to find their own _____ .

2. According to Erikson, the challenge of adolescence is _____ _____
_____ _____ .

3. The ultimate goal of adolescence is to establish a new identity that involves both repudiation and assimilation of childhood values; this is called _____ _____ .

4. The young person who prematurely accepts earlier roles and parental values without exploring alternatives or truly forging a unique identity is experiencing identity _____ .

5. An adolescent who adopts an identity that is the opposite of the one he or she is expected to adopt has taken on a _____
_____ .

6. The young person who has few commitments to goals or values and is apathetic about defining his or her identity is experiencing
_____ _____ .

7. A time-out period during which a young person experiments with different identities, postponing important choices, is called an identity
_____ .

8. Adolescents who have _____
_____ and those who have prematurely _____ tend to have a strong sense of ethnic identification. Those who have _____ tend to be high in prejudice, while those who are _____
_____ tend to be relatively low in prejudice.

9. The process of identity formation can take _____ or longer.

10. The surrounding culture can aid identity formation in two ways: by providing _____ and by providing _____ _____
and _____ that ease the transition from childhood to adulthood.

11. In a culture where most people hold the same moral, political, religious, and sexual values, identity is _____ (easier/more difficult) to achieve.

12. (In Person) For minority-group members, identity achievement is often _____ (more/

less) difficult than it is for other adolescents. This may cause them to embrace a _____ identity or, as is more often the case, to _____ on identity prematurely.

Family and Friends (pp. 439–449)

13. People who focus on differences between the younger and older generations speak of a _____ _____ . An exception occurs when the parents grow up in a very different _____ and _____ .

14. The idea that family members in different developmental stages have a natural tendency to see the family in different ways is called the _____ _____ .

15. Parent–adolescent conflict is most common in _____ (early/late) adolescence and is particularly notable with _____ (mothers/fathers) and their _____ (early/late)-maturing _____ (sons/daughters). This conflict often involves _____ , which refers to repeated, petty arguments about daily habits.

16. Among Chinese, Korean, and Mexican American teens, conflict tends to arise in _____ (early/late) adolescence possibly due the fact that these cultures encourage _____ in their children and emphasize family _____ .

17. Four other elements of family functioning that have been heavily researched include _____ , _____ , _____ , and _____ .

18. In terms of family control, a powerful deterrent to delinquency, risky sex, and drug abuse is _____ _____ . Too much interference, however, may contribute to adolescent _____ .

19. Overall, parent–teen relations in all family types and nations, and among children of both sexes, are typically _____ . If there is conflict, it is more likely to center on details like the adolescent's _____

_____
rather than on _____
_____ .

20. According to B. Bradford Brown, during adolescence the peer group serves four important functions.

   a. _____
   b. _____
      _____
   c. _____
      _____
   d. _____

21. The largely constructive role of peers runs counter to the notion of _____ _____ . Social pressure to conform _____ (falls/rises) dramatically in early adolescence, until about age _____ , when it begins to _____ (fall/rise).

22. For many immigrant families, the normal strain between the generations extends over a _____ (shorter/longer) period of time, because adolescents' physical and cognitive drives mature _____ (before/after) they would in traditional societies. This creates a severe _____ _____ in many minority families.

Outline the course of ethnic identity achievement in young Asian Americans.

23. Usually, the first sign of heterosexual attraction is a seeming _____ of members of the other sex. The pace at which adolescents "warm up" to the other sex _____ (is similar/varies) from culture to culture.

24. Another factor that affects heterosexual attraction is the _____ of puberty.

Adolescents who mature _____ (early/on time/late) generally are the first to reach out to the other sex. Other factors include _____ , _____ , _____ , and the availability of someone in a setting that allows sexual interaction.

(Research Report) Briefly outline the four-stage progression of heterosexual involvement.

25. (Research Report) Cultural patterns _____ (affect/do not affect) the _____ of these stages, but the basic _____ seems to be based on _____ factors.

26. (Research Report) For gay and lesbian adolescents, added complications usually _____ (slow down/speed up) romantic attachments. In cultures that are _____ , many young men and women with homosexual or lesbian feelings may _____ their feelings, or try to _____ or _____ them.

Adolescent Suicide (pp. 450–454)

27. Adolescents under age 20 are _____ (more/less) likely to kill themselves than adults are.

28. Thinking about committing suicide, called _____ _____ , is _____ (common/relatively rare) among high school students.

29. Research from around the world indicates that depression _____ (increases/decreases) at puberty, especially among _____ (males/females).

30. Most suicide attempts in adolescence _____ (do/do not) result in death.

A deliberate act of self-destruction that does not result in death is called a _____ .

31. List five factors that affect whether thinking about suicide leads to a self-destructive act or to death.

a. _____

b. _____

c. _____

d. _____

e. _____

32. (A Life-Span View) The rate of suicide is higher for adolescent _____ (males/females). The rate of parasuicide is higher for _____ (males/females).

33. (A Life-Span View) Around the world, cultural differences in the rates of suicidal ideation and completion _____ (are/are not) apparent.

34. (A Life-Span View) When a town or school sentimentalizes the "tragic end" of a teen suicide, the publicity can trigger _____ _____ .

(A Life-Span View) List several factors that correlate with suicide ideation and completion at any age.

(Table 16.4) Briefly describe ethnic differences in suicide rates in the United States.

35. Suicide rates in North America have _____ (risen/fallen) since 1960. This is due in part to less parental _____ and greater adolescent access to

_____ , _____ , and

_____ .

Breaking the Law (pp. 454–457)

36. Arrests are far more likely to occur during the

    _____ _____

    of life than during any other time period.
    Although statistics indicate that the
    _____ (incidence/prevalence) of
    arrests is highest among this age group, they do
    not reveal how widespread, or
    _____ , lawbreaking is among this
    age group.

37. If all acts of "juvenile delinquency" are included,
    the prevalence of adolescent crime is
    _____ (less/greater) than official
    records report.

Briefly describe data on gender and ethnic differences
in adolescent arrests.

38. (Changing Policy) Experts find it useful to distin-
    guish _____-_____
    offenders, whose criminal activity stops by age
    21, from _____-_____
    _____ offenders, who become
    career criminals.

39. (Changing Policy) Developmentalists have found
    that it_____ (is/is not) currently
    possible to distinguish children who actually will
    become career criminals.

40. (Changing Policy) Adolescents who later become
    career criminals are among the first of their
    cohort to _____

    _____ .

They also are among the least involved in
_____ activities, and tend to be
_____ in preschool and elementary
school. At an even earlier age, they show signs of
_____ _____ , such as
being slow in _____ development,
being _____ , or having poor
_____ control.

41. (Changing Policy) For most delinquents, residen-
    tial incarceration in a prison or reform school
    usually _____ (is/is not) the best
    solution.

(Changing Policy) List several background factors
that increase a child's risk of later becoming a career
criminal.

42. Research from several nations has shown that a
    major risk factor for becoming a violent criminal
    is _____ .

43. The victims of adolescent crime tend to be
    _____ (teenagers/adults).

Conclusion: (pp. 457–458)

44. For most young people, the teenage years overall
    are _____ (happy/unhappy) ones.

45. Adolescents who have one serious problem
    _____ (often have/do not usually
    have) others.

46. In most cases adolescent problems stem from ear-
    lier developmental events such as

    _____ .

Testing Yourself

After you have completed the audio and text review questions, see how well you do on the following quiz. Correct answers, with text and audio references, may be found at the end of this chapter.

1. As discussed in the audio program, "retrievability" refers specifically to the:
   a. cognitive capacity of adolescents to remember their own internalized ideologies.
   b. ability of troubled adolescents to bounce back from problem behaviors and benefit from "second chances."
   c. influence of authoritarian parenting on adolescent identity formation.
   d. permanent mark left on identity by problem behaviors during adolescence.

2. According to Erikson, the primary task of adolescence is that of establishing:
   a. basic trust.   c. intimacy.
   b. an identity.   d. integrity.

3. According to developmentalists who study identity formation, foreclosure involves:
   a. accepting an identity prematurely, without exploration.
   b. taking time off from school, work, and other commitments.
   c. opposing parental values.
   d. failing to commit oneself to a vocational goal.

4. When adolescents adopt an identity that is the opposite of the one they are expected to adopt, they are considered to be taking on a:
   a. foreclosed identity.
   b. diffused identity.
   c. negative identity.
   d. reverse identity.

5. The main sources of emotional support for most young people who are establishing independence from their parents are:
   a. older adolescents of the opposite sex.
   b. older siblings.
   c. teachers.
   d. peer groups.

6. (In Person) For members of minority ethnic groups, identity achievement may be particularly complicated because:
   a. their cultural ideal clashes with the Western emphasis on adolescent self-determination.
   b. peers, themselves torn by similar conflicts, can be very critical.
   c. parents and other relatives tend to emphasize ethnicity and expect teens to honor their roots.
   d. of all of the above reasons.

7. In a crime-ridden neighborhood, parents can protect their adolescents by keeping close watch over activities, friends, and so on. This practice is called:
   a. generational stake.   c. peer screening.
   b. foreclosure.   d. parental monitoring.

8. Conflict between adolescent girls and their mothers is most likely to involve:
   a. bickering over hair, neatness, and other daily habits.
   b. political, religious, and moral issues.
   c. peer relationships and friendships.
   d. relationships with boys.

9. If there is a "generation gap," it is likely to occur in _____ adolescence and to center on issues of _____ .
   a. early; morality   c. early; self-control
   b. late; self-discipline   d. late; politics

10. (In Person) Because of the conflict between their ethnic background and the larger culture, minority adolescents will *most often*:
    a. reject the traditional values of both their ethnic culture and the majority culture.
    b. foreclose on identity prematurely.
    c. declare a moratorium.
    d. experience identity diffusion.

11. (Changing Policy) In the long run, the most effective programs for preventing juvenile delinquency would include all of the following *except*:
    a. helping parents discipline in an authoritative manner.
    b. strengthening the schools.
    c. increasing the police presence in the area.
    d. shoring up neighborhood networks.

12. If the vast majority of cases of a certain crime are committed by a small number of repeat offenders, this would indicate that the crime's:
    a. incidence is less than its prevalence.
    b. incidence is greater than its prevalence.
    c. incidence and prevalence are about equal.
    d. incidence and prevalence are impossible to calculate.

13. Compared with normal adolescents, suicidal adolescents are:
    a. more concerned about the future.
    b. academically average students.
    c. rejected by their peers.
    d. less likely to have attempted suicide.

14. The early signs of life-course-persistent offenders include all of the following *except*:
    a. signs of brain damage early in life.
    b. antisocial school behavior.
    c. delayed sexual intimacy.
    d. use of alcohol and tobacco at an early age.

15. (A Life-Span View) Regarding gender differences in self-destructive acts, the rate of parasuicide is _____ and the rate of suicide is _____ .
    a. higher in males; higher in females
    b. higher in females; higher in males
    c. the same in males and females; higher in males
    d. the same in males and females; higher in females

16. Conflict between parents and adolescent offspring is:
    a. most likely to involve fathers and their early-maturing offspring.
    b. more frequent in single-parent homes.
    c. more likely between early-maturing daughters and their mothers.
    d. likely in all of the above situations.

LESSON GUIDELINES

Audio Question Guidelines

1. The biological changes associated with puberty are occurring among young people today earlier than in the past. Society, however, has not adapted to this change. The result is a relatively long period of time during which young people are physically mature, yet socially denied the privileges and responsibilities of adults.

   There is great diversity in biosocial development during early adolescence; some individuals continue to look like children, while others already resemble adults. This diversity is itself challenging for adolescents.

   Today there may be greater opportunity in the adolescent environment for experimentation and risk taking. This includes pressure from peers to experiment with risky behaviors such as delinquent acts, early sexual activity, and use of alcohol and other drugs.

   Compared to previous generations, adolescents today are exposed to much more lethal substances. This may account for the fact that the leading cause of death among young adolescents is accidents, often related to the diminished judgment that accompanies the use of drugs.

2. Approximately 75 percent of adolescents move through this season relatively easily; about 25 percent are at risk and do not make the transition as successfully.

   For those in early or middle adolescence who come from disadvantaged backgrounds and have already begun to experiment with risky behaviors, opportunities for "second-chance" interventions are especially important.

   Individuals who have been at risk need to perceive that they have a promising future economically and psychologically.

   Many young people have reserves of resiliency that make them eminently "retrievable" from their disadvantaged beginnings. For young people who do not possess this inner tenacity, early provision of social programs may make a major difference.

3. Peer counseling may help adolescents to learn about the dangers of high-risk behaviors, develop independence and social skills, forge a clearer sense of **identity**, and promote self-esteem. It can be helpful both to those who give it and those who receive it.

   Programs that link young people to consistent, caring adults have proven to be beneficial. So has the continuing involvement of parents.

Textbook Question Answers

1. identity
2. identity versus role confusion
3. identity achievement
4. foreclosure
5. negative identity
6. identity diffusion
7. moratorium
8. achieved identity; foreclosed; foreclosed; identity achievers
9. 10 years
10. values; social structures; customs
11. easier
12. more; negative; foreclose
13. generation gap; time; place
14. generational stake
15. early; mothers; early; daughters; bickering
16. late; dependency; closeness
17. communication; support; connectiveness; control
18. parental monitoring; depression
19. supportive; musical tastes, domestic neatness, sleeping habits; world politics or moral issues
20. **a.** a source of information and a self-help group

    b. a source of support for the adolescent who is adjusting to changes in the social ecology of adolescence

    c. a kind of mirror in which to check one's reflection

    d. a sounding board for exploring and defining one's values and aspirations
21. peer pressure; rises; 14; fall
22. longer; before; generation gap

The sequence begins with foreclosure on traditional values, continues with rejection of tradition in favor of mainstream values, is followed by a moratorium, and culminates in identity achievement by connecting with other young Asian Americans.

23. dislike; varies
24. biology; early; culture; peers; parents

The progression begins with groups of same-sex friends. Next, a loose, public association of a girl's group and a boy's group forms. Then, a smaller, heterosexual group forms from the more advanced members of the larger association. Finally, more intimate heterosexual couples peel off.

25. affect; timing; sequence; biological
26. slow down; homophobic; deny; change; conceal
27. less
28. suicidal ideation; common
29. increases; females
30. do not; parasuicide
31. **a.** the availability of lethal methods
    b. the extent of parental supervision
    c. the use of alcohol and other drugs
    d. gender
    e. the attitudes about suicide held by the adolescent's family, friends, and culture
32. males; females
33. are
34. cluster suicides

At any age, these include chronic depression, death of a close friend, drug abuse, loneliness, social rejection, and homosexuality.

Native American males have the highest rates, followed by European American males, Asian American males, African American males, and Hispanic American males.

35. risen; supervision; alcohol, drugs; guns
36. second decade; incidence; prevalent
37. greater

Boys are three times as likely to be arrested as girls, and African American youth are three times as likely to be arrested as European Americans, who are three times as likely to be arrested as Asian Americans.

38. adolescent-limited; life-course persistent
39. is
40. have sex, drink alcohol, and smoke cigarettes; school; antisocial; brain damage; language; hyperactive; emotional
41. is not

Children who have been abused or neglected, who have few friends, who are early substance users, or who are bullies are at higher risk.

42. being a victim of violence
43. teenagers
44. happy
45. often have
46. genetic vulnerability, prenatal insults, family disruptions, childhood discord, learning difficulties, aggressive or withdrawn behavior in elementary school, inadequate community intervention

Answers to Testing Yourself

1. **b.** is the answer. A major theme of the audio program is that the image of the troubled adolescent as irretrievable is incorrect. (audio program)

2. **b.** is the answer. (textbook, p. 435)

   a. According to Erikson, this is the crisis of infancy.

   c. & d. In Erikson's theory, these crises occur later in life.

3. **a.** is the answer. (textbook, p. 436)

   b. This describes an identity moratorium.

   c. This describes a negative identity.

   d. This describes identity diffusion.

4. **c.** is the answer. (textbook, p. 437)

5. **d.** is the answer. (textbook, pp. 443–444)

6. **d.** is the answer. (textbook, p. 440)

7. **d.** is the answer. (textbook, p. 442)

   a. The generational stake refers to differences in how family members from different generations view the family.

   b. Foreclosure refers to the premature establishment of identity.

   c. Peer screening is an aspect of parental monitoring, but it was not specifically discussed in the text.

8. **a.** is the answer. (textbook, p. 441)

9. **c.** is the answer. (textbook, pp. 440–441)

10. **b.** is the answer. (textbook, p. 440)

    a. This occurs in some cases, but not in *most* cases.

    c. Moratorium is a time-out in identity formation in order to allow the adolescent to try out alternative identities. It is generally not a solution in such cases.

    d. Young people who experience identity diffusion are often apathetic, which is not the case here.

11. **c.** is the answer. (textbook, p. 457)

12. **b.** is the answer. Incidence is how often a particular circumstance (such as lawbreaking) occurs; prevalence is how widespread the circumstance is. A crime that is committed by only a few repeat offenders is not very prevalent in the population. (textbook, p. 455)

13. **c.** is the answer. (textbook, p. 453)

14. **c.** is the answer. Most life-course persistent offenders are among the earliest of their cohort to have sex. (textbook, p. 456)

15. b. is the answer. (textbook, p. 452)

16. c. is the answer. (textbook, p. 441)

a. In fact, parent-child conflict is more likely to involve mothers and their early-maturing offspring.

b. The text did not compare the rate of conflict in two-parent and single-parent homes.

Reference

Jessor, R., & Jessor, S. (1977). *Problem behavior and psychosocial development: A longitudinal study of youth.* New York: Academic Press.

Professor Jessor, who is heard on the audio program, examines issues in high-risk adolescent behaviors.

Early Adulthood: Biosocial Development

AUDIO PROGRAM: Seasons of Eros

ORIENTATION

This is the first of a three-lesson unit on development between the ages of 20 and 40, the period of early adulthood. Lesson 17 focuses on biosocial development during this season.

In terms of our overall health, these years are the prime of life. However, with the attainment of maturity, a new aspect of physical development comes into play—that is, decline. Chapter 17 of *The Developing Person Through the Life Span 5/e*, takes a look at how people perceive changes that occur as the body ages as well as how decisions they make regarding lifestyle affect the course of their overall development.

Biosocial development during early adulthood is not without potential problems, however. The final section looks at three problems that are more prevalent during young adulthood than at any other period of the life span: drug abuse, compulsive eating and destructive dieting, and violence.

Audio program 17, "Seasons of Eros," explores how the expressions and meanings of sexuality, or **eros**, change over the life span. In a round table discussion featuring psychologists Janice Gibson, David Gutmann, and June Reinisch, psychiatrists Robert Butler and Thomas Carli, and psychotherapist Laura Nitzberg, it becomes clear that eros is more than intercourse; it is a capacity for pleasure that pervades the entire body and reflects the particular developmental needs of each individual and each age. The emerging life-span perspective makes it clear that, although its expressions and meanings may change, the life-giving force of eros manifests itself throughout the seasons of life.

LESSON GOALS

By the end of this lesson you should be prepared to:

1. Describe the changes in growth, strength, overall health, and physical appearance that occur during early adulthood.

2. Identify age-related trends in sexual responsiveness of women and men during early adulthod, the main causes of infertility in men and women, and techniques used to treat this problem.

3. Discuss the causes and consequences of drug abuse and repeated dieting during adulthood.

4. Describe the typical victims of anorexia nervosa and bulimia nervosa, and discuss possible explanations for these disorders.

5. Explain how restrictive stereotypes of "masculine" behavior may be related to the self-destructive behaviors of many young Americans.

Audio Assignment

Listen to the audio tape that accompanies Lesson 17: "Seasons of Eros."

Write answers to the following questions. You may replay portions of the program if you need to refresh your memory. Answer guidelines may be found in the Lesson Guidelines section at the end of this chapter.

1. Define "eros," and tell how its meaning changes from the beginning of life through adolescence.

2. Discuss the concept of sexual orientation and how experts believe it emerges in the individual.

3. Describe the ways in which the meaning and expression of eros change during adulthood.

Textbook Assignment

Read Chapter 17: "Early Adulthood: Biosocial Development," pages 465–487 in *The Developing Person Through the Life Span, 5/e*, then work through the material that follows to review it. Complete the sentences and answer the questions. As you proceed, evaluate your performance for each secdtion by consulting the answers on page 219. Do not continue with the next section until you understand each answer. If you need to, review or reread the appropriate section in the textbook before continuing.

1. The early 20s are the best years for

_____

_____

(three categories) .

Growth, Strength, and Health (pp. 465–471)

2. Girls usually reach their maximum height by age _____ , and boys by age _____ .

3. Growth in _____ and increases in _____ continue into the 20s.

4. Physical strength reaches a peak at about age _____ and then decreases.

5. Medical attention in early adulthood is more often necessitated by _____ than by illness.

6. Of the fatal diseases, _____ is the

leading killer of adults under age 75, with fewer than 1 in 10,000 being adults between _____ and _____ years of age.

7. When overall growth stops, _____ , or age-related decline, begins.

8. The earliest signs of aging include wrinkles, caused by loss of _____ in facial skin, and the first _____ _____ , caused by a loss of pigment-producing cells in the head.

9. The kidneys begin to lose their efficiency at about age _____ , declining about _____ percent per decade.

10. Lung efficiency, as measured by _____ _____ , decreases about _____ percent per decade beginning in the 20s.

11. Notable decline occurs in the ability of the eye's _____ to focus on _____ (near/far) objects. At about age _____ this decline reaches the point where it is labeled _____ , and reading glasses are needed.

12. Many of the body's functions serve to maintain _____ ; that is, they keep physiological functioning in a state of balance. The older a person is, the _____ (less time/longer) it takes for these adjustments to occur. This makes it more difficult for older bodies to adapt to, and recover from, _____ _____ .

13. (A Life-Span View) Male and female bodies _____ (do/do not) follow a similar sequence of sexual activation at every age.

14. (A Life-Span View) The sequence of sexual activation begins with _____ , followed by _____ _____ , release through _____ , followed by _____ and _____ .

15. (A Life-Span View) During the early years of manhood, sexual excitement, which includes

_____

_____

and _____

_____ , can

occur very quickly and frequently. As men grow older, they often need stimulation that is more _____ or _____ to initiate sexual excitement.

16. (A Life-Span View) Age-related trends in sexual responsiveness _____ (are/are not) as clear-cut for women. As they mature from adolescence toward middle adulthood, women become more likely to experience

_____ .

(A Life-Span View) State several possible reasons for this age-related trend in women.

17. For most of us, our bodies, if adequately maintained, are capable of functioning quite well until we are at least age _____ . The declines of aging primarily affect our

_____ _____ , which is

defined as _____

_____ .

18. The muscles of the body _____ (do/do not) have the equivalent of an organ reserve.

19. The average maximum heart rate _____ (declines/remains stable/increases) with age. Resting heart rate _____ (declines/remains stable/increases) with age.

Briefly explain why most of the age-related biological changes that occur during the first decades of adulthood are of little consequence to the individual.

20. Age-related biological changes *are* particularly noticeable in professional _____ and serious weekend players.

21. Performance in sports that demand vigorous _____ motor skills peaks in the 20s; in those that demand _____ motor skills, in the _____ . An important factor in the impact of aging on athletic performance, however, is the individual's

_____ .

The Sexual-Reproductive System (pp. 471–476)

22. In both sexes, sexual responsiveness, sexual preference, and sexual orientation vary for many reasons, including _____

_____ , _____

_____ , and _____

_____ as well as _____

_____ .

23. In early adulthood, sexual activity increases in both _____ and _____ . Moreover, individuals are more likely to be in _____ relationships, which partly explains why the use of _____ increases and _____ decreases over the years of early adulthood.

24. Most women can still bear a first child as late as age _____ , and most men can father a child _____ .

25. About _____ percent of all married couples experience infertility, which is defined as

_____ .

Age is _____ (often/rarely) a contributing factor to this problem.

26. The most common fertility problem in men lies in the _____ _____ of sperm or in the sperm's poor swimming ability, or _____ .

27. Sperm grow in the _____ over a period of _____ .

List several factors that can alter normal sperm development.

28. The above factors can also affect fertility in women. Two additional conditions that can contribute to female infertility are being _____ or _____ .

29. The most common fertility problem in women is difficulty with _____ . Most women find that ovulation becomes _____ (more/less) regular as middle age approaches. Older women take _____ (longer/less time) to conceive, and they are more likely to give birth to _____ when they do.

30. The other common fertility problem for women is blocked _____ _____ , often caused by _____ _____ _____ that was not treated promptly. Sexually transmitted diseases, such as _____ , can cause such infections.

31. A woman who has trouble conceiving may have _____ , a condition in which fragments of the _____ _____ block the reproductive tract. This disorder is most common after age _____ .

32. A final cause of female infertility is _____ problems that prevent _____ .

33. Most physicians recommend that women begin their childbearing before age _____ and would-be fathers before age _____ .

34. Many infertility problems can also be overcome by modern medical techniques, such as _____ to open blocked genital ducts or Fallopian tubes, or the use of _____ to stimulate ovulation. Another possibility is _____ _____ _____ , in which ova are fertilized outside the ovaries. The success rate of this technique is about one baby in _____ attempts. Two variations of this technique, _____ and _____ , involve inserting either sperm and unfertilized _____ or _____ into the Fallopian tube.

35. (In Person) These alternative paths to reproduction raise profound _____ and _____ questions. Another issue is the _____ _____ of alternative conception.

36. (In Person) About _____ of all infertile couples who remain untreated eventually have a baby, and about _____ of the couples who are treated never do.

Three Health Problems (pp. 476–486)

37. Three problems that are more prevalent in early adulthood are _____ _____ , _____ _____ , and _____ .

38. When the absence of a drug in a person's system causes physiological or psychological craving, _____ _____ is apparent.

39. The late teens and early 20s are the time of heaviest _____ and _____ consumption. The greatest use of other drugs, such as _____ , occurs at about age _____ .

40. In general, young adults are _____ (more likely/no more likely) to be addicts than are adolescence or older adults.

41. Women use drugs _____ (less often than/as often as/more often than) men do.

42. The temperament of those most likely to misuse drugs includes attraction to _____ , intolerance of _____ , and vulnerability to _____ . How powerfully these characteristics affect an individual is influenced by both _____ and early _____ _____ .

43. State four reasons for the high rate of drug use and abuse in the first years of adulthood.

    a. _____

    b. _____

    c. _____

    d. _____

44. Drug abuse and addiction generally _____ (increase/ decrease) from age _____ to _____ .

45. Compared to others their age, young adult drug users are more likely to _____ _____ .

46. Many scientists believe that each person has a certain _____ for his or her weight. List the factors that can affect this point.

47. To measure whether a person is too fat or too thin, clinicians calculate his or her _____ _____ _____ , defined as the ratio of _____ (in kilograms) divided by _____ (in meters squared).

48. (text and Changing Policy) The tendency to maintain body weight at a healthy level can be undermined by _____ _____ and specifics of the social context, such as the notion that an ideal body is _____- _____ . The subset of the population that is most susceptible to this notion is women in the _____ _____ (which country?) of _____ ancestry.

49. (Changing Policy) One survey of North American dieters found that those who were _____ , well-_____ , and _____ were the ones most likely to diet. The same survey reported that the average women during early adulthood would like to weigh _____ pounds less, and the average man about _____ pounds more.

50. (Changing Policy) Women who attempt to reach a target weight that is substantially below their set point generally _____ (do/do not) eventually regain it.

51. (Changing Policy) Crash dieting can result in _____ _____ , _____ _____ , and _____ to disease. As the dangers of eating disorders have become more widely known, women in the United States aged 20 to 34 _____ (are/are not) becoming less likely to be too thin. At the same time, the number of women who are obese has _____ (increased/decreased).

52. Dieting may also trigger physiological changes that lead to an eating disorder such as _____ , an affliction characterized by _____ , or the _____ (more/less) common disorder _____ _____ , which involves successive bouts of binge eating followed by purging through vomiting or massive doses of laxatives.

53. Binge-purge eating can cause a wide range of health problems, including damage to the _____ _____ and _____ _____ from the strain of electrolyte imbalance. A group that is at particular risk for eating disorders is _____ _____ .

Briefly summarize how each of the major theories of development views eating disorders.

Psychoanalytic theory

Learning theory

Cognitive theory

Sociocultural theory

Epigenetic systems theory

54. Stereotypes about "manly" behavior may lead to a problem that afflicts mostly young men—that is, behavior that leads to _____

_____ .

55. Many experts believe that _____

_____

are at the root of masculine violence. These values, however, can change, as evidenced by the decline in automobile crash rates involving young drunk men in response to the activism of groups such as _____ and

_____ .

56. Some experts believe that aggression is the result of an "explosive combination" of high _____ and dashed _____ . A blow to the individual's _____ is more likely to result in violence when the individual is under the influence of _____ ; when there is a _____ present; and when the individual lacks _____ .

57. (Research Report) The extent of masculine violence, as reflected in rates of _____ , _____ (varies/does not vary) from culture to culture.

58. (Research Report) A contextual factor frequently cited for the high rates of homicide among young American men is the availability of _____ . Research _____ (confirms/does not confirm) that the presence of a gun often transforms non-lethal aggressive impulses into deadly ones.

59. (Research Report) The leading cause of death for young African-American and Latino men is _____ , while among European-American men, _____ are the number one cause.

Testing Yourself

After you have completed the audio and text review questions, see how well you do on the following quiz. Correct answers, with text and audio references, may be found at the end of this chapter.

1. *Eros* is most broadly defined as:
   a. the biological drive to reproduce.
   b. the drive to obtain pleasure and avoid pain.
   c. our species' natural attraction to members of the opposite sex.
   d. the desire for sexual and sensual pleasure.

2. Approximately _____ percent of the population is estimated to have a homosexual orientation.
   a. 1
   b. 5
   c. 10
   d. 20

3. Which of the following is true regarding the development of a homosexual orientation?
   a. Homosexuality is the product of a combination of biological and environmental influences.
   b. Homosexuality arises out of fear of the opposite sex.
   c. Most homosexuals were sexually molested as children.
   d. Homosexuality develops most readily in families with domineering mothers and weak, ineffectual fathers.

4. During which season(s) of life does eros tend to be diffused throughout the body and sense organs?
   a. adolescence
   b. early adulthood
   c. later adulthood
   d. both a. and b.

5. During which season(s) of life does eros tend to be most narrowly focused?
   a. childhood
   b. early adulthood
   c. later adulthood
   d. both b. and c.

6. Senescence refers to:
   a. a loss of efficiency in the body's regulatory systems.
   b. age-related decline.
   c. decreased physical strength.
   d. vulnerability to disease.

7. When do noticeable increases in height stop?
   a. at about the same age in men and women
   b. at an earlier age in women than in men
   c. at an earlier age in men than in women
   d. There is such diversity in physiological development that it is impossible to generalize regarding this issue.

8. A difference between men and women during early adulthood is that men have:
   a. a higher percentage of body fat.
   b. lower metabolism.
   c. proportionately more muscle.
   d. greater organ reserve.

9. The majority of young adults rate their own health as:
   a. very good or excellent.
   b. average or fair.
   c. poor.
   d. worse than it was during adolescence.

10. The automatic adjustment of the body's systems to keep physiological functions in a state of equilibrium, even during heavy exertion, is called:
    a. organ reserve.   c. stress.
    b. homeostasis.   d. muscle capacity.

11. Which of the following temperamental characteristics was *not* identified as being typical of drug abusers?
    a. attraction to excitement
    b. intolerance of frustration
    c. extroversion
    d. vulnerability to depression

12. (A Life-Span View) As men grow older:
    a. they often need more direct stimulation to initiate sexual excitement.
    b. a longer time elapses between the beginning of sexual excitement and full erection.
    c. a longer time elapses between orgasm and the end of the refractory period.
    d. all of the above occur.

13. It is estimated that infertility affects:
    a. at least half of all married couples in which the woman is in her early 30s.
    b. men more than women.
    c. about one-third of all married couples.
    d. about 15 percent of all married couples.

14. Sperm develop in the testes over a period of:
    a. one month.
    b. four days.
    c. seventy-four days.
    d. one year.

15. Endometriosis is:
    a. a sexually transmitted disease.
    b. lack of ovulation or irregular ovulation in an older woman.
    c. a disease characterized by the presence of uterine tissue on the surface of the ovaries or the Fallopian tubes.
    d. a condition that invariably results from pelvic inflammatory disease.

16. In vitro fertilization is a solution for infertility that is caused by:
    a. endometriosis.
    b. low sperm count.
    c. low sperm count or ovulatory problems.
    d. PID.

17. A 50-year-old woman can expect to retain what percentage of her strength at age 20?

    a. 25

    b. 50

    c. 75

    d. 90

18. According to epigenetic systems theory, eating disorders such as anorexia nervosa are more common in young women who are genetically susceptible to:

    a. depression.

    b. alcohol abuse.

    c. obesity.

    d. suicide.

19. (Research Report) The leading cause of death among young adult African-American men is:

    a. cancer.

    b. homicide.

    c. fatal accidents.

    d. suicide.

20. Which of the following was *not* suggested as a reason for the high rate of drug use and abuse in the first years of adulthood?

    a. Young adults often have friends who use drugs.

    b. Young adults are trying to imitate their parents' behavior.

    c. Young adults may use drugs as a way of relieving job or educational stress.

    d. Young adults often fear social rejection.

NAME _____   INSTRUCTOR _____

LESSON 17: EROS IN THE MEDIA

Exercise

When sexuality is broadly defined as eros, it becomes clear that every season of life is sexual. Audio program 17 outlines the changing meanings of eros over the seasons of life.

Sexuality at various ages is often depicted in the popular media of television, magazines, motion pictures, novels, and radio. Television programs and advertising, for example, often employ sexual themes and stereotypes targeted to certain age groups.

The exercise for Lesson 17 asks you to look in the popular media for examples of advertising or programming that include portrayals of eros in various seasons. You may choose examples from current media sources or from your recollections of media portrayals in earlier seasons of your own life. After you have answered the following questions, hand the completed exercise in to your instructor.

Pick three stages of life (from infancy, childhood, adolescence, early adulthood, middle adulthood, or late adulthood) and, for each stage, find two contrasting portrayals of sexuality in the popular media. One portrayal, for example, might show someone in late adulthood as a "dirty old man"; a contrasting portrayal would show an older adult as being asexual. Then answer the following questions for each example.

1. Stage: _____

    a. Describe one portrayal of sexuality.

    b. Describe a contrasting portrayal of sexuality.

    c. Is sexual stereotyping present in either example? If so, in what ways?

  d. What aspects of sexuality during this stage of life are missing or misrepresented in the samples you have chosen?

2. Stage: _____

   a. Describe one portrayal of sexuality.

   b. Describe a contrasting portrayal of sexuality.

   c. Is sexual stereotyping present in either example? If so, in what ways?

   d. What aspects of sexuality during this stage of life are missing or misrepresented in the samples you have chosen?

3. Stage: _____

    a. Describe one portrayal of sexuality.

    b. Describe a contrasting portrayal of sexuality.

    c. Is sexual stereotyping present in either example? If so, in what ways?

    d. What aspects of sexuality during this stage of life are missing or misrepresented in the samples you have chosen?

LESSON GUIDELINES

Audio Question Guidelines

1. When sexuality is broadly defined as **eros**, it becomes clear that every season of life is sexual. Children derive pleasure from touching their bodies, and from the sensory experiences of their eyes, ears, and mouths. In this first season, pleasure is diffused throughout the body.

   As children grow older, they become interested in each other's bodies and curious about where babies come from.

   Around the age of 6, children come to understand that our society is uncomfortable about sexuality and so they become more private, entering what Freud called the period of **latency**.

   In adolescence and early adulthood, eros is directed at others and concentrated in the sexual organs. Sexuality centers on mating and reproduction, although it may not be focused on a particular partner or necessarily coupled with intimacy.

2. In addition to forging a personal identity, each individual develops a sexual orientation toward intimacy with members of the same or opposite sex. Approximately 10 percent of the population is homosexual.

   Experts still do not agree on what causes a person to develop a homosexual or heterosexual orientation. Some suggest that a biological predisposition is involved. One point of agreement is that sexual orientation does *not* appear to be learned. Children who grow up with gay or lesbian parents are no more likely themselves to be gay or lesbian than children who grow up with heterosexual parents. In all probability, it is a combination of certain biological factors and environmental influences that lead to the development of sexual orientation.

3. During early adulthood, eros is coupled with intimacy. A relationship with one special person becomes the basis for marriage and the bearing of children.

   Many couples report that the years of middle adulthood are the most sensual and sexual of their lives, as partners rediscover each other after the children have left home.

   Sex may become less frequent as one gets older, but it tends to be savored more fully, with pleasure diffused over all the senses, just as it was at the beginning of life.

Textbook Question Answers

1. hard physical work, problem-free reproduction, peak athletic performance
2. 16; 18
3. muscle; fat
4. 30
5. injuries
6. cancer; 20; 34
7. senescence
8. elasticity; gray hairs
9. 30; 4
10. vital capacity; 5
11. lens; near; 55; presbyopia
12. homeostasis; longer; physical stress
13. do
14. arousal; peak excitement; orgasm; refraction; recovery
15. faster heartbeat; penile erection; direct (or explicit); prolonged
16. are not; orgasm
    a. The slowing of the man's responses lengthens the sex act, providing the more prolonged stimulation that many women need to reach orgasm.
    b. With experience, both partners may be more likely to recognize and focus on those aspects of love-making that intensify the woman's sexual responses.
    c. The culture may teach women that sex is violent and that they should say no to it. It may take years for women to acknowledge and appreciate their sexuality.
    d. According to the ethological perspective, age-related increases in sexual passions among women are the result of the reduced likelihood of reproduction.
17. 70; organ reserve; the extra capacity that each organ has for responding to unusually stressful events or conditions that demand intense or prolonged effort
18. do
19. declines; remains stable

The declines of aging primarily affect our organ reserve. In the course of normal daily life, adults seldom have to call upon this capacity, so the deficits in organ reserve generally go unnoticed.

20. athletes

21. gross; fine; 30s; lifestyle

22. innate predispositions; childhood experiences; cultural taboos; daily circumstances

23. incidence; prevalence; committed; contraception; abortion

24. 40; at any age

25. 15; being unable to conceive a child after a year or more of intercourse without contraception; often

26. low number; motility

27. testes; 74 days

Anything that impairs normal body functioning, such as illness with a high fever, medical therapy involving radiation or prescription drugs, exposure to environmental toxins, unusual stress, or an episode of drug abuse, can affect the number, shape, and motility of the sperm.

28. underweight; obese

29. ovulation; less; longer; twins

30. Fallopian tubes; pelvic inflammatory disease (PID); gonorrhea or chlamydia

31. endometriosis; uterine lining; 25

32. uterine; implantation

33. 30; 40

34. surgery; drugs; in vitro fertilization (IVF); five; GIFT; ZIFT; ova; zygotes

35. legal; ethical; economic inequality

36. one-third; one-half

37. drug abuse; destructive dieting; violence

38. drug addiction

39. marijuana; alcohol; cocaine; 23

40. more

41. less often than

42. excitement; frustration; depression; genes; family experiences

43. a. For some young adults, drug abuse is a way of striving for independence from parents.

   b. Many abuse drugs in an effort to escape the life stresses that cluster during the 20s.

   c. The group activities of young adults, including large parties, concerts, and sports events, often promote drug use.

   d. Young adults are the group least likely to be regularly exposed to religious faith and practice.

44. increase; 18; 26

45. avoid, fail, or drop out of college; lose or quit jobs; be employed below their potential; be involved in transitory, uncommitted sexual relationships; die violently; and suffer from serious eating disorders

46. set point

Heredity, age, illness, hormones, childhood eating habits, and exercise levels can affect one's set point.

47. body-mass index (BMI); weight; height

48. cultural norms; fat-free; United States; European

49. young; educated; employed; 8; 5

50. do

51. nutritional imbalance; energy loss; vulnerability; are; increased

52. anorexia nervosa; self-starvation; more; bulimia nervosa

53. gastrointestinal system; cardiac arrest; college women

According to psychoanalytic theory, women with eating disorders have a conflict with their mothers, who provided their first nourishment. According to learning theory, disordered eating may set up a stimulus–response chain in which self-starvation relieves emotional stress and tension. Cognitive theory suggests that as women enter the workplace they try to project a strong, self-controlled, "masculine" image. Sociocultural explanations focus on the contemporary cultural pressures to be model-like in appearance. Epigenetic systems theory suggests that because self-starvation may cause menstruation to cease and sexual hormones to decrease, girls who are genetically susceptible to depression or addiction may resort to this self-destructive behavior to relieve the pressures to marry and reproduce.

54. violent death

55. social values; MADD; SADD

56. self-esteem; expectations; self-concept; alcohol; weapon; self-restraint

57. homicide; varies

58. firearms; confirms

59. homicide; accidents

Answers to Testing Yourself

1. **d.** is the answer. (audio program)

2. **c.** is the answer. About 10 percent of the population will eventually identify itself as homosexual. (audio program)

3. **a.** is the answer. (audio program)

4. **c.** is the answer. During later adulthood, as in childhood, eros is spread throughout the body and senses. (audio program)

5. b. is the answer. During early adulthood, eros tends to be focused on mating and reproduction. (audio program)

6. b. is the answer. (textbook, p. 466)

a., c., & d. Each of these is a specific example of the more general process of senescence.

7. b. is the answer. (textbook, p. 465)

8. c. is the answer. (textbook, p. 465)

a. & b. These are true of women.

d. Men and women do not differ in this characteristic.

9. a. is the answer. (textbook, p. 465)

10. b. is the answer. (textbook, p. 467)

a. This is the extra capacity that each organ of the body has for responding to unusually stressful events or conditions that demand intense or prolonged effort.

c. Stress, which is not defined in this chapter, refers to events or situations that tax the body's resources.

d. This simply refers to a muscle's potential for work.

11. c. is the answer. (textbook, p. 478)

12. d. is the answer. (textbook, p. 469)

13. d. is the answer. (textbook, p. 473)

b. Until middle age, infertility is equally likely in women and men.

14. c. is the answer. (textbook, p. 474)

15. c. is the answer. (textbook, p. 474)

a. Sexually transmitted diseases can cause infertility by contributing to pelvic inflammatory disease (PID).

b. This is another common fertility problem in women.

d. PID often is a cause of infertility; it is not, however, the same as endometriosis.

16. c. is the answer. (textbook, p. 475)

17. d. is the answer. (textbook, p. 468)

18. a. is the answer. Depression and low self-esteem often serve as stimulus triggers for fasting, bingeing, and purging, which may temporarily relieve these states of emotional distress. (textbook, p. 482)

19. b. is the answer. (textbook, p. 485)

a. Although this is the most common fatal disease in early adulthood, it certainly is not the most common cause of death.

c. This is the leading cause of death for young European-American men.

d. Suicide is much less frequently a cause of death for African-American men, partly because they tend to have extensive family and friendship networks that provide social support.

20. b. is the answer. In fact, just the opposite is true. Young adults may use drugs to express independence from their parents. (textbook, p. 478)

References

Hyde, J. S. (1996). *Understanding human sexuality* (6th ed.). New York: McGraw-Hill.

A comprehensive work on sexuality that includes discussion of human sexuality, sex-role development, and sexual disorders.

Whitbourne, Susan Krauss. (1996). *The aging individual: Physical and Psychological perspectives.* New York: Springer.

A comprehensive description of age-related changes in physical vitality.

Early Adulthood: Cognitive Development

ORIENTATION

Lesson 18 of the audio program is the fifth in a sequence of lessons that track cognitive development from infancy to late adulthood. The first two of these, Lessons 6 and 9, explored the acquisition of language. The next two, Lessons 12 and 15, presented the theory of Jean Piaget, who identified four stages of cognitive development culminating in the abstract logic of formal operations. In this lesson we step beyond Piaget and explore other ways of thinking.

As people grow from adolescence into adulthood, the commitments, demands, and responsibilities of adult life produce a new type of **postformal thinking** that is better suited than formal operations to solving the practical problems of daily life. Postformal thought is more adaptive, flexible, and **dialectical**. Dialectical thought, which some researchers consider the most advanced form of cognition, recognizes that most of life's important questions do not have single, unvarying, correct answers. It is grounded in the ability to consider both sides of an issue simultaneously.

Chapter 18 of *The Developing Person Through the Life Span, 5/e*, describes how adult thinking differs from adolescent thinking. The experiences and challenges of adulthood result in a new, postformal thought, evidenced by the dynamic, in-the-world cognitive style that adults typically use to solve the problems of daily life. The text also explores how the events of early adulthood can affect moral development. The final section examines how the college experience, parenthood, and other life events can trigger cognitive growth during young adulthood.

Thinking about questions of **faith** and ethics may also progress during adulthood, especially in response to significant life experiences such as participating in higher education and becoming a parent. Both the text and audio program 18, "The Development of Faith," present James Fowler's theo-

ry of how faith changes throughout the seasons of life. Fowler, a Christian minister and professor of theology, has bridged the fields of psychology and religion by creating a model in which faith is broadly conceived. Building on the cognitive and personality theories of Jean Piaget and Erik Erikson, Fowler's model extends the concept of faith beyond religious faith to include whatever each person really cares about—his or her "ultimate concern." Fowler's theory describes six stages, each of which has distinct features and is classified as typical of a certain age.

Although Fowler's theory is not without its critics, its emphasis on faith as a developmental process rings true. If Fowler is correct, faith, like other aspects of cognition, may mature from the simple self-centered and one-sided perspective of the child to the much more complex, altruistic, and multifaceted perspective of many adults.

LESSON GOALS

By the end of this lesson you should be prepared to:

1. Describe three approaches to the study of adult cognition.
2. Identify the main characteristics of postformal and dialectical thought, and describe how it differs from formal operational thought.
3. Explain Carol Gilligan's view of how moral reasoning changes during adulthood.
4. Outline James Fowler's stage theory of the development of faith.
5. Describe the relationship of adult cognitive growth to higher education and other significant life events.

Audio Assignment

Listen to the audio tape that accompanies Lesson 18: "The Development of Faith."

Write answers to the following questions. You may replay portions of the program if you need to refresh your memory. Answer guidelines may be found in the Lesson Guidelines section at the end of this chapter.

1. (Audio Program and A Life-Span View) List and describe the six stages in the development of faith proposed by James Fowler.

2. Discuss the relationship between cognitive development and faith.

3. Cite several criticisms of Fowler's theory.

Textbook Assignment

Read Chapter 18: "Early Adulthood: Cognitive Development," pages 489–509 in *The Developing Person Through the Life Span, 5/e,* then work through the material that follows to review it. Complete the sentences and answer the questions. As you proceed, evaluate your performance for each secdtion by consulting the answers on page 231. Do not continue with the next section until you understand each answer. If you need to, review or reread the appropriate section in the textbook before continuing.

1. Unlike the relatively "straightforward" cognitive growth of earlier ages, cognitive development during adulthood is _____ and _____ . Developmentalists have used three approaches to explain this develop-

ment: the _____ approach, the _____ approach, and the _____-_____ approach.

Postformal Thought (pp. 490–494)

2. Compared to adolescent thinking, adult thinking is more _____ , _____ , and _____ . Adults are also less inclined toward the "_____ _____ _____" as their thinking becomes more specialized and experiential.

3. Gisela Labouvie-Vief has noted that one hallmark of mature adult thinking is the realization that most of life's answers are _____ rather than _____ .

4. Reasoning that is adapted to the subjective real-life contexts to which it is applied is called _____ _____ .

5. Developmentalists distinguish between _____ thinking, which arises from the _____ experiences and _____ of an individual, and _____ thinking, which follows abstract _____ . The latter kind of thinking is _____ (more/less) adaptive for schoolchildren, adolescents, and young adults than for mature adults.

6. In her research, Labouvie-Vief found that although older adults recognize logical premises in solving real-life problems, they also explore the real-life possibilities and _____ _____ that might bear on an issue.

7. Other research demonstrates that the difference between adolescent and young adult reasoning is particularly apparent for problems that are _____ _____ .

8. (Research Report) In the Blanchard-Fields study of the effect of emotions on reasoning about social dilemmas, more mature thinkers scored higher because they were better able to take into account the _____

_____ of each party's version of events.

9. Some theorists consider _____ _____ the most advanced form of cognition. This thinking recognizes that every idea, or _____ , implies an opposing idea, or _____ ; these are then forged into a(n) _____ of the two. This type of thinking fosters a worldview that recognizes that most of life's important questions _____ (have/do not have) single, unchangeable, correct answers.

10. True dialectic thinkers acknowledge the _____ nature of reality _and_ the need to make firm _____ to values they realize will change over time.

11. All adults _____ (think/do not think) in a postformal manner, and everyone who thinks in a postformal way _____ (is/is not) also capable of formal operational thought. Dialectical thinking is more typical of _____-_____ adults than of _____ or _____ adults and is more evident in certain _____ than in others. For these reasons, developmentalists _____ (do/do not) all agree that postformal thought represents a distinct stage of cognitive development.

Adult Moral Reasoning (pp. 495–498)

12. According to James Rest, one catalyst for propelling young adults from a lower moral stage to a higher one is _____ .

13. Lawrence Kohlberg maintains that in order to be capable of "truly ethical" reasoning, a person must have experienced sustained responsibility for _____ .

14. Carol Gilligan believes that in matters of moral reasoning _____ (males/females) tend to be more concerned with the question of rights and justice, whereas _____ (males/females) are more concerned with personal relationships. Gilligan

also maintains that as people become responsible for the needs of others they begin to construct principles that are _____ and _____ , because they see that moral reasoning based chiefly on justice principles is inadequate to solve real-life moral dilemmas.

15. (A Life-Span View) The theorist who has outlined six stages in the development of faith is _____ . In the space below, identify and briefly describe each stage.

Stage One: _____
_____

Stage Two: _____
_____

Stage Three: _____
_____

Stage Four: _____
_____

Stage Five: _____
_____

Stage Six: _____
_____

16. (A Life-Span View) Although Fowler's stage theory of faith _____ (is/is not) widely accepted, the idea that religion plays an important role in human development _____ (is/is not).

17. The current approach to research on moral reasoning is based on a series of questions about moral reasoning called the _____ _____ _____ . In general, scores on this test increase with _____ and with each year of _____ _____ .

Cognitive Growth and Higher Education (pp. 499–506)

18. Years of education _____ (are/are not) strongly correlated with most measures of adult cognition. This relationship is _____ (stronger/weaker) than that

between socioeconomic status and adult cognition.

19. College education leads people to become more _____ of other viewpoints.

Briefly outline the year-by-year progression in how the thinking of college students becomes more flexible and tolerant.

20. William Perry found that the thinking of students, over the course of their college careers, progressed through _____ levels of complexity.

21. College seems to make people more accepting of other viewpoints because it makes people less _____ by them.

22. Research has shown that the more years of higher education a person has, the deeper and more _____ that person's reasoning is likely to become.

23. Over the past two decades, college students in the United States have become less concerned about developing a _____ _____ and more concerned about _____ _____.

24. Collegiate populations have become _____ (more/less) diverse and heterogeneous in recent years.

25. Worldwide, college has changed from an activity of the _____ to one of the _____.

26. As colleges have become more diverse, more and more _____ _____ are specifically organized for various interest groups. Today's cohort of college students tends to be more suspicious of _____ , _____ , and _____ that have no direct impact on college life.

27. Another cohort difference is that most of today's college students _____ (work/do not work) during their college years, so that cognitive growth depends more on the _____ and less on the _____ than in the past.

List several educational factors that appear to be unrelated to fostering cognitive growth in college students, and several factors that are important.

28. (Changing Policy) Young full-time students living on campus are _____ (more/less) likely to accept cheating than are students who commute. Many students have a _____ (broader/more limited) definition of cheating than professors. For example, many students seem unaware of the rules defining _____ .

29. (Changing Policy) Dr. Berger's analysis of cheating behavior led her to suspect that students may have a different _____ _____ that encourages cheating in order to cope with institutions that penalize those who are _____ _____ and those who are educationally _____ .

Cognitive Growth and Life Events (pp. 506–508)

30. It has been suggested that significant life events, such as _____

_____ ,

can trigger new patterns of thinking.

Testing Yourself

After you have completed the audio and text review questions, see how well you do on the following quiz. Correct answers, with text and audio references, may be found at the end of this chapter.

1. (Audio Program and a Life-Span View) According to James Fowler, the simplest stage of faith is the stage of:
   a. universalizing faith.
   b. intuitive-projective faith.
   c. mythic-literal faith.
   d. synthetic-conventional faith.

2. (Audio Program and a Life-Span View) At one stage in the development of faith, people learn to question the practices and philosophies of significant persons in their lives. This is the stage of:
   a. conjunctive faith.
   b. individual-reflective faith.
   c. synthetic-conventional faith.
   d. intuitive-projective faith.

3. (Audio Program and a Life-Span View) At the highest stages in the development of faith, people have incorporated a powerful vision of compassion and human brotherhood into their lives. This stage is called:
   a. conjunctive faith.
   b. individual-reflective faith.
   c. synthetic-conventional faith.
   d. universalizing faith.

4. (Audio Program and a Life-Span View) The stage of faith that corresponds with the age at which most individuals achieve concrete operational thought is called:
   a. mythic-literal faith.
   b. individual-reflective faith.
   c. synthetic-conventional faith.
   d. universalizing faith.

5. Fowler's theory of faith has been criticized for:
   a. focusing primarily on religious faith.
   b. proposing that faith develops in stages, rather than continuously.
   c. proposing stages of faith that many people will never reach.
   d. all of the above reasons.

6. Differences in the reasoning maturity of adolescents and young adults are most likely to be apparent when:
   a. low-SES and high-SES groups are compared.
   b. ethnic-minority adolescents and adults are compared.
   c. ethnic-majority adolescents and adults are compared.
   d. emotionally charged issues are involved.

7. Which of the following is *not* one of the major approaches to the study of adult cognition described in the text?
   a. the information-processing approach
   b. the postformal approach
   c. the systems approach
   d. the psychometric approach

8. Compared to adolescent thinking, adult thinking tends to be:
   a. more personal.   **c.** more integrative.
   b. more practical.   **d.** all of the above.

9. Labouvie-Vief has shown that the hallmark of adult adaptive thought is the:
   a. ability to engage in dialectical thinking.
   b. reconciliation of both objective and subjective approaches to real-life problems.
   c. adoption of conjunctive faith.
   d. all of the above.

10. (A Life-Span View) According to James Fowler, the experience of college often is a springboard to:
   a. intuitive-projective faith
   b. mythic-literal faith
   c. individual-reflective faith
   d. synthetic-conventional faith

11. Which approach to adult cognitive development focuses on life-span changes in the efficiency of encoding, storage, and retrieval?
   a. postformal
   b. information-processing
   c. psychometric
   d. dialectical

12. Postformal thinking is most useful for solving _____ problems.

    a. science   **c.** everyday
    b. mathematics   **d.** abstract, logical

13. The term for the kind of thinking that involves the consideration of both poles of an idea and their reconciliation, or synthesis, in a new idea is:

    a. subjective thinking.
    b. postformal thought.
    c. adaptive reasoning.
    d. dialectical thinking.

14. Thesis is to antithesis as _____ is to _____ .

    a. a new idea; an opposing idea
    b. abstract; concrete
    c. concrete; abstract
    d. provisional; absolute

15. Which of the following adjectives best describe(s) cognitive development during adulthood?

    a. multidirectional and multicontextual
    b. linear
    c. steady
    d. tumultuous

16. Which of the following most accurately describes postformal thought?

    a. subjective thinking that arises from the personal experiences and perceptions of the individual
    b. objective reasoning that follows abstract, impersonal logic
    c. a form of logic that combines subjectivity and objectivity
    d. thinking that is rigid, inflexible, and fails to recognize the existence of other potentially valid views

17. The Defining Issues Test is a:

    a. standardized test that measures postformal thinking.
    b. projective test that assesses dialectical reasoning.
    c. series of questions about moral dilemmas.
    d. test that assesses the impact of life events on cognitive growth.

18. According to Carol Gilligan:

    a. in matters of moral reasoning, females tend to be more concerned with the question of rights and justice.
    b. in matters of moral reasoning, males tend to put human needs above principles of justice.
    c. moral reasoning advances during adulthood in response to the more complex moral dilemmas that life poses.
    d. all of the above are true.

19. An important factor in determining whether college students learn to think deeply is:

    a. the particular interactions between students and faculty.
    b. the college's overall religious or secular philosophy.
    c. the college's size.
    d. all of the above.

20. Research has revealed that a typical outcome of college education is that students become:

    a. very liberal politically.
    b. less committed to any particular ideology.
    c. less tolerant of others' views.
    d. more tolerant of others' views.

NAME _____   INSTRUCTOR _____

LESSON 18: THINKING DURING ADULTHOOD

Exercise

One theme of the *Seasons of Life* series is that every age brings a different way of knowing. The cognitive patterns that emerge during adulthood are propelled by the commitments each individual makes during this time. These include commitments to personal achievement, family concerns, and the community at large. Such commitments give the individual a new understanding of the complexity of most of life's daily problems.

In this lesson we have explored several types of thinking, including formal and **post-formal thought, dialectical reasoning**, and **faith** Test your understanding of these ways of thinking by writing answers to the following questions. Hand the completed exercise in to your instructor.

1. Many different kinds of problems arise in daily life. Based on your own experiences, or those of a typical college student or person in your season of life, give an example of a problem likely to benefit from formal operational thinking. Why is a logical answer to this problem appropriate?

2. Imagine that you are a religious leader attempting to convince the members of your congregation to become more involved in their community's religious life. What kind of appeal might be most effective with members at Fowler's stage of "mythic-literal faith"? with members at the stage of "individual-reflective faith"?

3. Dialectical thinking involves the constant integration of one's beliefs and experiences with the contradictions and inconsistencies of daily life. Give an example of the use of dialectical thinking in your own life, or that of a typical person in your season.

4. The idea that personal commitment and assuming responsibility for others are hallmarks of adult thinking is central to several theories of adult cognition. Why would becoming a parent foster cognitive growth? In what ways might being a stepparent or grandparent influence cognitive growth? What other life experiences have influenced your own cognitive development?

LESSON GUIDELINES

Audio Question Guidelines

1. Stage One: **Intuitive-projective faith** refers to the imaginative faith that emerges as children acquire the use of symbols and language.

   Stage Two: **Mythic-literal faith** corresponds to Piaget's stage of concrete operations. In this stage children become interested in learning the stories of their culture, and often take these stories literally.

   Stage Three: **Synthetic-conventional faith** often emerges during adolescence as a result of young people's new awareness of who they are and what they believe in. Faith is characterized by a conformist, nonintellectual acceptance of the values and ideals of people who are important to the young person.

   Stage Four: **Individual-reflective faith** often begins in early adulthood, as individuals become critically reflective of their beliefs. Characterized by intellectual detachment from the values of the culture and the approval of others, faith in this stage may represent God in the abstract or as a philosophical concept. In the audio program, Fowler refers to this stage as "individuative."

   Stage Five: **Conjunctive faith** rarely develops before middle age. Considered the highest stage that most people experience, conjunctive faith recognizes the many paradoxes and inconsistencies of life.

   Stage Six: **Universalizing faith** refers to the behavior of rare individuals who develop a vision of universal compassion, justice, and love that often leads to the denial of their personal welfare in an effort to serve those beliefs.

2. James Fowler has delineated six stages of faith that progress from a simple, self-centered perspective to a more complex, altruistic, and multifaceted view.

   In developing this theory, Fowler was strongly influenced by Piaget's stages of cognitive development. Although Fowler's stages are not considered exclusive to a given age range, each is classified as typical of a certain age group and a certain stage of cognitive development. In the first stage of faith (intuitive-projective faith), for example, egocentric preschoolers, who are unable to take the perspective of another person, often form a highly imaginative and nonhuman image of God. In the second stage (mythic-literal faith)—equivalent to Piaget's stage of concrete operations—children begin to understand cause-and-effect rela-

tionships, but are limited to the concrete reality of the here and now. Their faith puts a correspondingly literal interpretation on the stories and myths of their religion and culture.

   Later in adulthood, the development of faith is also paced by cognitive development. When **postformal thought** is achieved, for example, faith can become dialectical in nature and recognize the often paradoxical nature of life. This is what happens in the conjunctive stage. At each season of life, therefore, the development of faith and thinking go hand in hand.

3. Like any pioneer, James Fowler is not without his critics. One criticism is that although Fowler defines faith broadly, he overemphasizes religious faith.

   Another criticism is that faith may develop continuously rather than in stages as Fowler proposed.

   A third objection is based on the reluctance of some critics to accept the notion that some stages of faith are higher than others.

Textbook Question Answers

1. multidirectional; multicontextual; postformal; psychometric; information-processing
2. personal; practical; integrative; game of thinking
3. provisional; enduring
4. postformal thought
5. subjective; personal; perceptions; objective; logic; more
6. contextual circumstances
7. emotionally charged
8. interpretive biases
9. dialectical thought; thesis; antithesis; synthesis; do not have
10. subjective; commitments
11. do not think; is not; middle-aged; younger; older; contexts; do not
12. college
13. the welfare of others
14. males; females; relative; changeable
15. James Fowler

Intuitive-projective faith is magical, illogical, filled with fantasy, and typical of children ages 3 to 7.

Mythic-literal faith, which is typical of middle childhood, is characterized by taking the myths and stories of religion literally.

Synthetic-conventional faith is a nonintellectual acceptance of cultural or religious values in the context of interpersonal relationships.

Individual-reflective faith is characterized by intellectual detachment from the values of culture and the approval of significant others.

Conjunctive faith incorporates both powerful unconscious ideas and rational, conscious values.

Universalizing faith is characterized by a powerful vision of universal compassion, justice, and love that leads people to put their own personal welfare aside in an effort to serve these values.

16. is not; is

17. Defining Issues Test; age; college education

18. are; stronger

19. tolerant

First-year students often believe that there are clear and perfect truths to be found. This phase is followed by a wholesale questioning of values. Finally, after considering opposite ideas, students become committed to certain values, at the same time realizing the need to remain open-minded.

20. nine

21. threatened

22. dialectical

23. meaningful life philosophy; finding a good job

24. more

25. elite; masses

26. student organizations; politicians; governments; philosophies

27. work; classroom; dorm

The unrelated factors include the college's overall philosophy (religious or secular), funding (public or private), and size. The related factors include the particular interactions between students and teachers and among students themselves, peer tutoring, structured group learning, and reflective teaching.

28. more; more limited; plagiarism

29. value system; culturally different; underprepared

30. the birth of a child, the loss of a loved one, a new intimate relationship or the end of an old one, a job promotion or dismissal, being the victim of an attack

Answers to Testing Yourself

1. **b.** is the answer. In this stage faith is magical, illogical, imaginative, and filled with fantasy. (audio program; textbook, p. 496)

2. **b.** is the answer. A person's ability to articulate his or her own values, separately from family and friends, is characteristic of individual-reflective faith. In the audio program, Fowler calls this stage "individuative." (audio program; textbook, p. 496)

3. **d.** is the answer. Persons reaching stage six in the development of faith (examples include Mahatma Gandhi, Martin Luther King, Jr., and Mother Teresa) are exceedingly rare. (audio program; textbook, p. 497)

4. **a.** is the answer. At this stage, the individual takes the myths and stories of his or her religion literally. (audio program; textbook, p. 496)

5. **d.** is the answer. (audio program)

6. **d.** is the answer. (textbook, pp. 491, 492)

   a., b., & c. Socioeconomic status and ethnicity do not predict reasoning maturity.

7. **c.** is the answer. (textbook, p. 489)

8. **d.** is the answer (textbook, p. 490)

9. **b.** is the answer. (textbook, p. 491)

10. **c.** is the answer. (textbook, p. 496)

11. **b.** is the answer. (textbook, p. 489)

    a. This approach emphasizes the emergence of a new stage of thinking that builds on the skills of formal operational thinking.

    c. This approach analyzes the measurable components of intelligence.

    d. This is a type of thinking rather than an approach to the study of cognitive development.

12. **c.** is the answer. (textbook, p. 490)

    a., b., & d. Because of its more analytical nature, formal thinking is most useful for solving these types of problems.

13. **d.** is the answer. (textbook, pp. 491–492)

    a. Thinking that is subjective relies on personal reflection rather than objective observation.

    b. Although dialectical thinking *is* characteristic of postformal thought, this question refers specifically to dialectical thinking.

    c. Adaptive reasoning, which also is characteristic of postformal thought, goes beyond mere logic in solving problems to also explore real-life complexities and contextual circumstances.

14. **a.** is the answer (textbook, p. 491)

15. **a.** is the answer. (textbook, p. 489)

    b. & c. Comparatively speaking, linear and steady are *more* descriptive of childhood and adolescent cognitive development.

16. **b.** is the answer. (textbook, p. 490)
17. **d.** is the answer. (textbook, p. 498)
18. **c.** is the answer. (textbook, p. 495)

   a. In Gilligan's theory, this is more true of males than females.

   b. In Gilligan's theory, this is more true of females than males.

19. **a.** is the answer. (textbook, p. 504)
20. **d.** is the answer. (textbook, p. 501)

Reference

Fowler, James W. (1981). *Stages of faith: The psychology of human development and the quest for meaning*. New York: HarperCollins.

   James Fowler outlines his influential theory of the development of faith.

Early Adulthood: Psychosocial Development

AUDIO PROGRAM: Not Being First

ORIENTATION

Lesson 19 of *Seasons of Life* is concerned with psychosocial development in early adulthood and the changing composition of the American family. Chapter 19 of the textbook begins with a discussion of the two basic psychosocial needs of adulthood, love and work. The next section addresses the need for intimacy in adulthood, focusing on the development of friendship, love, and marriage. The impact of divorce on families is also discussed. The final section is concerned with generativity, or the motivation to achieve during adulthood. It highlights the importance of work and parenthood and addresses the special challenges facing stepparents, adoptive parents, and foster parents.

For some, the question "Who's in your family?" is difficult to answer. Although many people tend to form very close-knit nuclear families consisting of a mother, a father, and one or more children, the number of **stepfamilies** is increasing. This increase is not due, as it was in the past, to death and remarriage, but to divorce and remarriage. For the first time in 1974 more marriages in the United States were ended by divorce than by death. Since people are living longer now than at any other time in history, divorced persons have more opportunities to remarry.

These trends in the composition of American families have created new notions about the words *family*, *mother*, and *father*. Unlike nuclear families, stepfamilies usually include children who are members of two households. Extra sets of in-laws and grandparents and the stress of the competition that often exists between a stepparent and the ex-spouse all serve to complicate family relationships.

Audio program 19, "Not Being First," poignantly illustrates the particular dilemma of the stepparent by introducing the listener to Penny and Lyn Beesley. Married for six years, both Penny and Lyn have had previous marriages that ended in divorce. As the program unfolds, we hear of Lyn's struggles to form a bond with Heather, Penny's daughter from her first marriage. We also hear commentary from counselor Elaine Horigian, a clinical psychologist, and Helen Weingarten, a professor of social work.

LESSON GOALS

By the end of this lesson you should be prepared to:

1. Discuss the ways in which adults meet their needs for love/affiliation and work/achievement during early adulthood.

2. Explain how the social clock influences the timing of important events during adulthood.

3. Review the developmental course of friendship during adulthood, and discuss the issues facing adults in meeting the need for intimacy.

4. Discuss the impact of social systems on divorce, the reasons for today's rising divorce rate, and the usual impact of divorce on families.

5. Describe the typical stages of the family life cycle, and discuss the special challenges facing stepparents, adoptive parents, and foster parents.

Audio Assignment

Listen to the audio tape that accompanies Lesson 19: "Not Being First."

Write answers to the following questions. You may replay portions of the program if you need to refresh your memory. Answer guidelines may be found in the Lesson Guidelines section at the end of this chapter.

1. In what ways do nuclear families and stepfamilies differ?

2. How and why has the prevalence of stepfamilies changed from the seventeenth century to the present day? Do experts predict that the current trend will continue?

3. Name and describe the three stages in stepfamily development described by clinical psychologist Elaine Horigian.

4. What are some of the typical problems faced by the members of stepfamilies?

5. Why is it that "every person in a stepfamily has experienced a significant loss"?

Textbook Assignment

Read Chapter 19: "Early Adulthood: Psychosocial Development," pages 511–540 in *The Developing Person Through the Life Span, 5/e*, then work through the material that follows to review it. Complete the sentences and answer the questions. As you proceed, evaluate your performance for each secdtion by consulting the answers on page 245. Do not continue with the next section until you understand each answer. If you need to, review or reread the appropriate section in the textbook before continuing.

The Tasks of Adulthood (pp. 511–514)

1. Developmentalists generally agree that two psychosocial needs must be met during adulthood. These are _____

_____

_____ .

2. According to Freud, the healthy adult was one who could _____ and _____ .

3. According to Maslow, the need for _____ and _____ was followed by a need for _____ and _____ .

4. In Erikson's theory, the identity crisis of adolescence is followed in early adulthood by the crisis of _____ _____ _____ , and then later by the crisis of _____ _____ _____ .

5. Today, most social scientists regard adult lives as less _____ and _____ than stage models suggest.

Briefly describe what was in the 1950s the most common pattern of development during the early and middle 20s.

6. Although most developmentalists _____ (take/do not take) a strict stage view of adulthood, they do recognize that development is influenced by the

   _____ _____ ,

   which is defined as _____

   _____ .

7. Internationally, societies in _____ (highly developed/less developed) regions have tended to be quite age-stratified.

8. A prime influence on the social clock is

   _____ _____ . The

   lower a person's SES, the _____ (younger/older) the age at which he or she is expected to leave school, begin work, marry, have children, and so forth.

9. The influence of SES is particularly apparent with regard to the age at which _____ (men/women) are expected to

   _____ and finish _____ .

10. Women from low-SES backgrounds may feel pressure to marry by age _____ , and most stop childbearing by age _____ , whereas wealthy women may not feel pressure to marry until age _____ or to stop childbearing until age _____ .

Intimacy (pp. 514–528)

11. Two main sources of intimacy in early adulthood

    are _____ _____

    and _____ _____ .

12. As a buffer against stress and a source of positive feelings, _____ are particularly important.

Briefly state why this is so.

13. Young adulthood is the prime time to solidify friendships and make new ones for two reasons:

    a. _____

    _____ .

    b. _____

    _____ .

14. Four factors that promote friendship by serving

    as _____ _____

    _____ are:

    a. _____

    b. _____

    c. _____

    d. _____

15. When it comes to our close confidants, most of us have two or three basic _____ , and everyone who has those traits is _____ from consideration.

16. During early adulthood _____ (men/women/both men and women) tend to be more satisfied with their _____

    _____ than with almost any other part of their lives.

17. (In Person) Gender differences in friendship _____ (are/are not) especially apparent during adulthood. In general, men's friendships are based on _____

    _____ and _____ ,

    whereas friendships between women tend to be more _____ and _____ .

Briefly contrast the types of conversations men and women are likely to have with their friends.

18. (In Person) Research has shown that _____ (women/men) are more likely to reveal their weaknesses to friends, whereas _____ (women/men) are more likely to reveal their strengths. Thus, men may view friendship as a means of maintaining a positive _____ , while women regard it as a

means of coping with _____
_____ .

19. (In Person) Another gender difference is that men's friendships are more clearly tinged with open _____ .

20. (In Person) List three reasons that men's friendships seem so much less intimate than women's.

a. _____
   _____ .

b. _____
   _____ .

c. _____
   _____ .

Describe some of the opportunities and problems of cross-sex friendships.

21. The typical _____ (female/male) friendship pattern seems to be better in terms of meeting intimacy needs.

22. A woman's tendency to seek mutual loyalty among confidantes may undermine her _____ performance and handicap her _____ . Men who cannot share problems with friends may be handicapped _____ .

23. (Research Report) Robert Sternberg has argued that love has three distinct components: _____ , _____ , and _____ . Sternberg also believes that the emergence and prominence of each component tends to follow a pattern that is _____ (unpredictable/predictable).

24. (Research Report) Early in a relationship _____ intimacy tends to be high, while _____ intimacy is much lower.

25. (Research Report) Relationships grow because _____ _____ intensifies, leading to the gradual establishment and strengthening of _____ .

26. (Research Report) When commitment is added to passion and intimacy, the result is _____ love.

27. (Research Report) With time, _____ tends to fade and _____ tends to stabilize, even as _____ develops.

28. Increasingly common among young adults in many countries is the living pattern called _____ , in which two unrelated adults of the opposite sex live together.

29. Cohabitation _____ (does/does not) seem to benefit the participants. Cohabitants tend to be less _____ , less _____ , and less satisfied with their _____ _____ than married people.

30. An estimated _____ percent of all adults in the United States spend part of adulthood in gay or lesbian partnerships. Homosexual couples _____ (have/do not have) the same relationship problems as heterosexual couples.

31. In the United States today, the proportion of adults who are unmarried is _____ (higher/lower) than in the previous 100 years; only _____ percent of brides are virgins; nearly _____ percent of all first births are to unmarried mothers; and the divorce rate is _____ percent of the marriage rate.

32. Adults in many developed nations spend about _____ of the years between 20 and 40 single.

33. The younger marriage partners are when they first wed, the _____ (more/less) likely their marriage is to succeed. According to Erikson, this may be because intimacy is hard to establish until _____ is secure.

34. Marriage between people who are similar in age, SES, ethnicity, and the like, called

_____ , is _____
(more/less) likely to succeed than marriage that
is outside the group, called _____ .
Similarity in leisure interests and
_____ preferences, called
_____ _____ ,
is particularly important to marital success.

35. A third factor affecting marriage is
_____ _____ , the
extent to which the partners perceive equality in
the relationship. According to
_____ theory, marriage is an
arrangement in which each person contributes
something useful to the other.

36. A final factor that predicts marital satisfaction is
the idea that the relationship is a _____
_____ _____ .

37. In the United States, almost one out of every
_____ marriages ends in divorce.
This rate _____ (varies/does not
vary significantly) from country to country.
Worldwide, divorce has
_____ (increased/decreased/
remained stable) over most of the past 50 years.

38. Many developmentalists believe that spouses
today expect _____ (more/less)
from each other than spouses in the past did.

39. Most people find the initial impact of divorce to
be quite _____ (negative/positive)
and adjustment to divorce
_____ (more/less) difficult than
they expected.

State two reasons why this is so.

40. Another adjustment problem is that the ex-
spouses' _____
_____ usually shrinks in the first
year after divorce.

41. Newly divorced people are more prone to
_____
_____
_____ .
In most cases, such effects _____
(do/do not) eventually dissipate with time.

42. Compared to others, single divorced adults are
_____ (most/least) likely to be very
happy with their lives. The presence of
_____ is a key factor that makes
adjustment to divorce more problematic, particularly for custodial _____ (mothers/
fathers).

43. _____ (Most/Only a minority of)
noncustodial fathers maintain intimate ongoing
relationships with their children.

44. The tendency of many custodial mothers to
express their financial and social frustration by
limiting the father's access to the children
_____ (is/is not necessarily)
destructive. Children do best with an involved,
_____ father who provides
_____ and _____ con-
sistent with the mother's caregiving.

(A Life-Span View) Identify several factors that contribute to spouse abuse.

45. (A Life-Span View) One form of spouse abuse,
_____ _____
_____ , entails outbursts of fighting,
with both partners sometimes becoming
involved. This type of abuse
_____ (usually leads/usually does
not lead) to worse abuse.

46. (A Life-Span View) The second type of abuse,
_____ _____ ,
occurs when one partner, almost always the
_____ , uses a range of methods to

punish and degrade the other. This form of abuse leads to the _____ _____ syndrome and _____ (becomes/does not usually become) more extreme with time.

47. (A Life-Span View) To break the cycle of abuse, the woman usually requires _____ _____ , which has helped to _____ (increase/reduce) the incidence of this abuse.

Generativity (pp. 528–539)

48. The motivation to _____ is one of the strongest of human motives. The observable expression of this motive _____ (varies/does not vary) significantly from culture to culture.

49. Even more important to workers than their paycheck is the opportunity that work provides to satisfy _____ needs by allowing them to:

    a. _____
       _____ .

    b. _____
       _____ .

    c. _____
       _____ .

    d. _____
       _____ .

50. The four traditional stages of the career cycle are _____ , _____ , _____ , and _____ . This pattern fit the _____- _____ job market that was typical in the 1950s. In such a market, low levels of _____ are needed, and employees are nearly _____ .

51. Today, the employment scene is very different. One reason for this is the shift in developing nations from an economy based on _____ to one based on _____ , and in developed nations from an economy based on _____ to one based on _____ and _____ .

52. Among the fastest-growing occupations in the United States are _____ _____ _____ .

53. Today, the work path for individuals is much less _____ and _____ than it once was. In many of today's jobs, although the skills are quite _____ , they may be obsolete tomorrow. This means that people in their 20s should seek educational and vocational settings that foster a variety of _____ and _____ skills.

54. Another reason for the variability in the job cycle is that workers today are more _____ . For example, in developed nations nearly _____ (how much?) the civilian labor force is female. Due to the increased proportion of _____ in the work force, _____ diversity in the work place is also much greater today than in the past.

State two implications of these trends for young adults just starting out in the work world.

55. Many women, members of minorities, and immigrants continue to experience difficulty in breaking through the _____ _____ , an invisible barrier to career advancement.

56. In the happiest couples, _____ (one/neither/both) spouse(s) work(s) either very long hours or very few hours.

57. Contemporary children generally _____ (suffer/do not suffer) when both parents work outside as well as inside the home.

58. Women who are simultaneously wife, mother, and employee _____

(inevitably/do not necessarily) experience the stress of multiple obligations called

_____ _____ .

In fact, among dual-earner families

_____ _____

is more prevalent as two people share obligations.

59. Generally speaking, adults who balance marital, parental, and vocational roles _____ (are/are not) happier and more successful than those who function in only one or two of them.

60. (Changing Policy) Today, family _____—coordinating housework, child care, work schedules, and so on—typically requires a level of planning and mutual agreement that was unnecessary in earlier generations. There _____ (are/are not) signs that today's younger couples are approaching greater equity in hours of domestic work and work outside the home.

61 (Changing Policy) An increasingly common kind of marital inequity occurs when the wife

_____

_____ . This can be particularly devastating to men who are _____-_____ workers or men who are _____ .

62. Proportionately, about _____ of all North American adults will become stepparents, adoptive parents, or foster parents at some point in their lives.

63. Strong bonds between parent and child are particularly hard to create when a child has already formed _____ to other caregivers.

64. Because they are legally connected to their children for life, _____ (adoptive/ step/foster) parents have an advantage in establishing bonds with their children.

65. Stepchildren, foster children, and adoptive children tend to leave home _____ (at the same age as/earlier than/later than) children living with one or both biological parents.

Testing Yourself

After you have completed the audio and text review questions, see how well you do on the following quiz. Correct answers, with text and audio references, may be found at the end of this chapter.

1. According to Erik Erikson, the first basic task of adulthood is to establish:
   a. a residence apart from parents.
   b. intimacy with others.
   c. generativity through work or parenthood.
   d. a career commitment.

2. Most social scientists who study adulthood emphasize that:
   a. intimacy and generativity take various forms throughout adulthood.
   b. adult lives are less orderly and predictable than stage models suggest.
   c. each culture has a somewhat different social clock.
   d. all of the above are true.

3. Which of the following was *not* identified as a gateway to attraction?
   a. physical attractiveness
   b. frequent exposure
   c. similarity of attitudes
   d. apparent availability

4. The social circles of ex-spouses usually _____ in the first year following a divorce.
   a. shrink
   b. grow larger
   c. become more fluid
   d. become less fluid

5. In the United States and other Western countries, the lower a person's socioeconomic status:
   a. the younger the age at which the social clock is "set" for many life events.
   b. the older the age at which the social clock is "set" for many life events.
   c. the more variable are the settings for the social clock.
   d. the less likely it is that divorce will occur.

6. According to Erikson, the failure to achieve intimacy during early adulthood is most likely to result in:
   a. generativity.   c. role diffusion.
   b. stagnation.   d. isolation.

7. Regarding friendships, most young adults tend to:
   a. be very satisfied.
   b. be very dissatisfied.
   c. find it difficult to form social networks.
   d. be without close friends.

8. Between ages 20 and 30:
   a. 60 percent of men and 46 percent of women have never married.
   b. 3 percent of men and women are already divorced.
   c. the unmarried are in the majority.
   d. all of the above are true.

9. (Research Report) According to Robert Sternberg, consummate love emerges:
   a. as a direct response to passion.
   b. as a direct response to physical intimacy.
   c. when commitment is added to passion and intimacy.
   d. during the early years of parenthood.

10. An arrangement in which two unrelated, unmarried adults of the opposite sex live together is called:
    a. cross-sex friendship.
    b. a passive-congenial pattern.
    c. cohabitation.
    d. affiliation.

11. Differences in religious customs or rituals are *most* likely to arise in a:
    a. homogamous couple.
    b. heterogamous couple.
    c. cohabiting couple.
    d. very young married couple.

12. Children in dual-earner families:
    a. are slower to develop intellectually.
    b. gain several benefits, including more active relationships with their fathers.
    c. often experience role overload.
    d. often have weak social skills.

13. The four stages of the traditional career cycle:
    a. are less applicable today than they were in the 1950s.
    b. derive from a time when workers were more specialized than they are today.
    c. accurately describe all but the least technical of occupations.
    d. fit the job market of today better than the job market of earlier cohorts.

14. Adults who combine the roles of spouse, parent, and employee tend to report:
    a. less overall happiness than other adults.
    b. more overall happiness than other adults.
    c. regrets over parental roles.
    d. problems in career advancement.

15. Compared to adolescents who live with their biological parents, stepchildren, foster children, and adoptive children:
    a. leave home at an older age.
    b. leave home at a younger age.
    c. have fewer developmental problems.
    d. have the same developmental problems.

16. In the seventeenth century most marriages were ended _____ ; today most are ended _____ .
    a. by divorce; by the death of a spouse
    b. by the death of a spouse; by divorce
    c. before children were born; after children are born
    d. after children were born; before children are born

17. Compared to the nineteenth century, the number of stepfamilies today is:
    a. significantly greater.   c. a little greater.
    b. about the same.   d. significantly less.

18. According to experts, one common mistake made by many stepfamilies is to:
    a. try to become the same as nuclear families.
    b. allow their stepchildren to do anything they want.
    c. discipline their stepchildren too harshly.
    d. avoid establishing any "deep" relationships within the stepfamily.

19. Concerning children within stepfamilies, which of the following is true?
    a. Small children tend to form new loyalties only with difficulty.
    b. Small children tend to think in terms of absolutes such as, "You can only love one mom and one dad."
    c. Small children often feel resentful and hostile toward a stepparent.
    d. All of the above are true.

20. According to counselor Elaine Horigian, in the final stage of stepfamily living:
    a. family members "let go" of unrealistic expectations and realize that their stepfamily will never be the same as a nuclear family.
    b. each family member "bends over backwards" trying to please other family members.
    c. family members become alienated to the extent that a sense of closeness is impossible.
    d. none of the above occurs; it is impossible to predict such stages.

NAME _____   INSTRUCTOR _____

LESSON 19: GENOGRAMS

Exercise

As an exercise in studying the trends described in the audio program, and reflecting on your own life experiences, construct a **genogram** of your own, or another, family. A genogram is a map of several generations within a family, something like a family tree. By convention, in genograms males are represented by squares and females by circles. Marriage is indicated by a solid line drawn from circle to square, and divorce by a dashed line. Death is indicated by drawing an "X" through the circle or square. The genogram is expanded horizontally to include additional individuals within a given generation, and vertically to document the family history across several generations. Here, for example, is the beginning of a genogram representing the Beesley family, whose members were introduced in the audio program.

This genogram would be completed by adding Penny's and Lyn's brothers, sisters, parents, and grandparents.

Since the turn of the century, family relationships and the typical structure of family genograms have changed in several ways. For one thing, families with multigenerational living members are much more common. For another, the average size of nuclear families has declined and there are more single-parent and stepparent households. These changes are resulting in more complex genograms. As Lyn Beesley said of Heather's family tree, "It had a whole lot of branches on it!" Is the same going to be true of your genogram?

Here are the symbols to be used in constructing your genogram. It might be a good idea to make a rough draft before drawing the final version on the back of this sheet. Hand the completed genogram in to your instructor.

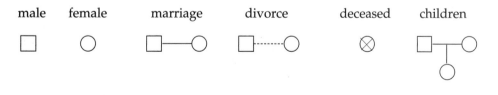

LESSON GUIDELINES

Audio Question Guidelines

1. **Stepfamilies** are much more complex than nuclear families for several reasons:

   When parents remarry, children become members of two households.

   Competition may exist within and among stepfamily relationships.

   There are more relationships—that is, extra in-laws, grandparents, and so on.

2. In the seventeenth century, stepfamilies were very common due to the deaths of spouses and a high rate of remarriage among widows and widowers. In the eighteenth and nineteenth centuries, the number of stepfamilies declined. In the middle of the twentieth century, as divorce rates began to soar and people continued to live longer than in the past, the number of stepfamilies began to rise again.

   Although it is not easy to count the number of stepfamily households, the rising trend is expected to continue.

3. Stage One (The "Honeymoon" Stage): For approximately six months after the remarriage, everyone "tries too hard" and avoids dealing with his or her true feelings of fear, resentment, and threat.

   Stage Two (The "Conflict" Stage): Negative feelings are now expressed. It's necessary for the natural parent to support the stepparent and give him or her credibility.

   Stage Three (The "Letting Go" Stage): The stepfamily begins to realize that it will never be the same as a nuclear family and lets go of some of the myths, ideals, and dreams it once held. This is a very rewarding stage because the stepfamily members realize that their relationships are deep and caring, even though they are different from those within a nuclear family.

4. The new stepfamily is often immediately faced with a set of very difficult problems involving deeply held feelings of loyalty. It takes a long time for children to develop new attachments. Stepparents often are disappointed that their relationships with stepchildren are not as close as they would like.

   Stepfamilies often attempt to re-create the exclusive, close-knit relationships of a nuclear family, which usually is not possible.

   The extra relationships within stepfamilies may create hostility and competition.

   Stepparents may feel alienated, awkward, and as if they are constantly "walking on eggs."

   With so many diverse relationships within a stepfamily, social etiquette is often difficult. Graduations and weddings can pose problems, for example. Issues of sexuality also are different than they are in nuclear families. Sexual feelings between husband and wife, between stepparents and stepchildren, and between unrelated youngsters suddenly brought together must all be dealt with.

5. Children may feel that they have "lost" a natural parent.

   Stepparents lose the sense of "being first" in their relationships with stepchildren.

   Stepparents may also experience a sense of loss of the dreams that accompany a first-time marriage.

   "Natural" parents feel a sense of loss of their former spouse.

Textbook Question Answers

1. affiliation and achievement (affection and instrumentality or interdependence and independence or communion and agency)
2. love; work
3. love and belonging; success and esteem
4. intimacy versus isolation; generativity versus stagnation
5. orderly; predictable

In the 1950s, men in their early 20s would finish their education, choose their occupation, marry, buy a house, and have children. Women would marry and have children.

6. do not take; social clock; the culturally set timetable that establishes when various events and endeavors are appropriate
7. highly developed
8. socioeconomic status; younger
9. women; marry; childbearing
10. 18; 30; 30; 40
11. close friendship; romantic partnership
12. friends

Friends choose each other, often for the very qualities that make them good sources of emotional support. They are also a source of self-esteem.

13. **a.** Most young adults try to postpone the over-riding commitments of marriage and having children.

   b. Because today's elderly are healthier, few young adults must provide care for aging parents.

14. gateways to attraction

   a. physical attractiveness

   b. availability

   c. absence of unwanted traits

   d. frequent exposure

15. filters; excluded

16. both men and women; friendship networks

17. are; shared activities; interests; intimate; emotional

Women talk more often about their intimate concerns and delve deeper into personal and family issues; men typically talk about external matters such as sports, politics, or work.

18. women; men; self-concept; problems via shared fears, sorrows, and disappointments

19. competition

20. **a.** Intimacy is grounded in mutual vulnerability, a characteristic discouraged in men.

   b. From childhood, boys are inclined to be more active and girls more verbal.

   c. Many men avoid any expression of affection toward other men because they fear its association with homosexuality.

Cross-sex friendships offer men and women an opportunity to explore their commonalities, to gain practical skills traditionally "reserved" for the other sex, and to expand their perspectives. Because each sex tends to have its own expectations for friendship, misunderstandings can occur in cross-sex friendships. Another hazard is that men are often inclined to try to sexualize friendships.

21. female

22. job; vocationally; psychologically

23. passion; intimacy; commitment; predictable

24. physical; emotional

25. personal intimacy; commitment

26. consummate

27. passion; intimacy; commitment

28. cohabitation

29. does not; happy; healthy; financial status

30. 2 to 5 percent; have

31. higher; 10; 50; 49

32. half

33. less; identity

34. homogamy; more; heterogamy; role; social homogamy

35. marital equity; exchange

36. work in progress

37. two; varies; increased

38. more

39. negative; more

First, until the divorce, ex-spouses often are unaware of things that *were* going well. Second, even after divorce, emotional dependence between the former partners often is strong.

40. social circle

41. loneliness, disequilibrium, promiscuous sexual behavior, and erratic patterns of eating, sleeping, working, and drug and alcohol use; do

42. least; children; mothers

43. Only a minority of

44. is; authoritative; guidance; discipline

Many factors contribute to spouse abuse, including social pressures that create stress, cultural values that condone violence, personality pathologies, and drug and alcohol addiction.

45. common couple violence; usually does not lead

46. patriarchal terrorism; husband; battered-wife; becomes

47. outside intervention; reduce

48. achieve; varies

49. generativity

   a. develop and use their personal skills or talents

   b. express their creative energy

   c. aid and advise co-workers

   d. contribute to the community

50. exploration; establishment; maintenance; decline (retirement); low-tech; expertise; interchangeable

51. agriculture; industry; industry; information; service;

52. physical or occupational therapist, human service worker, computer engineer, home health caregiver, systems analyst, medical assistant, paralegal, and special-education teacher

53. linear; secure; specific; psychosocial; cognitive

54. diverse; half; immigrants; ethnic

First, it is a mistake to plan on staying in one career forever. Second, to be successful today workers must be sensitive to cultural differences.

55. glass ceiling

56. neither

57. do not suffer

58. do not necessarily; role overload; role buffering

59. are

60. logistics; are

61. earns more, and is more committed to her career, than the husband; blue-collar; immigrants

62. one-third

63. attachments

64. adoptive

65. earlier than

Answers to Testing Yourself

1. **b.** is the answer. (textbook, p. 511)

2. **d.** is the answer. (textbook, p. 513)

3. **c.** is the answer. (textbook, p. 513)

4. **a.** is the answer. (textbook, p. 525)

   c. & d. The fluidity of social circles following divorce was not discussed.

5. **a.** is the answer. (textbook, p. 514)

   d. Low SES is actually a risk factor for divorce.

6. **d.** is the answer. (textbook, p. 511)

   a. Generativity is a characteristic of the crisis following the intimacy crisis.

   b. Stagnation occurs when generativity needs are not met.

   c. Erikson's theory does not address this issue.

7. **a.** is the answer. (textbook, p. 515)

   c. Because they are mobile and tend to have fewer commitments, young adults find it relatively easy to form friendships.

   d. Almost never do young adults feel bereft of friendship.

8. **d.** is the answer. (textbook, p. 521)

9. **c.** is the answer. (textbook, p. 519)

   d. Sternberg's theory is not concerned with the stages of parenthood.

10. **c.** is the answer. (textbook, p. 519)

11. **b.** is the answer. (textbook, p. 522)

    a. By definition, homogamous couples share values, background, and the like.

    c. & d. These may or may not be true, depending on the extent to which such a couple is homogamous.

12. **b.** is the answer. (textbook, p. 534)

    a. & d. It is a common *myth* that children in dual-earner families suffer neglect.

    c. Role overload more often pertains to adults who must balance the roles of parent, spouse, and employee.

13. **a.** is the answer. (textbook, p. 529)

    b. & d. In fact, just the opposite is true.

    c. The traditional career cycle is *more* typical of low-tech occupations.

14. **b.** is the answer. (textbook, p. 534)

    c. Most parents report that they are pleased that they have had children.

15. **b.** is the answer. (textbook, p. 539)

    c. & d. The text does not discuss variations in the incidence of developmental problems in the various family structures.

16. **b.** is the answer. Today, with higher divorce rates and longer life expectancy, marriages are ended more by divorce than by death. (audio program)

17. **a.** is the answer. Today, approximately one child in four will spend some time living with a stepparent before turning 17. (audio program)

18. **a.** is the answer. A stepparent can never replace a natural parent; to attempt to do so is, according to experts, disastrous. (audio program)

19. **d.** is the answer. For all of these reasons, stepparents are often disappointed that they cannot quickly develop close relationships with their stepchildren. (audio program; textbook, pp. 535, 538)

20. **a.** is the answer. According to Horigian, this final stage of "letting go" is very rewarding. Once families are freed from the disappointment of lost dreams, the relationships within a family are released to grow in their own unique ways. (audio program)

Reference

Schneider, D. M. (1980). *American kinship: A cultural account.* Saddlebrook, NJ: Prentice Hall.

An interesting anthropological/sociological description of cultural variations in family structure.

Middle Adulthood: Biosocial Development

AUDIO PROGRAM: Improving the Odds

ORIENTATION

How long do you think you will live? What are the odds that you will survive to be 100 years old? Is there anything you can do to improve these odds? An individual's **longevity** is limited by the biological clock, but the limit is flexible. As the author of *The Developing Person Through the Life Span, 5/e,* indicates, today's cohort of middle-aged persons is healthier than in previous years. Although many physical changes occur between the ages of 40 and 60, most have no significant health consequences. Variations in health are related to genetic, educational, and economic factors, as well as ethnicity and gender. The most important reason for individual variations in health, however, is personal lifestyle.

In audio program 20, "Improving the Odds," we meet two middle-aged individuals concerned about the health of their changing bodies. As the program unfolds, Susan, 47, and Larry, 59, complete the **life-expectancy questionnaire** designed by psychologist Diana Woodruff-Pak. Although the test obviously cannot predict how long each person will live, it is a useful tool that identifies factors likely to extend or shorten that life. These factors focus on each person's **genetic history**, **personal health habits**, **socioeconomic status**, and **social** and **personality characteristics**. As Susan and Larry work through the questionnaire, it becomes clear that certain factors related to longevity, such as how long one's ancestors lived, are beyond the individual's control. But factors under one's control can add or subtract 20 years to/from a life. We wonder what the questionnaire predicts for Larry and Susan.

LESSON GOALS

By the end of this lesson you should be prepared to:

1. Describe the typical pattern of physical development that occurs during middle adulthood.

2. Explain the relationship of an individual's life expectancy to lifestyle, genetic history, health practices, and personality.

3. Differentiate four measures of health, and explain the concept of quality-adjusted life years.

4. Describe age-related changes in the sexual-reproductive system and discuss their impact on sexual expression.

Audio Assignment

Listen to the audio tape that accompanies Lesson 20: "Improving the Odds."

Write answers to the following questions. You may replay portions of the program if you need to refresh your memory. Answer guidelines may be found in the section at the end of this chapter.

1. What is the difference in life expectancy for men and women and why do researchers believe that this difference is a biological rather than a social phenomenon?

2. What is the relationship between an individual's predicted longevity and his or her genetic history?

3. In what ways do personal health habits predict longevity?

4. What is the relationship between an individual's predicted longevity and his or her socioeconomic status?

5. What is the relationship between an individual's predicted longevity and his or her social and personality characteristics?

6. What does it mean when there is a correlation between two variables?

7. Several limitations of the life-expectancy test were mentioned in the program. What are they?

Textbook Assignment

Read Chapter 20: "Millde Adulthood: Biosocial Development," pages 545–569 in *The Developing Person Through the Life Span, 5/e*, then work through the material that follows to review it. Complete the sentences and answer the questions. As you proceed, evaluate your performance for each secdtion by consulting the answers on page ??. Do not continue with the next section until you understand each answer. If you need to, review or reread the appropriate section in the textbook before continuing.

Normal Changes in Middle Adulthood (pp. 545–550)

1. Some of the normal changes in appearance that occur during middle adulthood include

   _____

   _____

   _____

2. With the exception of excessive

   _____ _____ ,

   the physical changes that typically occur during middle adulthood usually _____
   (do/do not) have significant health consequences.

3. The physical changes of middle adulthood may have a substantial impact on a person's
   _____ ; this is particularly true for
   _____ (men/women).

4. (In Person) The overall impact of aging on the individual depends in large measure on the individual's _____ toward growing old.

5. Age-related deficits in the sense organs are most obvious in _____ and

   _____ .

6. Compared to women, who begin to show hearing deficits at around age _____ , men begin to show some deficits by age _____ . The rate of hearing loss is faster in _____ (women/men).

7. Most losses in hearing during middle adulthood are the result of the interaction of _____ and _____ .

8. Age-related hearing loss is the result of prolonged exposure to _____ .

9. With normal aging, the ability to hear differences in _____ _____ declines faster than the ability to understand _____ .

10. Speech-related hearing losses are first apparent for _____-(high/low) frequency sounds.

11. After puberty, _____ affects focusing much more than age does. Due to the fact that the _____ of their eyes are too _____ (flat/curved), people who need glasses before age 20 tend simply to be _____ (nearsighted/farsighted/astigmatic). In contrast, older adults tend to be _____ , due to the fact that the _____ of their eyes become _____ (too curved/flatter). A 50-percent decrease in the _____ of the lens results in many older adults wearing _____ .

12. Other aspects of vision that decline steadily with age are _____ _____ , _____-_____ , _____ , _____ , and _____ _____ . These changes are particularly likely to become apparent by age _____ .

13. Serious accidents are much more common in late _____ or late _____ than in middle adulthood, when most people are sufficiently _____ to compensate for minor visual losses.

14. A more serious vision problem is the disease _____ , a hardening of the eyeball caused by an increase of _____ within the eyeball. By age _____ , this disease is the leading cause of _____ . The incidence of this disease is especially high among those of _____ descent.

15. Systemic declines in the efficiency and the organ reserve of the _____ , _____ , and _____ _____ make middle-aged people _____ (more/less) vulnerable to disease. Declines are also evident in the _____ system, resulting in an increased risk of _____ diseases such as _____ _____ and _____ .

16. Thanks to better _____ _____ and _____ , the overall death rate among the middle-aged is _____ what it was sixty years ago, especially for the two leading causes of death in this age group: _____ _____ and _____ . The overall health of middle-aged adults _____ (varies/does not vary) significantly from one nation to another.

Health Habits over the Years (pp. 550–555)

17. For most conditions and diseases, it is a person's _____ _____ over the years that have the greatest influence on delaying and preventing physiological decline.

18. (Research Report) Cigarette-smoking is a known risk factor for most serious diseases, including _____ .

19. (Research Report) All smoking diseases are _____- and _____-sensitive. Although smoking rates have dropped in North America, rates in most _____ nations and _____ nations have not.

These statistics highlight the importance of
_____ and _____ ,
rather than _____ in smoking.

20. Some studies find that adults who drink moder-
ately may live longer, possibly because alcohol
increases the blood's supply of
_____ , a protein that helps reduce
the amount of _____ in the body.
Another possible explanation of the relationship
between moderate drinking and longevity is that
moderate drinking may reduce
_____ and aid
_____ .

21. Alcohol dependence and abuse are most common
at about age _____ .

List some of the damaging effects of heavy drinking
on the body.

22. Worldwide, alcohol is a leading factor in the
_____ _____
_____ , which is a measure that
combines indicators of premature
_____ and _____
worldwide.

23. Specific foods probably _____
(can/cannot) prevent, or cause, major health
problems. Nevertheless, research *does* support the
health benefits of avoiding too much
_____ and including sufficient
amounts of _____ in one's diet.

24. Adults in industrialized countries typically consume _____ percent of their calories
as fat. The National Cancer Institute recommends
that adults increase their consumption of fiber to
no more than _____ grams per day
and reduce their consumption of fat to less than
_____ percent.

25. High-fiber diets lower a person's risk of several
forms of _____ , particularly that of
the _____ .

26. Overweight, defined as _____
_____ , is present in
_____ (how many?) middle-aged
residents of the United States. Obesity, defined as
_____ ,
is a risk factor for_____
_____ , _____ , and
_____ , and a contributing factor
for _____ , the most common disability
for older adults.

27. Throughout much of the world, the percentage of
people who are overweight or obese is
_____ (less than/greater
than/about the same as) that of previous generations. Many experts believe that being slightly
overweight _____ (increases/does
not increase) a person's risk of disease, disability,
or death.

28. Women are more likely to be depressed if they
are _____ (overweight/under-
weight), while men are more likely to be
depressed if they are _____ (over-
weight/underweight)

29. Between ages 20 and 50, a person's metabolism
_____ (slows/increases) by about a
third, which means that middle-aged people need
to eat _____ (more/less) simply to
maintain their weight.

30. Even more important to health than eating less
during middle age is _____ more.
People who are active _____
(do/do not) have lower rates of serious illness
and death than inactive people. Exercise also
reduces the ratio of body _____ to
body _____ . An additional advantage is enhanced _____ functioning
due to improved circulation to the
_____ .

List some of the health benefits of regular exercise.

Variations in Health (pp. 555–563)

31. Individuals who are relatively well-educated, financially secure, and living in or near cities tend to live _____ (shorter/longer) lives and have _____ (more/ fewer) chronic illnesses or disabilities.

32. In the United States, people living in the _____ and _____ are healthier than those in the _____ and _____ _____ . The reasons for such differences include variations in

    _____

    _____ .

33. Perhaps the most solid indicator of health of given age groups is the rate of _____ , or death.

34. A more comprehensive measure of health is _____ , defined as _____ of all kinds; it can be sudden, or _____ , or it can be _____ , extending over a long time period.

35. To truly portray quality of life, we need to measure _____ , which refers to a person's inability to perform basic activities, and _____ , which refers to how healthy and energetic a person feels.

36. In terms of quality of life, _____ is probably the most important measure of health.

37. The concept of _____-_____ _____ _____ indicates how many years of full vitality are lost as a result of a particular disease or disability.

38. Between the ages of 45 and 55, the chance of dying is twice as high for _____ , and only half as high for _____ _____ , as it is for European Americans. In between are the mortality rates for

_____ and _____ _____ . Self-reported health status, morbidity, and disability _____ (do/do not) follow the same ethnic patterns as does mortality.

39. In all minority groups, the illness and death rates among recent immigrants are _____ (higher/lower) than among long-time U.S. residents.

State several possible explanations for this difference.

40. (Changing Policy) Categorizing people in racial terms may mistakenly cause people to conclude that _____ and ancestral _____ are the main explanations for group differences in health. In addition to these, other factors in group differences in health are _____ and _____ , as well as the pressures and opportunities provided by the larger society

41. (Changing Policy) The racial difference in the death rates of black and white Americans is greatest during the early _____ (what decade?), when U.S. blacks are _____ (how many?) times as likely to die as whites. Genetic predispositions and ancestry probably _____ (explain/do not explain) this pattern. Extrinsic factors, particularly _____ and _____ , are especially harmful between _____ and age 65.

42. (Changing Policy) Recent studies have also found that rates of _____

    _____

    among adults of West African ancestry rose as adults grew up farther away from rural Africa. Another study found that the _____ of breast cancer in middle-aged African American women is less than in European American women, but their rate of _____ from the disease is higher. This, too, demonstrates that ethnic health differences are influenced less by genes than by factors related to _____ , _____ , and _____ .

43. Compared to middle-aged women, middle-aged men are _____ as likely to die of any cause and three times as likely to die of _____ _____ . Not until age _____ are the rates equivalent.

44. Beginning in middle age, women have higher _____ and _____ rates than men. Contributing to the gender difference in mortality is the fact that men are more likely to_____ , _____ , be _____ , repress _____ , and ignore their _____ _____ .

45. Contributing to the gender difference in morbidity and disability is the tendency of the medical community to focus on treating _____ _____ rather than _____ _____ , and on preventing _____ rather than avoiding _____ . This has meant that more research money is dedicated to studying diseases that are more common in _____ (men/women).

The Sexual-Reproductive System (pp. 563–568)

46. At an average age of _____ , a woman reaches _____ , as ovulation and menstruation stop and the production of the hormones _____ , _____ , and _____ drops considerably.

47. All the various biological and psychological changes that precede menopause are referred to as the _____ . The first symptom is typically shorter _____ _____ , followed by variations in the timing of her _____ . Symptoms such as hot flashes and flushes and cold sweats

are caused by _____ _____ , that is, a temporary disruption in the body mechanisms that maintain body temperature.

48. Two other serious changes caused by reduced levels of _____ are loss of bone _____ , which can lead to the thin and brittle bones that accompany _____ , and an increase of arterial _____ that can set the stage for _____ _____ _____ .

49. Whether natural menopause is troubling depends, in part, on factors in the _____ context, such as _____ values and prevailing _____ views.

50. In the United States, approximately _____ percent of women going through natural menopause and _____ percent going through surgically induced menopause experience symptoms sufficiently difficult that they require _____ _____ _____ , or HRT.

51. Continued use of HRT beyond menopause has been shown to reduce the risk of _____ _____ disease, _____ fractures, and _____ disease. The long-term consequences of HRT, however, are not yet known.

(A Life-Span View) Briefly explain why menopause is more often welcomed by women today than in the past.

52. (A Life-Span View) Physiologically, men _____ (do/do not) experience anything like the female climacteric. Although the average levels of testosterone decline gradually, if at all, with age, they can dip if a man becomes _____ _____ or unusually worried.

53. Frequency of intercourse and orgasm usually _____ (declines/increases/ remains unchanged) during middle age.

54. During middle adulthood, sexual stimulation takes _____ (longer/less time) and needs to be _____ (more/ less) direct than earlier in life.

55. Most middle-aged men report that they _____ (are/are not) satisfied with their sex life. The physical changes that follow menopause generally _____ (impair/need not impair) sexual relationships.

Testing Yourself

After you have completed the audio and text review questions, see how well you do on the following quiz. Correct answers, with text and audio references, may be found at the end of this chapter.

1. The life expectancy advantage that females have over males is:
   a. found in no species other than humans.
   b. probably a social rather than a biological effect.
   c. probably a biological rather than a social effect.
   d. only a recent historical development.

2. Individuals whose diets are rich in _____ tend to live the longest.
   a. vegetables, fruits, and simple foods
   b. meat, fish, and other high-protein foods
   c. saturated fats
   d. simple carbohydrates

3. The leading cause of mortality in both sexes is:
   a. lung cancer.   c. heart disease.
   b. accidents.   d. stroke.

4. At age 80 there are about twice as many women as men alive; this is probably due to the fact that:
   a. although males are born at a higher rate than are females, they are more susceptible to the hazards of life at every age.
   b. estrogen protects females against the heart disease that kills many males.
   c. testosterone makes males more susceptible to heart disease.
   d. all of the above are true.

5. The major influence on longevity is an individual's :
   a. personal health habits.
   b. socioeconomic status.
   c. genetic history.
   d. personality.

6. During the years from 40 to 60, the average adult:
   a. becomes proportionally slimmer.
   b. gains about 5 pounds per year.
   c. gains about 1 pound per year.
   d. is more likely to be noticeably overweight.

7. (In Person) The overall impact of aging depends *largely* on the individual's:
   a. general physical health.
   b. genetic predisposition toward disease.
   c. attitudes about aging.
   d. health habits and lifestyle.

8. Age-related deficits in speech-related hearing are most noticeable for:
   a. high-frequency sounds.
   b. low-frequency sounds.
   c. mid-range-frequency sounds.
   d. rapid conversation.

9. Compared to the acuity problems of younger adults, which tend to be confined to _____ , those of older adults also tend to include _____ .
   a. farsightedness; nearsightedness
   b. farsightedness; nearsightedness and decreasing depth perception
   c. astigmatism; farsightedness
   d. nearsightedness; farsightedness and decreasing depth perception

10. Characterized by an increase in fluid within the eyeball, this eye disease is the leading cause of blindness by age 70. It is called:
    a. myopia.   c. cataracts.
    b. astigmatism.   d. glaucoma.

11. At midlife, individuals who _____ tend to live longer and have fewer chronic illnesses or disabilities.
    a. are relatively well educated
    b. are financially secure
    c. live in or near cities
    d. are or do all of the above

12. The term that refers to diseases of all kinds is:
    a. mortality.
    b. morbidity.
    c. disability.
    d. vitality.

13. On average, women reach menopause at age:
    a. 39.
    b. 42.
    c. 46.
    d. 51.

14. In explaining ethnic variations in health and illness during middle age, _____ factors are more important than_____ factors.
    a. genetic; social and psychological
    b. social and psychological; genetic
    c. intrinsic; cultural
    d. cultural; extrinsic

15. In middle age, _____ rates are higher for men than for women, whereas _____ rates are higher for women than men.
    a. mortality; morbidity
    b. morbidity; mortality
    c. vitality; disability
    d. disability; vitality

16. The leading cause of mortality in both sexes is:
    a. lung cancer.
    b. accidents.
    c. heart disease.
    d. stroke.

17. The concept that indicates how many years of full physical, intellectual, and social health are lost to a particular physical disease or disability is:
    a. vitality
    b. disability
    c. morbidity
    d. quality-adjusted life years.

18. (A Life-Span View) Today, decisions regarding childbearing are made to a large extent on the basis of:
    a. age.
    b. religion.
    c. education level.
    d. financial situation.

19. (Research Report) Which of the following is true of all smoking diseases?
    a. They are a natural result of smoking for ten years or more, whether or not the person eventually quit.
    b. They are related to dosage of nicotine taken in and to length of time the person has smoked.
    c. They are all incurable.
    d. They are all based on the psychological addiction to tobacco.

20. The first symptom of the climacteric is usually:
    a. shorter menstrual cycles.
    b. a drop in the production of progesterone.
    c. increased variation in the timing of ovulation.
    d. weight gain.

NAME _____   INSTRUCTOR _____

LESSON 20: HOW LONG WILL YOU LIVE?

Exercise

An individual's life span is determined by many factors, including genetic history, personal health habits, socioeconomic status, and personality. To see how these factors interact, complete the following life expectancy questionnaire for yourself (or for someone you know). The basic life expectancy for American males of all races today is 73.6 years; for females it is 79.4 years. Write this beginning number down; then, as you check through the list, add or subtract the appropriate number of years for each item.

Beginning Life Expectancy   _____

1. Longevity of grandparents
   Add 1 year for each grandparent living beyond age 80. Add one-half year for each grandparent surviving beyond the age of 70.   _____

2. Longevity of parents
   If your mother lived beyond the age of 80, add 4 years. Add 2 years if your father lived beyond 80.   _____

3. Cardiovascular disease among close relatives
   If any parent, grandparent, or sibling died from cardiovascular disease before age 50, subtract 4 years for each incidence. If any died from the above before the age of 60, subtract 2 years.   _____

4. Other heritable disease among close relatives
   If any parent, grandparent, or sibling died before the age of 60 from diabetes or peptic ulcer, subtract 3 years. If any died before 60 from stomach cancer, subtract 2 years. Women whose close female relatives have died before 60 from breast cancer should also subtract 2 years. Finally, if any close relatives have died before the age of 60 from any cause except accidents or homicide, subtract 1 year for each incidence._____

5. Childbearing
   Women who cannot or do not plan to have children, and those over 40 who have never had children, should subtract one-half year. Women who have had over seven children, or plan to, should subtract 1 year.   _____

6. Mother's age at your birth
   Was your mother over the age of 35 or under the age of 18 when you were born? If so, subtract 1 year.   _____

7. Birth order
   Are you the first-born in your family? If so, add 1 year.   _____

8. Intelligence
   If you feel that you are superior in intelligence, add 2 years.

   _____

9. Weight
   If you are more than 30 percent overweight, subtract 5 years.
   If you are more than 10 percent overweight, subtract 2 years.

   _____

10. Dietary habits
    If you eat a lot of vegetables and fruits, and usually stop eating
    before feeling full, add 1 year. If you drink five or more cups of
    coffee per day, subtract one-half year.

    _____

11. Smoking
    If you smoke two or more packs of cigarettes a day, subtract 12 years.
    If you smoke between one and two packs a day, subtract 7 years.
    If you smoke less than a pack a day, subtract 2 years.

    _____

12. Drinking
    If you are a moderate drinker, add 3 years. If you are a light
    drinker, add 1.5 years. If you are a heavy drinker, subtract 8 years.

    _____

13. Exercise
    If you exercise briskly at least three times a week, add 3 years.

    _____

14. Sleep
    If you sleep more than 10 hours or less than 5 hours a night, subtract 2 years.

    _____

15. Sexual activity
    If you enjoy sexual activity at least once a week, add 2 years.

    _____

16. Regular physical examinations
    If you have an annual physical examination by your physician, add 2 years.

    _____

17. Health status
    If you have a chronic illness at present, subtract 5 years.

    _____

18. Years of education
    If you graduated from college, add 4 years. If you attended college
    but did not graduate, add 2 years. If you graduated from high school
    but did not attend college, add 1 year. If you have less than an
    eighth-grade education, subtract 2 years.

    _____

19. Occupational level (former, if retired; spouse's, if you are not working)
    Professional, add 1.5 years; technicians, administrators, managers,
    and agricultural workers, add 1 year; semi-skilled workers should
    subtract one-half year; laborers should subtract 4 years.

    _____

20. Family income
    If your family income is above average for your education and
    occupation, add 1 year. If it is below average for your education
    and occupation, subtract 1 year.   _____

21. Activity on the job
    If your job involves a lot of physical activity, add 2 years. If your
    job requires that you sit all day, subtract 2 years.   _____

22. Age and work
    If you are over the age of 60 and still on the job, add 2 years.
    If you are over the age of 65 and have not retired, add 4 years.   _____

23. Rural vs. urban dwelling
    If you live in an urban area and have lived in or near the city for
    most of your life, subtract 1 year. If you have spent most of your
    life in a rural area, add 1 year.   _____

24. Married vs. divorced
    If you are married and living with your spouse, add 1 year.
    Men: If you are separated or divorced and living alone,
    subtract 9 years (not alone: subtract 4 years). If you are widowed
    and living alone subtract 7 years (not alone: subtract 3 years).
    Women: If you are separated or divorced and living alone, subtract
    4 years. If you are widowed and living alone, subtract 3 years.
    If you are separated, divorced, or widowed and not living alone,
    subtract 2 years.   _____

25. Single living status
    Unmarried women (living alone or with others) and unmarried men
    who live with family or friends should subtract 1 year for each
    unmarried decade past age 25. Unmarried men who live alone
    should subtract 2 years for each decade after 25.   _____

26. Life changes
    If you are always changing things in your life—jobs, residences,
    friends—subtract 2 years.   _____

27. Friendship
    If you have at least two close friends in whom you can confide
    almost all the details of your life, add 1 year.   _____

28. Aggressive personality
    If you have an aggressive and sometimes hostile personality,
    subtract 2 years.   _____

29. Flexible personality
    If you are a calm, easygoing, adaptable person, add 2 years.
    If you are rigid, dogmatic, and set in your ways, subtract 2 years. _____

30. Risk-taking personality
    If you take a lot of risks, including driving without seat belts, exceeding the speed limit, and taking any dare that is made, subtract 2 years. If you use seat belts regularly, drive infrequently, and generally avoid risks and dangerous parts of town, add 1 year.   _____

31. Depressive personality
    Have you been depressed, tense, worried, or guilty for more than a period of a year or two? If so, subtract 1 to 3 years depending upon how seriously you are affected by these feelings.   _____

32. Happy personality
    Are you basically happy and content, and have you had a lot of fun in life? If so, add 2 years.   _____

After you have completed the longevity questionnaire, fill in the information requested on the handout and return the response sheet to your instructor.

National Center for Health Statistics. 1999. *United States Department of Health and Human Services.*

1. By how many years did your predicted longevity change as a result of the factors listed below? For each factor, a negative change indicates a *decrease* in longevity; a positive change in years indicates an *increase* in predicted longevity.

    a. Genetic history. Subtract your beginning life expectancy from your total after item 8 (intelligence).   _____

    Number of years by which predicted longevity changed (indicate plus or minus)   _____

    b. Personal health habits. Subtract your total after item 17 (health status) from your total following item 8 (intelligence).   _____

    Number of years by which predicted longevity changed   _____

    c. Socioeconomic status. Subtract your total in years following item 22 (age and work) from your total following item 17 (health status).   _____

    Number of years by which predicted longevity changed   _____

    d. Social and personality characteristics. Subtract your total in years following item 32 (happy personality) from your total following item 22 (age and work).   _____

    Number of years by which predicted longevity changed   _____

2. By how many years did your predicted longevity change (increase or decrease from beginning life expectancy) as a result of factors that are under your direct control?

    Number of years by which predicted longevity changed

3. By how many years did your predicted longevity change (increase or decrease from beginning life expectancy) as a result of factors that you cannot control?

    Number of years by which predicted longevity changed

4. Did completing the questionnaire encourage you or your subject to make any changes in your personal habits or lifestyle? If so, what are those changes?

5. Which, if any, variables were you surprised to discover were related to life expectancy? Why did they surprise you?

6. a.   Are there variables that did not appear in the questionnaire that you would also expect to be related to longevity? Name them.

   b.   Which research methods might you use to determine whether such a relationship does, in fact, exist?

7.   What are the strengths and limitations of the correlational method of research?

LESSON GUIDELINES

Audio Question Guidelines

1. In all species of animals in the wild, the female of the species lives longer. The fact that this is true of all species, including humans, suggests a biological rather than a social effect.

   For humans, women maintain this biological edge from the first instant of life to the very end. About 120 males are conceived for every 100 females, but the hazards of male development are so great that at birth the ratio is down to 106 males for every 100 females. At age 80 there are only 50 males for every 100 females alive.

   Women are probably protected from cardiovascular disease (the most common cause of death in the United States) by the hormone estrogen. Because of their higher testosterone levels, men may be at an increased risk for cardiovascular disease.

2. Genetic history has the major influence on an individual's **longevity**. In order of importance, the longevity of one's mother, father, and grandparents is correlated with one's own life expectancy.

3. In promoting longevity, the following personal health habits are important: maintaining an ideal and stable body weight; eating a balanced diet rich in fruits, vegetables, and simple foods, yet low in fat and sugar; not smoking; drinking alcohol in moderation; engaging in regular exercise; and having regular physical examinations.

4. The higher a person's socioeconomic status, the longer he or she is likely to live. Longevity tends to be greater in people who have had more education, those who work in professional or managerial (rather than unskilled) professions, and in those with above average income for their age and occupation.

   The lower average socioeconomic status of African-Americans in the United States may explain why their life expectancy is approximately 6 years less than that of persons of European descent. Persons with low socioeconomic status are more likely to live in conditions less conducive to the maintenance of good health.

5. Greater longevity is found more commonly among persons who are socially integrated than among those who are not.

   Especially among men, divorce, widowhood, being single, and being separated predict shorter life expectancy.

   Experiencing many changes in one's life is also associated with reduced life expectancy.

   Being a happy person generally and having at least two close friends predicts a longer life expectancy.

   Being an aggressive personality is associated with reduced life expectancy.

6. When two factors or variables are correlated, it means that changes in one are predictive of changes in the other. A correlation between two variables, however, does not imply that changes in one *cause* changes in the other: A third factor might influence the two variables, which, although linked in a correlational fashion, do not influence one another.

7. Because the life-expectancy test is an example of correlational, rather than experimental, research, no conclusions about what "causes" a person to have lengthened or reduced life expectancy can be drawn.

   The life-expectancy test relies on the subjective assessment and memory of the respondent. The test's validity and accuracy are, therefore, subject to question.

   There has been no longitudinal "follow-up" of individuals who have taken the test to see if the predictions were accurate.

Textbook Question Answers

1. hair turns gray and thins; skin becomes drier and more wrinkled; pockets of fat settle on the upper arms, buttocks, and eyelids; back muscles, connecting tissues, and bones lose strength, causing some individuals to become shorter; many become noticeably overweight
2. weight gain; do not
3. self-image; women
4. attitude
5. hearing; vision
6. 50; 30; men
7. age; genes
8. noise
9. pure tones; conversation
10. high
11. heredity; corneas; curved; nearsighted; farsighted; corneas; flatter; elasticity; bifocals
12. depth perception; eye-muscle resilience; color sensitivity; dark adaptation; 50
13. adolescence; adulthood; cautious

14. glaucoma; fluid; 70; blindness; African-Americans

15. lungs; heart; digestive system; more; immune; autoimmune; rheumatoid arthritis; lupus

16. health habits; disease prevention; half; heart disease; cancer; varies

17. health habits

18. cancer of the lung, bladder, kidney, mouth, and stomach, as well as heart disease, stroke, pneumonia, and emphysema

19. dose; duration; European; developing; culture; cohort; genes

20. HDL (high-density lipoprotein); LDL (low-density lipoprotein); tension; digestion

21. 40

Heavy drinking is the main cause of cirrhosis of the liver; it also stresses the heart and stomach, destroys brain cells, hastens calcium loss, decreases fertility, and is a risk factor for many forms of cancer.

22. global disease burden; death; disability

23. cannot; fat; fiber

24. 40; 30; 30

25. cancer; colon

26. a BMI of 25 or higher; two of every three; a BMI of 30 or higher; heart disease; diabetes; stroke; arthritis

27. greater than; increases

28. overweight; underweight

29. slows; less

30. exercising; do; fat; weight; cognitive; brain

Regular aerobic exercise increases heart and lung capacity, lowers blood pressure, increases HDL in the blood, reduces the ratio of body fat to body weight, and enhances cognitive functioning. It also sometimes helps reduce depression and hostility.

31. longer; fewer

32. West; Midwest; South; Middle Atlantic; the quality of the environment and health care, as well as genetic, dietary, religious, socioeconomic, medical, and cultural patterns

33. mortality

34. morbidity; disease; acute; chronic

35. disability; vitality

36. vitality

37. quality-adjusted life years (QALYs)

38. African Americans; Asian Americans; Native Americans; Hispanic Americans; do

39. lower

One reason is that people who emigrate tend to be hardier. Another is health habits, which tend to be healthier in those less assimilated, particularly with regard to alcohol use, exercise, and diet. Recent immigrants also tend to be more optimistic, and have stronger family communication and support.

40. genes; culture; education; SES

41. 40s; three; do not explain; prejudice; poverty; adolescence

42. hypertension (high blood pressure); incidence; mortality; education; income; racism

43. twice; heart disease; 85

44. morbidity; disability; smoke; drink; overweight; emotions; medical symptoms

45. acute illnesses; chronic conditions; death; disability; men

46. 51; menopause; estrogen; progesterone; testosterone

47. climacteric; menstrual cycles; period; vasomotor instability

48. estrogen; calcium; osteoporosis; fat; coronary heart disease

49. social; cultural; medical

50. 10; 90; hormone replacement therapy

51. coronary artery; hip; Alzheimer's

Traditionally, the more children a couple had, the more fortunate they were considered to be. The impact of the loss of fertility was therefore much more significant. Today, the end of childbearing is determined less by age than by personal factors such as financial situation. Thus, as the time when sexual activity is no longer accompanied by fear of pregnancy, menopause is more often welcomed than regretted.

52. do not; sexually inactive

53. declines

54. longer; more

55. are; need not impair

Answers to Testing Yourself

1. **c.** is the answer. In all species of animals studied, including the human, the female of the species lives longer than the male. (audio program)

2. **a.** is the answer. People who live the longest are not overly concerned with food, but tend to eat diets that emphasize vegetables, fruits, and simple foods. (audio program)

3. **c.** is the answer. (audio program)

4. **d.** is the answer. (audio program)

5. **c.** is the answer. Personality, health habits, and socioeconomic status are all important, but personal genetic history is the *major* influence on how long a person will live. (audio program)

6. **d.** is the answer. (textbook, p. 545)

   b. & c. Weight gain varies substantially from person to person.

7. **c.** is the answer. (textbook, p. 546)

8. **a.** is the answer. (textbook, p. 547)

9. **d.** is the answer. (textbook, p. 548)

10. **d.** is the answer. (textbook, p. 548)

    a. This is the technical name for nearsightedness.

    b. & c. Although not discussed in the text, these are serious, but usually correctable, eye conditions.

11. **d.** is the answer. (textbook, p. 555)

12. **b.** is the answer. (textbook, p. 556)

    a. This is the overall death rate.

    c. This refers to a person's inability to perform activities that most others can.

    d. This refers to how physically, intellectually, and socially healthy an individual feels.

13. **d.** is the answer. (textbook, p. 563)

14. **b.** is the answer. (textbook, p. 560)

    c. & d. Genes and culture *are* intrinsic and extrinsic factors, respectively.

15. **a.** is the answer. (textbook, pp. 561–562)

16. **c.** is the answer. (textbook, pp. 561–562)

17. **d.** is the answer. (textbook, p. 557)

    a. Vitality is a measure of how healthy and energetic a person feels.

    b. Disability measures only the inability to perform basic activities.

    c. Morbidity refers only to the rate of disease.

18. **d.** is the answer. (textbook, p. 566)

19. **b.** is the answer. (textbook, p. 551)

20. **a.** is the answer. (textbook, p. 564)

Reference

Woodruff, D. (1977). *Can you live to be one hundred?* New York: New American Library.

Middle Adulthood: Cognitive Development

AUDIO PROGRAM: What Makes an Expert?

ORIENTATION

For most of this century, psychologists were convinced that intelligence peaks during adolescence and then gradually declines throughout adulthood. Within the past 35 years, however, research has led to the opposite conclusion, that in some ways intelligence actually improves during adulthood. Audio program 21 explores how intelligence changes through the adult years and describes the methodology by which developmental psychologists study these changes.

Chapter 21 of the textbook notes that researchers today believe that there are several kinds of intelligence, each of which may increase, decrease, or remain stable with age. Some experts maintain that **fluid intelligence**, based on the underlying abilities of short-term memory, abstract thought, and speed of thinking, declines with age, while **crystallized intelligence**, based upon accumulated general knowledge, increases. Each dimension of intelligence follows its own developmental pattern, which is determined in part by the individual's education and life experiences, and in part by cohort, or generational, differences. In fact, during middle adulthood **interindividual variation** is probably more important in influencing cognitive development than is chronological age.

The audio program, "What Makes an Expert?" states that as people grow older they get better and better at things that are important to them, while abilities that are not practiced decline. Focusing on the particular **expertise** of a musical savant and a professor of surgery, the program, like the text, explores the many ways in which experts are better than novices at what they do. They are more intuitive and flexible, use better problem-solving strategies, and often process information and perform automatically. During the program, commentary is provided by psychologist Neil Charness and Professor of Surgery George Zuidema.

As the program opens, we hear a piano sonata played by John LaFond. Although he has been blind since birth, suffers from severe epilepsy, is mentally retarded, and is nearly paralyzed on the right side of his body, LaFond has specialized very successfully in one domain: music.

LESSON GOALS

By the end of this lesson you should be prepared to:

1. Distinguish between fluid and crystallized intelligence, and explain how each is affected by age.

2. Outline the theories of intelligence put forth by Robert Sternberg and Howard Gardner.

3. Discuss the multidirectionality of intelligence.

4. Discuss the complexity and plasticity of the development of intelligence during the adult years.

5. Describe the distinguishing features of expertise.

Audio Assignment

Listen to the audio tape that accompanies Lesson 21: "What Makes an Expert?"

Write answers to the following questions. You may replay portions of the program if you need to refresh your memory. Answer guidelines may be found in the Lesson Guidelines section at the end of this chapter.

1. Explain what the abilities of a middle-aged musical savant, a chess grand master, and a skilled physician indicate about the nature of intelligence.

2. Describe the ways in which thinking changes as a person develops expertise in a particular area.

3. Discuss whether experts in different fields of specialization have different peak years of achievement and productivity during the life span.

Textbook Assignment

Read Chapter 21: "Middle Adulthood: Cognitive Development," pages 571–589 in *The Developing Person Through the Life Span, 5/e,* then work through the material that follows to review it. Complete the sentences and answer the questions. As you proceed, evaluate your performance for each secdtion by consulting the answers on page 279. Do not continue with the next section until you understand each answer. If you need to, review or reread the appropriate section in the textbook before continuing.

Multidimensional Intelligence: Not One, But Many? (pp. 571–578)

1. Historically, psychologists have thought of intelligence as _____ (a single entity/several distinct abilities).

2. A leading theoretician, _____ , argued that there is such a thing as general intelligence, which he called _____ .

3. In the 1960s, researchers _____ and _____ differentiated two aspects of intelligence, which they called _____ and _____ intelligence.

4. As its name implies, _____ intelligence is flexible reasoning used to draw infer-

ences and understand relations between concepts. This type of intelligence is also made up of basic mental abilities, including

_____ _____ ,
_____ _____ , and
_____ _____

_____ .

5. The accumulation of facts, information, and knowledge that comes with education and experience with a particular culture is referred to as _____ intelligence.

6. During adulthood, _____ intelligence declines markedly, along with related abilities such as _____ _____ and _____-_____ _____ . However, if a person's intelligence is simply measured by one _____ score, this decline is temporarily disguised by a(n) _____ (increase/decrease) in _____ intelligence.

7. Originally, psychologists thought that _____ intelligence was primarily genetic and that _____ intelligence was primarily learned. Today, most psychologists think that this distinction _____ (is/is not) valid.

8. Research reveals that _____ intelligence continues to expand throughout most of adulthood.

9. In the WAIS, total IQ is an average of two types of intelligence: _____ , which remains in the _____ range throughout adulthood, and _____ , which drops an average of _____ points during adulthood.

10. The theorist who has proposed that intelligence is composed of three fundamental aspects is _____ . The _____ aspect consists of mental processes fostering efficient learning, remembering, and thinking. This type of thinking is particularly valued at _____ (what stage of life?).

11. The _____ aspect enables the person to be flexible and innovative when dealing with new situations. This type of thinking is always _____ rather than _____ , meaning that such thinkers frequently find _____ solutions to problems rather than relying on the one that has always been considered correct. Different cultures value this type of thinking in some _____ more than others.

12. The _____ aspect concerns the ability to adapt to the contextual demands of a given situation. This type of thinking is particularly useful for managing the conflicting personalities in a _____ or _____ .

13. Most adults believe that practical intelligence _____ (increases/decreases/is stable) with age.

14. (Research Report) Researchers such as Paul Baltes have found that people devise alternative strategies to compensate for age-related declines in ability. He calls this _____ _____ _____ _____ .

15. The researcher who believes that there are eight distinct intelligences is _____ . Evidence from brain-damaged people _____ (supports/does not support) the multidimensional view of intelligence.

16. The value placed on different dimensions of intellectual ability _____ (varies/ does not vary) from culture to culture _____ (and/but not) from one stage of life to another.

Briefly explain why, according to the multidimensional view of intelligence, so few middle-aged adults do any regular exercise or engage in sports.

Multidirectional Intelligence: Not Just Increase or Decrease (pp. 578–579, 580–581)

17. The multiple dimensions of intelligence can follow different trajectories with age; that is, they are _____ . Some, such as _____-_____ _____ , generally fall steadily, whereas others, such as _____ , generally rise. Other abilities, such as _____ _____ , might rise, fall, and rise again, depending on how much they are used in daily life.

18. (A Life-Span View) For most of the twentieth century, psychologists were convinced that intelligence peaks during _____ and then gradually declines.

19. (A Life-Span View) During the 1950s, Nancy Bayley and Melita Oden found that on several tests of concept mastery, the scores of gifted individuals _____ (increased/ decreased/remained unchanged) between ages 20 and 50.

20. (A Life-Span View) Follow-up research by Bayley demonstrated a general _____ (increase/ decrease) in intellectual functioning from childhood through young adulthood. This developmental trend was true for _____ (most/a few) of the subtests of the _____ _____ _____ _____ .

21. (A Life-Span View) Bayley's study is an example of a _____ (cross-sectional/longitudinal) research design. Earlier studies relied on _____ (cross-sectional/longitudinal) research designs.

(A Life-Span View) Briefly explain why cross-sectional research can sometimes yield a misleading picture of adult development.

22. (A Life-Span View) Cite three reasons that longitudinal findings may be misleading.

    a. _____

    b. _____

    c. _____

23. (A Life-Span View) One of the first researchers to recognize the problems of cross-sectional and longitudinal studies of intelligence was

    _____ .

24. (A Life-Span View) Schaie developed a new research technique combining cross-sectional and longitudinal approaches, called

    _____-_____ research.

    (A Life-Span View) Briefly explain this type of research design.

25. (A Life-Span View) Using this design, Schaie found that on five _____

    _____ _____ , most people improved throughout most of adulthood. The results of this research are known collectively as the _____

    _____ _____ .

26. (A Life-Span View) Schaie's research on adult changes in intelligence reveals an increase in cognitive abilities from age _____ until the late _____ , except for

    _____ _____ , which begins to shift slightly downward by age_

    _____ .

Contextual Intelligence: Where You Are and Where You Were (pp. 579, 582–584)

27. Genetic makeup and each individual's unique experiences contribute to the _____ variation that is the basis for the variety of patterns of adult cognitive development. One source of variation that has been largely overlooked is variations in these experiences during

    _____ that are related to changes in _____ and _____ responsibilities. Other sources are variations in _____ level, _____ ,

    _____ , _____ , and _____ status.

28. The importance of context in the multidirectional nature of intelligence highlights the specifics of each person's _____ .

29. Schaie's research on cohort differences in cognitive growth found that more recently born cohorts outperformed earlier cohorts on two abilities: _____ _____ and _____ _____ .

    This improvement in recent cohorts is also reflected in scores on _____ tests. Two likely explanations for this are years of _____ and teachers who encouraged students to think for themselves. Changes in _____ _____ are a likely explanation for the improved arithmetic scores of recent cohorts.

Plastic Intellectual Change (pp. 584–588)

30. Intellectual abilities are characterized by their _____ , which means that abilities can become enhanced or diminished, depending on how, when, and why a person uses them. This characteristic _____ (declines somewhat/does not decline) with increasing age. A critical factor in whether proficiency in a particular area can be improved is _____ .

31. Some developmentalists believe that as we age, we develop specialized competencies, or _____ , in activities that are important to us.

32. There are several differences between experts and novices. First, novices tend to rely more on _____ (formal/informal) procedures and rules to guide them, whereas experts rely more on their _____ _____ and the immediate

_____ to guide them. This makes the actions of experts more _____ and less_____ .

33. Second, many elements of expert performance become _____ , almost instinctive, which enables experts to process information more quickly and efficiently.

34. A third difference is that experts have more and better _____ for accomplishing a particular task.

35. A final difference is that experts are more _____ .

36. In developing their abilities, experts point to the importance of _____ , usually at least _____ (how long?) before their full potential is achieved. This highlights the importance of _____ in the development of expertise.

37. Research studies indicate that expertise is quite _____ (general/specific), and that practice and specialization _____ (can/cannot) always overcome the effects of age.

38. A conclusion of this chapter is that in middle adulthood _____ _____ are more critical in determining the course of cognitive development than is age alone.

39. (Changing Policy) The fact that intelligence rises and falls with _____ and _____ means that age generally _____ (is/is not) the reason older workers are less able to do a job.

40. (Changing Policy) For the cohort that grew up during the _____ _____ retirement and leisure activities often were viewed with _____ (dread/eager anticipation).

41. (Changing Policy) A longitudinal study of 7,000 college seniors found that those who engaged in more extracurricular activities had grade point averages that were _____ (lower/as good as or better) than those of students who avoided all such activities.

Testing Yourself

After you have completed the audio and text review questions, see how well you do on the following quiz. Correct answers, with text and audio references, may be found at the end of this chapter.

1. Research on expertise indicates that during adulthood, intelligence:
   a. increases in most of the primary mental abilities.
   b. increases in specific areas of interest to the person.
   c. increases only in those areas associated with the individual's career.
   d. shows a uniform decline in all areas.

2. John LaFond, a musical savant, can easily reproduce a piano melody that he has heard for the first time. His ability to do so demonstrates expertise based on:
   a. superior short-term memory for individual notes.
   b. superior working memory for individual notes.
   c. superior ability to recognize and remember familiar musical patterns.
   d. compensation for retardation in other areas.

3. Which of the following is *not* characteristic of expertise, as described in the audio program?
   a. an intuitive approach to performance
   b. automatic cognitive processing
   c. a heightened ability to recognize familiar patterns *and* unusual cases
   d. superior intelligence and intellectual functioning

4. Compared to the peak years for achievement in mathematics, the peak years for achievement in history:
   a. tend to come at an earlier age.
   b. tend to come at a later age.
   c. tend to come at about the same age.
   d. cannot be predicted with any degree of accuracy.

5. (A Life-Span View) Most of the evidence for an age-related decline in intelligence came from:
   a. cross-sectional research.
   b. longitudinal research.
   c. cross-sequential research.
   d. random sampling.

6. (A Life-Span View) The major flaw in cross-sectional research is the virtual impossibility of:
   a. selecting subjects who are similar in every aspect except age.
   b. tracking all subjects over a number of years.
   c. finding volunteers with high IQs.
   d. testing concept mastery.

7. (A Life-Span View) Because of the limitations of other research methods, K. Warner Schaie developed a new research design based on:
   a. observer-participant methods.
   b. in-depth questionnaires.
   c. personal interviews.
   d. both cross-sectional and longitudinal methods.

8. Why don't traditional intelligence tests reveal age-related declines in processing speed and short-term memory during adulthood?
   a. They measure only fluid intelligence.
   b. They measure only crystallized intelligence.
   c. They separate verbal and non-verbal IQ scores, obscuring these declines.
   d. They yield a single IQ score, allowing adulthood increases in crystallized intelligence to mask these declines.

9. Which of the following is most likely to *decrease* with age?
   a. vocabulary
   b. accumulated facts
   c. speed of thinking
   d. practical intelligence

10. The basic mental abilities that go into learning and understanding any subject have been classified as:
    a. crystallized intelligence.
    b. plastic intelligence.
    c. fluid intelligence.
    d. rote memory.

11. Some psychologists contend that intelligence consists of fluid intelligence, which _____ during adulthood, and crystallized intelligence, which _____ .
    a. remains stable; declines
    b. declines; remains stable
    c. increases; declines
    d. declines; increases

12. Charles Spearman argued for the existence of a single general intelligence factor, which he referred to as:
    a. *g*.
    b. practical intelligence.
    c. analytic intelligence.
    d. creative intelligence.

13. The plasticity of adult intellectual abilities refers primarily to the effects of:
    a. fluid intelligence.
    b. experience.
    c. genetic inheritance.
    d. crystallized intelligence.

14. The shift from conscious, deliberate processing of information to a more unconscious, effortless performance requires:
    a. automatic responding.
    b. subliminal execution.
    c. plasticity.
    d. encoding.

15. Concerning expertise, which of the following is true?
    a. In performing tasks, experts tend to be more set in their ways, preferring to use strategies that have worked in the past.
    b. The reasoning of experts is usually more formal, disciplined, and stereotyped than that of the novice.
    c. In performing tasks, experts tend to be more flexible and to enjoy experimentation more than novices do.
    d. Experts often have difficulty adjusting to situations that are exceptions to the rule.

16. Because each person is genetically unique and has unique life experiences, _____ during middle adulthood is (are) more important in determining intellectual development than _____ .
    a. cohort differences; interindividual variation
    b. interindividual variation; cohort differences
    c. nature; nurture
    d. interindividual variation; age

17. (A Life-Span View) Which of the following describes the results of Nancy Bayley's follow-up study of members of the Berkeley Growth Study?
    a. Most subjects reached a plateau in intellectual functioning at age 21.
    b. The typical person at age 36 improved on two of ten subtests of the Wechsler Adult Intelligence Scale: Picture Completion and Arithmetic.
    c. The typical person at age 36 was still improving on the most important subtests of the intelligence scale.
    d. No conclusions could be reached because the sample of subjects was not representative.

18. Which of the following is *not* one of the general conclusions of research about intellectual changes during adulthood?
    a. In general, most intellectual abilities increase or remain stable throughout early and middle adulthood until the 60s.
    b. Cohort differences have a powerful influence on intellectual differences in adulthood.
    c. Intellectual functioning is affected by educational background.
    d. Intelligence becomes less specialized with increasing age.

19. The psychologist who has proposed that intelligence is composed of analytic, creative, and practical aspects is:
    a. Charles Spearman.   c. Robert Sternberg.
    b. Howard Gardner.   d. K. Warner Schaie.

LESSON 21 EXERCISE: CREATIVITY

One theme of this lesson is that contemporary psychologists take a broader view of intelligence than was the case in previous years. Experts recognize that earlier studies of intelligence failed to consider that generational differences, or **cohort effects**, may influence scores on standardized intelligence tests. Intelligence is now considered **multidimensional** and **multidirectional** in nature rather than being a single, fixed entity. One dimension of intelligence is the specialized knowledge that comes with the development of **expertise**. Another is creativity. The term "creativity" is used to describe the behavior of individuals who are able to find novel, and practical, solutions to problems.

How is creativity related to more traditional dimensions of intelligence? Research has shown that although a certain degree of intelligence is obviously necessary for creativity to be manifest, other factors, such as individual life experiences, are also important.

In attempting to study how creativity changes during adulthood, developmentalists have used several approaches. On the following page is a copy of the *Remote Associates Test* devised by Sarnoff and Mednick. This test is based on the idea that creativity reflects an ability to see relationships among ideas that are remote from one another. Several studies have reported that creative abilities tend to hold up well through middle adulthood, and may even extend into late adulthood. This is especially true for individuals who regularly engage in creative thinking, such as those whose professions require and call upon their creativity.

Arrange to administer the *Remote Associates Test* to two individuals, preferably a young adult or adolescent, and an older adult. If you wish to take the test yourself, do so first, and then test your other subject. Two copies of the test are printed, one for each of your subjects. Instructions for the test are given on the test sheet. You will need to time the number of minutes it takes for you and/or your subject(s) to complete the test. Correct answers to the test are given at the end of this lesson following the Lesson Guidelines section. When you have finished the testing, answer the questions on page 277 and hand that page in to your instructor.

REMOTE ASSOCIATES TEST

Instructions: In this test you are presented with three words and asked to find a fourth word that is related to all three. Write this word in the space to the right.

For example, what word do you think is related to these three?

paint   doll   cat   _____

The answer in this case is "house": house paint, doll house and house cat.

1. call   pay   line   _____
2. end   burning   blue   _____
3. man   hot   sure   _____
4. stick   hair   ball   _____
5. blue   cake   cottage   _____
6. man   wheel   high   _____
7. motion   poke   down   _____
8. stool   powder   ball   _____
9. line   birthday   surprise   _____
10. wood   liquor   luck   _____
11. house   village   golf   _____
12. plan   show   walker   _____
13. key   wall   precious   _____
14. bell   iron   tender   _____
15. water   pen   soda   _____
16. base   snow   dance   _____
17. steady   cart   slow   _____
18. up   book   charge   _____
19. tin   writer   my   _____
20. leg   arm   person   _____
21. weight   pipe   pencil   _____
22. spin   tip   shape   _____
23. sharp   thumb   tie   _____
24. out   band   night   _____
25. cool   house   fat   _____
26. back   short   light   _____
27. man   order   air   _____
28. bath   up   gum   _____
29. ball   out   jack   _____
30. up   deep   rear   _____

Source: Gardner, T. (1980). *Exercises for general psychology*. New York: Macmillan, 115–116.

REMOTE ASSOCIATES TEST

Instructions: In this test you are presented with three words and asked to find a fourth word that is related to all three. Write this word in the space to the right.

For example, what word do you think is related to these three?

paint   doll   cat   _____

The answer in this case is "house": house paint, doll house and house cat.

1. call   pay   line   _____
2. end   burning   blue   _____
3. man   hot   sure   _____
4. stick   hair   ball   _____
5. blue   cake   cottage   _____
6. man   wheel   high   _____
7. motion   poke   down   _____
8. stool   powder   ball   _____
9. line   birthday   surprise   _____
10. wood   liquor   luck   _____
11. house   village   golf   _____
12. plan   show   walker   _____
13. key   wall   precious   _____
14. bell   iron   tender   _____
15. water   pen   soda   _____
16. base   snow   dance   _____
17. steady   cart   slow   _____
18. up   book   charge   _____
19. tin   writer   my   _____
20. leg   arm   person   _____
21. weight   pipe   pencil   _____
22. spin   tip   shape   _____
23. sharp   thumb   tie   _____
24. out   band   night   _____
25. cool   house   fat   _____
26. back   short   light   _____
27. man   order   air   _____
28. bath   up   gum   _____
29. ball   out   jack   _____
30. up   deep   rear   _____

Source: Gardner, T. (1980). *Exercises for general psychology*. New York: Macmillan, 115–116.

NAME _____   INSTRUCTOR _____

LESSON 21: CREATIVITY

Exercise

1. What were the ages of your subjects?
   a. Younger subject's age _____
   b. Older subject's age _____

2. How long did it take your subjects to take the Remote Associates Test?
   a. Younger subject's time _____ minutes
   b. Older subject's time _____ minutes

3. Of the 30 items on the Remote Associates Test, how many did your subjects answer correctly?
   a. Younger subject's total _____
   b. Older subject's total _____

4. Do you consider that the Remote Associates Test is a valid test of creativity? of any kind of intelligence? Why or why not? What relationship (if any) would you expect to find between performance on a test of creativity and the test-taker's age? Why?

5. What (if any) cohort effects (historical events, education, etc.) do you believe would influence your performance (or that of someone in your cohort) on an instrument like the Remote Associates Test?

LESSON GUIDELINES

Audio Question Guidelines

1. LaFond's ability in music (compared to his severe general retardation) indicates that intelligence can be very narrowly specialized. LaFond's memory span for individual notes is not unusually high. Rather, as a result of spending thousands of hours at the piano, LaFond has developed an uncanny ability to recognize and remember familiar *patterns* of notes.

   This superior pattern memory is similar to the "Grand Master intuition" seen in expert chess players. After many years of experience, chess masters have built up a large memory repertoire of chess patterns that helps them to play more intuitively, recognize instantly the structure of a situation, and determine its likely outcome.

   Experienced physicians diagnose symptoms more quickly and spot rare cases as a result of recognizing familiar patterns.

   In general, then, these abilities indicate not only the specialized nature of intelligence, but also the growth of **practical intelligence** with experience.

2. Relying more than novices on their accumulated experience, experts are more intuitive and less stereotyped in their problem-solving behaviors.

   Many elements of expert performance become automatic and less tied to focused attention.

   As **expertise** is acquired, certain skills and cognitive processes become more specialized.

   Experts generally have more, and better, strategies for accomplishing particular tasks.

   Experts tend to be more flexible in their work.

3. Most people tend to do their greatest work in the decade of their 30s. This varies from field to field, however.

   In fields such as mathematics, the peak years of achievement tend to be a little earlier. This is because the individual needs fewer facts before he or she can go to work and be productive.

   In fields such as history, which require the accumulation of a greater knowledge base, the peak years of achievement tend to be somewhat later.

Textbook Question Answers

1. a single entity
2. Charles Spearman; *g*
3. Cattell; Horn; fluid; crystallized
4. fluid; inductive reasoning; abstract thinking; speed of thinking
5. crystallized
6. fluid; processing speed; short-term memory; IQ; increase; crystallized
7. fluid; crystallized; is not
8. crystallized
9. verbal; average; performance; 25
10. Robert Sternberg; analytic; the beginning of adulthood
11. creative; divergent; convergent; unusual; domains
12. practical; family; organization
13. increases
14. selective optimization with compensation
15. Howard Gardner; supports
16. varies; and

Kinesthetic ability is much less valued by middle-aged adults than by those who are younger. For this reason, older adults in cultures that emphasize competitive, strength-based sports for the young are less likely to value (or practice) any kinesthetic skills than their counterparts in cultures that value activities older adults can do.

17. multidirectional; short-term memory; vocabulary; mathematical reasoning
18. adolescence
19. increased
20. increase; most; Wechsler Adult Intelligence Scale
21. longitudinal; cross-sectional

Cross-sectional research may be misleading not only because it is impossible to select adults who are similar to each other in every important aspect except age, but also because each age group has its own unique history of life experiences.

22. a. People who are retested several times may improve their performance simply as a result of practice.
    b. because people may drop out of lengthy longitudinal studies, the remaining subjects may be a self-selected sample.
    c. Longitudinal research takes a long time.

23. Schaie
24. cross-sequential

In this approach, each time the original group of subjects is retested a new group is added and tested at each age interval.

25. primary mental abilities; Seattle Longitudinal Study

26. 20; 50s; number ability; 40

27. interindividual; adulthood; family; career; education; income, health, personality; marital

28. cohort

29. verbal memory; inductive reasoning; IQ; education; teaching strategy

30. plasticity; declines somewhat; education

31. expertise

32. formal; accumulated experience; context; intuitive; stereotyped

33. automatic

34. strategies

35. flexible (or creative)

36. practice; 10 years; motivation

37. specific; cannot

38. individual differences

39. training; experience; is not

40. Great Depression; dread

41. as good as or better

Answers to Testing Yourself

1. **b.** is the answer. The widespread belief that intelligence inevitably declines during adulthood is based on a misconception of intelligence as a single, fixed entity rather than a multidimensional and multidirectional entity. (audio program; textbook, p. 584)

2. **c.** is the answer. Experts do not have "better" memory per se; the key to their expertise lies in how their knowledge and memories are organized. (audio program)

3. **d.** is the answer. There is no evidence that experts are more "intelligent" than nonexperts; moreover, the concept of intelligence as a single general ability is probably not valid. (audio program)

4. **b.** is the answer. Success in fields such as history is based partly on the accumulation of knowledge over a long period of time. (audio program)

5. **a.** is the answer. (textbook, p. 580)

   b. Although results from this type of research may also be misleading, longitudinal studies often demonstrate age-related *increases* in intelligence.

   c. Cross-sequential research is the technique devised by K. Warner Schaie that combines the strengths of the cross-sectional and longitudinal methods.

d. Random sampling refers to the selection of subjects for a research study.

6. **a.** is the answer. (textbook, p. 580)

   b. This is a problem in longitudinal research.

   c. & d. Neither of these is particularly troublesome in cross-sectional research.

7. **d.** is the answer. (textbook, p. 581)

   a., b., & c. Cross-sequential research as described in this chapter is based on *objective* intelligence testing.

8. **d.** is the answer. (textbook, p. 573)

   a. & b. Traditional IQ tests measure both fluid and crystallized intelligence.

9. **c.** is the answer. (textbook, p. 573)

   a., b., & d. These often increase with age.

10. **c.** is the answer. (textbook, p. 572)

    a. Crystallized intelligence is the accumulation of facts and knowledge that comes with education and experience.

    b. Although intelligence is characterized by plasticity, "plastic intelligence" is not discussed as a specific type of intelligence.

    d. Rote memory is memory that is based on the conscious repetition of to-be-remembered information.

11. **d.** is the answer. (textbook, p. 573)

12. **a.** is the answer. (textbook, p. 571)

    b. Practical intelligence refers to the intellectual skills used in everyday problem solving.

    c. & d. These are two aspects of intelligence identified in Robert Sternberg's theory.

13. **b.** is the answer. Life experiences give intelligence its flexibility and account for the variety of patterns of adult cognitive development. (textbook, p. 584)

14. **a.** is the answer. (textbook, p. 586)

    b. This was not discussed in the chapter.

    c. Plasticity refers to the flexible nature of intelligence.

    d. Encoding refers to the placing of information into memory.

15. **c.** is the answer. (textbook, p. 586)

    a., b., & d. These are more typical of *novices* than experts.

16. **d.** is the answer. (textbook, p. 579)

    a. & b. Cohort differences are a source of interindividual variation.

    c. The text does not discuss the relative impact of nature and nurture on intelligence during adulthood.

17. c. is the answer. (textbook, p. 580)

    b. In fact, these were the only two subtests on which performance did *not* improve.

    d. No such criticism was made of Bayley's study.

18. d. is the answer. In fact, intelligence often becomes *more specialized* with age. (textbook, p. 587)

19. c. is the answer. (textbook, p. 574)

    a. Charles Spearman proposed the existence of an underlying general intelligence, which he called *g*.

    b. Howard Gardner proposed that intelligence consists of eight autonomous abilities.

    d. K. Warner Schaie was one of the first researchers to recognize the potentially distorting cohort effects on cross-sectional research.

Answers to the Remote Associates Test

1. phone   **2.** book   **3.** fire   **4.** pin   **5.** cheese   **6.** chair   **7.** slow   **8.** foot   **9.** party   **10.** hard   **11.** green   **12.** floor   **13.** stone   **14.** bar   **15.** fountain   **16.** ball   **17.** go   **18.** cover   **19.** type   **20.** chair   **21.** lead   **22.** top   **23.** tack   **24.** watch   **25.** cat   **26.** stop   **27.** mail   **28.** bubble   **29.** black   **30.** end

References

Charness, N. (1986). Expertise in chess, music, and physics: A cognitive perspective. In L. K. Obler & D. A. Fein (Eds.), *The neuropsychology of talent and special abilities*. New York: Guilford Press.

    Professor Charness, who is heard on the audio program, discusses further distinctions that can be made between those who are experts and those who are less skilled.

Schaie, K. W., & Herzog, C. (1983). Fourteen-year cohort–sequential studies of adult intelligence. *Developmental Psychology, 19,* 531–543.

    Professor Schaie, who was one of the earliest researchers to recognize the distorting effects of cohort differences, discusses issues raised by the assessment of cognitive development during adulthood.

Middle Adulthood: Psychosocial Development

AUDIO PROGRAM: The Life Course of Work

ORIENTATION

Lesson 22 is concerned with **middle age**, a period when the reevaluation of career goals, shifts in one's family responsibilities, and a growing awareness of one's mortality often lead to turmoil and change. Chapter 22 of *The Developing Person Through the Life Span, 5/e,* explores several issues concerning development during middle age. The first is the so-called **midlife crisis**. Is it fact or fantasy? The second issue concerns the stability of personality throughout the life span, which determines the impact of age-related events and changes. The third issue regards the changing relationships of middle-aged adults with their adult children and aging parents. Being "sandwiched" between the younger and older generations is often a source of stress, as middle-aged adults experience additional financial, emotional, and caregiving demands.

The program explores career development during middle age. Most of us define ourselves by the work we perform. But what happens when the basic structure of our job changes? or we change? At some point during middle age, most adults reach a plateau in their career development that prompts a reevaluation of career objectives.

In the program, the stories of Mary and Dan illustrate how the life course of work has changed. Mary, 48, returned to college when the youngest of her three children started high school. She has continued with graduate training in the hopes of beginning a new career. Sociologist Alice Rossi, who has done extensive research on the work and family lives of women, offers a historical perspective on women like Mary, who return to school and then to work after careers as mothers and homemakers.

Dan, 56, has practiced dentistry for 30 years. Although he would never think of quitting his profession, changes in the field have caused him to stop rec-

ommending it to others as a career. Professor of Business Stephen Lazarus, who has worked extensively with those threatened by occupational changes, discusses the impact of career crises on workers and offers advice to working adults of all ages.

As the program opens, we hear Professor Lazarus discussing the dramatic changes that have occurred in the life course of work.

LESSON GOALS

By the end of this lesson you should be prepared to:

1. Discuss psychosocial development during middle age, noting whether midlife is invariably a time of crisis for men and women.

2. Describe the Big Five clusters of personality traits, and discuss reasons for their relative stability during adulthood.

3. Explain the tendency toward gender-role convergence during middle adulthood.

4. Describe the ways in which family dynamics may change during middle adulthood.

5. Discuss the dynamics of career development during middle adulthood and the ways in which the life course of work may change.

Audio Assignment

Listen to the audio tape that accompanies Lesson 22: "The Life Course of Work."

Write answers to the following questions. You may replay portions of the program if you need to refresh your memory. Answer guidelines may be found in the Lesson Guidelines section at the end of this chapter.

1. What historical, economic, and demographic factors have led to the return of large numbers of married women to school and the labor force?

2. In what ways has the life course of work changed in recent generations?

3. What advice is offered in the program for those making occupational choices at ages 20, 40, and 60?

Textbook Assignment

Read Chapter 22: "Middle Adulthood: Psychosocial Development," pages 591–610 in *The Developing Person Through the Life Span, 5/e,* then work through the material that follows to review it. Complete the sentences and answer the questions. As you proceed, evaluate your performance for each secdtion by consulting the answers on page 297. Do not continue with the next section until you understand each answer. If you need to, review or reread the appropriate section in the textbook before continuing.

Changes During Middle Age (pp. 591–592, 593)

1. At about age _____ , people reach a point called _____ , which ushers in _____ _____ , which lasts until about age _____ .

2. Midlife is popularly thought of as a period of _____ .

List several sources of upheaval that may make middle age a troubling time.

3. At this time, some adults reassess the balance between _____ and _____ .

4. In recent years, the demands placed on middle-aged adults by the younger and older generations have _____ (increased/ decreased), so that this group is referred to as the _____ _____ .

5. (A Life-Span View) Approximately _____ (what proportion?) of middle-aged adults who have grown children find at least one of them still living with them. This is especially likely when the parents are in _____ _____ and when the children are _____ _____ .

6. (A Life-Span View) Middle-aged _____ (men/women) are especially likely to be called on to provide elder care. Those who are particularly likely to feel unfairly burdened with elder care are _____ - _____ - _____ . An added stress occurs when the adult children who are living with their parents have _____ _____ .

7. (A Life-Span View) Although having many _____ to fill might make some middle-aged adults feel _____ , it may also increase their _____ _____ .

8. (A Life-Span View) Although it has long been assumed that middle-aged women were _____ , research has revealed that this is less likely to be the case if the roles are _____ to the woman, her _____ are satisfying, and if the _____ requirements are not overwhelming.

9. (A Life-Span View) State three reasons why overwhelming demands are unusual in middle age.

   a. _____

   b. _____

   c. _____

10. The notion of a midlife crisis _____ (is/is not) accepted by most developmentalists as an inevitable event during middle age.

11. How people react to middle age has more to do with their overall _____ _____ than it has to do with calendar milestones.

Personality Throughout Adulthood (pp. 592, 594–597)

12. The major source of developmental continuity during adulthood is the stability of

    _____ .

13. List and briefly describe the Big Five personality factors.

    a. _____
       _____

    b. _____
       _____

    c. _____
       _____

    d. _____
       _____

    e. _____
       _____

14. Whether a person ranks high or low in each of the Big Five is determined by the interacting influences of _____ , _____ , early _____-_____ , and the experiences and choices made at a younger age. By age _____ , the Big Five usually become quite stable. This stability results not only from _____ but also from the fact that by this age most people have settled into an _____

    _____ .

15. (In Person) By age _____ , those high in _____ have likely found mates who share their _____ . Adults who are high in _____ are likely to choose a vocation that draws on their general _____ .

Draw several other comparisons of the ecological niches carved out by adults who are high in extroversion, and those who are high in neuroticism.

16. Certain traits such as _____ toward others and _____ about oneself show marked individual patterns.

17. Most adults settle into a niche that reinforces their basic _____ .

18. The cumulative experiences of living a life often lead to _____-_____ and greater _____ with age.

19. In many cultures, gender roles _____ (loosen/become more rigid) during middle age. Some researchers even believe that there is a _____ _____ of personality traits, as women become more _____ , while men become more able to openly express _____ or

    _____ .

20. One reason for gender-role shifts during middle age is that reduced levels of _____ _____ may free men and women to express previously suppressed traits.

21. The psychoanalyst who believed that everyone has both a masculine and feminine side is _____ . According to this theory, middle-aged adults begin to explore the

    _____ _____

    of their personality.

22. Longitudinal research suggests a _____ explanation for gender convergence in personality. The current cohort of middle-aged adults is _____ (more/less) marked in their convergence of sex roles because sex roles today are _____ (more/less) sharply defined than in the past.

Family Dynamics in Middle Adulthood (pp. 598–606)

23. Being the "generation in the middle," middle-aged adults are the _____ _____ of their families. This role is sometimes ignored because_____ is

often confused with _____ , the latter defined as _____

_____ .

24. American families today are _____ (more/less) likely to consist of several generations living under the same roof.

25. Because of their role in maintaining the links between the generations, middle-aged adults become the _____ . This role tends to be filled most often by _____ (women/men).

26. The relationship between most middle-aged adults and their parents tends to _____ (improve/worsen) with time. One reason is that, as adult children mature, they develop a more _____ view of the relationship as a whole.

Briefly explain why this is especially true *today*.

27. Three generations of a family living under one roof is more common among _____ and_____ Americans.

28. Whether or not middle-aged adults and their parents live together depends mostly on _____ , which is the belief that _____ .

29. Most middle-aged adults _____ (maintain/do not maintain) close relationships with their children.

30. Two out of every three Americans become a _____ during middle adulthood. Most react quite _____ (positively/negatively) to the occurrence of this event.

31. Grandparent–grandchild relationships take one of three forms: _____ , _____ , or _____ . A century ago, most American grandparents adopted a _____ role. The _____ pattern, which was prevalent

among grandparents for most of the twentieth century, is rare today among those who

_____ .

32. Most contemporary grandparents seek the _____ role as they strive for the love and respect of their grandchildren while maintaining their own _____ .

33. Some of the diversity in grandparent–grandchild relationships today results from differences in _____ , _____ traditions, and_____

_____ . Another factor is the _____ _____ of the three generations.

34. The grandparent–grandchild bond tends to be closer if the grandchild is relatively _____ , if the parent is the _____ ,

and if the grandparent is

_____ .

35. The trend toward relatively uninvolved grandparenting in middle age is particularly unfortunate in_____ and _____ groups, in which grandparents traditionally transmit the _____ , _____ , _____ , and _____ of the community.

36. (Research Report) Grandparents who take over the work of raising their children's children are referred to as _____ _____ . This role is more common when parents are _____ _____ .

37. (Research Report) Grandparents are most likely to provide surrogate care for children who need _____ _____ , such as infants who are _____ -_____ or _____ . If the relationship is the result of a legal decision that the parents were _____ or _____ , it becomes _____ _____ .

38. (Research Report) More than one in _____ (how many?) grandparents witnesses the divorce of their adult child. As a result, the parents of the _____ ex-spouse are often shut out of their grandchildren's lives.

39. For the majority of middle-aged adults, their most intimate relationship is with their _____ . For a growing minority, however, intimacy is achieved through _____ with a partner.

40. Throughout adulthood, the family relationship most closely linked to personal happiness, health, and companionship is _____ .

41 After the first decade or so, marital happiness tends to gradually _____ (increase/decrease).

List several possible reasons for this finding.

42. Divorce in middle adulthood is typically _____ (more/less) difficult than divorce in early adulthood.

43. Most divorced people remarry, on average, within _____ years of being divorced.

State several of the benefits that remarriage may bring to middle-aged adults.

44. Compared with people in first marriages, remarried people are _____ (more/less) likely to describe their marriage as either very happy or quite unhappy.

State two possible explanations for the divorce rate among remarried couples.

45. (Changing Policy) Middle-aged _____ (women/men) are disadvantaged when it comes to finding a marriage partner for three reasons:

    a. _____
    b. _____
    c. _____

Work (pp. 606–609)

46. Job security usually _____ (increases/decreases) during middle adulthood. During middle adulthood, the percentage of adults who work _____ (varies/does not significantly vary) by gender and _____ (varies/does not significantly vary) with whether the individual has children.

47. During middle adulthood there is often a shift in the balance among _____ , _____ , and _____ .

48. During _____ adulthood, the combined demands of the workplace and the individual's own aspirations for promotion often create _____ .

49. During the _____ stage of marriage, women and men with children often engage in a _____ _____ of their employment effort in order to combine work and _____ .

Briefly describe three different scaling-back strategies.

50. Some middle-aged workers assume the position of a _____ as they help an inexperienced worker "learn the ropes."

Testing Yourself

After you have completed the audio and text review questions, see how well you do on the following quiz. Correct answers, with text and audio references, may be found at the end of this chapter.

1. The return of large numbers of married women to the labor force was largely provoked by:
   a. the civil rights movement of the 1950s and 1960s.
   b. a shortage of unmarried women in the work force following World War II.
   c. efforts of lobbying groups such as the National Organization for Women.
   d. the increase in life expectancy during the past 75 years.

2. Today, more than _____ of women with preschool children are employed.
   a. one-fourth
   b. one-third
   c. one-half
   d. two-thirds

3. A recent national survey of men in their 50s and 60s found that _____ percent had changed occupations at least once in their lives.
   a. 25
   b. 50
   c. 75
   d. 90

4. Which of the following pieces of advice was offered in the audio program to workers at various stages in their occupational careers?
   a. "Don't expect that your life will be divided into three neat segments corresponding to school, work, and retirement."
   b. "Don't expect that your family will fully understand or support you if you make too dramatic a career change during adulthood."
   c. "Baby boomers will find reduced career opportunities in the years to come, due to shrinking promotional opportunity, pressure from younger workers, and an unwillingness of older workers to retire."
   d. All of the above were offered as advice.

5. According to the experts heard in the audio program, for most professions:
   a. 40 is not too late to begin a new career.
   b. people who do not begin their career until middle age will not have sufficient time to make a significant contribution to their field.
   c. productivity increases directly with the number of years of experience a person has in the field.
   d. all of the above are true.

6. The most important factor in how a person adjusts to middle age is his or her:
   a. gender.
   b. developmental history.
   c. age.
   d. race.

7. The Big Five personality factors are:
   a. emotional stability, openness, introversion, sociability, locus of control.
   b. neuroticism, extroversion, openness, emotional stability, sensitivity.
   c. extroversion, agreeableness, conscientiousness, neuroticism, openness.
   d. neuroticism, gregariousness, extroversion, impulsiveness, openness.

8. Concerning the prevalence of midlife crises, which of the following statements has the *greatest* empirical support?
   a. Virtually all men, and most women, experience a midlife crisis.
   b. Virtually all men, and about 50 percent of women, experience a midlife crisis.
   c. Women are more likely to experience a midlife crisis than are men.
   d. Few contemporary developmentalists believe that the midlife crisis is a common experience.

9. Middle-age shifts in personality often reflect:
   a. the particular traits that are valued within the culture at that time.
   b. rebellion against earlier life choices.
   c. the tightening of gender roles.
   d. all of the above.

10. During middle age, gender roles tend to:
    a. become more distinct.
    b. reflect patterns established during early adulthood.
    c. converge.
    d. be unpredictable.

11. Middle-aged adults who are pressed on one side by adult children and on the other by aging parents are:
    a. said to be in the sandwich generation.
    b. especially likely to suffer burnout.
    c. especially likely to suffer alienation.
    d. all of the above.

12. Which of the following statements *best* describes the relationship of most middle-aged adults to their aging parents?
    a. The relationship tends to improve with time.
    b. During middle adulthood, the relationship tends to deteriorate.
    c. For women, but not men, the relationship tends to improve with time.
    d. The relationship usually remains as good or as bad as it was in the past.

13. In families, middle-aged adults tend to function as the _____ , celebrating family achievements, keeping the family together, and staying in touch with distant relatives.
    a. sandwich generation
    b. nuclear bond
    c. intergenerational gatekeepers
    d. kinkeepers

14. Which of the following is *not* one of the basic forms of grandparent–grandchild relationships?
    a. autonomous   c. companionate
    b. involved   d. remote

15. During middle adulthood, *scaling back* refers to the tendency of both men and women to:
    a. limit their involvement in activities that take away from their careers.
    b. deliberately put less than full effort into their work.
    c. pull away from their spouses as they reevaluate their life's accomplishments.
    d. explore the "shadow sides" of their personalities.

16. Most grandparents today strive to establish a(n) _____ relationship with their grandchildren.
    a. autonomous   c. companionate
    b. involved   d. remote

17. Concerning the degree of stability of personality traits, which of the following statements has the greatest research support?
    a. There is little evidence that personality traits remain stable during adulthood.
    b. In women, but less so in men, there is notable continuity in many personality characteristics.
    c. In men, but less so in women, there is notable continuity in many personality characteristics.
    d. In both men and women, there is notable continuity in many personality characteristics.

18. People who exhibit the personality dimension of _____ tend to be outgoing, active, and assertive.
    a. extroversion   c. conscientiousness
    b. agreeableness   d. neuroticism

19. According to Jung's theory of personality:
    a. as men and women get older, gender roles become more distinct.
    b. to some extent, everyone has both a masculine and a feminine side to his or her character.
    c. the recent blurring of gender roles is making adjustment to midlife more difficult for both men and women.
    d. gender roles are most distinct during childhood.

20. Which of the following personality traits was *not* identified in the text as tending to remain stable throughout adulthood?
    a. neuroticism   c. openness
    b. introversion   d. conscientiousness

LESSON 22 EXERCISE: THE UNISEX OF LATER LIFE

The Developing Person Through the Life Span, 5/e, notes that as people get older, both men and women tend to become more androgynous. According to personality theorist Carl Jung, every individual has both a masculine and feminine side of personality. During early adulthood, the side that conforms to social expectations is dominant. Then during **middle age**, men and women become more flexible and feel freer to explore the opposite side of their characters. The sharp gender-role distinctions of earlier adulthood break down and each sex moves closer to a middle ground between the traditional gender roles. Many women become more assertive and self-confident. Many men become more considerate, more nurturant, and less competitive as career goals become less important.

Traditional measures of masculinity and femininity are based on the assumption that these traits represent endpoints of a single bipolar dimension that considers the sexes as opposites. Recently, however, several researchers have developed a measure of androgyny based on a reconceptualization of masculinity and femininity as independent dimensions. This test of androgyny—the PRF ANDRO scale—contains separate subscales for femininity and masculinity, and is shown on the next page.

To help you to better understand the concept of androgyny, administer the test to two adults of the same sex but in different seasons of life. For example, you might test an adult in his or her 20s, and one in his or her 50s. You might wish to include yourself as one of the subjects. Alternatively, you might ask an older adult to complete the test "as you see yourself now," and "as you were during your early adulthood."

After you have collected your data, determine separate masculinity and femininity scores for each of your respondents by giving them 1 point on each subscale for each answer that agrees with those in the following key. Then complete the questions on page 295 and hand only that page in to your instructor.

Masculinity Key

2. T	12. T	31. T	47. T
3. F	15. F	33. T	48. F
4. T	17. T	34. F	50. T
6. F	25. T	35. F	52. T
7. T	26. T	38. F	54. F
8. T	27. T	40. F	
10. F	29. T	42. T	
11. T	30. T	46. F	

Femininity Key

1. T	20. T	37. T	53. T
5. F	21. T	39. T	55. T
9. F	22. F	41. T	56. F
13. T	23. T	43. T	
14. T	24. F	44. T	
16. F	28. F	45. T	
18. T	32. F	49. T	
19. F	36. T	51. F	

THE PRF ANDRO SCALE*

For each statement below write (T) True or (F) False to indicate whether the statement applies to you or to the person you are testing.

_____ **1.** I like to be with people who assume a protective attitude with me.

_____ **2.** I try to control others rather than permit them to control me.

_____ **3.** Surfboard riding would be dangerous for me.

_____ **4.** If I have a problem I like to work it out alone.

_____ **5.** I seldom go out of my way to do something just to make others happy.

_____ **6.** Adventures where I am on my own are a little frightening to me.

_____ **7.** I feel confident when directing the activities of others.

_____ **8.** I will keep working on a problem after others have given up.

_____ **9.** I would not like to be married to a protective person.

_____ **10.** I usually try to share my problems with someone who can help me.

_____ **11.** I don't care if my clothes are unstylish, as long as I like them.

_____ **12.** When I see a new invention, I attempt to find out how it works.

_____ **13.** People like to tell me their troubles because they know I will do everything I can to help them.

_____ **14.** Sometimes I let people push me around so they can feel important.

_____ **15.** I am only very rarely in a position where I feel a need to actively argue for a point of view I hold.

_____ **16.** I dislike people who are always asking me for advice.

_____ **17.** I seek out positions of authority.

_____ **18.** I believe in giving my friends lots of help and advice.

_____ **19.** I get little satisfaction from serving others.

_____ **20.** I make certain that I speak softly when I am in a public place.

_____ **21.** I am usually the first to offer a helping hand when it is needed.

_____ **22.** When I see someone I know from a distance I don't go out of my way to say "Hello."

_____ **23.** I would prefer to care for a sick child myself rather than hire a nurse.

_____ **24.** I prefer not being dependent on anyone for assistance.

_____ **25.** When I am with someone else, I do most of the decision-making.

_____ **26.** I don't mind being conspicuous.

_____ **27.** I would never pass up something that sounded like fun just because it was a little hazardous.

_____ **28.** I get a kick out of seeing someone I dislike appear foolish in front of others.

*Source: Berzins, J., Welling, M.A., & Wetter, R.E. (1978). A new measure of psychological androgyny based on the Personality Research Form. *Journal of Consulting and Clinical Psychology, 46,* 126, 138. Reprinted with permission.

_____ 29. When someone opposes me on an issue, I usually find myself taking an even stronger stand than I did at first.

_____ 30. When two persons are arguing, I often settle the argument for them.

_____ 31. I will not go out of my way to behave in an approved way.

_____ 32. I am quite independent of the people I know.

_____ 33. If I were in politics, I would probably be seen as one of the forceful leaders of my party.

_____ 34. I prefer a quiet, secure life to an adventurous one.

_____ 35. I prefer to face my problems by myself.

_____ 36. I try to get others to notice the way I dress.

_____ 37. When I see someone who looks confused, I usually ask if I can be of any assistance.

_____ 38. It is unrealistic for me to insist on becoming the best in my field of work all of the time.

_____ 39. The good opinion of one's friends is one of the chief rewards for living a good life.

_____ 40. If I get tired while playing a game, I generally stop playing.

_____ 41. When I see a baby, I often ask to hold him.

_____ 42. I am quite good at keeping others in line.

_____ 43. I think it would be best to marry someone who is more mature and less dependent than I.

_____ 44. I don't want to be away from my family too much.

_____ 45. Once in a while I enjoy acting as if I were tipsy.

_____ 46. I feel incapable of handling many situations.

_____ 47. I delight in feeling unattached.

_____ 48. I would make a poor judge because I dislike telling others what to do.

_____ 49. Seeing an old or helpless person makes me feel that I would like to take care of him.

_____ 50. I usually make decisions without consulting others.

_____ 51. It doesn't affect me one way or another to see a child being spanked.

_____ 52. My goal is to do at least a little bit more than anyone else has done before.

_____ 53. To love and be loved is of greatest importance to me.

_____ 54. I avoid some hobbies and sports because of their dangerous nature.

_____ 55. One of the things that spurs me on to do my best is the realization that I will be praised for my work.

_____ 56. People's tears tend to irritate me more than arouse my sympathy.

THE PRF ANDRO SCALE*

For each statement below write (T) True or (F) False to indicate whether the statement applies to you or to the person you are testing.

_____   1. I like to be with people who assume a protective attitude with me.

_____   2. I try to control others rather than permit them to control me.

_____   3. Surfboard riding would be dangerous for me.

_____   4. If I have a problem I like to work it out alone.

_____   5. I seldom go out of my way to do something just to make others happy.

_____   6. Adventures where I am on my own are a little frightening to me.

_____   7. I feel confident when directing the activities of others.

_____   8. I will keep working on a problem after others have given up.

_____   9. I would not like to be married to a protective person.

_____   10. I usually try to share my problems with someone who can help me.

_____   11. I don't care if my clothes are unstylish, as long as I like them.

_____   12. When I see a new invention, I attempt to find out how it works.

_____   13. People like to tell me their troubles because they know I will do everything I can to help them.

_____   14. Sometimes I let people push me around so they can feel important.

_____   15. I am only very rarely in a position where I feel a need to actively argue for a point of view I hold.

_____   16. I dislike people who are always asking me for advice.

_____   17. I seek out positions of authority.

_____   18. I believe in giving my friends lots of help and advice.

_____   19. I get little satisfaction from serving others.

_____   20. I make certain that I speak softly when I am in a public place.

_____   21. I am usually the first to offer a helping hand when it is needed.

_____   22. When I see someone I know from a distance I don't go out of my way to say "Hello."

_____   23. I would prefer to care for a sick child myself rather than hire someone to nurse him or her.

_____   24. I prefer not being dependent on anyone for assistance.

_____   25. When I am with someone else, I do most of the decision-making.

_____   26. I don't mind being conspicuous.

_____   27. I would never pass up something that sounded like fun just because it was a little hazardous.

_____   28. I get a kick out of seeing someone I dislike appear foolish in front of others.

*Source: Berzins, J., Welling, M.A., & Wetter, R.E. (1978). A new measure of psychological androgyny based on the Personality Research Form. *Journal of Consulting and Clinical Psychology, 46,* 126, 138. Reprinted with permission.

_____ 29. When someone opposes me on an issue, I usually find myself taking an even stronger stand than I did at first.

_____ 30. When two persons are arguing, I often settle the argument for them.

_____ 31. I will not go out of my way to behave in an approved way.

_____ 32. I am quite independent of the people I know.

_____ 33. If I were in politics, I would probably be seen as one of the forceful leaders of my party.

_____ 34. I prefer a quiet, secure life to an adventurous one.

_____ 35. I prefer to face my problems by myself.

_____ 36. I try to get others to notice the way I dress.

_____ 37. When I see someone who looks confused, I usually ask if I can be of any assistance.

_____ 38. It is unrealistic for me to insist on becoming the best in my field of work all of the time.

_____ 39. The good opinion of one's friends is one of the chief rewards for living a good life.

_____ 40. If I get tired while playing a game, I generally stop playing.

_____ 41. When I see a baby, I often ask to hold him or her.

_____ 42. I am quite good at keeping others in line.

_____ 43. I like to be with people who are less dependent than I.

_____ 44. I don't want to be away from my family too much.

_____ 45. Once in a while I enjoy acting as if I were tipsy.

_____ 46. I feel incapable of handling many situations.

_____ 47. I delight in feeling unattached.

_____ 48. I would make a poor judge because I dislike telling others what to do.

_____ 49. Seeing a helpless person makes me feel that I would like to take care of him or her.

_____ 50. I usually make decisions without consulting others.

_____ 51. It doesn't affect me one way or another to see a child being spanked.

_____ 52. My goal is to do at least a little bit more than anyone else has done before.

_____ 53. To love and be loved is of greatest importance to me.

_____ 54. I avoid some hobbies and sports because of their dangerous nature.

_____ 55. One of the things that spurs me on to do my best is the realization that I will be praised for my work.

_____ 56. People's tears tend to irritate me more than arouse my sympathy.

NAME _____   INSTRUCTOR _____

LESSON 22: THE UNISEX OF LATER LIFE

Exercise

1. List the ages of your questionnaire respondents and their scores on the masculinity and femininity subscales.

	Age	Sex	Masculinity Score	Femininity Score
Respondent 1:	_____	_____	_____	_____
Respondent 2:	_____	_____	_____	_____

2. Do your respondents' masculinity and femininity scores support the viewpoint that both men and women tend to become more androgynous as they get older? If not, what possible explanation might there be for the discrepancy?

3. What are some of the masculine and feminine characteristics identified in the two subscales of the "PRF ANDRO" questionnaire? To what extent do you consider that these characteristics reflect only temporary settings of the social clock? That is, would these characteristics of masculine and feminine behavior hold true at other times in history?

4. Do you consider that the "PRF ANDRO" scale is a valid test of androgyny, masculinity, and/or femininity? Explain your response.

LESSON GUIDELINES

Audio Question Guidelines

1. Until World War II, female employment was largely restricted to young unmarried women. After their marriage or the birth of a child, most women withdrew from the labor force.

    After the war, in the early 1950s, there were approximately four million fewer unmarried women than before the war. Since jobs tended to be gender stratified, employers had no alternative but to begin hiring married women to fill jobs previously held by unmarried women.

    The emergence of continuing education programs for older students occurred in the 1960s.

    These changes have resulted in a resetting of the social clock, such that with each passing decade, the woman returning to the work force is younger because she has been absent from the labor force for a shorter period of time.

    Today, more than half of women with preschool children are employed.

2. One major change is that more and more women today are either returning to the work force or have never left it, despite establishing families and becoming mothers.

    Another change is that the "one job for life" rule no longer holds. In fact, the odds of staying in one occupation for life are getting slimmer all the time. One national survey found that 90 percent of men in their late 50s and 60s had changed occupations at least once in their lives.

    These changes have led some experts to recommend thinking of work as we do our lives—in terms of seasons.

3. Experts recommend that those just beginning a career spend time talking to people who are actually in that occupation to find out what the job is really like.

    Another recommendation is that young people no longer count on a "linear experience" of being educated in their early 20s, working until 65, and then retiring. Rather, experiences should occur in parallel, as people periodically break away from work in order to refresh themselves in school or acquire new skills.

    Experts warn those at **midlife**—the "outriders of the baby boom generation"—that shrinking promotional opportunity, pressure from the younger generation, and an unwillingness of those who are older to retire may result in fewer career opportunities in the years ahead.

For those nearing retirement without any previous commitment to leisure, experts warn that retirement may become a dull, boring trap. Their advice is for middle-aged people to start thinking about part-time work, hobbies, or other ways of maintaining identifiable and satisfying pursuits.

Textbook Question Answers

1. 40; midlife; middle age; 65
2. crisis

People become aware that they are beginning to grow old and often must make adjustments in their parental roles and achievement goals. For many adults, midlife is also a time to reexamine earlier choices regarding intimacy and generativity.

3. work; family
4. increased; sandwich generation
5. half; good health; financially needy
6. women; daughters-in-law; serious disabilities
7. roles; squeezed; life satisfaction
8. overburdened; important; relationships; time
9. a. Adult children's independence reduces their burden.

    b. Disabled adults usually require less care than when they were children.

    c. Major caregiving of the very oldest is often borne by other older adults.

10. is not
11. developmental history
12. personality
13. a. extroversion: outgoing, assertive

    b. agreeableness: kind, helpful

    c. conscientiousness: organized, conforming

    d. neuroticism: anxious, moody

    e. openness: imaginative, curious

14. genes; culture; child rearing; 30; genes; ecological niche
15. 30; extroversion; outgoingness; neuroticism; apprehensiveness

Extroverts often have established a busy social life and their jobs, recreational activities, and other details of their lives foster social contact. By contrast, adults who are high in neuroticism expect the worst from life and may alienate those around them. They also may be fearful of taking a new job and become stuck in a cycle of self-pity and unhappiness.

16. warmth; confidence
17. temperament
18. self-improvement; generativity

19. loosen; gender crossover; assertive; tenderness; sadness

20. sex hormones

21. Carl Jung; shadow side

22. historical; less; less

23. cohort bridges; family; household; people who eat and sleep together in the same dwelling

24. less

25. kinkeepers; women

26. improve; balanced

Most of today's elderly are healthy, active, and independent, giving them and their grown children a measure of freedom and privacy that enhances the relationship between them.

27. Hispanic; Asian

28. familism; family members should be close and supportive of one another

29. maintain

30. grandparent; positively

31. remote; involved; companionate; remote; involved; were born in the United States

32. companionate; independence (autonomy)

33. personality; ethnic; national background; developmental stage

34. young; first sibling to have children; neither too young nor too old

35. immigrant; minority; values; beliefs; language; customs

36. surrogate parents; poor, young, unemployed, drug- or alcohol-addicted, single, or newly divorced

37. intensive involvement; drug-affected; rebellious; abusive; neglectful; kinship care

38. three; noncustodial

39. spouse; cohabitation

40. marriage

41. increase

Families at this stage typically have greater financial security and have met the goal of raising a family. In addition, disputes over equity in domestic work and other issues of parenting generally subside. A third reason is that many couples have more time for each other.

42. more

43. 5

Divorced women typically become financially more secure, and divorced men typically become healthier and more social once they have a new partner. For men, it also improves their relationship with offspring.

44. more

The high divorce rate of the remarried may be due to the fact that some people are temperamentally prone to divorce.

45. women

    a. Middle-aged men tend to marry younger women.

    b. Men die at younger ages.

    c. Few marriages take place between a younger man and an older woman.

46. increases; does not significantly vary; does not significantly vary

47. work, family; self

48. early; workaholics

49. establishment; scaling back; parenthood

One spouse may choose to work part time. Or, both partners may work full time, one at a "job" to earn money and the other at a lower-paying "career." In another scaling-back strategy, the partners take turns pursuing work and domestic and child care.

50. mentor

Answers to Testing Yourself

1. **b.** is the answer. This shortage caused employers to begin hiring married women. (audio program)

2. **c.** is the answer. (audio program)

3. **d.** is the answer. The odds of staying in one occupation for life are getting slimmer all the time. (audio program)

4. **d.** is the answer. (audio program)

5. **a.** is the answer. Many experts consider that the freshness a 40-year-old brings to a new career may compensate for a limited number of years he or she has in which to contribute to the profession. (audio program)

6. **b.** is the answer. (textbook, p. 592)

7. **c.** is the answer. (textbook, p. 594)

8. **d.** is the answer. (textbook, p. 592)

    a. & b. Recent studies have shown that the prevalence of the midlife crisis has been greatly exaggerated.

    c. The text does not suggest a gender difference in terms of the midlife crisis.

9. **a.** is the answer. (textbook, p. 596)

    b. This answer reflects the notion of a midlife crisis—a much rarer event than is popularly believed.

c. Gender roles tend to loosen in middle adulthood.

10. **c.** is the answer. (textbook, pp. 596–597)

a. Gender roles become *less* distinct during middle adulthood.

b. Gender roles often are most distinct during early adulthood, after which they tend to loosen.

d. Although there *is* diversity from individual to individual, gender-role shifts during middle adulthood are nevertheless predictable.

11. **a.** is the answer. (textbook, p. 592)

b. & c. These are job-related problems.

12. **a.** is the answer. (textbook, p. 599)

c. The relationship improves for both men and women.

d. Because most of today's elderly are healthy, active, and independent, this gives them and their grown children a measure of freedom and privacy that enhances the relationship between them.

13. **d.** is the answer. (textbook, p. 598)

a. This term describes middle-aged women *and* men, who are pressured by the needs of both the younger and older generations.

b. & c. These terms are not used in the text.

14. **a.** is the answer. (textbook, pp. 600–601)

15. **b.** is the answer. (textbook, p. 608)

16. **c.** is the answer. (textbook, p. 601)

a. This is not one of the basic patterns of grandparenting.

b. This pattern was common for most of the twentieth century.

d. This pattern was common a century ago.

17. **d.** is the answer. (textbook, p. 594)

18. **a.** is the answer. (textbook, p. 594)

b. This is the tendency to be kind and helpful.

c. This is the tendency to be organized, deliberate, and conforming.

d. This is the tendency to be anxious, moody, and self-punishing.

19. **b.** is the answer. (textbook, p. 597)

a. Jung's theory states just the opposite.

c. If anything, the loosening of gender roles would make adjustment easier.

d. According to Jung, gender roles are most distinct during adolescence and early adulthood, when pressures to attract the other sex and the "parental imperative" are highest.

20. **b.** is the answer. (textbook, p. 594)

References

Gutmann, David L. (1985). The parental imperative revisited: Towards a developmental psychology of later life. *Contributions to Human Development*, 14, 30–60.

Rossi, Alice S. (1980). Life-span theories in women's lives. *Signs*, 6, 4–32.

> An eminent psychologist and sociologist, both of whom are heard in the *Seasons of Life* series, discuss issues pertaining to psychosocial development during adulthood.

Late Adulthood: Biosocial Development

AUDIO PROGRAM: Opening the Biological Clock

ORIENTATION

Lesson 23 of *Seasons of Life* is about the biosocial changes that occur during late adulthood. As indicated in the text, most people's perceptions of these changes are much worse than the reality. **Ageism**, or prejudice against the elderly, fosters stereotypes that are harmful to older adults and serves to isolate the older generation. As the next three lessons will indicate, this season of life, more than any other, has been subject to misinformation and mistaken assumptions.

Is the physical decline that occurs during an individual's 60s, 70s, or 80s an inevitable product of the **biological clock**? In the audio program, "Opening the Biological Clock," Dr. Robert Butler and biologist Richard Adelman point out that many physical changes of late adulthood that once were attributed to aging may be caused by disease, variation in social context, and other factors that are not intrinsic to aging itself.

Another issue addressed in the program and text is why aging, and ultimately death, occur. Since 1900 over 25 years have been added to the **average life expectancy** of the average newborn, largely as a result of better health practices and the elimination of certain childhood diseases, accidents, and other events that led to an early death. Although the number of years a newborn can look forward to has increased, the **maximum life span**—the biological limit of life—remains fixed at about 100 to 120 years of age.

As science continues to unravel the mysteries of the biological clock, a number of fascinating questions are raised for future research. Why do we die? Can our life span be increased? Is there a master gene that programs when the hour of death will come? What effect will added years of life have on intellectual potential? on the family? on society? What is surprising is the reaction of old people themselves to the prospect of living for 130 to 140 years.

LESSON GOALS

By the end of this lesson you should be prepared to:

1. Define ageism, and identify two reasons for changing views about old age.

2. Distinguish among three categories of the aged, and explain the current state of the dependency ratio.

3. Give a realistic description of the physical changes that are due to aging itself and those that are a result of such external factors as social context and disease.

4. Outline the wear-and-tear and cellular accidents theories of aging, and explain senescence from an epigenetic systems perspective.

5. Discuss the role of genetics in aging, and explain what the Hayflick limit is and how it supports the idea of a genetic clock.

Audio Assignment

Listen to the audio tape that accompanies Lesson 23: "Opening the Biological Clock."

Write answers to the following questions. You may replay portions of the program if you need to refresh your memory. Answer guidelines may be found in the Lesson Guidelines section at the end of this chapter.

1. Define and differentiate biological clock, life span, and life expectancy. What (if any) changes have occurred in each of these during the past century?

biological clock

life span

life expectancy

2. Explain the "watch in the water" metaphor introduced in the audio program. If the biological clock is the watch, what in the water influences its operation and has an impact on older bodies?

3. (Audio Program and Text) How did the age-related incidence rates of acute and chronic disease changed during the twentieth century? In what ways do these changes complicate efforts to isolate the causes of physical changes associated with aging?

4. Discuss why researchers are "rewriting the book on aging and sexuality," by addressing the following questions.

  a. What causes the changes in sexual response that occur with age?

b. What is the impact of social context on sexuality? How did the policy decision to segregate older men and women living in nursing homes lead to an erroneous conclusion regarding the biology of aging and sexuality?

5. Identify three physical features of growing old that are probably intrinsic to the process of aging.

6. Explain the concept of programmed death at the cellular level. What research evidence supports the idea of a genetically based limit to the life of a cell, and the possibility of resetting this limit?

Textbook Assignment

Read Chapter 23: "Late Adulthood: Biosocial Development," pages 615–645 in *The Developing Person Through the Life Span, 5/e*, then work through the material that follows to review it. Complete the sentences and answer the questions. As you proceed, evaluate your performance for each secdtion by consulting the answers on page 311. Do not continue with the next section until you understand each answer. If you need to, review or reread the appropriate section in the textbook before continuing.

Ageism (pp. 616–620)

1. The prejudice that people tend to feel about older people is called _____ .

2. The cultural bias that labels teenagers as irresponsible and trouble-prone and older people as senile and rigid _____ (is/is not) weakening.

3. The scientific study of aging is called
_____ .

4. The study of populations and the social statistics associated with them is called _____ .

5. (A Life-Span View) In the past, when populations were sorted according to age, the resulting picture was a(n) _____ , with the youngest and _____ (smallest/largest) group at the bottom and the oldest and _____ (smallest/largest) group at the top.

(A Life-Span View) List two reasons for this picture.

a. _____
_____

b. _____
_____

6. (A Life-Span View) Today, because of
_____ _____
_____ and increased
_____ , the shape of the population is becoming closer to a(n)
_____ .

7. (A Life-Span View) The fastest-growing segment of the population is people age _____ and older.

8. (A Life-Span View) The shape of the demographic pyramid _____ (varies/is the same) throughout the world.
_____ (What country?) has the longest average life span and the lowest _____ _____ of all nations with large populations.

9. (A Life-Span View) As birth rates fall, young adults tend to _____ (accelerate/postpone) life transitions, such as completing their education. In the United States, the average age of retirement has _____ (increased/decreased) in recent years.

10. The ratio of self-sufficient, productive adults to dependent children and elderly adults is called the _____ _____ . Because of the declining _____ rate and the small size of the cohort just entering

_____ _____ , this ratio is _____ (lower/higher) than it has been for a century.

List several possible benefits and problems that will result from the increasing number of older people.

11. Approximately _____ percent of the elderly live in nursing homes.

12. Older adults who are healthy, relatively well-off financially, and integrated into the lives of their families and society are classified as
_____-_____ .

13. Older adults who suffer major physical, mental, or social losses are classified as
_____-_____ . The
_____-_____ are dependent on others for almost everything; they are _____ (the majority/a small minority) of those over age 65.

Primary Aging (pp. 620–627)

14. Developmentalists distinguish between the irreversible changes that occur with time, called
_____ _____ ,
and _____ _____ ,
which refers to changes caused by particular
_____ or _____ . This latter category of age-related changes _____ (is/is not) inevitable with the passage of time.

15. Every body system experiences a gradual reduction in _____ and
_____ _____ with age.

16. As people age, the skin becomes
_____ , _____ , and
_____ (more/less) elastic, which

produces wrinkling and makes blood vessels and pockets of fat more visible. Dark patches of skin known as _____ _____ also become visible.

17. Most older people are more than _____ shorter than they were in early adulthood, because their _____ have settled closer together.

18. With age, body fat tends to collect more in the _____ and _____ _____ than in the arms, legs, and upper face.

19. Body weight is often _____ (higher/lower) in late adulthood, particularly in _____ (men/women), who have more _____ and less body _____ than the other sex.

20. Another reason for the change in body weight is the loss of bone_____ that causes bones to become more porous and fragile.

21. (In Person) Changes in appearance can have serious _____ and _____ consequences. When older-looking people are treated in a stereotyped way—such as by using _____-they may feel (and become) less competent.

22. More than _____ (what proportion?) of those older than 80 have one of the three major eye diseases of the elderly. The first of these, _____ , involves a thickening of the _____ of the eye. The second, _____ , involves the _____ of the eyeball because of a buildup of _____ within the eye. The disease _____ _____ _____ involves deterioration of the _____ .

23. The leading cause of legal blindness among the elderly is _____ _____ _____ .

24. Age-related hearing loss, or _____ , affects about _____ percent of those aged 65 and older. Some elderly persons experi-ence a buzzing or ringing in the ears called _____ . The only treatment for this condition is _____ .

25. Because hearing aids are regarded as a symbol of agedness, less than _____ percent of the elderly use them.

26. Four hearing losses associated with aging are:

    a. _____

    b. _____

    c. _____

    d. _____

27. Sometimes younger adults automatically lapse into _____ when they talk to older adults.

Describe this form of speech.

28. The examples of the young-old, old-old, and oldest-old indicate that aging may be _____ , _____ , or _____ .

29. Optimal aging requires _____ _____ to body changes, not _____ _____ . To have the most beneficial impact, _____ interventions and _____ changes should take place during usual aging—typically during _____ or _____ adulthood.

30. Two statistics that indicate that many elderly people understand the importance of active adjustment to aging are:

    a. _____

    b. _____

31. Scientists _____ (agree/do not agree) on how much sleep people need. A fre-

quent sleep complaint among older adults is

_____ , which is often treated by

prescription _____ drugs.

Explain why this medical intervention may be particularly harmful in late adulthood.

32. Frequent waking during the night becomes more common during late adulthood because the decrease in the brain's _____

_____ with advancing age means sleep is not as deep and _____ are not as long.

33. (Research Report) Many gerontologists now recommend _____ , rather than pharmacological solutions, to treat insomnia in the elderly. In one study, elderly volunteers in the _____ (experimental/control) group received four weekly sessions of sleep education and counseling, while volunteers in the _____ (experimental/control) group received no treatment. In this study, the independent variable was the _____ and _____ , and the dependent variable was _____ _____ .

(Research Report) Briefly summarize the results of this study.

Secondary Aging (pp. 627–632)

34. It _____ (is/is not) inevitable that aging brings on disease.

35. In a recent survey, most older adults reported that their health limited their activities _____ (very little/a great deal).

36. The incidence of chronic diseases _____ (increases/does not increase) with age. However, whether a person becomes ill depends less on age than on _____ factors, past _____ , current _____ and _____ habits, and _____ factors such as social support.

37. Give two reasons for the increased incidence of chronic diseases.

    a. _____

       _____

    b. _____

       _____

38. Older people take _____ (less/more) time to recover from illnesses and are _____ (less/more) likely to die of them.

39. A goal of many researchers is a limiting of the time any person spends ill, that is, a(n) _____ _____ _____ .

Causes of Senescence (pp. 632–638)

40. The oldest theory of aging is the _____-_____- _____ theory, which compares the human body to a(n) _____ . Overall, this analogy _____ (is a good one/doesn't hold up).

41. A more promising theory suggests that some occurrence in the _____ themselves, such as the accumulation of accidents that occur during _____ _____ , causes aging. According to this theory, toxic environmental agents and the normal process of _____ repair result in _____ that damage the instructions for creating new cells.

42. Another aspect of the cellular theory of aging is that metabolic processes can cause electrons to separate from their atoms, resulting in atoms called _____ _____ _____ that scramble DNA molecules or produce errors in cell maintenance and repair.

43. Free radical damage _____ (is/is not) inevitable, and may be slowed by certain _____ that nullify the effects of free radicals. These include vitamins _____ , _____ , and _____ , and the mineral _____ .

44. The body's self-healing processes include a gene called _____ , which causes a flawed cell to stop_____ . Women may be protected against heart disease by the hormone _____ . Postponing or limiting childbearing may _____ (extend/shorten) a woman's life.

45. The "attack" cells of the immune system include the _____ from the bone marrow, which create _____ that attack invading _____ and _____ , and the _____ from the _____ gland, which produce substances that attack any kind of infected cells.

46. The first notable change in the immune system involves the _____ _____ , which begins to shrink during _____ . Over the course of adulthood the power, production, and efficiency of T- and B-cells _____ (increases/decreases/remains constant).

47. Additional support for the immune theory of aging comes from research on AIDS, or _____ _____ _____ _____ , which is caused by_____ , or _____ _____ _____ .

48. Individuals with stronger immune systems tend to live _____ (longer/shorter) lives

than their contemporaries. This has led some researchers to conclude that the _____ of the immune system is *the* cause of aging.

49. Females tend to have _____ (weaker/stronger) immune systems than males, as well as _____ (smaller/larger) thymus glands. However, as a result, women are more vulnerable to _____ diseases such as rheumatoid arthritis.

50. Some theorists believe that, rather than being a mistake, aging is incorporated into the _____ plans of all species.

51. The oldest age to which members of a species can live, called the _____ _____ _____ , which in humans is approximately 120 years, is quite different from _____ _____ _____ , which is defined as _____ _____ .

52. Life expectancy varies according to _____ , _____ , and _____ factors that affect frequency of _____ in childhood, adolescence, or middle age. In the United States today, average life expectancy at birth was about _____ for men and _____ for women. In 1900, in developed nations, the average life expectancy was about age _____ .

Briefly state two possible explanations for senescence according to epigenetic systems theory.

53. According to another theory of senescence, DNA acts as a genetic _____ , switching on genes that promote aging at a genetically pre-

determined age. Support for this theory comes from several diseases that involve premature signs of aging and early death, including

_____ _____

and the rare disease _____ .

54. When human cells are allowed to replicate outside the body, the cells stop replicating at a certain point, referred to as the _____ _____ . Cells from people with diseases characterized by accelerated aging replicate _____ (more/fewer) times before dying.

Can Aging Be Stopped? (pp. 638–644)

55. Researchers have been able to extend the life of some animal species by reducing their

_____ .

56. Most scientists believe that aging occurs at the level of the _____ , with _____ at least partly responsible. Except in the case of rare diseases, aging probably _____ (is/is not) directly controlled by one or several particular genes. This means that human aging probably can't be slowed with a specific _____ or via

_____ _____ .

57. The availability of universal health care has resulted in a steady increase in average life expectancy in _____ (which country?). Conversely, the average life span has been reduced in _____ , where _____ , _____ , and other epigenetic factors have recently increased; and in several nations of _____ , where _____ kills young adults who would have survived a generation ago.

58. (Changing Policy) Vitamin and mineral needs _____ (increase/decrease) with age. However, calorie requirements _____ (increase/decrease) by about _____ percent from those of early and middle adulthood. During late adulthood, a diet that is _____ and healthy is even more important than earlier.

59. (Changing Policy) Getting enough nutrients is more problematic for the aged than for younger adults primarily because the senses of _____ and _____ diminish with age.

List three external factors that make getting enough nutrients more difficult for some older adults.

   a. _____

   b. _____

   c. _____

60. (Changing Policy) Many of the elderly also take _____ that affect nutritional requirements.

61. (Changing Policy) For the very old, regular exercise _____ (is/is not) beneficial.

Describe the most beneficial type and frequency of exercise for older adults.

62. (Changing Policy) The gap between research, public policy, and practice is revealed by the fact that less than _____ percent of those over age 50 currently eat a _____ _____ or use _____ _____ to build their muscles.

63. The places famous for long-lived people are in _____ , _____ regions where pollution is minimized. Furthermore, in these places, tradition ensures that the elderly are _____ and play an important social role. Because of the absence of _____ , some researchers believe the people in these regions are lying about their true age.

List four characteristics shared by long-lived people in these regions.

   a. _____

   b. _____

   c. _____

   d. _____

Testing Yourself

After you have completed the audio and text review questions, see how well you do on the following quiz. Correct answers, with text and audio references, may be found at the end of this chapter.

1. Which of the following best expresses the concept of the biological clock?
   a. a gene that scientists have discovered that determines life expectancy
   b. a gene that determines life span
   c. a metaphor for the body's many way of timing its physical development
   d. the time frame in which human evolution takes place

2. What is the most probable explanation for the increase in life expectancy that has occurred since 1900?
   a. The biological clock has been reset as a natural result of the evolution of the human species.
   b. Cultural, rather than biological, evolution has occurred, in the form of increased knowledge leading to the control of disease.
   c. A decrease in chronic disease has occurred in older people.
   d. The rate of accidents in older people has decreased.

3. Why do researchers find it difficult to determine the physical effects of aging per se?
   a. The biological clock is sensitive to social context.
   b. It is difficult to differentiate the effects of disease from those of aging.
   c. The range of individual differences in behavior increases in older people.
   d. Researchers find it difficult for all of the above reasons.

4. What, if any, changes have occurred in life span and life expectancy during the past century?
   a. Life span has increased by 25 years; life expectancy has not changed.
   b. Life span remains the same; life expectancy has increased.
   c. Both life span and life expectancy have increased.
   d. There have been no changes in life span or life expectancy.

5. "Programmed death" refers to the fact that when normal human or animal cells are grown under artificial laboratory conditions:
   a. the cells from species with longer life spans survive longer than cells from species with shorter life spans.
   b. the cells from young individuals survive longer than those from older individuals.
   c. cells will reproduce a finite number of times and then die.
   d. all of the above occur.

6. Ageism is:
   a. the study of aging and the aged.
   b. prejudice or discrimination against older people.
   c. the genetic disease that causes children to age prematurely.
   d. the view of aging that the body and its parts deteriorate with use.

7. (A Life-Span View) The U.S. demographic pyramid is becoming a square because of:
   a. increasing birth rates and life spans.
   b. decreasing birth rates and life spans.
   c. decreasing birth rates and increasing life spans.
   d. rapid population growth.

8. Primary aging refers to the:
   a. changes that are caused by illness.
   b. changes that can be reversed or prevented.
   c. irreversible changes that occur with time.
   d. changes that are caused by poor health habits.

9. Auditory losses with age are more serious than visual losses because:
   a. they affect a far larger segment of America's elderly population.
   b. they are more difficult for doctors to diagnose than are visual losses.
   c. hearing aids, in contrast to glasses, are ineffective as a corrective measure.
   d. those who suffer from them are less likely to take the necessary corrective steps.

10. Which disease involves the hardening of the eyeball due to the buildup of fluid?
    a. cataracts
    b. glaucoma
    c. senile macular degeneration
    d. myopia

11. Factors that explain the increased incidence of chronic diseases during late adulthood include all of the following *except*:
    a. increased hypochondria.
    b. accumulated risk factors.
    c. decreased efficiency of body systems.
    d. diminished immunity.

12. A direct result of damage to cellular DNA is:
    a. errors in the reproduction of cells.
    b. an increase in the formation of free radicals.
    c. decreased efficiency of the immune system.
    d. the occurrence of a disease called progeria.

13. Which theory explains aging as due in part to mutations in the cell structure?
    a. wear and tear
    b. immune system deficiency
    c. cellular accidents
    d. genetic clock

14. According to the theory of a genetic clock, aging:
    a. is actually directed by the genes.
    b. occurs as a result of damage to the genes.
    c. occurs as a result of hormonal abnormalities.
    d. can be reversed through environmental changes.

15. Laboratory research on the reproduction of cells cultured from humans and animals has found that:
    a. cell division cannot occur outside the organism.
    b. the number of cell divisions was the same regardless of the species of the donor.
    c. the number of cell divisions was different depending on the age of the donor.
    d. under the ideal conditions of the laboratory, cell division can continue indefinitely.

16. Presbycusis refers to age-related:
    a. hearing losses.
    b. decreases in ability of the eyes to focus on distant objects.
    c. changes in metabolism.
    d. changes in brain activity during sleep.

17. Highly unstable atoms that have unpaired electrons and cause damage to other molecules in body cells are called:
    a. B-cells.   c. free radicals.
    b. T-cells.   d. both a. and b.

18. In triggering our first maturational changes and then the aging process, our genetic makeup is in effect acting as a(n):
    a. immune system.
    b. cellular accident.
    c. demographic pyramid.
    d. genetic clock.

19. Age-related changes in the immune system include all of the following *except*:
    a. shrinkage of the thymus gland.
    b. loss of T-cells.
    c. reduced efficiency in repairing damage from B-cells.
    d. reduced efficiency of antibodies.

20. Women are more likely than men to:
    a. have stronger immune systems.
    b. have smaller thymus glands.
    c. be immune to autoimmune diseases such as rheumatoid arthritis.
    d. have all of the above traits.

LESSON GUIDELINES

Audio Question Guidelines

1. The **biological clock** is a metaphor for the body's way of timing its physical development.

   Life span refers to the biological limit of life.

   Life expectancy refers to the number of years a typical newborn can expect to live, allowing for the hazards of his or her particular historical time.

   Although life expectancy has increased by 25 years since 1900, the biological clock (and therefore life span) has not changed. Then and now we are timed genetically to have a **maximum life span** of between 100 and 120 years.

2. In investigating the biosocial effects of aging, it is important to remember that aging, or the operation of the biological clock (or watch), occurs in a specific historical context in which social, biological, and other types of influences (the water) interact with those of aging itself.

   Chronic disease, for example, produces many physical changes (e.g., in balance) that once were thought to be intrinsic to the process of aging.

   Social context manifests itself in many behaviors, including sexual response, hormone levels, and even neural connections in the brain.

3. **Acute diseases**, such as influenza or the common cold, occur frequently in early life but diminish with age. They have nearly been eliminated as causes of death among older persons in the United States.

   Chronic diseases, such as cancer and heart disease, are uncommon in the young but increase in incidence with age.

   Chronic diseases themselves often produce behavioral changes that are difficult to isolate from the effects of aging per se because the diseases are much more common in older persons. As stated in the program, "You can't say the cause is aging unless you're sure it's not disease."

4. a. Sexual response does slow down with age, but the cause may be chronic disease rather than aging. Changes in the physiology of circulation and the nervous system, possibly brought on by disease, may account for this slowing down, rather than themselves being an inevitable result of aging. These changes may therefore be correctable through the use of certain medications or surgery.

   b. It was once accepted as fact that the level of the male hormone testosterone declines with age. Dr. Robert Butler has discovered that this "fact" came from studies of older men living separately from women in institutions. When these studies have been repeated in recent years, either in community-dwelling men or in institutionalized men who are socialized with women, not only do testosterone levels fail to diminish, but sexual capability is shown not to be lost in normal, healthy elderly men. Thus, social context has a significant effect on sexuality.

5. Three physical features that appear intrinsic to the process of aging are a slowing down of behavior (e.g., reflexes, cognitive functioning), an increased variation in behavior, and the longer lives of women.

6. Biologists are convinced that components of our bodies are genetically programmed to die. Biologist Leonard Hayflick discovered that when normal human cells are grown in the laboratory, they will reproduce a finite number of times and then die.

   Cells from older individuals do not survive as long as cells from younger individuals.

   Cells from longer-lived animal species survive longer than cells from species with shorter life spans.

   Introducing genetic material from cells that are nearly dead into younger cells will cause premature death.

   This evidence suggests that at the level of the cell there is some mechanism that is counting and that prescribes the moment of death for the cell.

   Biologists have also found that infecting cells with certain viruses will cause them to divide infinitely, in effect resetting the biological clock so that the cell will not die. Biologists are also acquiring the ability to remove, add, and modify genes—techniques that might affect the biological clock.

Textbook Question Answers

1. ageism
2. is
3. gerontology
4. demography
5. pyramid; largest; smallest

   a. Each generation of young adults gave birth to more than enough children to replace themselves.

   b. A sizable number of each cohort died before advancing to the next higher section of the pyramid.

6. falling birth rates; longevity; square

7. 75

8. varies; Japan; birth rate

9. postpone; decreased

10. dependency ratio; birth; late adulthood; higher

Some experts warn of new social problems, such as increased expenses for medical care and decreased concern for the quality of education for children. Fortunately, in several European nations, this has led to social policies that benefit all the generations, such as publicly funded health care and continuing education.

11. 5

12. young-old

13. old-old; oldest-old; a small minority

14. primary aging; secondary aging; conditions; illnesses; is not

15. capacity; organ reserve

16. dryer; thinner; less; age spots

17. one inch; vertebrae

18. torso; lower face

19. lower; men; muscle; fat

20. calcium

21. social; psychological; elderspeak

22. one-third; cataracts; lens; glaucoma; hardening; fluid; senile macular degeneration; retina

23. senile macular degeneration

24. presbycusis; 40; tinnitus; surgery

25. 10

26. a.   difficulty in detecting where a sound is coming from

   b.   difficulty in deciphering electronically transmitted speech

   c.   difficulty in noticing high-frequency sounds

   d.   mishearing conversation

27. elderspeak

Like babytalk, elderspeak uses simple and short sentences, exaggerated emphasis, slower talk, higher pitch, and repetition.

28. optimal, usual; impaired

29. active adjustment; passive acceptance; medical; lifestyle; early; middle

30. a.   The aged are less likely to be victims of crime than are younger adults.

   b.   The elderly are less likely to be the driver in a serious auto accident.

31. do not agree; insomnia; narcotic

These drugs may mask age-related physiological problems for which sleep disturbances are a symptom, not a cause. In addition, prescription doses are often too strong for an older person, causing confusion, depression, or impaired cognition.

32. electrical activity; dreams

33. cognitive; experimental; control; education counseling; sleep patterns

Subjects in the experimental groups showed more improvement in their sleep patterns than the control subjects did.

34. is not

35. very little

36. increases; genetic; lifestyle; eating; exercise; psychosocial

37. a.   Older people are more likely to have accumulated several risk factors for chronic diseases.

   b.   Many of the biological changes that occur with aging reduce the efficiency of the body's systems, making the older person more susceptible to disease.

38. more; more

39. compression of morbidity

40. wear-and-tear; machine; doesn't hold up

41. cells; cell reproduction; DNA; mutations

42. oxygen free radicals

43. is; antioxidants; A; C; E; selenium

44. P53; duplicating; estrogen; extend

45. B-cells; antibodies; bacteria; viruses; T-cells; thymus

46. thymus gland; adolescence; decreases

47. acquired immune deficiency syndrome; HIV; human immunodeficiency virus

48. longer; decline

49. stronger; larger; autoimmune

50. genetic

51. maximum life span; average life expectancy; the number of years the average newborn of a particular species is likely to live

52. historical; cultural; socioeconomic; death; 74; 80; 50

One explanation is that since reproduction is essential for the survival of our species, it was genetically important for deaths to occur either very early in life or after childbearing and child rearing. Another is that genetic abnormalities usually cause the organism to die long before parenthood, thus ensuring that those genes are not passed on.

53. clock; Down syndrome; progeria
54. Hayflick limit; fewer
55. diet
56. cell; genes; is not; vitamin; genetic engineering
57. Sweden; Russia; pollution, stress; Africa; AIDS
58. decrease; decrease; 10; varied
59. smell; taste
    a. poverty
    b. living alone
    c. dental problems
60. drugs
61. is

Activities that involve continuous rhythmic movement three or four times a week for at least half an hour are more beneficial than those that require sudden, strenuous effort. In addition, strength training to stave off age-related muscle loss is highly recommended for older adults.

62. 1; restricted diet; resistance training
63. rural; mountainous; respected; verifiable birth or marriage records
    a. Diet is moderate, consisting mostly of fresh vegetables.
    b. Work continues throughout life.
    c. Families and community are important.
    d. Exercise and relaxation are part of the daily routine.

Answers to Testing Yourself

1. **c.** is the answer. Although a number of actual mechanisms have been proposed, the "biological clock" is only a metaphor for these mechanisms. (audio program)

2. **b.** is the answer. Life span has not increased, therefore "a" is incorrect. The incidence rates of chronic diseases and accidents in older people have not decreased, therefore "c" and "d" are also incorrect. (audio program)

3. **d.** is the answer. (audio program)

4. **b.** is the answer. Life expectancy, but not life span, has increased. (audio program; textbook, p. 637)

5. **d.** is the answer. Programmed death is exemplified by all of these. (audio program; textbook, p. 638)

6. **b.** is the answer. (textbook, p. 616)
   a. This is gerontology.
   c. This is progeria.
   d. This is the wear-and-tear theory.

7. **c.** is the answer. (textbook, p. 618)

8. **c.** is the answer. (textbook, p. 620)
   a., b., & d. These are examples of secondary aging.

9. **d.** is the answer. (textbook, p. 624)
   a. Visual and auditory losses affect about the same number of aged persons.
   b. & c. Hearing losses are no more difficult to detect, or to correct, than vision losses.

10. **b.** is the answer. (textbook, p. 623)
    a. Cataracts are caused by a thickening of the lens.
    c. This disease involves deterioration of the retina.
    d. Myopia, which was not discussed in this chapter, is nearsightedness.

11. **a.** is the answer. (textbook, pp. 629–630)

12. **a.** is the answer. (textbook, p. 633)
    b. In fact, free radicals damage DNA, rather than vice versa.
    c. The immune system compensates for, but is not directly affected by, damage to cellular DNA.
    d. This genetic disease occurs too infrequently to be considered a *direct* result of damage to cellular DNA.

13. **c.** is the answer. (textbook, p. 633)

14. **a.** is the answer. (textbook, p. 638)
    b. & c. According to the genetic clock theory, time, rather than genetic damage or hormonal abnormalities, regulates the aging process.
    d. The genetic clock theory makes no provision for environmental alteration of the genetic mechanisms of aging.

15. **c.** is the answer. (textbook, p. 638)

16. **a.** is the answer. (textbook, p. 623)

17. **c.** is the answer. (textbook, p. 634)
    a. & b. These are the "attack" cells of the immune system.

18. **d.** is the answer. (textbook, p. 638)
    a. This is the body's system for defending itself against bacteria and other "invaders."

b. This is the theory that aging is caused by mutations in the cell structure or in the normal course of DNA repair.

c. This is a metaphor for the distribution of age groups, with the largest and youngest group at the bottom, and the smallest and oldest group at the top.

19. c. is the answer. B-cells create antibodies that *repair* rather than damage cells. (textbook, p. 635)

20. a. is the answer. (textbook, p. 635)

b. & c. Women have *larger* thymus glands than men. They are also *more* susceptible to autoimmune diseases.

Reference

Schneider, Edward L., & Rowe, J. W. (1990). *Handbook of the biology of aging* (3rd ed.). San Diego: Academic Press.

This work is considered a definitive source for research on aging.

Late Adulthood: Cognitive Development

AUDIO PROGRAM: The Trees and the Forest

ORIENTATION

Each season of life has its own way of thinking. Lesson 24 centers on thinking during late adulthood. Chapter 24 of the textbook describes the changes in cognitive functioning associated with late adulthood and examines the use of standardized tests and artificial situations in the study of cognition in the elderly. While intellectual declines are observable for most people in their 60s, and in virtually everyone by age 80, these declines are more apparent in persons performing laboratory tasks than in real life. They are also limited in scope and greatly affected by health, education, and other experiences. In daily life, most older adults are not hampered by changes in their cognitive abilities.

Audio program 24, "The Trees and the Forest," points out that many of the fears of adults as they approach old age are exaggerated. **Alzheimer's disease**, for example, is not nearly as common as public anxiety would suggest. For most people today, late adulthood brings neither a loss nor a disease of memory, but a change of memory. Conscious memory for the short term (**primary memory**) and memory for the very long term (**tertiary memory**) change very little with age. What does decline with age appears to be memory for the immediate term—the kind of memory researchers refer to as **secondary memory**. But, as the audio program and the text point out, even this loss may be more the result of disuse and poor strategies of memorization than aging per se. When older persons are taught better strategies, they often are able to use them effectively.

In this program, psychologist K. Warner Schaie discusses the cognitive changes that are likely to come with each decade after 60. Marion Perlmutter, another psychologist, reflects on **wisdom**, which may be the special gift of this season.

LESSON GOALS

By the end of this lesson you should be prepared to:

1. Discuss cognitive changes in information processing in old age.

2. Explain why different measures of cognition may be needed to assess thinking in older and younger adults.

3. Suggest several reasons, other than the aging process itself, that might contribute to age-related declines in cognitive functioning.

4. Summarize the causes and effects of the different dementias.

5. Discuss the potential for new cognitive development, cognitive growth, and wisdom during late adulthood.

Audio Assignment

Listen to the audio tape that accompanies Lesson 24: "The Trees and the Forest."

Write answers to the following questions. You may replay portions of the program if you need to refresh your memory. Answer guidelines may be found in the Lesson Guidelines section at the end of this chapter.

1. Discuss how the focus of the study of intelligence in older persons has changed in recent years.

2. Describe each of the following memory stages and whether the function of each stage normally changes as an individual ages.

a. primary memory

b. secondary memory

c. tertiary memory

3. Discuss whether the decline in secondary memory is intrinsic to older age or is the result of deficiencies in strategies of encoding and retrieval.

4. Describe the normal changes in intellectual functioning that occur in most persons during their 60s, 70s, and 80s.

5. Discuss the concept of wisdom as introduced in the audio program. What kinds of wisdom may come in later life?

Textbook Assignment

Read Chapter 24: "Late Adulthood: Cognitive Development," pages 647–675 in *The Developing Person Through the Life Span, 5/e*, then work through the material that follows to review it. Complete the sentences and answer the questions. As you proceed, evaluate your performance for each secdtion by consulting the answers on page 329. Do not continue with the next section until you understand each answer. If you need to, review or reread the appropriate section in the textbook before continuing.

1. Adult cognitive development becomes even more _____ than before, meaning that some abilities increase, others wane, and some remain stable. It is also more complex and _____ than during early and middle adulthood.

Changes in Information Processing (pp. 647–653)

2. In Schaie's longitudinal study, older adults began to show significant declines on the five "primary mental abilities": _____

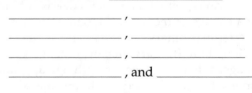

3. Variability in intellectual ability tends to be _____ (less/greater) in later life.

4. The _____ _____ stores incoming sensory information for a split second after it is received. Research suggests that senescence _____ (has no impact on/causes small declines in) the sensitivity and power of the sensory register.

5. Age-related changes in the sensory register _____ (can/cannot) easily be compensated for.

6. In order for sensory information to be registered, it must cross the _____ _____ . Due to sensory-system declines, some older people _____ (can/cannot) register certain information.

7. Research has found that differences in the subjects' _____ and _____ acuity accounted for half the variance in their _____ scores.

8. Because declines in sensory _____ can be much larger than declines in the sensory register, some experts believe that sensory function may be a fundamental index of _____ _____ .

9. Once information is perceived, it must be placed in _____ _____ .

10. Working memory has two interrelated functions: to temporarily _____ information and then to _____ it. Compared to younger adults, older adults seem to have _____ (smaller/larger/about the same) working-memory capacity.

11. Older adults are particularly likely to experience difficulty when they are asked to remember several items of information while _____ them in complex ways. This is especially true if the new information is mixed with material that is _____ . In general, increasing the number of things an adult must _____ to, or must _____ , reduces performance even more in late adulthood than earlier.

12. Of all the aspects of information processing, _____ _____ is the component that shows the most substantial declines with age.

13. The _____ _____ consists of one's storehouse of information held in _____-_____ memory. This storehouse is far from perfect, since

_____ _____ and _____ _____ allow most of this material to be forgotten.

14. Research on memory reveals that _____ (short-term/ long-term/both short- and long-term/neither short- nor long-term) memory is (are) diminished in older adults.

15. Memory takes two forms: _____ memory is "automatic" memory involving _____ , _____ responses, _____ procedures, and the _____ . This type of memory is _____ (more/less) vulnerable to age-related deficits than is _____ memory. This latter type of memory involves _____ , _____ , _____ , and the like, most of which was _____ (consciously/unconsciously) learned.

16. As people get older, differences in implicit- and explicit-memory might be reflected in their remembering how to _____ a particular task but not being as able to _____ its actions.

17. (A Life-Span View) Definitive research assessing long-term memory is difficult because it is hard to verify _____ _____ . For adults of any age, events that occurred between ages _____ and _____ are remembered better than earlier or later events. A common memory error is _____ _____ , not remembering who or what was the source of a specific piece of information.

18. (A Life-Span View) One solution to the assessment problem has been to make _____-_____ comparisons of people's memories of public events or facts. Another has been to probe memory of _____ learning.

19. (A Life-Span View) Overall, how much of their knowledge base is available to older adults seems to depend less on _____ _____ and more on _____ _____ .

20. The _____ _____ of human information processing function in an executive role and include _____ mechanisms, _____ strategies, _____ _____ , and _____ _____ . Older adults tend to use _____ (simpler and less efficient/more complex but less efficient/about the same) control processes as younger adults.

21. Older adults are more likely to rely on prior _____ , general _____ , and _____ _____ .

22. A significant part of the explanation for memory difficulties in the aged may be inadequate _____ _____ .

Reasons for Age-Related Changes (pp. 653–657)

23. Declines in cognitive functioning may be due to the primary aging process and result from _____ and _____ changes. Declines may also be associated with secondary factors, including disparaging _____ , diminished opportunities for _____ , and difficulty with the methods psychologists use to _____ cognition.

24. Stereotyping is most harmful to an individual who _____ the prejudice and reacts with _____ .

25. Older adults may _____ (overestimate/underestimate) their memory skills when they were younger; consequently, they tend to _____ (overestimate/underestimate) their current memory losses. As a result of this misperception, older adults may lose _____ in their memory.

26. The impact of ageist stereotypes on cognitive functioning is revealed in a study in which the memory gap between old and young _____ (deaf/hearing) _____ (Chinese/American) students was twice as great as that for _____ (deaf/hearing) _____ (Chinese/American) students and five times as great as that for _____ .

27. Laboratory tests of memory may put older persons at a disadvantage because they generally use _____ material, which reduces motivation in older adults. Also, they are constructed to minimize spontaneous _____ , or the use of one item to recall another. Many tests also focus on abstract _____ memory, but in so doing, exclude _____ and _____ memory, as well as any benefit that a large _____ _____ might provide.

28. Laboratory experiments also do not reflect differences in _____ and _____ , causing many older adults to question their purpose.

29. By the end of adulthood, the brain has lost at least _____ percent of its weight and _____ percent of its overall volume. Much of this loss is due to the death of _____ at an increasing rate after about age _____ .

30. The age-related changes that have the greatest impact on cognitive declines are related to the brain's _____ processes, which become _____ with age beginning in the late _____ . This can be traced to reduced production of _____ , including _____ , _____ , _____ , and _____ . It is also due to reductions in the volume of _____ _____ , the speed of the _____ _____ , and the activation of various parts of the cortex.

31. According to some experts, the slowing of brain processes means that thinking becomes

_____ , _____ , and
_____ with advancing age. One
way to compensate for this change is to provide
older adults with more _____ to
analyze information.

32. Intellectual ability _____ (is/is not)
directly related to the brain's size, weight, or
number of cells.

33. When brain cells die, existing cells
_____ (take over/do not take over)
their function. Throughout adulthood,
_____ continue to grow from each
neuron, allowing connections among surviving
neurons to become more extensive.

34. Scientists have recently discovered that
_____ cells in the brains of humans
can generate new neurons and that there is less
brain shrinkage in the _____
_____ than in lower portions of the
brain.

Cognition in Daily Life (pp. 657–662)

35. To an older adult, one of the most salient changes
associated with aging is _____
_____ ,
particularly _____ failure.

36. Most older adults _____ (do/ do
not) consider memory problems a significant
handicap in daily life.

37. Research has shown that problem solving in daily
life _____ (is/is not) less impaired
with age than problem solving in a laboratory setting. In general, the less _____ the
circumstances, the better an older person remembers.

38. (Research Report) Efforts to improve memory in
older adults by teaching them memory techniques such as the _____
_____ _____ are not
always effective.

State four general conclusions regarding age-related
changes in memory and cognition.

   a. _____

b. _____

c. _____

d. _____

39. In problem-solving tasks, older adults tend to be
_____ (slower/faster) to abandon
old strategies

40. A hallmark of successful aging is
"_____ _____
_____ _____ ," or the
capability to compensate for age-related declines
in intellectual functioning.

State several methods older adults use to compensate
for intellectual declines associated with aging.

41. Through regular _____ adults may
be able to halt or even reverse the slowing of
thinking processes that accompanies aging.
In addition, _____ _____
can help by stimulating _____ to
develop new connections. It is also possible to
slow brain deterioration with low-fat diets that
reduce _____ , by consumption of
_____ such as vitamin
_____ , by replacement of
_____ in women, and the use of
_____ steroids as well as
_____ and _____ .

42. Four factors that have a direct impact on thinking
during adulthood are _____ func-
tioning, _____ _____ ,
past _____ , and the individual's
sense of _____ .

43. (Changing Policy) Because many nursing homes
reinforce _____ ,
_____ , and _____
behaviors in residents, they may not foster the
kinds of practical competencies that are experienced by older adults who live independently.

Research has shown that giving patients the freedom to make mistakes in order to preserve their health—an approach called _____ _____ _____—may slow the more rapid decline observed in traditional nursing homes.

Dementia (pp. 662–670)

44. Although pathological loss of intellectual ability in elderly people is often referred to as _____ , a more precise term for this loss is _____ , which is defined as _____ .

45. Traditionally, when dementia occurred before age _____ , it was called _____ _____ ; when it occurred after this age, it was called _____ _____ . This age-based distinction is arbitrary, however, because the same _____ may occur at any age.

46. Dementia, which can be caused by more than 70 diseases and circumstances, has several general symptoms, including _____ _____ .

47. The most common form of dementia is _____ _____ . This disorder is characterized by abnormalities in the _____ _____ , called _____ and _____ , that destroy normal brain functioning.

48. Plaques are formed _____ (inside/outside) the brain cells from a protein called _____ ; tangles are masses of protein found _____ (inside/outside) the cells. Plaques and tangles usually begin in the _____ of the brain.

49. Physiologically, the brain damage that accompanies this disease _____ (does/does not) vary with the age of the victim.

50. When Alzheimer's disease appears in _____ (middle/late) adulthood, which is quite _____ (common/rare), it usually progresses _____ (less/more) quickly, reaching the last phase within _____ years. In such cases, the disease is caused by one of several _____ abnormalities.

51. With age, Alzheimer's disease becomes _____ (more/no more/less) common, affecting about one in every _____ adults over age 65 and about 1 in every _____ over age 85.

52. About _____ (what proportion?) of the population inherits the gene _____ , which increases the risk of Alzheimer's disease. Up to _____ percent inherit the protective _____ allele of the same gene, which may dissipate the _____ that cause the formation of plaques. More than _____ (what proportion?) of all adults have neither the protective nor the destructive gene.

53. The first stage of Alzheimer's disease is marked by _____ about recent events. Most people _____ (recognize/do not recognize) that they have a memory problem during this stage, which is often indistinguishable from the normal decline in _____ memory called _____ _____ _____ .

54. In the second stage, there are noticeable deficits in the person's _____ and _____-_____ . The third stage begins when memory loss becomes dangerous and _____ because the person can no longer manage _____ _____ _____ . People in the fourth stage require _____-_____ _____ . In the fifth stage, people become completely _____ and do not respond with any action or emotion at all. In general, death comes _____ (how many years?) after stage one.

55. There _____ (is/is not) a cure for Alzheimer's disease. One promising treatment is the use of _____ _____ _____ to delay the disease in women. Other approaches aim to slow the buildup of the protein _____ or use _____ therapy to teach victims and caregivers ways to make the disease less devastating.

56. The second major type of dementia is _____-_____ _____ . This condition occurs because a temporary obstruction of the _____ _____ , called a(n) _____ , prevents a sufficient supply of blood from reaching the brain. This causes destruction of brain tissue, commonly called a(n) _____ .

57. The underlying cause of MID is systemic _____ , which is common in people who have problems with their _____ systems, including those with _____ _____ , _____ , tingling or _____ in their extremities, and _____ . Measures to improve circulation, such as _____ , or to control hypertension and diabetes through _____ and _____ , can help to prevent or control the progress of MID.

58. Unlike the person with Alzheimer's disease, the person with MID shows a _____ (gradual/sudden) drop in intellectual functioning. The prognosis for a person with MID is generally quite _____ (good/poor).

59. Another form of dementia, called _____ _____ , originates in brain areas that do not directly involve thinking and memory. These dementias, which cause a progressive loss of _____ control, include _____ disease, _____ disease, and _____ _____ .

60. The best known of these dementias is _____ _____ , which produces muscle tremors or rigidity. This disease is related to the degeneration of neurons that produce the neurotransmitter _____ . Among the factors implicated as contributors to this disease are _____ _____ and certain _____ .

61. Another organic cause of dementia is _____ disease, which involves atrophy of the _____ and _____ lobes of the brain. The symptoms of this disease include _____ changes such as the loss of _____ skills and _____ .

62. Many AIDS and syphilis patients develop a brain _____ that causes dementia.

63. Chronic alcoholism can lead to _____ syndrome, the chief symptom of which is severely impaired _____-_____ _____ .

64. Oftentimes the elderly are thought to be suffering from brain disease when, in fact, their symptoms are caused by some other factor such as _____ , _____ , _____ , _____ , _____ , or _____ .

65. Symptoms of dementia can result from drug _____ that occur when a person is taking several different medications. This problem is made worse by the fact that many of the drugs prescribed to older adults can, by themselves, slow down _____ _____ .

66. In general, psychological illnesses such as schizophrenia are _____ (more/less) common in the elderly than in younger adults. Approximately _____ percent of the elderly who are diagnosed as demented are actually experiencing psychological illness.

67. At some time during their later years, _____ (many/a small percentage of) older adults experience symptoms of depression. Generally speaking, depression _____ (is/is not) very treatable in late adulthood.

68. One consequence of untreated depression among the elderly is that the rate of _____ is higher for those over age _____ than for any other group.

69. In most cases, the precipitating event for suicide is a(n) _____ _____ , with _____ and _____ being the most common such events. A related cause is _____ , particularly _____ or diseases that affect the _____ .

New Cognitive Development in Later Life
(pp. 670–674)

70. According to Erik Erikson, older adults are more interested in _____ _____ than younger adults and, as the "social witnesses" to life, are more aware of the _____ of the generations.

71. According to Abraham Maslow, older adults are more likely to achieve _____ .

72. (In Person) Many people become more appreciative of _____ and _____ _____ as they get older.

73. Many people also become more _____ and _____ than when they were younger.

74. One form of this attempt to put life into perspective is called the _____ _____ , in which the older person connects his or her own life with the future.

75. The reflectivity of old age may explain why professional productivity in the fields of _____ and _____ peaks in the 60s and 70s.

76. One of the most positive attributes commonly associated with older people is _____ , which Baltes defines as expert knowledge in the _____ _____ of life.

List five features that distinguish wisdom from other forms of human understanding.

Testing Yourself

After you have completed the audio and text review questions, see how well you do on the following quiz. Correct answers, with text and audio references, may be found at the end of this chapter.

1. The longest-lasting kind of memory is called:
   a. primary memory.
   b. secondary memory.
   c. tertiary memory.
   d. sensory register.

2. The two basic functions of working memory are:
   a. storage that enables conscious processing and processing of information.
   b. temporary storage and processing of sensory stimuli.
   c. retrieval of information stored for several minutes.
   d. retrieval of information stored for years or decades.

3. New cognitive development in late adulthood is characterized by Professor Perlmutter as:
   a. dementia.   c. wisdom.
   b. tertiary memory.   d. encoding.

4. Which type of material would most likely *not* be lost from the memory of a person in his or her 70s?
   a. the names of former business associates
   b. phone numbers of favorite shops
   c. early experiences with the family
   d. dates of appointments

5. The information-processing component that is concerned with the temporary storage of incoming sensory information is:
   a. working memory.   c. the knowledge base.
   b. long-term memory.   d. the sensory register.

6. Older adults tend to have the greatest difficulty picking up sensory stimuli that are:
   a. very loud or bright.
   b. ambiguous or of low intensity.
   c. abstract or meaningless.
   d. all of the above.

7. The two basic functions of working memory are:
   a. storage that enables conscious use and processing of information.
   b. temporary storage and processing of sensory stimuli.
   c. automatic memories and retrieval of learned memories.
   d. permanent storage and retrieval of information.

8. Memory for skills is called:
   a. explicit memory.   c. episodic memory.
   b. declarative memory.   d. implicit memory.

9. Strategies to retain and retrieve information in the knowledge base are part of which basic component of information processing?
   a. sensory register   c. control processes
   b. working memory   d. explicit memory

10. The plaques and tangles that accompany Alzheimer's disease usually begin in the:
    a. temporal lobe.
    b. frontal lobe.
    c. hippocampus.
    d. cerebral cortex.

11. Secondary aging factors that may explain some declines in cognitive functioning include:
    a. fewer opportunities for learning in old age.
    b. disparaging self-perceptions of cognitive abilities.
    c. difficulty with traditional methods of measuring cognitive functioning.
    d. all of the above.

12. (Changing Policy) Research showing that special training can remediate age-related cognitive declines must be interpreted cautiously because:
    a. it generally has involved relatively healthy and independent adults rather than those who are in poor health.
    b. there is evidence that intellectual plasticity increases with age.
    c. the studies are few in number and are based on very small sample sizes.
    d. of all of the above reasons.

13. Which of the following is a characteristic of laboratory experiments that inhibits the older adult's memory abilities?
    a. practice   c. motivation
    b. priming   d. time limitations

14. Dementia refers to:
    a. pathological loss of intellectual functioning.
    b. the increasing forgetfulness that sometimes accompanies the aging process.
    c. abnormal behavior associated with mental illness and with advanced stages of alcoholism.
    d. a genetic disorder that doesn't become overtly manifested until late adulthood.

15. Which of the following diseases does *not* belong with the others?
    a. Huntington's disease
    b. Parkinson's disease
    c. multiple sclerosis
    d. multi-infarct dementia

16. Alzheimer's disease is characterized by:
    a. a proliferation of plaques and tangles in the cerebral cortex.
    b. a destruction of brain tissue as a result of strokes.
    c. rigidity and tremor of the muscles.
    d. an excess of fluid pressing on the brain.

17. Multi-infarct dementia and Alzheimer's disease differ in their progression in that:
    a. multi-infarct dementia never progresses beyond the first stage.
    b. multi-infarct dementia is marked by sudden drops and temporary improvements, whereas decline in Alzheimer's disease is steady.
    c. multi-infarct dementia leads to rapid deterioration and death, whereas Alzheimer's disease may progress over a period of years.
    d. the progression of Alzheimer's disease may be halted or slowed, whereas the progression of multi-infarct dementia is irreversible.

18. Medication has been associated with symptoms of dementia in the elderly for all of the following reasons *except*:
    a. standard drug dosages are often too strong for the elderly.
    b. the elderly tend to become psychologically dependent upon drugs.
    c. drugs sometimes have the side effect of slowing mental processes.
    d. the intermixing of drugs can sometimes have detrimental effects on cognitive functioning.

19. The primary purpose of the life review is to:
    a. enhance one's spirituality.
    b. produce an autobiography.
    c. give advice to younger generations.
    d. put one's life into perspective.

LESSON 24 EXERCISE: PERSONAL WISDOM IN OLDER ADULTS

One theme of Lesson 24 is that each season of life has its own way of thinking and its own gift of knowledge. Both the text and audio program note that despite the cognitive declines of late adulthood, positive changes occur as well, as the elderly develop new interests, new patterns of thought, and what Professor Marion Perlmutter and others have referred to as **personal wisdom**. Many older adults become more responsive to nature, more appreciative of the arts, more philosophical, and more spiritual. To examine cognitive development in later life, ask an older adult whom you know well to complete the following Life/Values/Goals questionnaire. If you are an older adult, complete the questionnaire yourself. You, or the person you ask to complete the questionnaire, should answer the question from two life-cycle perspectives: as you (or your subject) felt during early or middle adulthood, and as you (or your subject) feel now, during late adulthood. Then answer the questions on page 327 and hand only that page into your instructor.

Source: Bugen, Larry A. (1979). *Death and dying: Theory, research, practice*. Dubuque, IA: Wm. C. Brown, p. 457.

LIFE/VALUES/GOALS QUESTIONNAIRE

As you see your life now, try to answer the following questions.

1. What three things would your friends say about you and your life if you died today?

2. Given the likelihood that you will not die today, and have some time left to change some things in your life, what three things would you most like to have said about you and your life?

3. If someone were to witness a week of your life, what assumptions would that person make about your values, that is, what matters most to you?

4. What values do you hold that are not evident from the way you live your daily life?

5. What three goals are important to you as you plan your life?

LIFE/VALUES/GOALS QUESTIONNAIRE

Try to answer the following questions as you might have answered them when you were a younger adult.

1. What three things would your friends say about you and your life if you died today?

2. Given the likelihood that you will not die today, and have some time left to change some things in your life, what three things would you most like to have said about you and your life?

3. If someone were to witness a week of your life, what assumptions would that person make about your values, that is, what matters most to you?

4. What values do you hold that are not evident from the way you live your daily life?

5. What three goals are important to you as you plan your life?

NAME _____   INSTRUCTOR _____

LESSON 24: PERSONAL WISDOM IN OLDER ADULTS

Exercise

Based on your responses to the Life/Values/Goals questionnaire, or those of your subject, answer the following questions.

1. Do your responses, or those of your subject, indicate a shift in life values, or goals, from early adulthood to later adulthood? What kind of shift?

2. Has the relationship between the way your subject lives life and his or her personal values changed during late adulthood? In what ways?

3. Would you say that the answers to the Life/Values/Goals questionnaire show evidence of a philosophical turn in thinking, or of the emergence of a special personal wisdom, during late adulthood? Why or why not?

LESSON GUIDELINES

Audio Question Guidelines

1. At one time the study of intelligence in old age was a study of what was believed to be the inevitable loss of function.

   Today researchers realize that each time of life has its own way of thinking, its own gift of knowledge that compensates for other losses.

   For the first time in history, as more people reach their 60s, 70s, and 80s, researchers are testing older persons in an effort to understand how thinking changes as people age.

2. a. **Primary memory** refers to memory that lasts for a minute or two. It is used to keep information in a person's conscious mind. Primary memory changes very little with age.

   b. **Secondary memory** refers to the storage of long-term memories that we are not consciously aware of. Secondary memory often becomes less reliable with age.

   c. **Tertiary memory** refers to memory for things over the long, long term, often involving experiences from early life. Tertiary memory does not decline with age, perhaps because we go over these distinctive memories time and time again.

3. Older persons do not automatically use the best strategies to put information into secondary memory (encoding). This may simply be a result of disuse of such strategies following retirement.

   Older persons can successfully use more efficient encoding and retrieval strategies when they are taught how.

   Examples of encoding and retrieval strategies include the use of imagery, context cues, the formation of rhymes and acronyms (e.g., "H-O-M-E-S," to retrieve the names of the five Great Lakes: Huron, Ontario, Michigan, Erie, Superior).

4. Using a **sequential research** program, in which the same group of people are periodically tested and retested (longitudinal research), and a new sample is added at each testing (cross-sectional research), Professor Schaie has studied people in their 60s, 70s, and 80s.

   The intellectual functioning of people in their 60s is not significantly different from that of people in their 50s.

   Beginning in the decade of the 60s, when most people are entering retirement, the saying "Use it or lose it" becomes an accurate description of intellectual change. There is often a loss of the selective skills once used in work but no longer needed after a person has retired.

   Sometime in the 70s many people experience an acceleration of *physical* decline. As a consequence, they restrict their environment and exposure to new and interesting things, which may accelerate *mental* decline.

   Among persons in their 80s there are wide individual differences in intellectual functioning, but as a rule, there are some losses in performance as compared to the 60s and 70s.

5. Professor Perlmutter believes that many older adults possess a form of **personal wisdom** that is characterized by:

   a. a greater sensitivity to perspective in life, and knowing what is important, and what is not.

   b. a more global and less self-centered view.

   c. a better integration of emotion and cognition.

   d. knowing what to remember and what to forget.

   e. knowing how to compensate for some of the cognitive losses that accompany age.

Textbook Question Answers

1. multidirectional; multicontextual
2. verbal meaning; spatial orientation; inductive reasoning; number ability; word fluency
3. greater
4. sensory register; causes small declines in
5. can
6. sensory threshold; cannot
7. visual; auditory; cognitive
8. acuity; cognitive aging
9. working memory
10. store; process; smaller
11. analyzing; distracting; attend; ignore
12. working memory
13. knowledge base; long-term; selective attention; selective memory
14. both short- and long-term
15. implicit; habits; emotional; routine; senses; less; explicit; words; data; concepts; consciously
16. perform; describe
17. personal recollections; 10; 30; source amnesia
18. cross-sectional; high school

19. how long ago information was learned; how well it was learned

20. control processes; storage; retrieval; selective attention; logical analysis; simpler and less efficient

21. knowledge; principles; rules of thumb

22. control processes

23. neurophysiological; biological; self-perceptions; learning; measure

24. internalizes; helplessness, self-doubt, or misplaced anger

25. overestimate; overestimate; confidence

26. hearing; American; deaf; American; Chinese

27. meaningless; priming; explicit; implicit; contextual; knowledge base

28. context; motivation

29. 5; 10; neurons; 60

30. communication; slower; 50s; neurotransmitters; dopamine; glucamate; acetylcholine; serotonin; neural fluid; cerebral blood flow

31. slower; simpler; shallower; time

32. is not

33. take over; dendrites

34. stem; cerebral cortex

35. cognitive decline; memory

36. do not

37. is; artificial

38. method of loci

   a. Mental processes slow down with age.

   b. The elderly do show memory declines.

   c. The elderly are less likely to use memory strategies.

   d. Memory in late adulthood is not as weak as anticipated.

39. slower

40. selective optimization with compensation

Older adults compensate by using mnemonic devices and written reminders, by allowing additional time for problem solving, by repeating instructions that might be confusing, and by focusing on meaningful tasks and ignoring those that are irrelevant.

41. exercise; cognitive stimulation; dendrites; atherosclerosis; antioxidants; E; estrogen; anti-inflammatory; aspirin; ibuprofen

42. pulmonary; physical exercise; education; control

43. passive; dependent; predictable; therapeutic risk taking

44. senility; dementia; severely impaired judgment, memory, or problem-solving ability

45. 60; presenile dementia; senile dementia (or senile psychosis); symptoms

46. severe memory loss, rambling conversation and language lapses, confusion about place and time, inability to function socially or professionally, and changes in personality

47. Alzheimer's disease; cerebral cortex; plaques; tangles

48. outside; B-amyloid; inside; hippocampus

49. does not

50. middle; rare; more; 3 to 5; genetic

51. more; 100; 5

52. one-fifth; apoE4; 10; apoE2; proteins; half

53. absentmindedness; recognize; explicit; benign senescent forgetfulness

54. concentration; short-term memory; debilitating; basic daily needs; full-time care; mute; 10 to 15

55. is not; estrogen replacement therapy; APP; group and family

56. multi-infarct dementia; blood vessels; infarct; stroke (or ministroke)

57. arteriosclerosis; circulatory; heart disease; hypertension; numbness; diabetes; exercise; diet; drugs

58. sudden; poor

59. subcortical dementia; motor; Parkinson's; Huntington's; multiple sclerosis

60. Parkinson's disease; dopamine; genetic vulnerability; viruses

61. Pick's; frontal; temporal; personality; social; motivation

62. infection

63. Korsakoff's; short-term memory

64. medication; alcohol abuse; mental illness; depression

65. interactions; mental processes

66. less; 10

67. many; is

68. suicide; 60

69. social loss; retirement; widowhood; illness; cancer; brain

70. arts, children, and the whole of human experience; interdependence

71. self-actualization

72. nature; aesthetic experiences

73. reflective; philosophical

74. life review

75. history; philosophy

76. wisdom; fundamental pragmatics

Wisdom is unspecialized and concerns all of human experience; entails practical and procedural knowledge; defines a contextual approach to life problems; accepts uncertainty in defining and solving life's problems; and recognizes individual differences in values, goals, and priorities.

Answers to Testing Yourself

1. **c.** is the answer. Tertiary memory is memory for the long, long term. It includes our very first memories of life. (audio program)

2. **a.** is the answer. (audio program; textbook, p. 648)

3. **c.** is the answer. Perlmutter is just beginning research into wisdom, the ability to "see the trees rather than the forest." (audio program)

4. **c.** is the answer. Early, meaningful life experiences seem to last forever. (audio program)

5. **d.** is the answer. (textbook, p. 648)
   a. Working memory deals with mental, rather than sensory, activity.
   b. & c. Long-term memory, which is a subcomponent of the knowledge base, includes information that is stored for several minutes to several years.

6. **b.** is the answer. (textbook, p. 648)

7. **a.** is the answer. (textbook, p. 648)
   b. These are the functions of the sensory register.
   c. This refers to long-term memory's processing of implicit and explicit memories, respectively.
   d. This is the function of long-term memory.

8. **d.** is the answer. (textbook, p. 650)
   a. & b. Explicit memory is memory of facts and experiences, which is why it is often called declarative memory.
   c. This type of memory, which is a type of explicit memory, was not discussed.

9. **c.** is the answer. (textbook, p. 651)

10. **d.** is the answer. (textbook, p. 663)

11. **d.** is the answer. (textbook, p. 653)

12. **a.** is the answer. (textbook, p. 661)
    b. Plasticity tends to *decrease* with age.

c. The text did not mention this as a limitation of such studies.

13. **d.** is the answer. (textbook, p. 655)

14. **a.** is the answer. (textbook, p. 662)

15. **d.** is the answer. Each of the other answers is an example of subcortical dementia. (textbook, pp. 666–667)

16. **a.** is the answer. (textbook, p. 663)
    b. This describes multi-infarct dementia.
    c. This describes Parkinson's disease.
    d. This was not given in the text as a cause of dementia.

17. **b.** is the answer. (textbook, p. 667)
    a. Because multiple infarcts typically occur, the disease *is* progressive in nature.
    c. The text does not suggest that MID necessarily leads to quick death.
    d. At present, Alzheimer's disease is untreatable.

18. **b.** is the answer. (textbook, p. 668)

19. **d.** is the answer. (textbook, p. 670)

References

Perlmutter, M., & List, J. A. (1982). Learning in later adulthood. In T. M. Field, A. Houston, H. C. Quay, L. Troll, & G. E. Finley (Eds.), *Review of human development*. New York: Wiley.

> Psychologist Marion Perlmutter, who is introduced in the audio program, offers a lucid critique of the laboratory research findings showing that older adults learn less well than younger adults.

Averyt, A., Furst, E., & Hummel, D. D. (1987). *Successful aging: A source book for older people and their families*. New York: Ballantine.

> Written in a sprightly but matter-of-fact tone, this book is a useful resource for the older adult. In addition to dispelling a number of myths of aging, it discusses such major topics as Alzheimer's disease, alcoholism, divorce, and death.

Late Adulthood: Psychosocial Development

AUDIO PROGRAM: Three Grandparents

ORIENTATION

How is psychosocial development affected by old age? In discussing three categories of theories—**self theories**, **stratification theories**, and **dynamic theories**—the text notes that the elderly are more diverse in lifestyle, income, and personality than people in any other season of life. This great diversity is not adequately explained by any single theory. The chapter also discusses pressures that come with old age, including retirement, changing relationships with children, grandchildren, and friends, decreased income, widowhood, and failing health. It concludes with a section on the most distressing aspect of this period—frailty in old age.

In audio program 25, "Three Grandparents," we meet three very different grandparents whose stories address three questions: What is the right age to become a grandparent? How has the dramatic rise in divorce rates affected grandparents? What are the effects of this century's great increase in length of life on the experience of being a grandparent?

Most people become grandparents during their 40s or 50s. Developmentalist Linda Burton has found that **on-time** grandparents are happier and better prepared than those who have the role of grandparent thrust on them early, in their 20s or 30s.

Sociologist Andrew Cherlin notes that in the wake of divorces grandparental ties are normally weakened on the father's side and strengthened on the mother's side. He points out that increased longevity means that many grandparents can now expect to spend half their lives with their grandchildren and that many will become great-grandparents. Although grandparenthood has changed, it still remains a central role in the family structure.

As the program opens, we hear the voices of three grandparents, each beginning his or her own unique story.

LESSON GOALS

By the end of this lesson you should be prepared to:

1. Discuss the psychosocial development of older persons from a variety of theoretical perspectives.

2. Discuss the impact of retirement on the individual, and identify several alternative sources of achievement during late adulthood.

3. Describe the components of the social convoy, and explain this convoy's increasing importance during late adulthood.

4. Explain how being a grandparent has changed during the past century, and discuss the relationships between the generations as it exists today.

5. Describe the frail elderly, explain why their number is growing, and identify various factors that may protect the elderly from frailty.

Audio Assignment

Listen to the audio tape that accompanies Lesson 25: "Three Grandparents."

Write answers to the following questions. You may replay portions of the program if you need to refresh your memory. Answer guidelines may be found in the Lesson Guidelines section at the end of this chapter.

1. Discuss the impact of being an "on-time" or "off-time" grandparent.

2. Discuss how grandparents are affected by the divorce of their children. What effect does divorce usually have on grandparental ties on the mother's side? on the father's side?

3. Describe the three phases of grandparenting. How does the grandparent's relationship to the grandchildren change during these phases?

4. Contrast the typical role of today's grandparent with that of grandparents at the turn of the century.

5. Discuss the typical role of today's grandparent in the family. How is this role likely to change in the future?

Textbook Assignment

Read Chapter 25: "Late Adulthood: Psychosocial Development," pages 677–706 in *The Developing Person Through the Life Span, 5/e,* then work through the material that follows to review it. Complete the sentences and answer the questions. As you proceed, evaluate your performance for each secdtion by consulting the answers on page 343. Do not continue with the next section until you understand each

answer. If you need to, review or reread the appropriate section in the textbook before continuing.

Theories of Late Adulthood (pp. 677–684)

1. Theories of psychosocial development in late adulthood include _____ theories, _____ theories, and _____ theories.

2. _____ theories emphasize the active part that individuals play in their own psychosocial development.

3. The most comprehensive theory is that of _____ _____ , who called life's final crisis _____ versus _____ .

4. Another version of self theory suggests that the search for _____ is lifelong. This idea originates in Erikson's crisis of _____ versus _____ .

5. Partly as a result of changes in _____ , _____ , and _____ , maintaining identity during late adulthood is particularly challenging. In the strategy _____ _____ , new experiences are incorporated unchanged. This strategy involves _____ reality in order to maintain self-esteem.

6. The opposite strategy is _____ _____ , in which people adapt to new experiences by changing their self-concept. This process can be painful, since it may cause people to doubt their _____ and _____ , leading to what Erikson called _____ .

7. Paul Baltes emphasizes _____ _____ _____ , which is the idea that individuals set their own _____ , assess their own _____ , and then figure out how to accomplish what they want to achieve despite the _____ and _____ of life.

8. People who have a strong sense of _____ believe that they can master any situation life presents, including aging.

9. Self theories have recently received strong support from research in the field of _____ _____ , which has shown that various life events seem to be at least as much affected by _____ as by life circumstances. Studies of twins have found that genetic influences often _____ (weaken/become more apparent) later in life.

10. Theorists who emphasize _____ maintain that _____ forces limit individual _____ and direct life at every stage. One form of this theory focuses on _____ _____ , reflecting how industrialized nations segregate the oldest generation.

11. According to _____ theory, in old age the individual and society mutually withdraw from each other. This theory is _____ (controversial among/ almost universally accepted by) gerontologists.

12. The opposite idea is expressed in _____ theory, which holds that older adults remain socially active. According to this theory, if older adults do disengage, they do so as a result of _____ .

13. The dominant view is that the more _____ the elderly play, the greater their _____ _____ and the longer their lives.

14. The most recent view of age stratification is that disengagement theory and activity theory are too _____ . According to this view, older adults become more _____ in their social contacts.

15. Another stratification theory, which draws attention to the values underlying the gender divisions promoted by society, is _____ theory. According to this theory, _____ policies and _____ values make later life particularly burdensome for women.

16. Currently in the United States, women make up nearly _____ (what proportion?) of the population over age 65 and nearly three-fourths of the elderly who are _____ .

17. According to the _____ _____ theory, race is a _____ _____ , and racism and racial discrimination shape the experiences and attitudes of both racial _____ and racial_____ .

18. Some theorists believe that stratification theory unfairly stigmatizes _____ and _____ groups. They point out that compared to European Americans, elderly _____ and _____ Americans are more often nurtured by _____ families. As a result of this _____ , fewer are put in nursing homes. Similarly, elderly women are less likely to be _____ and _____ than elderly men because they tend to be _____ and _____ .

19. An important concept in age stratification theory is that _____ shifts often change the meaning of gender and ethnicity.

20. According to _____ theory, each person's life is an active, changing, self-propelled process occurring within ever-changing _____ contexts.

21. According to _____ theory, people experience the changes of late adulthood in much the same way they did earlier in life. Thus, the so-called _____ _____ personality traits are maintained throughout old age.

22. The dynamic viewpoint stresses that the entire _____ _____ works toward _____ , even as elements of _____ _____ change.

23. Self theories echo _____ theories in the importance they place on childhood _____ and _____ .
Social stratification theories apply many concepts

from _____ theory. And the stress on dynamic change is an extension of _____ _____ theory.

Keeping Active (pp. 684–690)

24. Today, retirement is a much more varied experience than _____ theory suggests.

25. Mandatory retirement is _____ (legal/illegal) in many countries. Today, adults are retiring at _____ (a younger age than/about the same age as) in the past.

26. Early retirement is often the result of _____ _____ . A second problem faced by retirees is whether their _____ will last.

27. Between 1980 and 1997 the percentage of Americans over age 65 living in poverty _____ (increased/remained stable/decreased). Compared to other groups, _____ and _____ continue to have higher poverty rates, although their situation has improved.

28. Many of the elderly use the time they once spent earning a living to pursue _____ interests.

29. The eagerness of the elderly to pursue educational interests is exemplified by the rapid growth of _____ , a program in which older people live on college campuses and take special classes.

30. Compared to younger adults, older adults are _____ (more/less) likely to feel a strong obligation to serve their community.

31. Although the political activism of the older generation causes some younger adults to voice concerns regarding _____ _____ , the idea that the elderly are narrowly focused on their self-interest is unfair.

32. The major United States organization affecting the elderly is the _____ .

33. (Changing Policy) Ironically, while the financial circumstances of the American elderly have improved in recent years, other age groups, notably _____ , have grown poorer.

More than one American child in five now lives below the poverty line. This has led to calls for _____ _____ , defined as _____ _____ .

34. (Changing Policy) Because _____ is at the heart of intergenerational relationships, it is unfair and counterproductive to blame the elderly for the financial plight of the younger generations.

35. Many older adults stay busy by maintaining their _____ and _____ . This reflects the desire of most elderly people to _____ (relocate when they retire/age in place). One result of this is that many of the elderly live _____ .

The Social Convoy (pp. 690–697)

36. The phrase _____ _____ highlights the fact that the life course is traveled in the company of others.

37. Most elderly Americans _____ (are/are not) married, and they tend to be _____ , _____ , and _____ than those who never married or who are divorced or widowed.

38. The best predictor of the nature of a marriage in its later stages is _____ _____ .

Give two possible reasons that marriages may improve with time.

39. Poor health generally has a _____ (major/minor) impact on the marital relationship.

40. The death of a mate usually means not only the loss of a close friend and lover but also a lower _____ , less _____ ,

a(n) _____ social circle, and disrupt-
ed _____ _____ .

41. In general, living without a spouse is somewhat
easier for _____ (widows/widow-
ers).

State several reasons for this being so.

42. Only about _____ percent of those
currently over age 65 in the United States have
never married. A large portion of these are
_____ and _____ ,
many of whom have long-time
_____ and _____ net-
works.

43. Divorce is very _____ (rare/com-
mon) in late life. As a group, older divorced
_____ (men/women) tend to fare
better.

Briefly explain this gender difference.

44. A study of loneliness found that adults without
partners _____ (were/were not)
lonelier than adults with partners, and that
divorced or widowed adults
_____ (were/were not) lonelier
than never-married adults. The loneliest of all
were _____
_____ . The least
lonely were _____
_____ .

45. Older people's satisfaction with life is more
strongly correlated to contact with
_____ than to contact with younger
members of their own family.

46. Compared to men, women tend to have
_____ (larger/smaller) social circles, including _____ and a close
_____ (male/female) friend who is
not related.

47. (In Person) Although bonds between siblings
often _____ (intensify/weaken) in
late adulthood, rivalries that began in childhood
_____ (may/may not) continue
throughout life.

48. Because more people are living longer, more
older people are part of _____
families than at any time in history. Sometimes,
this takes the form of a _____
family, in which there are more
_____ than in the past but with only
a few members in each generation.

49. While intergenerational relationships are clearly
important to both generations, they also are likely
to include _____ and
_____ . The _____–
_____ relationship is an example of
this.

The Frail Elderly (pp. 698–705)

50. Elderly people who are physically infirm, very ill,
or cognitively impaired are called the
_____ _____ .

51. The crucial sign of frailty is an inability to perform the _____
_____ ,
which comprise five tasks: _____ ,
_____ , _____ ,
_____ , and _____ .

52. Actions that require some intellectual competence
and forethought are classified as _____
_____ .
These include such things as _____
_____ .

53. The number of frail elderly is _____
(increasing/decreasing). One reason for this
trend is that the fastest-growing segment of the
American population is people aged

_____ and older. As more people reach old age, the absolute numbers of frail individuals will _____ (increase/decrease). A second reason is that medical care now _____ _____ . A third is that health care emphasizes _____ _____ more than _____ _____ . The result has been an increasing _____ (morbidity/ mortality) rate, even as _____ (morbidity/mortality) rates fall. A final reason is that adequate nutrition, safe housing, and other preventive measures often don't reach those who _____ .

54. Long life _____ (does/does not) inevitably include years of frailty. Nor does being _____ , or a member of a _____ , or being _____ . One of the best defenses against frailty is an active drive for _____ , _____ , and _____. The dynamic systems perspective also reminds us that some people enter late adulthood with protective _____ in place. These include _____ .

55. (A Life-Span View) Many elderly persons never become frail because of four protective factors: _____ , _____ _____ , _____ _____ , and _____ _____ .

56. In caring for the frail elderly, cultures such as that of _____ (which country?) stress the obligation of children to their parents, rather than of the elderly caring for each another, as in _____ .

State three reasons that caregivers may feel unfairly burdened and resentful.

a. _____

b. _____

c. _____

57. An especially helpful form of caregiver support is _____ , in which a professional caregiver takes over to give the family caregiver a break.

58. (Research Report) Most cases of elder maltreatment _____ (involve/do not involve) family members.

59. Many older Americans and their relatives feel that _____ _____ should be avoided at all costs.

Testing Yourself

After you have completed the audio and text review questions, see how well you do on the following quiz. Correct answers, with text and audio references, may be found at the end of this chapter.

1. Most people become grandparents during their _____ or _____ . Since the beginning of this century, the average age has _____.
   a. 40s; 50s; increased   c. 40s; 50s; not changed
   b. 50s; 60s; increased   d. 50s; 60s; not changed

2. Which of the following is true of women who become grandmothers during their 20s and 30s?
   a. Because of inexperience, they usually do not do as good a job as women who become grandmothers later.
   b. They often are not as happy with their roles as are "on-time" grandmothers.
   c. Later, when the grandchildren are grown, they are more likely to reject the role of great-grandparent.
   d. All of the above are true.

3. Concerning the effects of divorce on grandparents, which of the following most often occurs?
   a. Grandparental ties weaken on the father's side and strengthen on the mother's side.
   b. Grandparental ties strengthen on the father's side and weaken on the mother's side.
   c. Grandparental ties strengthen on both the father's side and the mother's side.
   d. Grandparental ties weaken on both the father's side and the mother's side.

4. How does the great-grandparent/great-grand-child relationship usually differ from the grand-parent/grandchild relationship?
   a. It is often closer because the great-grandchildren tend to be more spoiled.
   b. It is usually more distant as a result of the additional layer of family in between.
   c. It is about the same as that between grandparent and grandchild.
   d. It is often much more argumentative since the generational gap between them reflects very different cultural values.

5. Sociologist Andrew Cherlin suggests that grandparents are in the difficult position of having to balance two different desires with respect to their role in the family:
   a. the desire to maintain equally close relationships with their children and their grandchildren.
   b. to make sure the grandchildren are brought up "in the right way" and yet do so without insulting their children by questioning their competence as parents.
   c. to feel secure that they will be cared for in their old age and yet not be a burden to their children or grandchildren.
   d. the desire to be autonomous and yet retain an important role in the family.

6. According to disengagement theory, during late adulthood people tend to:
   a. become less role-centered and more passive.
   b. have regrets about how they have lived their lives.
   c. become involved in a range of new activities.
   d. exaggerate lifelong personality traits.

7. (Changing Policy) Regarding generational equity, which of the following is implicit in a life-span perspective?
   a. The current distribution of benefits is particularly imbalanced for racial minorities.
   b. The outlay of public funds for health care is weighted toward preventive medicine in childhood and adolescence.
   c. As a group, the elderly are wealthier than any other age group.
   d. Each age and cohort has its own particular and legitimate economic needs that other generations might fail to appreciate.

8. Elderhostel is:
   a. a special type of nursing home in which the patients are given control over their activities.
   b. a theory of psychosocial development advocating that the elderly can help each other.
   c. an agency that allows older people of the opposite sex to live together unencumbered by marriage vows.
   d. a program in which older people live on college campuses and take special classes.

9. Longitudinal studies of monozygotic and dizygotic twins have recently found evidence that:
   a. genetic influences weaken as life experiences accumulate.
   b. strongly supports disengagement theory.
   c. some traits seem even more apparent in late adulthood than earlier.
   d. all of the above are true.

10. A former pilot, Eileen has always been proud of her 20/20 vision. Although to the younger members of her family it is obvious that her vision is beginning to fail, Eileen denies that she is having any difficulty and claims that she could still fly an airplane if she wanted to. An identity theorist would probably say that Eileen's distortion of reality is an example of:
    a. identity assimilation.
    b. identity accommodation.
    c. selective optimization.
    d. disengagement.

11. In general, older people are:
    a. more likely to retire at a later age.
    b. likely to retire for health-related reasons.
    c. likely to retire simply because they want to.
    d. more likely to retire at their employers' request.

12. The idea that individuals set their own goals, assess their abilities, and figure out how to accomplish what they want to achieve during late adulthood is referred to as:
    a. disengagement.
    b. selective optimization with compensation.
    c. dynamic life-course development.
    d. age stratification.

13. After retirement, the elderly are likely to:
    a. get a part-time job.
    b. become politically involved.
    c. do volunteer work because they feel a particular commitment to their community.
    d. do any of the above.

14. Which of the following theories does *not* belong with the others?
    a. disengagement theory
    b. feminist theory
    c. critical race theory
    d. continuity theory

15. Which of the following is most true of the relationship between the generations today?
    a. Because parents and children often live at a distance from each other, they are not close.
    b. Older adults prefer not to interfere in their children's lives.
    c. Younger adults are eager to live their own lives and do not want to care for their parents.
    d. The generations tend to see and help each other frequently.

16. (In Person) The importance of longstanding friendships is reflected in which of the following?
    a. the intensification of friendly bonds between in-laws
    b. the mother–daughter relationship becoming more like one between two friends
    c. the intensification of friendly bonds between siblings
    d. a change in the husband–wife relationship to one of friendship

17. In general, during late adulthood the *fewest* problems are experienced by individuals who:
    a. are married.
    b. have always been single.
    c. have long been divorced.
    d. are widowed.

18. Which of the following is true of adjustment to the death of a spouse?
    a. It is easier for men in all respects.
    b. It is initially easier for men but over the long term it is easier for women.
    c. It is emotionally easier for women but financially easier for men.
    d. It is determined primarily by individual personality traits, and therefore shows very few sex differences.

19. According to dynamic theories:
    a. self-integrity is maintained throughout life.
    b. adults make choices and interpret reality in such a way as to express themselves as fully as possible.
    c. people organize themselves according to their particular characteristics and circumstances.
    d. each person's life is largely a self-propelled process, occurring within ever-changing social contexts.

20. Which of the following most accurately expresses the most recent view of developmentalists regarding stratification by age?
    a. Aging makes a person's social sphere increasingly narrow.
    b. Disengagement is always the result of ageism.
    c. Most older adults become more selective in their social contacts.
    d. Older adults need even more social activity to be happy than they did earlier in life.

NAME _____   INSTRUCTOR _____

LESSON 25: GRANDPARENTS

Exercise

A number of issues pertaining to grandparents are raised in the text and audio program. These include the changing role of grandparents due to increased life expectancy, greater geographical mobility of offspring, greater financial independence, rising divorce rates, and the trend toward egalitarian relationships with grandchildren.

To help you apply the information in this lesson to your own life, reflect on the changing role of grandparents by writing brief answers to the questions that follow, then hand the completed exercise in to your instructor.

1. Describe your relationship with one of your grandparents. Was (is) it close and loving? How frequently did (do) you see him or her? To what extent did he or she participate in your upbringing?

2. In what ways is (was) your relationship to your grandparents different from that between your parents and *their* grandparents?

3. If you are a grandparent, in what ways does your role as grandparent differ from that of your grandparents? If you are not a grandparent, but hope to be one some day, how would you *like* your role as grandparent to differ from that of your grandparents?

4. The text notes that styles of grandparenting vary by gender, age at which one becomes a grandparent, and ethnic group, for example. If you would care to, describe how any of these factors have influenced your own relationships as a grandchild or grandparent.

LESSON GUIDELINES

Audio Question Guidelines

1. Developmentalist Linda Burton has found that grandmothers who assumed the role early (in their 20s or 30s) were not as happy with their new role as were **on-time** grandmothers (those who became grandmothers in their 40s or 50s). The early transition to grandmotherhood seemed to throw their life course out of synchronization. According to Burton, their rejection of the grandmother role amounts to their putting up a "speed bump" in their developmental cycle, saying in effect, "Stop, you're trying to push me into a middle-age stage of development."

   On-time grandmothers were much happier with their transition to the grandmother role because it came at a time in their lives when they expected it and when they were prepared for it.

2. The 1960s and 1970s saw a dramatic rise in divorce rates. Today one of every two marriages is likely to end in divorce. It is therefore not surprising that divorce is having a tremendous impact on grandparents, often weakening their ties to their grandchildren.

   Sociologist Andrew Cherlin has found that whether a daughter or son is getting the divorce often makes a big difference. In most cases of divorce, mothers keep custody of the children. For a grandparent, that means that if a daughter is getting divorced, the grandparent is likely to have a closer relationship with the grandchildren because he or she is more likely to be called on to help. If a son is getting divorced, it often is more difficult for the grandparent to maintain a relationship with the grandchildren.

3. Phase one of grandparenting begins with the birth of the grandchild. This phase is the best, according to most grandparents. Sociologist Cherlin has found that grandparental ties and emotional investment are highest during this phase.

   Phase two occurs during the grandchild's adolescence. During this phase the grandchild needs to establish independence from his or her parents and grandparents. The relationship between grandparents and grandchild becomes more distant.

   Phase three begins when the grandchild becomes an adult. During this phase the relationship often again becomes close. In many cases the usual roles of grandparent and grandchild start to be reversed: it is the grandchild who is likely to provide more in the way of support to his or her elderly grandparent.

4. In this century grandparenthood has become a much lengthier period of life and more distinct from the period of parenthood.

   Because of the increase in life expectancy, most people can now spend an entire career—perhaps even half their lives—as grandparents.

   Increased longevity has made great-grandparenting much more common today than it was at the turn of the century.

   Unlike grandparents, great-grandparents almost never become involved in a "hands-on" way with their great-grandchildren. This may be due to the fact that there are too many layers of family (parents and grandparents) insulating them from their great-grandchildren. In addition, most great-grandparents are fairly elderly and, although they love their great-grandchildren, they are not as interested in, or capable of, helping out as they were with their grandchildren.

5. Although grandparents today range in age from their 20s on up, and come in infinite varieties, grandparents share several common features.

   For one, they are a kind of family insurance policy, standing in the background ready to help out in the case of a family crisis, such as parental illness, divorce, or unemployment.

   A second common feature is the norm of noninterference. Grandparents are supposed to leave parenting to the parents; as a result, they must balance two very different desires: retaining their own autonomy, while maintaining a strong role in the family.

   Andrew Cherlin believes that grandparents' role as symbols of family continuity and love may actually increase in the future: as family size declines there are fewer grandchildren for grandparents to spend time with, giving the average grandparent more resources and more time to devote to a grandchild.

Textbook Question Answers

1. self; stratification; dynamic
2. Self
3. Erik Erikson; integrity; despair
4. identity; identity; role confusion
5. appearance; health; employment; identity assimilation; distorting
6. identity accommodation; values; beliefs; despair

7. selective optimization with compensation; goals; abilities; limitations; declines

8. self-efficacy

9. behavioral genetics; genes; become more apparent

10. stratification; social; choice; age stratification

11. disengagement; controversial among

12. activity; ageism

13. roles; life satisfaction

14. extreme; selective

15. feminist; social; cultural

16. two-thirds; poor

17. critical race; social construct; minorities; majorities

18. women; minority; African; Hispanic; multigenerational; familism; lonely; depressed; caregivers; kinkeepers

19. cohort

20. dynamic; social

21. continuity; Big Five

22. social system; continuity; individual lives

23. psychoanalytic; self-concept; identity; sociocultural; epigenetic systems

24. disengagement

25. illegal; a younger age than

26. failing health; money

27. decreased; minorities; widows

28. educational

29. Elderhostel

30. more

31. generational equity

32. American Association of Retired Persons (AARP)

33. children; generational equity; equal contributions from, and fair benefits for, each generation

34. interdependence

35. home; yard; age in place; alone

36. social convoy

37. are; healthier; wealthier; happier

38. its nature early on

One reason may be traced to the effects of their children, who were a prime source of conflict when they were younger but are now a source of pleasure. Another is that all the shared contextual factors tend to change both partners in similar ways, bringing them closer together in personality, perspectives, and values.

39. minor

40. income; status; broken; daily routines

41. widows

One reason is that elderly women often expect to outlive their husbands and have anticipated this event. Another is that in most communities widows can get help from support groups. A third is that many elderly men were dependent on their wives to perform the basic tasks of daily living.

42. 4.4; gays; lesbians; companions; social

43. rare; women

For divorced older women life is likely to improve with age, especially if they have successfully raised children or succeeded in a career against all odds. Because women are usually the kinkeepers, many former husbands find themselves isolated from children, grandchildren, and old friends.

44. were; were; men currently without a partner who had lost two or more wives through death or divorce; wives still in their first marriage

45. friends

46. larger; relatives; female

47. intensify; may

48. multigenerational; beanpole; generations

49. tension; conflict; mother–daughter

50. frail elderly

51. activities of daily life (ADLs); eating; bathing; toileting; dressing; transferring from a bed to a chair

52. instrumental activities of daily life (IADLs); shopping, paying bills, driving a car, taking medications, and keeping appointments

53. increasing; 85; increase; prolongs life; death postponement; life enhancement; morbidity; mortality; need them the most

54. does not; female; minority; poor; autonomy; control; independence; buffers; family members and friends, past education and continued educational opportunity, pensions, good health habits

55. attitude; social network; physical setting; financial resources

56. Korea; the United States

   a. If one relative is doing the caregiving, other family members tend to feel relief rather than an obligation to help.

   b. Care-receivers and caregivers often disagree about the nature and extent of care that is needed.

   c. Services designed for caregivers are difficult to obtain from social agencies.

57. respite care

58. involve

59. nursing homes

Answers to Testing Yourself

1. **c.** is the answer. Most people become grandparents during their 40s or 50s. This figure has not changed significantly during the past century. (audio program)

2. **b.** is the answer. (audio program)

3. **a.** is the answer. Grandparental ties usually strengthen on the mother's side following divorce. This is due to the fact that in most cases of divorce the mother retains custody of the children. (audio program)

4. **b.** is the answer. Great-grandparental ties are usually weaker than grandparental ties. (audio program)

5. **d.** is the answer. (audio program)

6. **a.** is the answer. (textbook, p. 680)

   b. This answer depicts a person struggling with Erikson's crisis of integrity versus despair.

   c. This answer describes activity theory.

   d. Disengagement theory does not address this issue.

7. **d.** is the answer. (textbook, p. 691)

   a. Some people believe this, but it is not advocated by life-span developmentalists.

   b. Just the opposite is true.

   c. Although some of the elderly are among the richest, most are in the middle-income bracket.

8. **d.** is the answer. (textbook, p. 686)

9. **c.** is the answer. (textbook, p. 679)

   a. Such studies have found that genetic influences do not weaken with age.

   b. This research provides support for self theories rather than disengagement theory.

10. **a.** is the answer. (textbook, p. 678)

    b. Accommodating people adapt to new experiences (such as failing vision) by changing their self-concept.

    c. People who selectively optimize are more realistic in assessing their abilities than Eileen evidently is.

    d. There is no sign that Eileen is disengaging, or withdrawing from her social relationships.

11. **c.** is the answer. (textbook, p. 685)

    a. & b. Workers are retiring earlier than in the past, and not always for health-related reasons.

    d. Mandatory retirement is illegal in many nations.

12. **b.** is the answer. (textbook, p. 679)

    a. This is the idea that the elderly withdraw from society as they get older.

    c. This is the theory that each person's life is a self-propelled process occurring within ever-changing social contexts.

    d. According to this theory, the oldest generation is segregated from the rest of society.

13. **d.** is the answer. Contrary to earlier views that retirement was not a happy time, researchers now know that the elderly are generally happy and productive, spending their time in various activities. (textbook, pp. 686–689)

14. **d.** is the answer. Each of the other theories can be categorized as a stratification theory. (ptextbook, p. 680–683)

15. **d.** is the answer. (textbook, p. 697)

16. **c.** is the answer. (textbook, p. 696)

    a., b., & d. These may occur in some cases, but they are not discussed in the text.

17. **a.** is the answer. (textbook, p. 692)

18. **c.** is the answer. (textbook, p. 693)

19. **d.** is the answer. (textbook, p. 683)

    a. This expresses continuity theory.

    b. This expresses self theory.

    c. This expresses stratification theory.

20. **c.** is the answer. (textbook, p. 681)

    a. This is the central idea behind disengagement theory.

    b., & d. These ideas are expressions of activity theory.

Reference

Cherlin, A., & Furstenberg, F. (1986). *The new American grandparent.* New York: Basic Books.

Professor Andrew Cherlin, who is heard in the audio program, discusses the changing roles of grandparents in contemporary society.

Death and Dying

AUDIO PROGRAM: Of Seasons and Survivors

ORIENTATION

The final lesson of *Seasons of Life* is concerned with death and dying. Depending on a person's age, experiences, beliefs, and historical and cultural context, death can have many different meanings. The Epilogue of *The Developing Person Through the Life Span*, 5/e, explores these meanings, including the pivotal work of Elisabeth Kübler-Ross, whose findings, based on interviews with terminally ill patients, helped make professionals and the general public more aware of the needs of the dying.

The text also discusses the concept of a "good death," which most agree is a death that comes swiftly and with dignity. It describes the hospice as an alternative to the dehumanization of the typical hospital death and explores the controversial issue of whether and when we should hasten the death of a loved one.

The chapter concludes with a discussion of bereavement, mourning, and the many factors that influence how people think about death. Consistent with our culture's tendency to conceal death by placing the dying in institutions, the process of grieving has recently been denied, which can have a crippling effect on the lives of the bereaved.

Audio program 26, "Of Seasons and Survivors," examines how the ending of one person's life affects the continuing stories of the family members who survive. Through the stories of two very different deaths, the listener discovers that losing a loved one "in season," at the end of a long life, has a very different impact than losing a loved one "out of season," in the prime of life. Expert commentary is provided by psychologist Camille Wortman, who has studied the grieving process extensively.

As the program opens, we hear the voice of a father describing the tragic death of his 30-year-old son.

LESSON GOALS

By the end of this lesson you should be prepared to:

1. Identify Kübler-Ross's stages of dying, and discuss these stages in light of more recent research.

2. Discuss the steps that patients, family members, and medical personnel can take to plan for a swift, pain-free, and dignified death.

3. Explain the concept of palliative care, focusing on the advantages and disadvantages of hospices.

4. Describe cultural and religious variations in how death is viewed and changes in the mourning process.

5. Contrast the impact of an "in-season" death and an "out-of-season" death on surviving family members.

Audio Assignment

Listen to the audio tape that accompanies Lesson 26: "Of Seasons and Survivors."

Write your answers to the following questions. You may replay portions of the program if you need to refresh your memory. Answer guidelines may be found in the Lesson Guidelines section at the end of this chapter.

1. Identify two misunderstandings the general public has about the grieving process.

2. Describe two ways in which well-intentioned persons are often not helpful to those who are grieving.

3. Explain how people *can* be helpful to those who have lost a loved one and identify another factor that facilitates the recovery process.

4. Contrast the impact of "in-season" and "out-of-season" deaths on surviving family members.

Textbook Assignment

Read the Epilogue: "Death and Dying," pages 709–721 in *The Developing Person Through the Life Span, 5/e,* then work through the material that follows to review it. Complete the sentences and answer the questions. As you proceed, evaluate your performance for each secdtion by consulting the answers on page 355. Do not continue with the next section until you understand each answer. If you need to, review or reread the appropriate section in the textbook before continuing.

The Dying Person's Emotions (pp. 709–710, 711)

1. A major factor in our understanding of the gamut of emotional reactions among the dying was the pioneering work of _____ . Her research led her to propose that the dying go through _____ (how many?) emotional stages. .

2. In order, the stages of dying are

_____ , _____ ,

_____ , _____ , and

_____ .

3. The final stage _____ (is/is not) a happy stage; it is a stage in which the person is

_____ .

4. Other researchers typically _____ (have/have not) found the same five stages of dying occurring in sequence.

5. In her interviews with the dying, Kübler-Ross quickly discovered the importance of _____ (concealing/not concealing) information about their condition.

6. (A Life-Span View) The age of the dying person _____ (does/does not) significantly affect his or her emotional response to death.

(A Life-Span View) Briefly describe the typical reactions of the following individuals to their own impending death:

a young child: _____

_____

an adolescent: _____

_____

a young adult: _____

_____

a middle-aged adult: _____

_____

an older adult: _____

_____

7. (A Life-Span View) The emotional response to death also depends on the age of the _____ . Little children, for example, are often _____ that the dying person _____ them. Generally speaking, deaths that are expected _____ (are/are not) easier to cope with because they permit _____ _____ .
A common emotion in mourners of every age is

_____ .

Deciding How to Die (pp. 710–714, 715)

8. Many adults hope to die _____ , with little _____ and great

_____ .

9. Because of modern medical techniques, a swift and peaceful death is _____ (more/less) difficult to ensure today than in the past.

10. Adults often die in pain, largely because analgesic medicines are _____ because of a fear of causing _____ . Pain is particularly likely for the _____-_____ patients in _____ _____ .

11. There is a growing consensus, both in _____ and in _____ practice, that the ultimate authority regarding what measures are to be used in terminal cases should be the _____ .

12. Some people make a _____ _____ to indicate what medical intervention they want if they become incapable of expressing those wishes. To avoid complications, each person should also designate a _____ , someone who can make decisions for them on the spot if needed.

13. Proxies _____ (do/do not) guarantee a problem-free death. One problem is that _____ members may disagree with the proxy; another is that more than _____ (how much?) the time proxy directives are ignored during emergencies.

14. Usually, if a patient prefers to die naturally, the order _____ _____ _____ is placed on that person's hospital chart. A situation in which medication relieves pain and hastens death is called _____ _____ .

Together, DNR orders and pain medication are a form of _____ _____ .

15. Generally speaking, _____ (most/few) doctors and nurses are trained to handle the psychological demands of palliative care. The institution called the _____ provides this type of care to terminally ill patients.

16. (Changing Policy) The hospice was conceived in response to the _____ of the typical hospital death.

17. (Changing Policy) Hospice patients are assigned a _____ _____ _____ , who is present much of the time and is responsible for some of the routine care.

18. (Changing Policy) The hospice concept _____ (does/does not) solve all the problems of dying.

(Changing Policy) State several criticisms of hospice care.

19. (Changing Policy) There are _____ (few/many) hospices for children. In the United States, about _____ percent of all deaths occur with hospice care.

20. Two other factors that help to determine whether or not a person will have a good death are _____ values and _____ practices.

21. Especially controversial are issues concerning _____-_____ _____ , in which a doctor provides the means for a person to end his or her life, and _____ , in which someone intentionally acts to terminate the life of a suffering person.

22. (Research Report) In 1993, the _____ legislature passed a law guaranteeing that doctors would not be prosecuted for assisting suicide if they followed several guidelines.

23. (Research Report) In the United States, the state of _____ has allowed physician-assisted suicide since 1998. Since that time, concerns that physician-assisted suicide might be used more often with minorities, the poor, and

the disabled _____ (have/have not) been proven to be well-founded.

The Social Context of Dying (pp. 714, 716–721)

24. Through the study of death we have learned that perceptions of death are _____ (variable/the same) in all cultures.

25. In most _____ traditions, elders take on an important new status through death.

26. In many _____ nations, death affirms faith in Allah and caring for the dying is a holy reminder of mortality.

27. Among Buddhists, disease and death are inevitable sufferings, which may bring _____ . Among _____ and _____ , helping the dying to relinquish their ties to this world and prepare for the next is considered an obligation for the immediate family.

28. Preparations for death are not emphasized in the _____ tradition because hope for _____ should never be extinguished.

29. Many _____ believe that death is the beginning of eternity in _____ or _____ , and thus welcome or fear it.

30. The study of death reveals that _____ often has more influence on variations in death practices than _____ does. Customs of _____ also vary tremendously.

31. Two themes that emerge in cultural variations of death practices are:

    a. _____

    b. _____

32. In recent times, mourning has become more _____ , less _____ , and less _____ . Younger generations are likely to prefer _____ _____ , while older generations prefer _____ _____ . One

result of trends is that those who have lost a loved one are more likely to experience _____ _____ and _____ _____ than in the past.

33. List two steps that others can follow to help a bereaved person.

    a. _____

    b. _____

34. A frequent theme of those who work with the bereaved is the value of a(n) _____ _____ .

35 (In Person) Particularly among younger people, grieving is sometimes aided today by an _____ _____ to the dead.

Testing Yourself

After you have completed the audio and text review questions, see how well you do on the following quiz. Correct answers, with text and audio references, may be found at the end of this chapter.

1. In her research with grieving families, Professor Wortman has found that:
   a. most people lose their attachment to the lost loved one within a year of the death.
   b. people often remain attached to a lost loved one for many years.
   c. people who remain attached to a lost loved one need professional counseling.
   d. women are better than men at adjusting to the loss of a loved one.

2. Which of the following statements would probably be the *most* helpful to a grieving person?
   a. "It must have been his or her time to die."
   b. "Why don't you get out more and get back into the swing of things?"
   c. "It must have been God's will that he or she was taken from you."
   d. "If you need someone to talk to, call me at any time."

3. Professor Wortman found that the single *most* helpful element in a person's recovery from the loss of a loved one was:
   a. the person getting back to his or her normal routine.
   b. the person's religious faith.
   c. having an understanding relative.
   d. having a friend who has experienced a similar loss.

4. Which of the following is true concerning the timing of death?
   a. Today, death is more likely than ever to come in any season of life.
   b. Today, death is more likely to come at the end of a long life.
   c. The timing of death has not changed significantly over the course of human history.
   d. Death is less predictable today than ever before.

5. In helping a person cope with the loss of a loved one, it is *not* a good idea to:
   a. rush the person through his or her grief.
   b. provide a philosophical perspective on death.
   c. encourage the person to forget and get on with life.
   d. do any of the above.

6. Kübler-Ross found that doctors often chose not to inform terminally ill patients of their condition and sometimes concealed the information from families as well. Such an approach would tend to:
   a. minimize possibilities for grief.
   b. increase feelings of isolation and sorrow.
   c. discourage the family from retaining memories of the deceased.
   d. maximize possibilities for passive euthanasia.

7. (A Life-Span View) Medical advances have meant that death today is more often:
   a. far less painful for the dying individual.
   b. emotionally far less painful for the bereaved.
   c. a solitary, lengthy, and painful experience.
   d. predictable, and therefore a less traumatic experience.

8. Kübler-Ross's stages of dying are, in order:
   a. anger, denial, bargaining, depression, acceptance.
   b. depression, anger, denial, bargaining, acceptance.
   c. denial, anger, bargaining, depression, acceptance.
   d. bargaining, denial, anger, acceptance, depression.

9. (text and A Life-Span View) Recent research regarding the emotions of terminally ill patients has found that:
   a. all patients reach the stage of acceptance.
   b. emotional stages generally follow one another in an orderly sequence.
   c. age has an important effect on emotions.
   d. most experience depression.

10. Most adults hope that they will die:
    a. with little pain.
    b. with dignity.
    c. swiftly.
    d. in all of the above ways..

11. A pain-free death is least likely to be experienced by:
    a. the oldest-old patients in nursing homes.
    b. hospice patients.
    c. children dying of cancer.
    d. patients who fail to make a living will.

12. *Hospice* is best defined as:
    a. a document that indicates what kind of medical intervention a terminally ill person wants.
    b. mercifully allowing a person to die by not doing something that might extend life.
    c. an alternative to hospital care for the terminally ill.
    d. providing a person with the means to end his or her life.

13. Palliative care refers to:
    a. heroic measures to save a life.
    b. conservative medical care to treat an illness.
    c. efforts to relieve pain and suffering.
    d. allowing a terminally ill patient to die naturally.

14. A situation in which, at a patient's request, another person acts to terminate his or her life is called:
    a. involuntary euthanasia
    b. voluntary euthanasia
    c. a physician-assisted suicide
    d. DNR

15. Which of the following is a normal response in the bereavement process?
    a. experiencing powerful emotions
    b. culturally diverse emotions
    c. a lengthy period of grief
    d. All of the above are normal responses.

16. A "double effect" in medicine refers to a situation in which:
    a. the effects of one drug on a patient interact with those of another drug.
    b. medication relieves pain and has a secondary effect of hastening death.
    c. family members disagree with a terminally ill patient's proxy.
    d. medical personnel ignore the wishes of a terminally ill patient and his or her proxy.

17. (Changing Policy) Criticisms made against hospices include all of the following *except*:
    a. the number of patients served is limited.
    b. in some cases a life is being ended that might have been prolonged.
    c. burnout and the rapid growth of hospices might limit the number of competent hospice workers.
    d. the patient is needlessly isolated from family and friends.

NAME _____   INSTRUCTOR _____

LESSON 26: COPING WITH DEATH AND DYING

Exercise

A central theme of this lesson is that death has many meanings, depending on a person's age, experience, beliefs, and his or her historical and cultural context. A number of issues are discussed, including our culture's tendency to institutionalize and deny death, the decline of "good deaths" as medical technology has provided new ways of prolonging life, developmental shifts in the way people view death, **euthanasia, assisted suicide**, and the pros and cons of the **hospice** as an alternative to hospitals for those who are dying.

To stimulate your thinking about these issues, complete the following questions. If you would like to ask these questions of someone other than yourself, feel free to do so. If you need more space for the answers, you may use additional sheets of paper. Hand the completed exercise in to your instructor.

1. What kind of ceremony or mourning ritual would you like to have when you die? What are your reasons for that choice?

2. What would you want to do if you had just six months to live?

3. A very close friend is in the hospital with a terminal illness, but no one has told her anything about the illness and the doctors are cheerily reassuring her she is going to get better. Your friend asks you if she is dying. What would you say?

4. How would you explain the death of a grandparent to a 7-year-old child? (Be aware of a 7-year-old's understanding of death.)

5. Your 40-year-old friend has recently been widowed. List three things you should *not* say or do to her, and explain why.

6. Knowing that you have a terminal illness, would you prefer to be kept alive by artificial means for as long as possible or to be allowed to die in a hospice?

LESSON GUIDELINES

Audio Question Guidelines

1. In her research on the process of grieving, Professor Camille Wortman has found that the general public has many misconceptions about grief. One is the belief that those who are bereaved are eventually able to break their attachment to the lost loved one. In reality, it is very common for the bereaved to remain attached to the loved one for a long time.

   Another misunderstanding is that after a year or two those who have lost a loved one will recover and get back to their normal routine. Professor Wortman has found that the vast majority of people who have lost a loved one experience permanent changes in their lives as a result.

2. Well-intentioned people often attempt to relate to people who are grieving in ways that are not helpful. For example, it is usually not helpful to provide a philosophical perspective on the event, such as the comment, "Well, it was her time to die."

   In addition, it is not helpful to try to hurry people through their grief by encouraging them to "get back into the swing of things."

3. Professor Wortman suggests that bereaved persons are comforted by social support, such as a friend who listens, sympathizes, and does not ignore the real pain and complicated emotions that accompany **mourning**.

   Those who would comfort the bereaved should also realize that bereavement is likely to be a demanding process that may last for months or even years.

   Professor Wortman found that recovery from the loss of a loved one was facilitated by some form of religious faith.

4. Every life, short or long, leaves a legacy and lasting effect on surviving family members. The impact of losing a loved one in the prime of his or her life is different from that of losing a loved one at the end of a long life. The sudden death of a person who is not "supposed" to die, such as the young man in the audio program, is usually the most difficult to bear. Surviving members of the family are often tormented by conflicting emotions of guilt, denial, anger, and sorrow.

   Death is somewhat easier to cope with when it is expected. Losing someone unexpectedly does not allow family members to come together with the dying person and share their affection for one another. Having time to anticipate and prepare for the death does not necessarily reduce the pain of loss, but it can reduce the conflicting emotions associated with it.

Textbook Question Answers

1. Elisabeth Kübler-Ross; five
2. denial; anger; bargaining; depression; acceptance
3. is not; almost void of feelings
4. have not
5. not concealing
6. does

Young children, who may not understand the concept of death, are usually upset because it suggests being separated from those they love.

Because they tend to focus on the quality of present life, *adolescents* may primarily be concerned with the effect of their condition on their appearance and social relationships.

Young adults often feel rage and depression at the idea that, just as life is about to begin in earnest, it must end.

For *middle-aged adults*, death is an interruption of important obligations and responsibilities.

An *older adult*'s feelings about dying depend on the particular situation. If one's spouse has already died, for example, acceptance of death is comparatively easy.

7. mourner; angry; abandoned; are; anticipatory grief; fear of isolation and pain
8. swiftly; pain; dignity
9. more
10. underprescribed; addiction; oldest-old; nursing homes
11. law; hospital; individual who must undergo those treatments
12. living will; proxy
13. do not; family; half
14. DNR (do not resuscitate); double effect; palliative care
15. few; hospice
16. dehumanization
17. lay primary caregiver
18. does not

The fact that hospice patients must be diagnosed as terminally ill and give up all hope of recovery severely limits the number of participants. Patients and their families must accept this diagnosis, agreeing that life or a cure is virtually impossible. Also, hospice care is expensive and therefore not available to everyone. Finally, hospices are much better prepared to meet the needs of young adult patients with cancer than older patients with combinations of illnesses.

19. few; 17
20. cultural; community
21. physician-assisted suicide; voluntary euthanasia
22. Dutch
23. Oregon; have not
24. variable
25. African
26. Muslim
27. enlightenment; Hindus; Sikhs
28. Jewish; life
29. Christians; heaven; hell
30. culture; religion; mourning
31. a. Religious and spiritual concerns often reemerge.
    b. Returning to one's roots is a common urge.
32. private; emotional; religious; small memorial services after cremation; burial after a traditional funeral; social isolation; physical illness
33. a. Be aware that powerful, complicated, and culturally diverse emotions are likely.
    b. Understand that bereavement is often a lengthy process.
34. intimate, caring relationship
35. electronic letter

Answers to Testing Yourself

1. **b.** is the answer. It is a common misconception that the bereaved are eventually able to break their attachments to loved ones who have died. (audio program)

2. **d.** is the answer. Professor Wortman's research has consistently found that the social support of a friend who is available to listen is an important aspect of the recovery process. (audio program)

3. **b.** is the answer. Having "c" an understanding relative and/or "d" a friend who has experienced a similar loss are/is also helpful to recovery, but religious faith seems to be the most beneficial of all. (audio program)

4. **b.** is the answer. Death is more likely to come "in season" today as a result of improved health practices and control of disease. (audio program)

5. **d.** is the answer. Altering the natural process of grieving by "a" rushing it, "b" attempting to rationalize it, or "c" denying it can have a crippling effect on the bereaved. (audio program)

6. **b.** is the answer. (textbook, p. 710)

7. **c.** is the answer. (textbook, p. 711)

8. **c.** is the answer. (textbook, p. 709)

9. **c.** is the answer. (textbook, pp. 709, 711)

10. **d.** is the answer. (textbook, p. 710)

11. **a.** is the answer. (textbook, p. 710)

12. **c.** is the answer. (textbook, p. 712)
    a. This is a living will.
    b. & d. These are forms of euthanasia.

13. **c.** is the answer. (textbook, p. 712)

14. **b.** is the answer. (textbook, p. 714)
    a. There is no such thing as involuntary euthanasia.
    c. In this situation, a doctor provides the means for a *patient* to end his or her own life.
    d. DNR, or *do not resuscitate*, refers to a situation in which medical personnel allow a terminally ill person who has experienced severe pain to die naturally.

15. **d.** is the answer. (textbook, pp. 718–719)

16. **b.** is the answer. (textbook, p. 712)

17. **d.** is the answer. A central feature of hospices is that the dying are *not* isolated from loved ones, as they might be in a hospital. (textbook, p. 713)

Reference

Kastenbaum, R. (1985). Dying and death: A life-span approach. In J. Birren & K. W. Schaie (Eds.), *Handbook of the psychology of aging*. New York: Van Nostrand Reinhold.
This excellent chapter provides a comprehensive overview of attitudes toward death across the life span.

The Television Term Project

The five television programs of *Seasons of Life*, hosted by David Hartman, present the stories of people at all stages of life. The programs may be viewed any time during the semester and perhaps more than once. After you watch each one, respond to the questions designated. These questions will help you integrate the television programs with other aspects of the course.

If possible, watch the television programs with other people—students in the course, family, or friends. Feel free to discuss the questions with them. Then write your own answers.

In some cases you will have to choose between questions for "younger" and "older" students. No matter what your age, pick the question better suited to you. Once you have answered all twenty-five questions, send the entire set of answers to your instructor.

PROGRAM ONE: INFANCY AND EARLY CHILDHOOD
(Conception to Age 6)

Program One follows the biological, social, and psychological clocks through the first six years of life. It explores the development of attachment, autonomy, gender identity, autobiographical memory, and the sense of self. In addition, it addresses the controversial issues of day care and expert "advice" on how to raise children. The program also discusses the dramatic changes that have occurred in the seasons of life, and introduces some of the families and experts who will appear throughout the series.

STORIES

- The Kennedy family of Butler, Pennsylvania, takes great pride in the 50 years and four generations they have worked the family dairy farm. At the head of the family are Martha, 72, and Francis, 69. Grandson Jeffrey and his wife Janice, both 22, have just become the proud parents of the newest Kennedy, Justin, whose birth brings back memories for each member of the family. Martha and Francis remember the birth of Jim, Justin's grandfather, and ponder how different the world will be for Justin as he grows up. Jim and wife Rita, both 45, wonder if Jeffrey and Janice are too young to be having a baby. Says Rita, "When I see people today with babies, I think, 'Oh boy! Are they young!' But we were at that stage one time too. I have to remember that."

- A day-care center in Pittsburgh is the setting for several vignettes about the effects of multiple caregivers on children. One such child is 5-week-old Grant Templin, whose mother Diane is returning to her full-time job. "It's very difficult for me as a new mother to leave such a little baby," she worries, "even though I know I'm leaving him in very competent hands."

- Meredith Wilson, at age 2, is racing into early childhood, the period when toddlers begin to establish independence and develop a sense of self. As Meredith struggles to draw a line—sometimes a battle line—between herself and others, mother Patty sighs, "It's hard to keep up with her." But keep up with her she does, for each time Meredith claims her independence she also wants to return to Mom and reestablish the bond of basic trust that was the legacy of her infancy.

- Gilberto Agosto, at age 3, is old enough to have his own cubbyhole at the day-care center he attends in East Harlem, New York. Although he and his friends are only beginning to understand the differences between boys and girls, already they prefer to play with others of the same sex. One of the things Gilberto shares with boys his own age is a biological tendency to be more aggressive than girls.

- James McManus, at age 4, not only knows that he's a boy and acts like one, but he also is forming autobiographical memories that will both shape and reflect his self-identity. When he's an adult, perhaps his first memory of life will be of running faster than the wind as he plays a game of ghost with his mother.

- At an art class in Boston, children eagerly paint pictures depicting themselves, their families, and important events, such as the loss of a pet. According to art educator Nancy Smith, a child's drawings are "the roots of it all—the first emergings of a great enormous tree" that is the child's sense of self.

- It's the first day of school for 6-year-old Jamillah Johnson, who lives with her grandmother in the Boston suburb of Roxbury, Massachusetts. At the end of early childhood, Jamillah is about to take a big step into the world of teachers, classmates, and formal education. Walking to the school, Jamil-lah's grandmother offers her granddaughter some loving admonitions.

Now answer questions 1–4, pages 363–364.

PROGRAM TWO: CHILDHOOD AND ADOLESCENCE (Ages 6–20)

Program Two presents the stories of nine young people who spell out different versions of growth and development during a sometimes tumultuous season. The biological clock slows growth in childhood, giving humans a latent period in which to learn the skills and information critical to their culture. According to the social clock, this is the time to go to school, to work at acquiring a sense of industry, and to develop feelings of being useful and competent. At the close of childhood, the biological clock again ticks loudly, bringing on adolescence and what probably is the most challenging and complicated season of life. By the time they reach early adulthood, adolescents have formed a fragile sense of who they are and have taken up authorship of their life stories.

STORIES

- Six-year-old Jamillah Johnson carries a pink backpack and a serious expression to her first day at kindergarten in her neighborhood elementary school. Her grandmother is holding her hand now, but schoolteachers are about to exert a very significant influence on her cognitive and social development. In class the teacher reminds Jamillah and her classmates: "Raise your hand. Stand straight. Stand still and quiet. Stand right behind the person in front of you." On the playground Jamillah makes overtures to a potential

friend. Her grandmother's words to her ring true: "You're going to be on your own. Everything you learn now is important to you."

- Nine-year-old Karl Haglund learns to love his handicapped brother Gerry. Describing her sons' sometimes argumentative relationship, the boys' mother comments, "We tried to explain to Karl that at times he has to be more understanding of Gerry's special needs. That can be frustrating for a nine-year-old to understand. Yet, when push comes to shove, Karl wants to be where Gerry is." Karl has a reading problem, but is nevertheless developing a sense of industry.

- Eleven-year-old Jason Kennedy does his part on the family farm—raising calves, doing chores, and working in the field. "Our kids are not smart 'street-wise' like kids in town," says his father Jim, "but you tell a farm kid to do anything and he'll give it a shot." Jason loves to show animals. Though he has lost his share of competitions, he revels in first-place ribbons and his father's pride.

- Twelve-year-old Candy Reed finds her way amid the social stresses of junior high school. Her grandfather, who helps his single-parent daughter raise Candy, says fondly, "She wants to feel she's a big girl, but we don't feel she's quite big enough yet." Her mother worries that some day discipline may alienate her daughter. "You can't be too permissive," she says, "you can't always just be a teenager's friend."

- Fifteen-year-old Kim Henderson must be responsible for her 18-month-old Angela at the same time she works to finish high school herself. Although her mother and sister care for the toddler during the day, Kim's after-school time is spent with her daughter. Kim is trying hard to be the best mom she can be—a blend of her own mother and grandmother—but she wants her daughter's experiences to be different from her own. "I hope Angela doesn't turn out like me," she says, "I don't want her to have a baby the same time I did. It could ruin her life."

- Seventeen-year-old Nuket Curran may be the most rebellious of the program's protagonists. Through her choices of music, clothing, and hair, she tries to distance herself from the crowd in her urban Pittsburgh high school. A talented artist, she has filled an autobiographical canvas with starkly drawn symbols of her emotions. Despite her rebelliousness, Nuket has some sound advice for adults, reminding them that, "Being a teenager is not easy. We're growing up and should be allowed to make stupid mistakes from time to time—to a point!"

- Eighteen-year-old Michael Shelton clashes with his stepfather over the family car. Unrepentant about his speeding, he jokes that his next investment will be a radar detector. Michael, who is about to enter a college program in commercial art, discusses his complex feelings about his biological parents and stepparents. Michael wants the girls he dates to be good looking. Although his dating habits have been tempered by the threat of AIDS, "Nobody in his right mind would go with a girl only for her personality and mind," he says.

- Eighteen-year-old Trey Edmundson gets ready for the senior prom. Although his mother died when he was 12, he has had a loving aunt and uncle looking out for him. "Thank God we went through that period quickly," says his uncle, Reverend Charles Stith, of Trey's adolescence. "At times," Trey admits, "teens want to be treated as adults; other times they want to do things kids would do."

- Seventeen-year-old Heather Robinson finds time to give love and attention to young children and an elderly woman. She volunteers at the local library, reading stories to preschoolers. And for three years she has enjoyed a very special relationship with Ida Rhine, an elderly, blind, retired musician she calls her advisor, confessor, and confidante. Soon Heather will be going away to college, where she has been accepted into a prestigious writing program. What has helped her, she says, "is just knowing that I've actually done something for somebody and not always feeling like there's so much out there that's wrong and that there's nothing I can do."

Now answer questions 5–8, pages 365–366.

PROGRAM THREE: EARLY ADULTHOOD
(Ages 20–40)

Program Three of *Seasons of Life* explores development during early adulthood by telling the stories of young people at different ages and of different statuses. As children and teenagers, we impatiently await the "rites of passage" that officially signal our entry into this season. But for young adults today, the vast array of lifestyle choices may be intimidating as well as exciting. The social clock ticks very loudly for people in their 20s and makes enormous demands all at once. The messages are urgent: Get a job. Find a mate. Start a family. In early adulthood we form a dream of the future and try to make that dream a reality.

STORIES

- It's an important day in the life of Justin Miller, age 21. On the threshold of early adulthood, he prepares to graduate from Carnegie-Mellon University with a degree in artistic design and hopes for a promising career. "My biggest fear is that I won't be successful," he worries. "You can easily get stagnant in some place and not move anywhere. That would be the worst that could happen to me." Like many college graduates today, Justin is putting his personal life on hold until his career is successfully launched. Still, he admits to thinking a lot about having a family, especially at the end of the day when he returns to his empty apartment.

- May-Ling Agosto's life, at age 21, has never been easy. Raised by her mother in New York City's Spanish Harlem, May-Ling married at 15 and now has a 3-year-old son. She is separated from her husband. "We're very strong pigheaded women in our family," she smiles. "If a husband is not going to do anything for you, what do you need him for?" May-Ling has fought her way back from cocaine addiction and looks ahead with excitement. She is training as a computer technician and has just moved into a one-bedroom, subsidized apartment in the Bronx after a three-year wait. "Now it's just up to me," she vows.

- Anthony and Julianne Cugini, 28 and 23, belonged to the same Catholic church all their lives before they met at a youth organization event. Religion and family are strong supports for them. The Cuginis have been married one year and have a baby girl. "My dreams aren't farfetched at all," Julianne says. "I want to have a marriage that works." Her husband agrees, "I'm as happy as I've ever been in my life," he confides.

- Donna Radocaj, 31, feels her dreams have been shattered. Divorce has left her struggling to cope with her two small children; in contrast to her comfortable married life, she now suffers through days with "no food and no money." Resolve and bitterness come together for Donna at this point in her life: "I thought by now I'd have my house in the country," she reflects. "I'm settling for second best."

- Phillip and Patti Wilson, both 30, were married 9 years before their daughter Meredith was born. They admit that marriage and parenting have revamped earlier dreams. "When I was 20," Patti says, "I never thought I'd be in Pennsylvania. I never thought I'd be married. I *never* thought I'd have kids." Phillip confesses that he had a TV image of what a husband was. "When the husbands came home the wives were relaxed." Despite the fact that their marriage has had its ups and downs, Patti speaks poetically about their baby: "I feel like I found something that I had before, but I just didn't know it. Like a new room in the house. You've passed the door so many times, but you never bothered to open it. Then I opened it, and it's the best room in the house."

- Thirty-one-year-old Bronwyn Reed was an unwed mother at 19. Now she supports her daughter Candy with a job she enjoys, but is not committed to. She is a physical therapist at a local hospital. "I don't have a career I can be proud of," she says in disappointment, "but when you have a job you don't want to do, you have to seek fulfillment in other ways." For Bronwyn that is music; she is an accomplished vocalist. Bronwyn feels ambiguous about her status as a single mother. "Sometimes I'm glad I'm not married," she says, "and sometimes I'd give an arm and a leg to have somebody else to talk to."

- Free-lance writer David Nimmons and union organizer David Fleischer are an openly gay couple in their early 30s. Like many adults his age, Nimmons was ready to settle down when he and Fleischer met. "People I know who are in couples are really working at something that seems like a good and valiant challenge," he says. "How lucky I am to have found this, because it fits so well for me."

- The idea that she may never marry and have children is a painful one for Christine Osborne, 39. While she is a very successful Chicago ad executive, personally she longs for a family. "I feel very envious of people who not only have happy marriages, but who have children," she says. Ruefully she notes her grandmother's dying words to her: "You're too picky." "It hasn't happened," she shrugs, tears in her eyes. "Now what?"

- Deborah and Charles Stith, both in their late thirties, would seem to have it all. He is an ordained Methodist minister in Boston. She is a physician and the State Commissioner of Public Health. They have two small children Charles calls "major events," and Deborah jokes about wanting seven more. Yet they too admit to struggling. They also raised Deborah's now-teen-age nephew after her sister died. "There are many points

along the way we could have gotten divorced," Deborah acknowledges. "I'm not going anywhere," says Charles. "I picked the best I'm capable of picking."

Now answer questions 9–12, pages 367–368.

PROGRAM FOUR: MIDDLE ADULTHOOD (Ages 40–60)

Program Four explores development during the fifth and sixth decades of life. Gray hair, wrinkles, and reading glasses are signals from the biological clock that life is half over—that there is more "time lived" than "time left." This is the season in which the biological and social clocks fade in importance and the psychological clock ticks more loudly. For those who have reached positions of expertise and power, middle age will be a time of personal and social command. For others who have experienced great losses—that of a child, of a spouse, or of a job—it will demand new directions. It is a season that ushers in androgyny: Women find new strength and men become more nurturing. Caring for others—what Erikson called generativity—is also emblematic of the middle years, as both sexes provide help to their extended families and the larger "human family," and begin to create a legacy for those who will come after them.

STORIES

- Former Cleveland Browns quarterback Brian Sipe faces the "precipice" of middle age at 37—after a lifetime of sports. "We all wish we were kids a little longer than we were," he says, "but I'll always be proud of what I did." Sipe is anxious to redirect his future. He thinks he might like to be an architect. And although he misses the regimen of professional sports, he's ready to take a next step. "There's nothing stopping me," he declares.

- Born January 1, 1946, Kathleen Wilkins was America's first official "baby boomer" and is now the first of her cohort to reach middle age. Recently separated from her husband, Kathleen has returned to college to study for an MBA while continuing her career in restaurant management. Not afraid of growing older, she says, "At 40, as a 'boomer,' I have more to offer than a 22-year-old. I can bring not only an expertise that I went back and studied for, I can bring life experiences."

- Daniel Cheever, 44, is the president of Wheelock College in Boston. At one time he considered leaving the field of education, but after 10 years as a public school superintendent, "I decided I had paid my dues in one field and that's where I would reap my reward." Cheever and his wife Abby both have professional careers, and Cheever has done most family chores since Abby entered law school more than 10 years ago. Both he and Abby look forward to the challenge of their life together now that their children will be in college.

- Jim Kennedy, 45, is celebrating his 25th wedding anniversary on the family dairy farm Jim's father mortgaged to him two decades ago. Although he and wife Rita once considered going out of business and can remember struggling to find 24 cents to buy a loaf of bread, today they sell 1.25 million pounds of milk a year. Jim has accumulated enough acreage to be able to offer any or all of his five children part of the family business. "The money isn't in farming," he says, "but it's a darned good life."

- The good life is gone for Matt Nort, 52, who lost his job at a Pittsburgh steel mill some time ago. Nort, who does not have a high school education, gets by on part-time work and hopes for a chance. "The dream is gone, probably gone forever," he worries. As he struggles to reconnect his life, he confronts many new feelings, including depression, bewilderment, and even thoughts of suicide. Yet Nort has strong faith, and a loving family. "It's just you and me against the world," his wife says, smiling at him.

- Kris Rosenberg, 55, fought her way back from a crippling bout with polio, a divorce, and perhaps most important, a devastating loss of self-esteem. Today she directs "Returning Women," a training program for older women who want to reenter the work force. "I can be real to them," she explains, noting that she was once as frightened and tentative as her students. Kris and her husband have reunited since her comeback, but they maintain separate lives, checking accounts, and rooms in the house. Having, in effect, turned her losses into gains, Kris notes, "For the first time I feel like an individual person."

- Harriet Lyons, 59, climbed out of despair and totally reconstructed her life after losing everything, including family mementos, when she lost her job. Eventually she found work with the Bank of Boston, and is setting goals for herself once again. Lyons raises her granddaughter Jamillah because her daughter, Jamillah's mother, is addicted to drugs. Despite this sadness, she is excited about the friendships she is strengthening with her six children and grandchildren, noting, "I guess in a lot of ways I'm coming to where I wanted to be in the first place. I feel good about myself. I've got a lot to offer."

- Dave and Ruth Rylander, 57 and 53, have lived a parent's nightmare. Their daughter Lynn died of leukemia when she was 19. As a result of their love for her and their own longing for meaning in their lives, both Rylanders have taken up careers in social service. Ruth runs peace movement activities for the Presbyterian church and Dave is the director of a local food bank. "I think she'd like what I'm doing today," Dave says. "She was the kind of young woman who cared about people." Ruth speaks eloquently about their lives today: "We've seen tragedies, joys. We have done our apprenticeship. Sometimes I am more cautious, but in many ways I'm less cautious. After all, what do I have to be afraid of?"

Now answer questions 13–16, pages 369–370.

PROGRAM FIVE: LATE ADULTHOOD (Ages 60+)

Late adulthood is a season of great diversity. It is the season upon which the twentieth century, with World Wars I and II, the Great Depression, and a 25-year increase in life expectancy, has had its most telling impact. Late adulthood is one kind of season if you have your health and financial resources; it is quite another if you don't. Some older adults extend the activities of middle age into their 70s. Others take advantage of their newly found leisure to change their lives completely. As the biological clock eventually runs down and the end of life comes into view, individuals work to achieve a sense of integrity. Now the lifelong suspense leaves their story, and they see how it will end. And they wonder: Was it a good story? Was it true to who I was? And are there a few last things I might do to give my life a better ending?

STORIES

- Harry Crimi, 61, has operated the family butcher shop in south Philadelphia for as long as he has been married—40 years. His wife Antoinette, 60, was born in the house they live in now, and her 93-year-old father is still with her. "He deserves the honor and glory of dying at home," she says. Harry and Antoinette dote on their family. Their children and grandchildren visit often. "You don't have time to cater to your children," Harry explains, "but you make time for your grandchildren." Where did the time go? "When you're 20 or 30," Harry shakes his head, "you don't imagine being 61 years old. But now that I'm 61, I wonder where all the years went."

- In Detroit, Tom and Vivian Russell, 61 and 60, are buying a new home in retirement. He has worked 40 years for the post office; she has been a social worker. Tom grew up in an African-American family in the segregated South where he remembers life as a constant struggle. Vivian was also raised in a poor family, one of nine children. They are a remarkably giving couple. Tom meets in Christian fellowship with inmates of a Federal penitentiary and Vivian is training as a hospice volunteer. As Tom says, "I hope we can continue to help people, continue to show our warmness, continue to do it together."

- Seventy-four-year-old Lyman Spitzer will leave an important scientific legacy. NASA will soon put into space a telescope designed by the astronomer/physicist. Spitzer remains fascinated with knowledge and continues the vigorous physical activities he has enjoyed all his life, not the least of which is mountain climbing. "No one has reproached me for being overly rash at my age," he contends. Spitzer has been married 51 years to Doreen Spitzer, who heads the American School in Greece. After all he and his wife have studied and experienced, life is still a fascinating puzzle. "I can well imagine," Spitzer says, "long after we know all that we need to know about the universe, we may still be trying to understand the nature of life."

- Milton Band, 78, and wife wife Rowena, enjoy the "good life" at a retirement center in Holiday Springs, Florida, where the relaxed atmosphere has afforded them a new intimacy in their marriage. "I feel like I'm 16 years old," Rowena says. "It's a wonderful, unbelievable thing (retirement), all of it, like a dream." Milton, who left his law career nine years ago, celebrates time to himself and an escape from the rat race.

- Francis Kennedy, 70, jokes about a few aches and pains and a forgetful moment or two, but he is still active on the family farm, baling hay and milking cows. "You could sit down, and I could sit down, and we could really cry the blues with each other. That wouldn't do any good," he claims. "We've got to get going. Tomorrow's another day. Be ready for it."

- Ellen Hanes is not as fortunate as her peers in good health. She is one of the frail elderly who requires constant care, and she lives in a private nursing home in Flushing, New York. Thirty-five percent of all sick elderly Americans will spend their life savings in a nursing home before they die. "If I had known I would be like this, I would have made more arrangements for myself. The doctors put me here," she says.

- Miriam Cheifetz lost her husband a year ago. When she found her loneliness unbearable, she moved to a group home in Chicago where she feels more comfortable. The women in the home share facilities, chores, and the stories of their lives. Miriam treasures memories of her husband and frequent visits from her affectionate family: "There's a thread that goes through your whole life, and when you see some of that in your children, you feel that your life was not in vain."

- "I hope I don't lose my upper plate when I blow," is Minna Citron's comment as she blows out the candles on her 90th birthday cake. After a long, unconventional life (her ex-husband once said, "Why can't you be like other people and just stay put?"), Citron enjoys her position as "curator of a career"—her own, as a prominent artist. Mobbed by friends at her birthday party, she is in high spirits: "I love my friends. . . I want to go on enjoying life if I can."

- George Nakashima, 84, chose a life of contemplation and art. Although he began work as a railroad gandy dancer in the Northwest, a career in architecture and design eventually took him to Paris, India, and Japan. During World War II, Nakashima, his wife, and 6-week-old daughter were forced into a detention camp set up by the U.S. government. There he began to train under a fine Japanese carpenter, schooled in the traditional manner. Nakashima came to love working with wood and developed a spiritual affinity for nature. Today he and his son and daughter painstakingly fashion works of art. "I take great pride in being able to take living things that will die, and give them a second life. It is a great feeling to be a part of nature, and to be a part of life itself," he says.

Now answer questions 17–25, pages 371–377.

NAME _____   INSTRUCTOR_____

The Television Term Project

Return pages 363–377 to your instructor.

1. Imagine that you had been born at a different point in history—for example, 100 years ago, or in your parents' generation. Select one setting of the social clock (one "age norm") that was different back then. How might your development have been altered had you lived at that time?

2. Give an example of how the biological, social, and psychological clocks each exert their influence in the first few years of life.

3. What important developments occur during the first year of life? What do the experts say and what is your own personal view?

4. **Younger students** (or those who are not parents): Of all the changes that occur between birth and age 6, which is the most remarkable to you? Why? Do you believe that someone's personality is well set by the time he or she goes to school?

    Older students (or parents): Did any of the episodes or experts in this first program provide insight into the development of your own child or children? Explain.

5. Did any of the stories provide insight into your own childhood or adolescence or those of your children? What did you learn about yourself or your children?

6. Which qualities and experiences of the people in the program would you hope to see in any children you might have? Why? Which qualities and experiences would you prefer not to see?

7. What experiences of childhood and adolescence were *not* portrayed in this program? Which of these should have been included?

8. What are some of the losses that occur during childhood and adolescence? What new potentials emerge during this stage of life? In what ways do these losses and gains relate to developmental events specific to childhood?

9. Did any of the stories provide insight into yourself as you are now or when you were a young adult? What did you learn about yourself?

10. **Younger students:** Which qualities and experiences of the people depicted in the program would you like to have during your own early adulthood? Why? Which would you like to avoid?

    Older students: What experiences of early adulthood were *not* portrayed in this program? Which of these should have been included?

11. What are some of the losses that occur during early adulthood? What new potentials emerge?

12. Based on your own experiences, and/or those of the people in the program, in what ways are the events of early adulthood a reflection of the developmental legacies of earlier stages of life? How might the experiences of early adulthood influence later life?

13. **Younger students:** Did any of these stories provide insight into your parents' lives and experiences? Why or why not? Do you see them differently in any way as a result? Explain.

    Older students: Did any of these stories provide insight into your own middle adulthood? Why or why not? Did you learn anything about yourself? Explain.

14. **Younger students:** Which qualities and experiences of these people would you like to have in your middle years? Why? Which would you like to avoid?

    Older students: What experiences of middle adulthood were *not* portrayed in this program? Which of these should have been included?

15. What are some of the losses that occur during middle adulthood? What are the potential gains of this stage?

16. Based on your own experiences and/or those of the people in the program, in what ways are the events of middle adulthood related to the earlier stages of life? How do the events of middle adulthood influence later life?

17. Did any of the stories provide insight into yourself, your parents, or your grandparents? Do you see yourself or your relatives differently as a result?

18. **Younger students:** Which qualities and experiences of the people in the program would you like to have in your later years? Why? Which would you like to avoid?

    Older students: What experiences of late adulthood were *not* portrayed in this program? Which of these should have been included?

19. What are some of the losses that occur during late adulthood? What are the potential gains of this season?

20. Based on your own experiences and/or those of the people in the program, in what ways do the events of late adulthood build on what happened in earlier seasons of life? Can you predict how a life will turn out from the way it began?

SUMMING UP

Your answers to the following questions should draw on the content of the entire *Seasons of Life* series, as well as your own life experiences.

21. Draw a family tree of the Kennedys, including only those members who appear in the television programs. Briefly identify each member of the family tree and describe at least one memorable characteristic about each person.

22. For each of the seasons of life—infancy, childhood, adolescence, early adulthood, middle adulthood, and late adulthood—think of someone in your family or from among your acquaintances. Does each of these people share similarities with one (or more) of the people in the series? Briefly describe similarities (and differences) below.

Infancy

Childhood

Adolescence

Early Adulthood

Middle Adulthood

Late Adulthood

23. Using bar graphs on the lines below, indicate how loudly the biological, social, and psychological clocks are "ticking" during each stage of life. During which stages is each clock most influential? The relative control exerted by the three developmental clocks should be indicated by the height of the bar—the greater the control, the higher the bar. Be sure to label each bar with a B, S, or P. In the example below, during early adulthood the social clock is ticking the loudest, followed by the biological clock, and then the psychological clock.

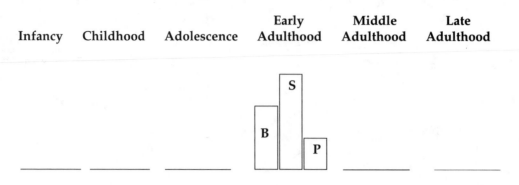

			Early	Middle	Late
Infancy	Childhood	Adolescence	Adulthood	Adulthood	Adulthood

Comment on the pattern you see across the life span.

24. One theme of the *Seasons of Life* series is that lives become more diverse as people age. Do you find this increasing diversity to be true, based on your own life experiences? Why or why not? What are some of the reasons life's paths tend to "fan out" as people grow older?

25. Another theme of *Seasons of Life* concerns how the life story evolves as we get older. For each stage—infancy, childhood, adolescence, early adulthood, middle adulthood, and late adulthood—state briefly how well-formed the life story is likely to be and what issues it is likely to address.

Infancy

Childhood

Adolescence

Early Adulthood

Middle Adulthood

Late Adulthood